Worst Case Scenario is a compelling read. Adventure, romance, exotic places, faith on trial, all in the context of a mom raising her children. It's not so much a missionary story as it is a story about following Jesus wherever He leads. Michelle's descriptions ring true from the Southern California coast to the Lesotho Mountains to the Great Rift Valley; from selling her home to meeting new colleagues to adopting her children. She tells it like it is even as she confronts her worst fears and learns to live through them without anyone to lean on but Jesus, and then has to decide whether that is enough. This book contains plenty to chew on, a lot of flavor and texture and not much sugar coating. I heartily recommend it.

Colin McDougall,
US Director, Africa Inland Mission

My soul doesn't resonate with the uninitiated. Reading through Michelle's story of tremendous challenges and losses, I was struck not only with the hugeness of the ordeals themselves, but more so, with her dedicated commitment to keep her eyes focused on the One who could get her through the hard times. She chose to trust God's perspective when she didn't understand what He was doing, knowing that His ways were higher than hers. It is clear that these hard times have refined her and I'm quite certain her resilience has only come from the Spirit Himself. I'm certain anyone who has suffered anything close to what Michelle has gone through will find themselves encouraged, moved, and changed after reading this heartfelt and honest trove.

I was.

Sylvia Lange,
Recording Artist and Women's Speaker

D1732728

Michelle Gennaro Lapp walks beside the reader on uncharted paths—roads that are spiritual and dirt all in one. A journey of faith that few on earth have taken. And yet it smells familiar; even with missionary work, adoptions, love, loss, finding love again, and finding a deeper level of faith that only comes through true suffering and challenges, it still somehow seems tangible and relatable to the reader.

Worst Case Scenario is a must read for all audiences. After turning the final page, one will discover the true brilliance that Michelle has crafted: that no matter what your circumstances look like, no matter what detours life throws at you, your faith in God and His plan for your life is what keeps you forging forward, never quitting. Each new day is exactly that: a new day and opportunity to discover the wonder of God and His plan for you.

Russ Womack,
Author of *Orange*

Jennifer,
I pray my story brings you encouragement from God's Word — straight to you!

WORST CASE SCENARIO

Finding
Overwhelming Rescue
in the
Promises of God

A Memoir   *Michelle G Lapp*

MICHELLE GENNARO LAPP

2 Cor 1

XULON ELITE

Xulon Press Elite
2301 Lucien Way #415
Maitland, FL 32751
407.339.4217
www.xulonpress.com

*The photo used in the cover design is an actual photo taken
from our house in the mountains of Lesotho, Africa.*

Paperback ISBN-13: 978-1-66286-927-3
Ebook ISBN-13: 978-1-66286-928-0

prov·i·dence

/ˈprävədəns/

Providence, noun[1]

1. the protective care of God or of nature as a
   spiritual power.
   "they found their trust in divine providence to be a
   source of comfort"
2. Similar: destiny, God's will, divine intervention,
   predetermination, fortuity, serendipity, one's lot
   (in life), one's portion.
3. God or nature as providing protective or spiritual care.
   noun: **Providence**
   "I live out my life as Providence decrees"
   o   timely preparation for future eventualities.
       "it was considered a duty to encourage providence"

---

[1]   Providence, n. "Providence, n. 1-3." OED Online. Oxford University Press, September 2022.

To my late, great husband, Chris Gennaro.

You showed me what unconditional love was, challenged me with your fierce determination, led us with courage, and laid it all down for the God you trusted. Thank you for leaving a legacy for your children, loving one person at a time for who they were made to be, and especially for choosing me to be your wife, come what may. We nailed it. You're never forgotten.

Table of Contents

Contents

Preface |

Call It What It Is

"Life has made me skeptical and anxious;
being an eyewitness to God's providence has kept me hopeful
and increasingly peaceful."
– 5/12/21 3:40 a.m.

Just this morning, my husband asked a simple question that sent me into thoughtful silence. "Why, in a week that has been relatively calm, is your back in knots?" It was an honest question! Why do I feel like I'm on the verge of tears, as if grief has just arrived? The answer eventually came to me in a flood of insight. It's because my body remembers. It remembers every milestone, every birthday, every place Chris, and I experienced together—the ease of our companionship, and the absence by my side. Without cognitive effort, a melancholy cloud descends on my spirit and the memories flood in at unexpected times.

I've never thought of myself as a "worrier." In fact, I get offended if someone refers to whatever this knotted up, grief-filled, fear-of-impending catastrophe anguish is as "worry." Worry is a lack of faith! My counselor recently gave it a name that is equally appalling to me: "Anxiety." To clarify, I don't worry that something bad will happen. I don't perseverate on negative thoughts about people or circumstances as one would picture "worry." No, I live in a constant state of waiting for the next tragedy to strike, the next call that something life-changing has happened, for my world to get turned upside down, and for something that is completely out of my control to suddenly crush me. That, my friends, is why I find myself in a place where Jesus is calling me to "Come to me, (all) Michelle, you who are weary and burdened, and I will give you rest."

Jesus has been so tender with me. As I verbalized the truth of the knotted back aloud, shame started to well up, but just as quickly, passages of Scripture replaced the shame with comfort.

"The Lord will surely comfort Zion (and Michelle!) and will look with compassion on all her ruins; he will make her deserts like Eden, her wastelands like the garden of the Lord. Joy and gladness will be found in her, thanksgiving and the sound of singing."
— Isaiah 51:3

"He will cover you with his feathers, and under his wings you will find refuge."
— Psalm 91:4

While there is a long, rolling scroll of a list of things that sets Jesus apart from us mere humans, the fact that He, being fully God, can see how all of eternity will play out is a godly trait none of us can claim to have. Yet, as I look over my life on the handwritten pages of my journal, the margins of my Bible, my blog posts, the outlines of my speaking notes, and the milestones etched in my heart, I can clearly see evidence of His presence in my life. He has equipped me, even when I was unaware, for each step He has asked me to take. Whether I felt prepared or not, He has always carried me through, given me hints of what was to come, and has kept His promise to be *with me* no matter what. I am an eyewitness to His living presence and faithfulness to go before, guide, carry, comfort, provide, strengthen, prune, instruct, and whatever else I've needed to have or experience in order to be both shaped for eternity AND a living *advertisement* that He IS who He says He is.

It is with that comfort and purpose that I gather bits of my life together for you; a slideshow of real stories and snapshots that have become solid evidence that the God of the universe has prepared me for the steps He has asked me to take—and then He carried me through them. I've lived long enough that He's even revealed His eternal purposes in some of them *and* has shown fruit from our lives, and even Chris's death. It's as if each of the stories gathered here are stones of remembrance, stacked high in memory of the One True God who has revealed Himself to me.

Besides, two of my favorite things to do in life are to gather special rocks from places I visit and to write. As a matter of fact, one of the very *first* ways God prepared me to live out the life He created me for was to give me plenty of words to work with. According to both of my parents, I have talked, read, written, and sung my way through life. As a result, I have dated notes in the margins of my well-worn Bibles, hand-written journal entries, outlines tucked in the pages of notebooks, blog posts that both Chris and I wrote over the years, and raw and intense prayers to my God whom I have needed desperately.

A note about my kids.

As I delve into recollections of my past, even circumstances I have never had the courage to revisit, it is important to quantify this work as a memoir from *my* perspective. There have been six beloved souls on this ride with me; most of them have weathered every transition and braced themselves through every twist and turn, and all of them are on their own growth journey of healing and restoration. Their personal journeys are sacred and deeply personal, so I've left most of their stories out for them to tell when they're ready. I wouldn't be where I am today without them. Most days they were the only reason to rise and face a new day. They are part of my "ruins" and will be part of the majestic splendor of new life someday when the pieces are all patched up and we're all whole.

I pray you will see the hand of our Heavenly Father who keeps His promise to work all things for the good. I've always told my students, "All means all." You know what that means?! This train wreck of a life, this trauma and grief, will be used for eternal good. To Him be the glory!

Part One |
Family Life

1 | "God's Doing Something Big"

"I am telling you now BEFORE it happens, so that when it DOES happen you will believe that I am who I am."
— John 13:19

We were in our early forties with six children when we got rid of everything we owned and moved to Africa in obedience to what we knew God was asking us to do. We were in it for the long haul. This was a career move, not a trip, and we were assimilating to the culture and staying until the task was done. There was no turning back; no house to run back to, no cars, no jobs, no safety net. We had given all of that up. It was about a year after we moved to the remote village in Lesotho when we had learned enough of the language to talk like preschoolers, that my husband Chris invited me outside into the yard of our cinder block house that looked over a village that felt to us like the "Middle of Nowhere Africa."

I followed him down the cement steps of the front porch avoiding the hole where the cement was crumbling and begging for repair. The ground was crunchy and hard, and my boots ground the sandy soil against wayward rocks as I walked the twenty paces or so to the fence where we could have privacy away from the kids. It was an unusually warm and still day as we looked out over the clusters of round, stone huts with thatched roofs and dirt paths that wound through the community we were just beginning to belong in.

I turned toward him, familiar with the furrow in his brow and the smooth, tanned features of his face. Although there was no social reason to be groomed in this remote place, I could count on Chris's face to be soft and clean-shaven. Whiskers seemed to understand their place on his face and stayed toward the edge of his jaw and chin, leaving his cheeks bare and touchable. I turned and met his thoughtful gaze. There was no need to look up or down; our bodies were made so that our eyes met naturally. We stood shoulder-to-shoulder, side-by-side.

The fact that he had invited me outside for a private conversation added enough apprehension to make me fidget. As we leaned against the rough, weather-worn fence of the garden, I reached for my wedding ring and twisted it round and round as I turned to focus on his blue eyes. A wistful and distant look fell over his face as he shared what was on his heart. *"I can't put my finger on it, but I keep getting a sense that we won't be here as long as we thought. It seems like God is about to do something big."*

Only hindsight reveals how accurate Chris's sense was. By the time four months were checked off the calendar from that conversation, he was gone from the earth and had received his Heavenly "well done." My husband of twenty-three years, the father to my six children, and my partner in life and ministry was dead and gone. In my mind, nothing could have prepared me for such a sudden tragedy, but my faith said otherwise.

2 | Saved, Called, and Not in Control

Point Loma Nazarene College, 1988

"Therefore, if anyone is in Christ, he is a new creation. The old has passed away; behold, the new has come."
— 2 Corinthians 5:17 ESV

"I want to be a missionary."

These words were written in ink on the first page of Chris Gennaro's Bible when I met him. He had penned them in junior high during a youth group "mission trip" to a Navajo reservation in Arizona. It was a call that would eat at him throughout his whole life. I was a new follower of Jesus, so the thought was foreign to me. Plus, I figured that we'd get married, pursue the American Dream, have a bunch of kids just like he wanted to do, and that little calling would eventually fade. I really had no idea what being a missionary really was. The impression I had of missionaries up to that point was that God sent them to scary places to do difficult things and that it would be miserable. Why would anybody sign up for *that*?!

It's easy to understand why I didn't have a clear picture of what missions was. I met Christ AND Chris in the same year! We were both students at Point Loma Nazarene College located in San Diego, California. He was a church kid, raised in the Nazarene Church and the son of a music pastor. I followed my best friend Rhonda to Point Loma, knowing it was a Christian school, but was not committed nor surrendered to Christ. I think I must have been longing for a new start and had experienced the love of Christ through Rhonda's family. The small size of the campus community was attractive to me, having primarily grown up in a small town in Northern California. I'd be lying if I didn't admit that the stunning ocean views from every part of campus didn't lure me a little, too. Perched on the cliffs above the Pacific Ocean, the breathtaking beauty of the campus was irresistible to me. Once I saw it, I didn't want to go anywhere else.

Living in a campus community with so many Christians was pivotal for me. Like any collection of humans, my peers weren't perfect. There were those who were there at a Christian college because they were living out a legacy—like the third generation to attend the university. Others came seeking a sheltered and conservative environment. It wasn't hard to find the rebellious ones who had grown up in Christian homes and were ready to experiment, explore, challenge, and decide for themselves if they believed as their parents did. This was my chosen group at first, and I found plenty in common with them until I started to sense a stirring in myself to pursue something eternal in my life.

A tension began to form inside of me, and my inner being was troubled. Shame entered my thoughts as I realized that what I was doing was actually sinful. My desperate thoughts plagued me as I learned more about Jesus, the Savior of the world. *"Of course Jesus forgives THESE people. They're good and what they do is mild and harmless. There's no way He'll forgive ME for all of the despicable things I have done."*

Spiritual Emphasis Week brought Tony Campolo to campus as a guest speaker, and his direct, shocking stories about the radical transformations of women from the streets revealed to me the Truth that set me free. If Jesus would forgive *them*, I figured there was hope for *me*! I repented, made a sudden turnaround in my choices for my social life, and received the gift of salvation. After that decision, my life would never be the same. The beginning of life-long learning, change, and growth in Christ had begun.

Receiving the gift of salvation in Jesus didn't change my desire to be loved and accepted, though, and it wasn't long after that when I met Chris. We were skipping chapel and landed at the same donut shop with friends. I had observed him from a distance for a while and had confessed my interest in him to only Micky, who wasn't in our circle of mutual friends. I had a sense that if I made my interest known to him, that I'd have to act on those feelings as new and fickle as they were. Chris was so different from any guy I had ever dated. He wasn't a sports guy, he was a little shorter than I was, AND he was a brilliant artist and dressmaker. Yes, Chris Gennaro sewed like nobody I'd ever seen! When worldly, passionate, flirtatious Michelle met conservative, creative, and persistent Christopher at the donut shop that day, the sparks were obvious, and I couldn't resist them! Our junior/senior "Banquet" was coming up and I didn't have a date. Without even thinking, I blurted out, "Want to go to the banquet with me?"

My gut instinct about Chris was accurate. We were serious from that point on; inseparable, compatible soulmates whose hearts connected immediately. We dated for nearly two years before the shame showed up again. As we got closer and closer, and our relationship was serious enough to talk about the future, doubts overwhelmed me. This man was clearly too good, and too pure for me. I needed to come clean about my past. I sat him down one evening, wracked by tears, and stumbling over my words. He sat there on the couch as if frozen in time; his vivid, steel blue eyes fixed on mine. Although he was a little shorter than me standing, he hovered over me at that moment seated there on the couch. The intensity of my repentance had led me to slip from my place and kneel in front of him so I could look straight into his welcoming, smooth face.

I started to confess the things I had done that I was ashamed of and wanted him to know before he chose me forever. His gentle, pristinely soft fingers over my mouth stopped me and his tender voice taught me a profound spiritual lesson that helped me understand Jesus's forgiveness with a depth I hadn't grasped up until that point. He said, "Michelle, I don't know that person. She's gone. The Bible says that when someone receives forgiveness from Jesus, *the old is gone and the new has come.* I don't need to know any of that."

We were married on August 26th, 1989, surrounded by family and friends in the historic Organ Pavilion at Balboa Park in San Diego. It would be a dream come true for any young woman to have a custom wedding gown made according to every detail they've ever pictured; but how many brides can say that their husband made their wedding dress?! I walked down the aisle in a cathedral length train with two of my guy friends in tuxedos as "train bearers." A weightless veil even longer than my train blew in the breeze making me feel like I was the luckiest girl in the whole world. We had a number of gifted friends sing and play the piano AND organ that day, but I'll never forget the song that Brad sang (You and Me and Jesus by Cliff Richard). It captured our prayers for our marriage and summed up how we wanted to live out our life together.

"You and me and Jesus
Jesus, me and you;
On our own we'd break,
With Him we'll make it through.
Jesus, take us make us
What you want us both to be;
I give myself to her,
She gives herself to me."[2]

---

2   Richard, Cliff. "You and Me and Jesus," On *Little Town,* EMI Records Ltd, 1982, vinyl.

3 | A Church to Call Home

As soon as we returned from our Canadian honeymoon, our college friends invited us to visit the church they had recently started attending. Their invitation came with a promise that we'd love it. They described it as a place where the people were real and the messages were biblical. Besides that, there was a group of newly married couples who met on Sunday's, but continued their friendships into the week, doing life together and loving each other in a way they hadn't experienced anywhere else. Once we stepped foot in that group of believers, we never looked back. Emmanuel would be my first and only church home for the next 30 plus years.

I had been to a few churches in my lifetime by the time we were married, but had never belonged to one. My parents took us when we were young, so I have positive memories of attending large gatherings of people who raised their voices in song, shook hands, and listened to long sermons. My vantage point was usually the cool, cement floor of the movie theater where followers gathered for services on Sundays. Once my mom granted me freedom from sitting properly in my seat, I would slip from my chair and hold my hand on the edge of it waiting for it to spring into its resting position. Pulling my coloring books and crayons from the bag Mom had packed to keep me busy, I escaped into my own creative world. The drone of the pastor's voice and the dim light faded into the background as I practiced outlining the pictures with careful, dark lines and filling the main parts of the pictures with perfect, soft strokes of waxy color.

Later, in high school, visits to a couple of other churches expanded my view. Since my home was tucked up in the mountains almost forty-five minutes from town, there were plenty of circumstances that led to me needing a place to sleep over. Whether I was snowed

9

in or committed to events with the marching band, Rhonda's family welcomed me into their home generously. If my stay included a Sunday, it also included attending the Nazarene church where her father was the associate pastor. I was drawn to the family-feel of that place. Although the building was simple and plain with brown carpet and simple wood furnishings on and around the stage area, the warmth of the people made me willing to return whenever I was invited. The youth group had fun events that brought teens together in pure, harmless ways that were new to me. The faithful dedication and love of the people in that church were my first impression of the Body of Christ, and they formed my first sense that God's people were a family who loved each other.

I learned a reverence for God at St. Thomas the Apostle Catholic church in my hometown through compulsory attendance with my friend Christin's father. Sliding into the smooth, warm wooden pew properly dressed made me want to sit up straight. My senses were overwhelmed with the glory around me. At that time, with my limited exposure to the rest of the world outside of our small town, I would have described it as a cathedral. Tall, stained glass windows lined the sides of the church with scenes of Jesus on the cross and then held dead in Mary's arms. Breathing in the mustiness left from years of routine reverence, I entertained myself with a study of each colorful, glass scene. Although I didn't understand the Latin mass, each time I went, a respect and awe of the majesty of God grew in me.

College ushered in my understanding of my own sin as I attended chapel three times a week with a campus full of church kids who were exploring their recent freedom from the structure and protective accountability they had been raised with. Weekends of carousing with students at nearby state universities or all-night dancing at discotheques across the Mexican border led to crowded altars at Monday's chapel. I would watch as my friends became overwhelmed with something that looked like guilt and then tearfully and reverently shuffled forward to the front of the church with heads bowed. Kneeling at the altar, they would pray and then rise with new peace to begin the week with a clean conscience.

Eventually, Spiritual Emphasis Week ushered in my deliverance. When I rose from my own altar experience, I sincerely felt the change inside of me and a new spirit led me to make different choices from then on. I still had the same passion and fleshly urges, but there was a power that gave me an urgency to grow in Christ.

It was during this season of change that I met Chris. His baby-faced innocence captivated me, and his blue, sparkling eyes brought an intriguing mischief that drew me in. He had been raised in the Church and had never even kissed a girl beyond a peck when we met. That level of purity made me feel safe and respected, and I grew in my relationship with God and Chris simultaneously.

By the time the invitation came to visit Emmanuel, we were ready to dive into married life with a church family. We were still in our early twenties, tightly connected with our college friends, and soaking up all we were learning from the Bible. The people around us didn't just listen to eloquent sermons on Sunday, they digested the truth throughout the week, starting their days in their Bibles and in prayer and discussing it when they hung out. As I learned to be a student of God's Word, I was drawn into a true depth of relationship with the One who made me. Church was no longer just a building or a place to enter for temporary cleansing, it was a family to do life and grow with.

4 | A New Kind of Border Crossing

*"The real voyage of discovery consists not in seeking
new landscapes, but in having new eyes."*
– Marcel Proust

My entrance into cross-cultural ministry
exposed the drastic transition my life had taken after my decision
to follow Christ. During the first two years of my college experience,
I spent most weekends crossing the border to Mexico because the
drinking age was eighteen and the discotheques were loud and
exciting. As a twenty-something married woman getting to know life
as the member of a church family, trips south of the border were a
little different. When given the opportunity, I found myself writing
my name down on a sign-up sheet to go on a work-trip to Mexico.
This was cross-cultural service, not partying. Dave, a member at
Emmanuel and missionary with the larger denomination, was just
beginning the house building and mobilization ministry of Mexico
Caravan Ministries. He was inviting adult Sunday School classes to
come down, see the work, and get dirty helping out.

Crossing the border was different this time. We were piled into
a van with friends from church and we wore work clothes without
make-up and shoes without heels. Looking out of the window, I
watched the familiar downtown area near "Avenida Revolucion"
fade into the distance as the vast, brownish-gray, dusty frontier
of the rapidly developing fringes of Tijuana came into view. Early
morning smelled of smoky cooking fires mixed with the exhaust
from the commuting cars, and my senses reminded me I was in
a place vastly different from where I lived thirty minutes away in
San Diego.

Getting my hands dirty that day and witnessing the hospitality and gratitude of the people we worked with exposed me to a new side of Mexico—and of myself. With new eyes, I saw the felt need of those around me and felt compassion for them well up inside of me. No longer did this place represent a chance to indulge my flesh, but rather an opportunity to spend my time, resources, and energy looking outside of myself to help others. As I experienced a new side of myself emerging, I saw a deeper side of Chris too. It was as if pulling gloves over his clean, soft hands transformed him from an artist with fabric to a workhorse. He volunteered for the dirtiest, hardest jobs with gusto, and his spirit seemed to soar as he quietly came alongside people to serve them. While all of this was new to me, it was familiar to Chris and evoked the same completeness he had on those junior high trips to the reservation.

Our new church home was a place of *doing* God's Word, not just hearing it, and we both grew spiritually as our friendships deepened. We continued to return to Mexico to serve regularly whenever our work schedules lined up with the opportunities to serve. Those days were hot, long, and dusty. Clothed in work clothes and armed with simple construction tools, we would leave the rapidly developing community of El Florido and head out into the hills where arid slopes were becoming the backdrop to the population boom that was happening in the early nineties. People from all over Mexico were descending on Tijuana to try to get jobs and found themselves without adequate housing. That lack was the open door for ministry in that area where a simple structure and a roof over a family's head brought them shelter and an opportunity to share the love of Jesus in a place where people were often without hope and help.

The climate seemed more intense on the other side of the border, and exposure to the hot sun often turned my body into a swollen, sweaty mess. When we were on the worksite surrounded by profound need and getting to know the families who we were building for, we both fully immersed ourselves in the task and our own discomfort faded into the background. Swinging a hammer and pounding nails brought a familiar joy as I used the skills my father had instilled in me as a kid building our house in Northern California. The physical labor took me back to the simplicity of my childhood and working next to Chris in that way brought a new depth to our partnership. He came alive in that setting; his eye for detail was as well-placed on the building team as it was with any other medium. He quickly rose to the occasion, and his cheerful, tenor voice could be heard above the others offering encouragement or playful jokes above the rhythm of the work.

"I've got it! Let me bring that to you."
"Anybody else need anything?"

Late in the afternoon, when the heat of the sun had sucked our energy from us and the window holes were shuttered with hinged plywood doors, we would all cram into the house with the family and pray for them. On one particularly sweltering trip, when we had crammed into vans to head back to the dorm, my attention returned to my own condition. Looking around at my teammates, I could see that we all shared the tinge of dust head-to-toe and the occasional shading of darker areas that had piled on thicker where the sweat had trapped it. Returning to the sloping, dirt driveway of the Caravan headquarters building brought a sigh of relief. Shade, water, and rest were imminent.

Swinging my legs around to follow the team as they piled from the van, I noticed discomfort in my left hand. When I stripped off my work glove, the throbbing led me to my ring finger where my narrow, channel set, sparkly diamond wedding band glistened from its sinking spot on my red, swollen finger. After alerting Chris, he found our friend Jake who was on staff there and spoke Spanish. He rushed next door and asked the neighbor to come with his metal cutting shears. Huddled there with the sweat of our heads touching, we watched as the neighbor carefully pushed the curved blade between the gold band and my puffy finger. His gentle, melodic voice counted as I held my breath, "*Uno, dos, tres...*"

Snip! That one cut set my finger free, and we bent the gold band gingerly until I was able to remove it. Suddenly, that symbol of our never-ending love and commitment was an object held in my dirty hand. My breath halted for a moment while my mind caught up to what we had just done. The precious metal and sparkling diamonds glistened through dust and reminded me of the sentimental value of the object in my hand. As I stared at it, the truth came to me. That severed, bent shape was symbolic of a change in our hearts; a willingness to release our possessions and time for the benefit of God's eternal work. We just had no idea what the future would bring.

5 | Parenthood

*"Pregnancy is a process that invites you to surrender
to the unseen force behind all life."*
— Unknown

I thought I knew all about love before I had
children, but I was mistaken. Each of them took me deeper and
deeper into the kind of love that has you doing things you never
even thought you would do; like analyzing and counting bowel
movements or scooping up little barf-covered kids into your arms
to comfort them in the middle of the night. Every one of our children
were prayed for and labored over. Each of the six is completely
unique and showed up ready to teach me more than I was ready
to learn.

Chris and I dreamed of traveling the world before we had
children. We were also going to settle down into our "careers" and
buy a house. We were in our early twenties and those things seemed
logical and attainable, until we set out to do it. Chris had his own
dressmaking business in La Jolla, California—a wealthy, coastal
community in San Diego. I taught ninth grade English in the local
mountains, so we decided to live halfway between our jobs in a little
town in the foothills. We lived in a rented newish apartment, spent
time with our college friends, and got more and more involved at our
church, Emmanuel. Before we knew it, four years had flown by, and
we hadn't traveled *nor* purchased a home. We were twenty-six and
twenty-seven and, after "practicing" taking care of small children
by babysitting our friends' babies, we started talking about having
a family. I guess we figured we knew everything by then. The
conversation went something like this:

"There's really no way we're going to be able to buy a house
in San Diego anytime soon."

"We don't really have the money to go on any fancy, travel-the-world vacations either."

"We have health insurance, though."

"Let's start praying and try to get pregnant. It'll happen in God's timing, right?"

Praying for a child isn't unlike other big things you bring to your Heavenly Father. For me, it was initially a graceful asking, followed by an increase in desire that eventually morphed into begging God for a baby like a young child without eloquence. Like I said, marriage and having babies sets your heart up for feeling things humans can't begin to process without supernatural help. Once I started praying for that first baby, I entered into a vulnerability that changed my life. If I were to make a list of the things I had to trust God for—knowing that I wasn't in control of whether I got it or not—having a child would be second on the list. Marrying Chris was number one. My brain thinks in lists, so I might as well tell you about a list I could have written simultaneously at that point in my life—"People I Love So Much that I Fear Losing Them."

When my little answer to prayer grew to full term in my womb and my due date passed, I realized this wasn't an event I could schedule neatly and prompt according to my own wishes. Hot, summer evening walks were the setting for our prayers as we waited for the first labor pains. It only took one contraction's worth of stabbing pain to show me that my life was now out of my control. We had attended Lamaze classes in preparation for childbirth and had written a detailed plan for the birth of our first child. Not only that, but we had the timing figured out as well. The baby would come RIGHT as I finished teaching for the school year because we were due to have a June baby. I would have the summer off and then go back to teaching while Chris would take care of the baby and run his dressmaking business. It made perfect sense to me! The due date came and went; a week overdue turned into two weeks overdue and we had to take waddling walks through the local mall because the summer heat showed up before the baby did.

Slam! Jab! Sharp, shocking pain jolted me awake at 5:00 a.m. on June 29th, 1993. Less than five minutes later, another cramp-like wave bigger than the first started deep in the hollow of my lap and spread like a wave up my whole belly. When the agonizing tightness reached my abdomen, my stomach convulsed with nausea. I was in labor! As it turned out, studying about labor and delivery didn't prepare me adequately for actually experiencing it. There wasn't a position I could get into that would relieve the harrowing tightness that pulled on my swollen belly, nor the stabbing throbs that emanated from my cervix as it dilated. As I hunched over and writhed to find relief, I knew that it was the one sentence advice from mothers who had gone before that described this best. Each one had given me the annoying truth and preparedness that was all I needed to know in that moment, "When it happens, YOU'LL KNOW!"

Chris frantically called the hospital to report that I was in labor. A calm nurse on the other end explained to him that "it may not be the real thing. Since this is your first baby, monitor the contractions and call us back when they're less five minutes apart."

As he was trying to explain that they were *already* five minutes apart, I vomited. I guess the nurse could hear it over the phone because she told Chris to get me to the hospital. On the way there, with every bump in the road triggering another contraction, I told Chris he better ask for an epidural as soon as we get to the hospital. "Our plan is to try it naturally first," he reminded me.

"I CHANGED MY MIND! GET.ME.THE.EPIDURAL!"

That, my friends, was the beginning of my parenting journey. There was no way to know what to expect even though I had read all of the latest books on the topic. It was a bitter pill to swallow, the realization that there wasn't a curriculum adequate to prepare me properly for the season I was entering into. Our first baby girl arrived after a little over eight hours of labor. We had lists of boy and girl names picked out, but suddenly that choice seemed so serious and final. After almost two days in the hospital, we chose the name Julia Rose because she had the sweetest "rosebud" lips.

Before we could take Julia home, a couple of things had to happen. The first requirement was that she had to pee so they could do a urine test on her in order to make sure she was clear of infection. The second, and equally as difficult a task to accomplish was that my fever had to go down. Our baby, who came according to a timeline we didn't plan and in a way we never pictured, was also born during a breakout of Group B Strep at the hospital. They were having to test every baby and mother for it so that they could treat the babies, preventing fatalities with life-saving antibiotics.

All of the things that had to happen before we could spring from that hospital seemed to be beyond my ability and control. I couldn't *will* my body to produce breast milk fast enough, I couldn't *make* my newborn guzzle with perfect form, nor could I force my fever down. They wouldn't give me a pill for reducing the fever because they needed to see my symptoms and monitor what my body was telling them. In a desperate attempt to take matters into my own hands, I even strategically drank ice water before the nurse came in to take my temperature. When she did and my temperature was drastically lower, she asked if I had had anything to drink in the last few minutes. There was no hiding my charade without downright lying to her face, so my shenanigans only led to me waiting longer for her to check it again.

Eventually, after a couple of days, my fever went down and Julia eeked out enough urine for them to test it. With all of her vitals looking good, her feeding on track, and her weight maintaining well, they cleared us to take her home with the promise to let us know the results of her test. Within minutes of sitting down at home, the phone rang with news that would propel us into the first trial of our parenting journey. Julia's test was positive. I had picked up Group B Streptococcus from my routine, pre-labor exam at the hospital, and then she contracted the bacteria from me as she passed through the birth canal. There was no choice of outcomes now; we had to take her back to the hospital.

We had to leave our helpless, precious baby in the NICU for a ten-day round of intravenous antibiotics. This was a life-saving treatment, and we had no choice other than to place her in the hands of God and the doctors. Leaving her there alone felt like the ultimate abandonment. We had prayed for her, and God had answered; so why did we have to give her up? My arms hung limp with the desire to hold her, and I wrapped them around myself to quell the ache of it. Chris put his arm around me as we hung our heads and processed what we had to do. Up to that point, I hadn't felt emotional pain nor fear intense enough to paralyze me. I was frozen with it. I could only stand in place with limp extremities and pull in short, weak breaths that withheld sufficient oxygen from my body. I had to tell my feet to move just to leave the hospital that night without my baby. It didn't matter that I could return in the morning and hold her; it felt like a part of me was torn away.

Our families and church family rallied around us. I remember our Sunday School class signing up for meals like they normally did when couples in the class had a baby; only this time they brought the meals to the picnic tables outside of the hospital. Those were intimate, special times that made us feel loved and supported. Our friends would sit with us, listen, and pray as we tried to stomach a few bites of food during the nurses' shift changes. Every one of our needs was met at that time and we left that hospital with an eagerness to parent more fierce than it was before.

This wasn't just the beginning of my "Mama Bear instinct" that rose to confront danger when it threatened my child, it was also the maiden voyage of a long, storm-filled journey of seeing God as more than an invisible, distant force. I'm pretty sure that leaving my newborn in the Intensive Care Unit was the first time I truly had a sense that I was not in control, but fully in His faithful and powerful hands.

6 | Juggling Life 101

"Being a parent is a weird juggling act -
and nobody does it right. Everybody does it wrong."
– Jamie Lee Curtis

The only neat and tidy thing about Julia's
unique entrance into the world was that her labor and delivery were
right on schedule with my workday as a ninth grade English teacher
out in a mountain community east of San Diego. My first contraction
happened at the time my alarm usually woke me up and her first
cry happened as the last bell of the day would have sounded at the
end of sixth period. Now that I think about it, that had to be the last
shred of routine normalcy that our marriage would ever see.

At the end of that summer, I continued my commute east into
the rural community where the students were bussed from outlying
areas, and Chris took on the diaper changing and bottle feeding
duties while trying to keep his business going. He drove west to
the coast where he had his own dressmaking studio and designed
custom, special-occasion gowns in between burping his infant
daughter.

The plan seemed completely attainable before we actually held
Julia in our arms, but the reality of it rendered me a complete basket
case. Leaving my baby was excruciating. It felt like that day in the
hospital all over again. I would get in the car and cry halfway to work,
arriving at my first period English class with puffy eyes and a half-
hearted devotion. By third period I was warmed up and focused as
my love for my students and passion for teaching rejuvenated my
purpose for being there. Once my day was complete, I would leave
school, make the drive home in anticipation of getting back to my
little family, and then begin the process all over again the next day.

Clearly, our seamless plan wasn't sustainable for the long term.
We had prayed for a family, and I wanted to actually *be* with my

daughter. For Chris, trying to bottle feed a baby that preferred to breastfeed and changing diapers made it pretty hard to make designer dresses and meet with clients. One morning in particular, he had four-month-old Julia in his arms to carry her to the car seat when she had a "blow out." Bright yellow poop the color of spicy mustard had oozed and squished out of her diaper and soiled his tidy work outfit. It was difficult for him to even make it to the shop without being frazzled and late. By the end of the school year, I made arrangements to take a leave of absence that eventually led to me realizing that working outside of the home was no longer feasible. We'd have to trust God to provide and be creative to make ends meet.

That one sentence, *We'd have to trust God to provide and be creative to make ends meet*, characterizes the rest of our life as partners and parents. We were a team in a great balancing act, and we navigated each feat by utilizing our combined talents to hold everything together. Chris took pride in the fact that he had an equal role in Julia's care. When people referred to what he was doing as "babysitting," he'd stand up tall and correct them without a second thought, "I'm her DAD. I don't babysit my own kid."

He despised the pop culture term "Mr. Mom" more than the label of babysitter and that brought more sass from him in response. "I'm just as much her parent as my wife is. I'm not stupid."

It was that confidence in our teamwork that led us to make the decision for me to apply for a position as a Resident Director at Point Loma. The job would require us to live in a small apartment attached to the dorm, and I would be responsible for overseeing three hundred freshman women. Since I was pregnant with our second child and nobody had ever done the job with children, it was decided that I would have an assistant to help me with the daunting task. We moved back to our alma mater full of expectation because I would be able to be home with the babies and work at the same time.

One of the many perks of that life was that the position offered housing, salary, and benefits. With the pressure off of him for a time, Chris saw his opportunity to be involved in ministry across the border. He cut his hours at his dressmaking business to part-time and spent the rest of his work week down at Caravan helping with the housebuilding side of the ministry. The contrast that characterized his weeks were as vast as his taste in magazines. I don't know if I've ever known anyone else who subscribed to both Bride Magazine and Car and Driver. Who, then, would be more suited to use soft, clean hands to sew ornate, perfectly-fitted special occasion garments in one of the most affluent communities in the United States for part of the week, and then don work gloves to build ten-by-twelve houses for the poorest of the poor in Mexico the rest of the week?

My juggling act was no less dramatic. Since we already had a baby on the way when I accepted the position, the transition to having a toddler and an infant was balanced with the responsibility of three hundred eighteen year olds. For some reason, that number was smaller in my mind when I was dead set on doing the job than when I was actually trying to live it out. Thankfully, my assistant quickly became a beloved and trusted friend, and our twelve upper class resident assistants were our counterparts in both work and play.

When Olivia arrived during finals week after our first term in the job, we had a crew of people to help us. Since I was pioneering the job with children and her delivery was aligned perfectly with Christmas break, there was no maternity leave beyond that vacation. That meant that my infant daughter went to her first college retreat when she was three weeks old. Most of my RAs were eager to help, so I would breastfeed her, burp her, put her in a front carrier, and then nestle her onto one of the college students to bounce her while I led the sessions. She slept in a buggy right by my bunk as if nothing phased her, and we kept right on with college life together just as we had when she was in the womb.

This pace continued for over two years until we had a visit from our own college friends, Greg, and Jan. It was Homecoming and we capitalized on the opportunity to spend some extended time with them. At the very end of their visit, Jan pulled me to the side and gave me inside information that woke me up and brought the impetus for a change in that life pace. She had asked Chris how he was doing and how life was living with three hundred women. His response said all that I needed to hear: "I want my wife back."

After finishing three years juggling a toddler, an infant, three hundred eighteen year olds, a thriving dressmaking business, and a ministry in Mexico, we decided together that we needed to take a huge step of faith and have me stay home with our daughters. Julia was going to start kindergarten in the fall and life would be different. Chris rightfully longed for us to have evenings together as a family without me handing the kids off to him and rushing out to a meeting or event. In order to make it work, though, we had to continue our strategy for life: trust God to provide and be creative to make ends meet.

Our move out of the dorm didn't mean we wouldn't live in community, though. We invited my assistant and one of my RAs to move with us as rent-paying roommates so that we could afford to live in a house in a central suburb of San Diego, manage to keep Chris's business, and keep me at home. Being a family of four with two roommates may have been unconventional, but it worked for all of us. We were like an extended family, sibling-like friends from separate decades who loved and cared for each other. After three years of juggling all of the college students and our growing family, we settled in to focus our attention more fully on our family. Although our house was rented, it felt like we were almost grown-ups.

7 | Handful of Roses

Four unique little humans to raise

"For you created my inmost being; you knit me together in my mother's womb. I praise you because I am fearfully and wonderfully made; your works are wonderful, I know that full well. When I was woven together in the depths of the earth, your eyes saw my unformed body."
– Psalm 139:13-15

Once I was home and solely focused on being a mom, that became my primary focus and mission. At the time, in our twenty-something minds, it would make perfect sense to ask God for another baby! From that time on, for the next ten years or so, this was our "family planning method": pray, get pregnant, have a baby; and then Chris would declare in the delivery room, "Let's have another!" The discomfort of pregnancy and pain of childbirth would fade in my memory and then we'd start praying again. God graciously and generously answered our prayers four times. Once we got the hang of taking care of Julia Rose, He entrusted us with Olivia Rose, Jedidiah Rose, and Sicilia Rose. In His creative mercy and grace, God continued to teach us new things with every single one of them.

We approached certain parts of this family growing business with the methodical planning of gestational engineers. Name origins were studied before we chose a list of options for our beloved offspring. We practiced possible mean nicknames for future middle school classmates and crossed out the ones that were too easily mangled. Then, when we thought we had just the right name picked out for our second daughter, we found a flaw in our formula. There was no way we could give Julia the middle name of the flower known to be the ultimate symbol of love and then curse the second daughter with a name that was any less regal. With only one option that made sense, we gave Olivia the same middle name, Rose.

Although we doubted our bodies could work together to produce the genetic combo necessary to make a boy, ultrasounds revealed that it was highly likely that we had a son on the way. When he was almost ready to make his appearance, I met a woman who gave me the next idea for our naming strategy. She knew a family who had six children, each of them with the middle name "Rose." They had reasoned that if all of their kids, both boys and girls, had at least one name in common, they'd still be united with a family name when the girls eventually married. We loved the symbol of such unity and already had a head start on the idea, so we took the risk and also gave our son the middle name Rose. We had at least two good reasons a man could carry that name proudly. We had a family friend at the time, a man we respected deeply, who had the surname "Rose," and there was a rock star with the same last name. Our little guy's name held a powerful promise, "Beloved of the Lord," and the middle name would forever unite him with his sisters. It seemed like the perfect pattern to continue if God chose to add more children to our growing herd.

After two creatively engaged, precocious, and content girls, we were completely unprepared for how differently things would go with Jedidiah. Labor and delivery was relatively short with the first two, with them making their squishy appearances in eight hours or less. Jed, on the other hand, seemed to insist we do things in HIS timing, waiting out the night until his birthday changed and then taking his sweet time to exit the womb in fourteen and a half hours.

According to the baby books, the girls walked early by about eleven months, but Jed walked at nine months! He had us on our toes before then, though. One time I left him crawling in the living room as I went to use the bathroom and returned to find that he had used one of the dining room chairs to climb up on the table and was sitting there happily drizzling syrup all over himself and the tabletop. He rode a Razor scooter like a pro, zipping down the sidewalk before he was two and his bumps and bruises ushered in a new season of my medical training.

There's a snapshot from this time that sums up this "childbearing season" well. I'm hunched over the keyboard of a '90s edition personal computer in our TV room. In the background, toys are strewn on the carpet as a reminder of the chores that are waiting patiently to be finished. My focus and concentration are on the screen in front of me, but there's an added appendage. Infant Jed lies relaxed in my lap breastfeeding contentedly while I work on my Master's thesis. By the third baby, I was hands-free nursing and finishing my Master's of Education. I wore the black robe again and graduated with my degree from Point Loma to the cheers of my family who bounced Jed and held him while I soaked in the accomplishment and relief of having finished.

By the time Sicilia joined the family, we were used to the chaos and cacophony of life with a full house. She was the realization of Chris's dream to have a big family like he did growing up, and my drive and inability to sit very well made me well-equipped for the pace of our life. The miracle of her birth would be the grand finale in a harrowing, wonder-filled four-round line-up of birth stories. It was as if, by the fourth one, we needed to be humbled and reminded that we should proceed with parenthood from a position of dependence on the One who had made our kids rather than on our own expertise. Anything could happen, after all.

It did. A routine ultrasound revealed concerning markers that alerted doctors to the potential that our baby may have Down's Syndrome. High blood sugar readings, a scheduled induction, plummeting heart rates, and preparation for an emergency C-section followed that. When her heart rate rallied, we were able to return to the labor and delivery suite for the expected Lamaze breathing and pushing we were more accustomed to.

Relief washed over us when Sicilia Rose Gennaro was pushed from the birth canal with the cord loosely draped around her neck. What *could* have happened didn't and our baby girl breathed her first breath and belted her first cries with gusto. As I held her in my arms for the first time and smelled the sweet, musty aroma of the last lingering dampness of the womb, I breathed a sigh of relief. This would be the grand finale of a four-scene birth drama, and I would retire my body from growing nine-pounders no matter what Chris said.

8 | Our Grand Adventure

*"Family is like music: some high notes, some low notes,
but always a beautiful song."*
– Jesse Joseph

Reflecting back on that season of life feels a lot like watching a romcom on fast forward. The rented house on Mt. Casas eventually became ours with a little help from my parents and, with our family filling every room, we had to phase out of our long streak of living with roommates. How perfectly fitting that the name of the street was literally "House Mountain" in Spanish. While life wasn't perfect, that thirteen-year season was a long, sweet mountaintop experience with vivid scenes of dynamic days.

Turning from the highway-like main street into our neighborhood was like entering a much less affluent version of Wysteria Lane. Streets bended with the shape of the canyon and houses built in the sixties set the scene for a community transitioning into a second generation of child-rearing. As the first homeowners retired and moved out, young families purchased the homes, added on, and updated them so that a drive down the street felt like a glance over a quilt of many fabrics. Turning left down our street, there was a single-story original on the corner with drought resistant rocks in the front, while nearby a two-story painted in brown tones brought the more modern, beachy vibe with tropical-tinged landscaping; and sprinkled in were houses like ours. There was nothing that made it stand out—no fancy cars in the driveway and no lavish curb appeal. The brown-trimmed, three bedroom, single-story was an ordinary setting for the dynamic life that happened on the inside.

Names of neighbors who became trusted friends to share life with scroll through my mind as I think about those days. The location was a pretty easy fifteen-minute commute for Chris to get to his dressmaking shop and we were about a mile from the elementary school. For four years, I lived the mom-dream—packing lunches, doing school drop-offs, potty-training, planning meals, keeping a tight budget to creatively plan outings, meeting friends for playdates, and remaining active in our church.

As homeowners with four growing kids in "America's Finest City," we depended on God to provide and saw His generosity again and again. Eventually, though, His provision came in the form of a job that combined my gifts, teaching experience, and mom season to serve our church family as the Director of Children's Ministry. The role provided much-needed health insurance and a salary while still allowing me to drop off and pick up my kids from school. There was even a preschool on the church campus where my youngest two could learn, grow, and play while I worked upstairs in the office. I brought back my juggling skills and balanced work, parenting, and church life. All of those roles blurred together during that time into a rich medley of bustling activity.

Each child remembers our "early years" from their own unique perspective, but pieced together, the cast and colorful scenes of our screenplay begin to emerge. In birth order, their memories are precious indications of lives well-lived.

"I remember Sea World and zoo passes, beach days in the summer, family thrift shopping on Saturdays," Julia begins the reminiscing.

Olivia adds, "The long bike rides we would do all the way around the bay when you were training for a run."

No matter what hobby or activity Chris and I started, we made sure to include the whole family somehow. Those runs must have looked like a parade with Dad taking up the lead pushing a stroller, two girls on bikes, a trickster little brother zipping in and out of the action on a Razor scooter, and a mom keeping a steady clip toward the back to make sure everyone stayed together. Chris called out directions with the confidence of a traffic cop, bold and loud, "We'll turn left up here! Slow down a little. Stop, stop... Jed, stop! Everyone look both ways..."

We all fell in line as he led us through the adventure. Sometimes we'd stop along the way to notice something, find a bathroom, or have a snack we had packed and carried in the basket of the stroller. Those were times the kids looked forward to special treats for good listening and positive attitudes. We never shied away from rewards for good behavior. Sometimes they were special privileges, but they often took the form of something delicious. On hot days, we'd stop at 7-Eleven on the way home and treat them to the coveted small Slurpees and watch them sip with delight as they weighed up stained tongues and squealed as they compared the severity of brain freeze.

Jed's memories come out in flashbacks that span large chunks of time: "Last minute cramming for AWANA even though Mom ran the thing... Mini Cooper mileage milestones, rolling slowly on the side of the 805 so Dad could watch it roll over to 100,000... 'G-Strings,' the band that traveled the world."

Those sentences beg for added detail but describe our life with absolute precision. Days were so crammed with the busyness of life that the Mom-commander of the Bible club was usually reduced to a frazzled taxi driver who collected kids from the neighborhood to transport everyone to church. I'd push the Bible verse song cassette into the tape player in the van and let it roll as everyone sang their verses. Someone would usually call out from the back, "Rewind it again!" and we'd sing over and over again until they had locked it into their brains.

Chris's attention to detail and milestones come through in his determination to actually see the numbers roll over on his odometer. There's a picture of it and a memory etched in his son's mind of time shared together, deliberate pause taken to slow down and experience something. He cared about the little things, and we celebrated simple victories with loud cheers, dance parties, or just simple group hugs and shared moments.

The band name came much later, so it's a foreshadow to when they're all teenagers. It's a cheeky ode to a rule Chris held the girls to. He refused to allow them to wear thong underwear. Most of them had instruments to play and needed a name for themselves. Seeing them obey him while being able to joke about it is a reminder of Chris's humor and the witty way he kept things hilariously real and edgy. Most of them have carried his sparkly sense of humor into adulthood.

Creative, raucous play characterized our leisure activities. We put our heads together to devise schemes that would appeal to all of them, were affordable enough, and packed the most active punch without being an organized sport. Chris didn't love those, and the kids didn't long for them either. When Julia was in kindergarten and I asked her if she wanted to join the little soccer league like her playmates, her response set a boundary for all future expectations. My verbose five-year-old quickly challenged me with a question: "Don't you know what they do?!"

"They play soccer. What do *you* think they do?"

"All they do is run the WHOLE time! No way."

Sicilia's memories click through like a slide show of snapshots that need wordy captions of interpretation:

"Remember the blind lady who would walk by and ask us to splash her on hot days?"

"How about riding to Target on bikes and riding in the parking lot like we were a car?"

"Dad purposely picked us up in the Mini just so he could see if all of us could fit in it. He even let us 'drive' around the block sometimes."

"Or what about when he drove the Mini on the sidewalk and chased us?"

Now that demands a backstory of epic proportions. Having a husband and father like Chris Gennaro was never boring. It was as if the vibrancy and verve of his personality were too big for the package it contained. Although he was on the short side, he was bigger than life. His style exuded incomparable flair and colorful boldness. Everything he wore was well thought out, from the jewelry he wore to express himself to the outfits, and even down to the car he drove. That chili red Mini Cooper with the black and white checkered top was the perfectly matched carriage for his matchless zest for life.

At the end of the day, as they rode their bikes and scooters up and down the sidewalk, their eyes darted east toward the turn where his car would eventually appear. It was a race to see who would spot him first, "Here he comes!" Working the clutch like a pro, Chris held a modest pace while revving the engine to make it seem like he was racing toward them. Then, with an exaggerated swerve, he'd turn into the slope of our neighbor's driveway, turn onto the sidewalk, and drive the five or six feet of cement between our houses until taking a left up the slight incline of our driveway. The dramatics of his entrance sent the kids into screeching delight as their voices rose to screams of declaration. "Daddy's home! Daddy's home!"

As soon as they turned around and boldly returned to the house, Chris would burst forth from the driver's seat with the beaming smile of a Formula 1 driver at the finish line. Arms wide open, he'd rush them for hugs and tickles as they giggled and screeched with delight.

It's the joy that lingers now. Laughter and play wash over the bumps, bruises, and speed bumps of life casting colorful hues of vibrancy over a life that should have been ordinary.

9 | Born in the Wrong Country

"I want to be a missionary."
– Chris

This wee little sentence written in the front of Chris's Bible from the time I met him didn't disappear from his heart; it just got choked out by the cacophony of life. By 2003, we were both busy with work and raising four children. Chris still had his dressmaking business and took on additional jobs in the lean seasons. Weddings, bat mitzvahs, and other formal events ebbed and flowed. My role as the Director of Children's Ministry at Emmanuel and balancing the care of our own kids kept us busy with our vibrant but ordinary life. It seemed as if we had finally achieved the stability of the American dream.

We navigated life like explorers, eager to try new things that busted the assumptions of the status quo. New things were exciting to us, and we looked forward to new adventures. When the colorful press release about a visiting Ugandan choir landed on my desk at work, I had no idea that hosting a concert would change the course of our daily life. The flier announced that a choir of orphans from Uganda was coming to our area on a Southern California tour. This wouldn't be just a concert; the touring group would need host homes that could house one of the auntie or uncle chaperones and two or three of the kids while they set up for their performance and had a day off. Pictures of dynamic, bright-eyed, smiling faces hooked me and I made the commitment to host a performance and provide housing for the group during their stay.

Our church family has always oozed with generosity so it wasn't hard to find seven or eight families who would be willing to open their homes to the group. Although our own home was already pretty full with four kids by then, we figured that displacing our kids to couches and carpet in order to give them the full experience of meeting kids from another culture would be worth it.

We sat in the front on the evening of the concert, our kids captivated by the rhythms of the music, the drums, the vibrant colors of their costumes, and the choreographed movements of their dancing. The overwhelming joy and redemptive nature of their testimonies is what drew Chris and me into their lives the most. Every one of the children was a true orphan—no mother or father—and they were being raised in villages run by the ministry. Despite the tragedies those kids had endured, they exuded hope and sang with genuine delight.

The deep attachments we had with those kids after having them in our home for only a few days led us to follow them to most of their concerts after that. Like a group of shameless groupies, our whole family would pile into the van and drive as much as two hours to see them again, experience the concert, and then steal a few minutes with them before they would head out to their host families. This routine nurtured our friendships with the directors and the other adults with the choir to the point that we were invited to join the choir for their end-of-tour, celebratory trip to Magic Mountain.

There are few things as exciting as experiencing roller coasters for the first time with people who have never been on one. Of course the reviews were mixed on whether the terrifying rides were fun or not. The aunties and uncles set the expectation as reasonably as possible, each of the kids had to ride at least once. As we rumbled along at break-neck speed on one of the rides with an upside down, out, and back loop, one of the sweet girls screamed desperately, "JESUS, SAVE MEEEEEE!!!" And then, on the way back when the ride hadn't stopped and she had to repeat the upside-down loop, she cried out again, "JESUS, ARE YOU THERE?!"

The day ended with a special meal at a local restaurant where we sat in amazement as the wife of the director calmly ordered for twenty plus children. The meal was spent remembering the concerts and experiences of their tour through our home place. We had built memories with them that would last a lifetime. We savored the privilege of the time we had been given with them and dreaded their return to their home country that was a world away from our own. The thought of never seeing them again was one we didn't want to face, yet it still came as a shock when Chris blurted out the next promise that would change our lives forever, "The next time we see you, we'll be on YOUR soil."

There's nothing practical, effective, nor advisable about traveling half a world away without a solid plan or goal, so we welcomed the wise advice of people within the organization. There were a couple of key staff members there who were especially invested in making sure our first visit to Uganda was a good one, not just from our perspective, but also for those we cared about and intended to help. Once it was suggested that we join a team from Tulsa, Oklahoma who was already scheduled to go later that year, our plans started falling into place. There were even enough spots available on the team for four of us, so we started the process of getting passports, raising some support, and praying that God would provide for what seemed like a crazy dream.

The team welcomed us with open arms and included us in their training and preparation for the trip scheduled for October of 2003. Chris and I brought Julia and Olivia who were ten and eight years old, which brought the size of our team to a total of eighteen people. There were couples, singles, and a variety of ages, which only added to the depth of learning and growth we shared as most of us took our first steps onto African soil. We were all transitioning from choir groupies to being hands-on ministry partners with an organization and cause we cared deeply about.

According to statistics and reports we were hearing at the time, there were more than two million orphans in the country of Uganda alone. No longer was this just an empty fact on a page, but there were faces we knew and loved who were living with the reality of it. We were excited and motivated to contribute even a little bit to a ministry that was making great strides to raise up the next generation of leaders for the country of Uganda. All of the money the team raised went to building a home for a widow and eight orphans in the new village Watoto was building to accommodate the growing need.

The excitement and anticipation of seeing our friends again in Uganda worked like the sugar coating on a pill that would have otherwise been difficult to swallow. As I mentioned before, we had a lean budget with very narrow margins for things like vacations and unneeded luxuries. This time, the immunizations required to prepare four members of our family to travel to an African country like Uganda had the potential to drain a bank account. Yet, God's provision poured in and sustained us as we took one step at a time toward each preparation deadline for the trip.

The day of our departure finally came, and after almost twenty-four solid hours of travel, the plane touched down in Kampala, Uganda. Our bodies screamed from the lack of sleep and the cramped seats of the airliner, but our spirits soared with elation and butterflies at the realization that our dreams were coming true. We were in Africa!

The doors of the plane opened and the crew gave instructions to weary travelers. With no gate or walkway that connected the plane to the terminal, passengers exited down the stairs of the airplane and walked across the tarmac to the simple building. Stepping into the crisp, outside air of the early morning in Kampala was a sharp contrast to the chaotic crowds of the vast indoor terminals of Heathrow. My body was stiff with the evidence of a couple of long days on the airplane, but my brain was slow to catch up to the reality of how far from home we were.

My senses were in a state of heightened awareness from stepping into a foreign place, and I found it difficult to take in all of the new sights and smells that confronted me at every turn. The land surrounding the airport seemed rural with sporadic trees and low shrubs popping out of a blanket of red dirt. A warm wind swept across my face and blew my hair back as smoky air shocked my nostrils. Years later, the smell of fresh air mixed with the smoke of cooking fires would take me back to those precious first minutes in Uganda.

Each of us held the hands of our daughters tightly as we approached the terminal building with our passports and visas. As we shuffled along with the crowd, Chris summed up all he was feeling in one sentence, "I feel like I was born in the wrong country."

As soon as the words left his lips, my instincts told me to brace myself. It was already becoming clear that the desire God had placed on Chris's heart back in junior high to take the Gospel somewhere else in the world someday was intersecting with our actual lives. As we boarded the bus with our teammates to drive into the city to the place we were staying, the team chatted with excited energy while our eyes fixated on the scenes we were passing outside. Shops made from shipping containers lined the street with their metal doors open. Hand-built inventory sat on display in various stages of completion: furniture, metal tools and bars for windows, caskets, clothing. My mind raced with the newness of it and the terror of Chris's statement. If he was feeling those feelings already, my life was about to change.

Getting to the actual worksite brought a sense of familiarity and anticipation. Our prior team building experience at Mexico Caravan Ministries came in handy when we got to the worksite as we worked alongside the local men to build the simple, four-room structure from bricks they made on-site. Mixing concrete and stacking up blocks that were formed a stone's throw away in the hot sun sapped us of energy but allowed us the priceless opportunity to learn more about the culture and people we were building with. All of us went about our tasks with gusto, learning new ways to construct a house and assisting in any way we could. Each time I looked for Chris, I'd find him working closely with one of the local guys, his attention locked on his face to understand what he was saying in a mixture of the local language and English with a strong, unfamiliar accent. His face gave away his passion for this, and he was fully alive.

Days were long and hot with quiet evenings at the guesthouse where we would shower, have a hot meal on the covered patio family style, and then share a debrief and time of study with the team. Friendships with a few members of the team quickly deepened so that we felt like we had a new extended family. We were all learning eternal lessons that would impact our lives forever. For me, my time in the village and the opportunity to get acquainted with people who lived simple lives with vastly different levels of material need challenged my own definitions of "need," "want," and "happiness." I had felt this contrast before in the dirt-floored, one-room, pallet-constructed houses of El Florido, Mexico, and it hit me again with even more power. Joy didn't come from having money or things but from a deep place of spiritual fulfillment and gratitude, regardless of possessions.

While all of us were observing similar things as we fully engaged every moment we could throughout the trip, it was Chris who seemed to be finding the place where God was calling him. One day, as we bumped along in the back of the sweltering bus with dust blowing into the windows and traffic slowing our progress through the chaos of the city, he turned to me and voiced the depth of the impact Uganda was having on him. What he said brought me back to that anxious place of bracing myself for whatever God was about to do: "I want to live and die here."

That truth, along with my own growing passion and love for the people of Uganda, fueled our motives to help as much as we could. There were endless needs in the ministry as they set out to address the orphan crisis, and we now had an understanding of what it took to do trips like the one we had just experienced. Before we had even left Uganda, a handful of us on the team had conspired to return together to fund and build a classroom in the new secondary school where the growing teens in the village could continue their education. We were back in Uganda by August of 2004, this time we led "Team *Amaka*" (Family) and brought Julia and five-year-old Jedidiah while the other two stayed in the care of their grandparents.

It's important to say here that it wasn't the work we did with our hands that made the biggest difference. Those buildings still stand and I'm sure they're still used; but the hands that built them aren't thought about as the orphan children go through their days at the school on the top of the hill and then walk down the dusty, red-dirt path to their humble homes and their foster mamas. It is God, their Heavenly Father, who gets the glory for all that He has done there and that's an answer to our prayers during the time we had with them. All of us had a clear and powerful sense that God was doing big things in our midst, but there was no way we could see out over our future lives to see the fruit from it. Years later, as the fruit begins to be seen, the eternal view is stunning.

For Chris and me, these trips were like the unveiling of our purpose. It was as if each day held snapshots of glory that we could assemble together and see truths about God that we couldn't see in our routines back home. By the end of the second trip, it was becoming clear to Chris that Africa was the place where he was to live out his calling to be a missionary. That revelation was just as evident to me, but my reaction to it was opposite to Chris's. He was ready to drop everything and move. I looked way ahead and felt the pain of the goodbyes and letting go. I was overwhelmed and filled with fear.

It was in that headspace that we arrived at Kampala Pentecostal Church on the last Sunday morning of our trip. Our driver pulled the van up to the main entrance of the historic, art deco theater building the church used as their main sanctuary. The huge structure stood as a tan ancient relic surrounded by the bustling city that rose up around it. The drab color of the outside left worshippers unaware of what awaited them inside.

We received a gracious welcome as honored visitors and partners in the ministry and were ushered to our seats in the front row. Thumping Christian music played in the background as people found their seats. As I stood in front of my seat and turned my head to see behind me, my eyes took in a heavenly sight. We were a fraction of the throng of more than a thousand Ugandan brothers and sisters dressed in their vibrant Sunday best crowding into the tri-level sections of the old theater. The worship team began to file onto the stage dressed in matching outfits, a choir of coordinated back-ups lined up behind them, and the energy in the room swelled to match the anticipation I felt just being there.

As the first song began to play and the worship leader shouted the welcome, the congregation spontaneously stood and broke out into applause. Swaying and dancing with arms raised, adorers praised the One who had set them free. The music swelled with an intoxicating crescendo and the worshippers rose to their feet with their arms in the air; but I remained seated, frozen in place as I wrestled with the Lord. Chris stood next to me enthralled and caught up in the spiritual journey he was on while I sat next to him praying. Surrounded and caught up in the moment, we both cried out to God about our future. Later, as we processed the experience, Chris poured out his feelings about the prayer he was led to pray during that powerful experience, "Lord, don't make me leave here."

My eyes must have bulged as my head dropped with the realization of how polarized our experiences had been. Sitting next to him in exactly the same space and time, with similar experiences and perspective, my prayers were desperate and filled with fear as I pleaded for the exact opposite: "Lord, don't make me stay."

Begging God not to make me stay in Uganda wasn't disobedience, it was the cry of a terrified daughter. I felt like I was on the precipice of something big and I couldn't put my finger on it.

Chris had been sewing since he was a child and had been a dressmaker for our whole marriage. As our family grew, we both had to work to make ends meet. He was well-respected in the wealthy, coastal community where he had his shop and where his business had grown steadily. Still, the nature of the business was feast or famine. In lean years, Chris had to work outside of his passion to bring home a paycheck, and that wore on him. I was well aware that stepping onto African soil had awakened his calling to be a missionary and that this awakening had made him dissatisfied and restless working the daily grind.

The more Chris testified to God's work in his life and the clarity of what God was calling him to do, the more afraid I became. I begged God to show me whether this was Him working in Chris's heart or if it was just a mid-life crisis. Was Chris simply feeling like the grass was greener in Uganda than in the routine of our life in San Diego? Was he just escaping his frustration with his search for fulfillment in life and work? I was willing to follow God to Africa, but I couldn't bring myself to simply uproot my family to follow the whim of a man, even if he was my husband.

"Oh, God, show me if it's YOU telling him what to do!"

The answer came more clearly than I had ever heard God; not quite audible, but yet louder than I'd ever heard Him. It was almost like a loud whisper I had in my head from a voice that was clearly not my own: "**GET ON BOARD**."

With my own calling clear, I began a journey to find the strength to obey. Where we were supposed to go was unclear and what our task would be was yet to be revealed, but we knew a few things. *Chris was called to be a missionary way back in junior high. It was indeed God who was preparing our hearts to live that out, and my calling from Him was to get on board with the plan as it unfolded.* This was a lot for me to process and led to the beginning of a much more intense and personal prayer life. It wasn't a neat and tidy morning ritual with knees bowed and hands folded, but an unplanned, unstructured, and unceasing desperate conversation with a Heavenly Father I couldn't see.

10 | Crossing My Own Jordan

Preparing to move

"When you see the ark of the covenant of the Lord your God, and the Levitical priests carrying it, you are to move out from your positions and follow it. Then you will know which way to go, since you have never been this way before."
– Joshua 3:3-4a

On one particular day during this season of traveling back and forth to Uganda, I was alone on a huge stretch of grass on the cliffs of the lavish seaside town of La Jolla, California. As a mom of four young children, it was rare to have times of solitude, and I'm not sure how I happened to have the time to myself. It may have been motivated by exercise; after all, that was one of my favorite places to run. I would often end my run in the expansive lawn of the park overlooking the crashing waves of the ocean into the Cove. Shaded by trees and cooled by the ocean breeze, it was a breathtaking, peaceful place to stretch. The stillness provided the opportunity to listen to God rather than just send up my usual frenzied requests for help. I felt raw and exhausted from my effort to be strong. I wanted to be obedient and faithful, but I was so afraid. Here I was in ministry, and yet I couldn't work up the faith I needed to follow Him without reservation. And then, as if on cue, the song playing in my ears began to speak to my weary heart:

> *"How did you know that I'm all alone today*
> *Oh, I feel so scared and I wanna go away*
> *I bleed so deep underneath*
> *My soul is screaming*

44

I'm not gonna hide
I'm not gonna run away
I'll uncover the scars and show you every mistake
Your love is mending my blisters and the bruising shame
Here with you,
I am safe." [3]

With the song still filling my ears with the calming truth that I was safe, my mind drifted to the passage I had read recently. I could picture the page in my mind—Joshua 3:1-17. The capital letters written in the margin of my old Bible illuminated the words: "MOVE OUT IN FAITH."

The same God who held back the floodwaters of the Jordan River was the One whose presence I felt as I pondered the weight of our future. I still didn't know all of the answers, but for the first time in my life I was willing to take risks for God knowing I was safe with Him being in control.

It's important to note here that these events were all unfolding at the same time in our lives. As I sit here remembering, it's difficult to organize the stories in an order that makes sense. The best I can do is present it as it actually was—earth shattering, confusing at times, mind-numbing, overwhelming, exciting—and most-of-all, messy. If your mind darts back and forth in whiplash fashion as you try to find your bearings in all of it, you've almost got it. Buckle up. Transitions like this aren't sequential and tidy, they're cataclysmic.

---

[3] Grant, Natalie. "Safe." On *Relentless.* Curb Records – D2-79025, 2008, CD, record.

11 | A Full Quiver

"Your greatest contribution to the kingdom of God may not be something you do but someone you raise."
– Andy Stanley

Being on Ugandan soil and growing to love people in their own home country did more than just broaden our world views and reveal our personal callings from God. It broke our hearts and wrecked us. How could we sit by in our privileged life and ignore the pain and hopelessness that we saw all around us? By American standards, we were probably hovering at the humble bottom of the working middle class, yet we owned a home, had two cars, great health insurance, and had never been hungry. The more time we had in Uganda, the more we realized that we *did* have resources God could use to make a difference.

Our hearts seemed to grow in size and capacity with each visit to Uganda. Knowing and loving orphans there nurtured a passion to do something, but we weren't sure *what* we could do. Although Chris was convinced that he was supposed to live and die in Africa, I hadn't yet received that same message, so we hadn't begun making plans to move. It seemed like most things we were equipped to do would just be a little, tiny Band Aid on a gargantuan humanitarian wound. A couple of things began to be clear to both of us as we wrestled with these things: we had enough love and resources for at least one more child and, as parents of four children, we were a solid team and could manage a large family.

The children we had been working with weren't available for adoption, so after our second trip to Uganda in 2004, there were only two steps we had taken toward a plan. We started praying and we shared our dream and prayer with our team so they could pray with us. They were the perfect ones to join with us in praying as their hearts were broken for the children of Uganda as well. It must have been toward the end of 2004 that our friend Brent met Debbie and her daughter Sonia on a plane when he was on his way back to the States from a business trip. It was clear that Sonia was adopted, so Brent took a bold risk and asked about how that came to be. It resulted in Debbie handing him a business card that would guide us to the next monumental milestone of our lives.

Now that we had a name and a contact for someone who knew about adopting from Uganda, our prayers intensified and our networking began. We already had plans in the works to lead another team back to Uganda to finish an administrative building in October of 2005, so we started there. We called our contact in the ministry office and asked her if she had heard of the small baby home in Jinja. Her answer shocked us in a profound, providential way. Not only had she heard of it, but she personally knew the director because she had worked with their organization for a time. Brent's chance meeting on the airplane now seemed like a lit arrow propelling us toward our next step in figuring out if we were supposed to grow our family through adoption.

The whole team was eager to see a new part of Uganda, so we planned a weekend for the adults on the team to raft the Nile and the rest of us to see the source of the raging, iconic river. After the team heaved their way out of the river soaking wet and sharing survival stories, we made the short drive through Jinja town to visit the baby home we had heard about.

Approaching the first blocks of the downtown felt more like we were entering into a small city perched on the lake. *Boda bodas* (motorcycles and bicycles used as taxis) zipped and weaved through the streets sharing the aged, rough pavement with cars and pedestrians carrying heavy loads. Markets full of fresh fruits and veggies from the region swarmed with local people. Everything you needed for daily, fresh meals could be found there. Colorful, plastic household goods hung on display and sat piled up and stacked around crowded stalls. Historically, this was a place where people converged to trade, and the town still had the electric feel of people from all over the world mingling in search of goods or enjoying time away in the lush, green landscape of the lakeside town.

We turned onto a red, rutted dirt road lined with tall walls and gates that blocked compounds with lush trees and vines. Occasionally, the shine of the lake could be seen through the trees to the south. Eventually, our driver Godfrey slowed the bus, turned left toward a large, red double gate, and tooted the horn twice. The alarm cued Joseph, the quiet and friendly groundskeeper, to come to the gate. He opened the locked, small door that was fashioned into the gate and stepped through it to talk to Godfrey, confirming that we had arranged for our visit. Once he properly cleared us, he gave a warm smile and welcome before swinging the gates open to let us in.

The main house stood tall and bold in the front of the property. It was a two story building capped off with an orange-red tile roof that seemed to match the rich redness of the dirt that stained the bottom of every building on the compound. Multiple dwellings of different sizes were situated toward the back of the property, each wearing a worn majesty that hinted of a colonial past. In the foreground was a large grass yard with a giant tree. A tire swing hung from it and there was a wooden treehouse and slide built into it.

As we inched up the short drive, the crunch of deep gravel under the tires alerted the children and we slowly began to see them appear from the various buildings on the compound. Miniature toddler-sized, black plastic toy *boda* motorcycles were parked neatly along the wall of the long building at the top of the property awaiting active toddlers who would scoot and zip around the slate rock paths that connected each house on the compound. A long clothesline was strung across the grassy yard between the main house and the smaller cottages. Cloth diapers hung like colored banners across the line and blew in the wind like party decorations.

This visit wasn't just a friendly visit or a volunteer project; for Chris and me it was really a reconnaissance mission. We weren't alone in our desire to learn more about other organizations who were working tirelessly to help with the orphan crisis that was a crushing reality in that beautiful country. The whole team had been looking forward to the weekend visit to volunteer in any way we could. Chris and I prayed that our providential meetings and time at Amani would be the next step in learning if adopting from there was even remotely possible.

As we arrived and piled out of the bus, the whole team was prepared for anything. Some of us helped hold and feed babies, others pushed toddlers on the swing, some painted, and others sat and folded endless piles of clean diapers. Silly left evidence of our contribution to the betterment of the clinic by leaving a precariously placed, indelible green handprint in oil based paint. Chris had a fever that day, so he did the responsible thing and stayed on the bus resting most of the time, although his determination to meet Danyne, the director of the baby home, wasn't quelled by his illness. Resisting the urge to hold any of the babies, he escaped his sick bed to seek her out.

It was at the tail end of nap time that we found Danyne in the infant rooms of the main house. She gave us a tour of those rooms as the babies and toddlers slowly stretched and roused from their afternoon sleep. I remember the room being darkened somehow for naptime. As Danyne walked slowly in a broad U-turn through the room, she passed built in cribs on every wall. The individual beds were constructed so that they were stacked like bunk beds. Latched rungs on the front side allowed for mamas and volunteers to pick the children up out of them. Like a proud mama, she gave a little background on toddlers as she passed their cribs. Her introductions and stories stopped when she came to one of the lower cribs on the far side of the room. As she stood there, she whispered the story of the tiny boy as he roused from his sleep and peeked up at us. "This is Joseph. He's one of my first twelve babies who came with me when we started. We call them the 'dirty dozen.'" She continued her description as we all giggled a little, "We've been praying for a family for Joseph for a long time. He is a precious boy, but he has club feet and will need some medical help."

Chris and I glanced at each other and, after comparing notes about the experience, I know now that we were thinking the same thing. Looking back and forth from each other and then glancing down at Joseph's twisted feet, we agreed and declared, "We have health insurance. We can help with that." Since Chris was keeping his distance, Danyne turned to me and asked me if I wanted to hold him. My body tingled with something like a mixture of adrenaline and compassion. It felt different from when I had scooped up numerous other babies to hold them on my hip. As I took him in my arms, Chris verbalized the question that was burning in our minds: "So, does he need a family?"

This was one of those Chris Gennaro moments where persistence and courage fed his resolve, and he took leaps of faith assuming that he knew what was going on in *my* brain too. He wasn't wrong this time. As he spoke the words, my grip on Joseph tightened and I didn't want to put him down. "We'll adopt him."

I don't even remember what Danyne's response was as my whole body and mind were flooded with some kind of eternal fog. This felt like those first moments with your newborn infant after they squished from the womb, only this time he was clothed and could look up at me with eyes that held a thousand longings. Filled with emotion, I followed Chris and Danyne in a dizzied trance as they entered the sparse room where the children ate their meals. We stood in the middle of the empty room. A clean, neatly swept mat was spread out on the cement floor where the toddlers sat in a circle and ate their meals from large, plastic bowls. Each room had a Ugandan mama who was in charge and volunteers from around the world made their rounds helping with all of the daily tasks. I struggled to focus on the details of the tour and Danyne's animated voice was distorted by the distraction of my realization that I was holding the answer to our prayers in my arms.

Chris's voice broke through my musings like the brash and sudden noise of an alarm, "Are there any other toddler boys available for adoption? I think it would be best if we brought two home at the same time."

He was on a roll now. My body pivoted in reflex as I found his eyes with mine. "What?!"

Glancing at me with a look of confident assurance, he turned to Danyne, and they continued their conversation about the possibility of adopting not one, but *two* toddler boys. She quickly jumped on board with Chris's idea to bring two toddlers home at once. Her first reason was obvious—the boys would have each other as they grew up. They would look similar and share the same story, which we all assumed would diminish the feeling of isolation they may feel growing up in our white, middle class American family. The brief meeting was suddenly interrupted by Danyne's brainstorm, "I know JUST the one!"

Time was frozen. I have no memories of the moments in between that decision and the arrival of my sixth child. I stood stunned holding Joseph as Mama Danyne bounced into the room carrying a younger, smaller, wide-eyed, sleepy toddler boy. "This may not be an appropriate reason to pick a child, but he's my cutest one! This is Duane, named after my Uncle Duane. We just had another family fall through for him, he can be adopted too."

The growth of our family happened just like that. It was sudden and clear. Three people united in purpose by the Holy Spirit stood in a room in Jinja, Uganda, and shared the supernatural beginning of a forever family. *"Whether you turn to the right or to the left, your ears will hear a voice behind you saying, 'This is the way, walk in it.'"* Isaiah 30:21. All three of us believed that God had ordained this meeting and we committed to move forward together in faith one step at a time until they made it home.

Our adoption journey was the longest labor of all. Saying we took one step at a time in faith doesn't describe it well enough. We had held Joseph and Duane and, in the scope of that first day with them, began seeing them as our sons. It was that vision that had two opposite and equally powerful emotional effects as we walked through nearly two and a half years of red tape and legal hoops to make them ours legally. It kept us fighting for them at all costs and held us in an emotional state very similar to pregnancy. We had the anticipation of having two little guys in our arms but had no control over whether it would actually happen. Once again, we had to place our hope and trust in God and His promises.

Along the way, through each mess of paperwork and the confusion of navigating a foreign legal system, there were circumstances in our adoption process that served as "markers" that God was in control. Rather than being false warnings about potential challenges like the ones we got during the ultrasound with Sicilia, these markers were signs to us that God was indeed working behind the scenes on our behalf. One of my most vivid memories was when our lawyer in Uganda gave them their names. The court was requiring them to have the standard number of legal names rather than just first names, so she set out to name them properly. In many African countries, this process has deep meaning and tells a story. On our side, we were going about the process in our own customary way, brainstorming names that would blend with the names of our other children with a *Lugandan* middle name that would be reminders of their home country and our journey to bring them home.

Although we hadn't yet communicated our process to those who were working on the paperwork in Uganda, we had gotten as far as choosing Joseph's middle name. With our very limited knowledge of the forty native languages in Uganda, we chose the name "Mukisa" for him because it meant "blessing" or "gift from God." We had decided to leave their first names the same because they were too old to change them, and they had been given to them intentionally.

As we were dreaming and going through the process at home, our lawyer was going through her own process to give them legal names for the court paperwork. When we heard them, it was like a message from God that He was indeed present in our process. Out of all of the names she could have chosen for Duane, she picked the name Mukisa. Then, it was Joseph's name that caused us to ask for more information. She had given him the name *"Kuteesa,"* which we had never heard of. Her explanation was like a message from

Heaven, *"Kuteesa* means 'to sit down and discuss.' It is as if we sat down to discuss this with God and He said it is His will."

Whether or not that is indeed the correct etymology of the word was irrelevant. To us, the name gave us hope that God was working behind the scenes on our behalf as we begged Him for help in a process that was taking place thousands of miles away. Once those papers were submitted to the court, the next thing we waited for was a court date. Family and friends from around the world prayed very specifically for every step of the process and we went about our daily lives restlessly waiting for the next call.

Facebook couldn't have entered the scene at a better time. Looking back, it looks as if we started using it simply to update our friends and family about where we were in the adoption process so they could pray. The first post after the details of my history on my profile is one posted on March 8, 2007. I was clearly a novice at writing posts back then, or maybe it was that there was a maximum number of words allowed. Either way, the updates were short and sweet and tell a very condensed version of the story.

+ March 8, 2007: "Chris and Michelle, along with their family, are excited to bring home Joseph and Duane!"
+ June 4, 2007: "Praying for our new June 29th court date."
+ June 7, 2007: "Packing again!"
+ June 14, 2007: "Praising God in the HIGHEST! Our judge CAN say YES!"
+ June 23, 2007: "Excited to see her boys in just a FEW DAYS!"
+ August 1, 2007: "Learning to trust God MORE!"
+ August 14, 2007: "Michelle is wanting her boys home... BADLY!"
+ August 30, 2007: "Praying for rulings!"
+ September 2, 2007: "Praying, this week, Lord..."
+ September 24, 2007: "Wanting to hold her boys."
+ October 7, 2007: "Finding her hope in the LORD."
+ October 15, 2007: "Wishing Joseph a happy 4th birthday!"
+ November 11, 2007: "IN Uganda now!"

Court dates were announced and then changed a number of times, each date bringing a wave of excitement that ended with the crash of disappointment when the date was delayed. There were a few other families in the process at the same time, so we weren't in it alone. Without rhyme or reason, other people seemed to sail through the process while we watched from the sidelines waiting for our turn. In those times, all we could do was trust God for the timing. Finally, the judge started giving favorable rulings and we began to see families coming home. Our hope began to rise with that news. Maybe we would be next!

Milestones started ticking by. We worked together with the staff at the orphanage to use the time to build relationships with the boys as well as we could despite the distance and length of time. They brought the boys together for play dates and began to tell them that they were brothers and that their parents were coming for them. We had one-sided conversations with them on the phone where we would call, and the staff would put it on speaker so they could hear our voices. We made little padded, fabric photo albums with pictures of our family and other extended family so they could look at us and we'd look familiar when we finally came for them. We had cozy blankets embroidered with their names on them so that they'd have something special to sleep with from us. Nothing we could do was an adequate substitute for our presence, but we prayed that God would comfort them and prepare them for our arrival.

By the end of June of 2007, almost two years after we met the boys in Uganda, our bags were partially packed and ready for the call to go. We planned to take Silly with us since she would be the sibling closest to them in age. It seemed logical for us to bring a "sibling ambassador" for them to bond with so that we could ease their transition from there to our home. My mom was also on call and ready to make the trip. She was in the delivery room for each of our four other babies, so we invited her along to witness Joseph and Duane's "entrance" into our family too. We were prepared with everything we could think of: gently used clothes I had been stocking up on from hand-me-downs and thrift stores, matching new outfits for Joseph and Duane to wear to court, shoes for each of them, a collection of healthy snacks we could give them for long car rides or waits at the courthouse, and little Hot Wheels cars and other toys and books to use as we bonded with them through play times.

Our excitement and anticipation to return to Uganda to see Joseph and Duane again had built to anxious sleep-depriving, head-spinning proportions. Thoughts of bringing them home with us and having them join our family were dizzying, with our minds racing with all of the firsts we looked forward to sharing with them. We anticipated so many God-inspired blessings and eternal lessons for all of us that our conversations usually turned to talking about what-ifs and imaginings of what was to come. This trip was different from the last three. This time we were coming to take care of family business, but we still saw the opportunity to connect with our driver Godfrey who had been a faithful friend and guide for us over the years. Having him welcome us at the airport, meet my mom, and drive us to Jinja was a comfort and joy that calmed our nerves as we entered the next huge step of faith in our journey.

As we entered through the gates, this time our weary eyes scanned the property for two familiar faces. As I remember, it was just after breakfast. The travel from LAX usually took nearly twenty-four hours and the time difference meant arriving in the early morning. We knew that Joseph and Duane had been moved up to the toddler house and into the same room so that they could get used to being together, so we made our way there. The mamas caring for them shared our excitement and squealed and yipped with delight when they saw us. It took no time for them to deliver them to our arms, and we received the answers to our prayers and held them again.

My mom was the first to hold Joseph this time, and my heart swelled as I held myself together to take a picture of all of them in those moments. Tears filled my eyes, and my hands shook as I took in the scene. Those were the moments I had been daydreaming about for so many months. It was a different kind of delivery room experience, but my mom was still there for this one like she'd been with the four others. Rather than looking at her holding our new baby in the sterile environment of a hospital, she stood there in Uganda among the banana trees holding a wide-eyed toddler.

It took a while to put the boys down, but it was playtime and it seemed like Joseph was excited to get out there with his little friends. Duane, on the other hand, was silent, contemplative, and content to be held as long as someone was willing to carry him. As we sat on the back porch and watched the kids play, we noticed something different about Joseph. He was running! Wait... he was wearing SHOES! Both Chris and I thought we were seeing things. Nobody had told us anything about Joseph receiving any kind of treatment! When we last saw him, he hobbled and walked on his right ankle bone because of his twisted foot! How was he running?! Stunned and curious, I found the nearest mama, pointed to Joseph, and asked, "What happened to Joseph's feet?! How is he able to run?!"

Her answer was confident but didn't explain the phenomenon and left us standing there stupefied in wonder. In her thick accent, she told us her perspective: "One day we just told him to get up and run, and he ran."

Further investigation confirmed that Joseph had not had surgery, nor had he had any treatments since we had seen him last. We had one picture of him as a young infant with casts on his legs, but medical records show that he had nothing else done to his legs after that. From the time we met him with curved legs and a turned-up right foot, Joseph had been miraculously healed. The very thing that had been a roadblock for Joseph being placed in a family had been straightened by the healing hand of His Heavenly Father. There was no other explanation. That little, bright-eyed boy running before us was a moving picture of a God who is present and powerful. We were eyewitnesses to a modern, Acts-like miracle.

"In Lystra there sat a man who was lame. He had been that way from birth and had never walked. He listened to Paul as he was speaking. Paul looked directly at him, saw that he had faith to be healed and called out, 'Stand up on your feet!' At that, the man jumped up and began to walk."
– Acts 14:8-10

There's a book's worth of triumphs and disappointments as we went through the adoption process in a place that had no system or reference for what we were trying to do. After our official hearing with the high court judge, we waited for more than a week before we found out that he had gone on a holiday without writing up his ruling for our case. Nobody could tell us when he would return, nor when his decision might be granted. Without his decision, we couldn't even begin the process of getting the boys' passports. There was nothing else that could be done. We had no choice but to leave them and return home.

There's a group picture of all of us that was taken on the day we had to leave them again. Chris and I are holding Joseph and Duane. We're posed as a happy little family on a gravel driveway in front of a taxi van. Our pasted smiles hide the grief and dread that were building up inside of us. The time came for us to hand the boys over to the staff and the tears flooded to the surface. We couldn't hold them back when Duane clung to Chris with his little legs. He had to be pried from his arms and we were forced to turn and quickly board the vehicle for our ride to the airport. Without understanding, it's hard to imagine what the despairing, confused toddler must have been feeling. We had made great strides in bonding with them and now we had to leave them behind, not knowing when we'd see them again or even if the judge would grant us permission to raise them as our own.

"God is not human, that he should lie, not a human being, that he should change his mind. Does he speak and then not act? Does he promise and not fulfill?"
– Numbers 23:19

I wish I had been journaling through that time so that I could pull back the memories with precision, but life didn't really allow for sitting. We returned to San Diego and back to life with our kids with the dull pain of waiting hearts aching under the surface. This was when Facebook and email became a lifeline. We watched the status updates of other waiting families, keeping in touch with the ones who were in Jinja with us for court dates, and prayed every day. We prayed for everything we could think of, down to the last detail.

Waiting times have taught me to pray more unceasingly. Each time a thought about that judge would surface, I'd stop and pray for him. I remember asking God to supernaturally move our stack of papers to the front of his desk so that he'd see them first thing in the morning. Based on what people said to us in this waiting time, I think it was hard to encourage us when there were no guarantees. We loved these boys and believed that God had placed them in our paths in order for them to be our sons, and yet there was nothing we could do to make it happen. The fact that we were depending on a largely corrupt system made it even more risky and tenuous. What a perfect recipe for learning to trust God rather than our own limited resources and intellects.

Chris was always the persistent one in times when we needed to stick to something, and that character kicked in with a vengeance during that time. He thought of all of the things we could accomplish while we waited: researching immigration and adoption laws in California, acquiring gently used clothing for the boys, and rearranging Jed's room to accommodate two more brothers. By American standards, we really didn't have room for two more children, but we had seen how the rest of the world lived and were willing to live dorm style in order to bring Joseph and Duane into our family. We already had the three girls bunked in one room, so once the boys came home we'd even the score and have the three boys share the small room with the camo-painted wall. With bunk beds and a toddler bed for tiny Duane, it would work for a while.

Finally, sometime in November, we got the call. The judge said yes! There was one problem: we had spent most of our money to get to this point in the process. We decided that I would fly solo so that I could begin the immigration process on that side and Chris would stay back with the kids. By this time, we had a huge network of people praying and waiting with us, so we put out what felt like the biggest, most humbling prayer request of all time: if God compels your hearts to give, please help us get Joseph and Duane home.

Without the ability to see the future, we had no idea how meticulously God was using this part of the process to equip us for the next season of our lives. We were getting our training in support raising, international immigration, filling out forms, navigating embassies and government offices, and especially prayer. With all of those systems in the works at the same time, I boarded a plane for the first trip I had EVER taken alone toward a destination where I would have to navigate a foreign system without Chris. Even with this, God was instilling independence, confidence, and courage in me that I had no idea I would need someday.

There was so much to do when I hit the ground in Uganda. With that signed document from the judge, we had permission to bring them home with us and eventually legally adopt them in our home country. Other families had gone through this stage of the process before us, despite the fact that we had been waiting the longest. From where we sat in the waiting place, there was no rhyme or reason for how the legal operation got these things done. However, as it turned out, by the time I arrived for this phase, the lawyer and staff had been oriented and they had paperwork drawn up and ready for me to submit at the necessary government offices because of the practice they'd had with the other families.

Navigating the heavily trafficked roads of Kampala and the chaotic government offices on different compounds became routine as we took each necessary legal step. Days started early so that we could get to the city before travel time increased as more and more travelers flooded the route to get there. We had to pluck the boys out of their beds, clothe them in the city clothes we had brought for them, and bring the little picnic bag of provisions we had put together with the help of the cook at the baby home. Hard boiled eggs were a staple for their breakfasts anyway and they were perfect for "take away."

Setting the stage for the victories God orchestrated throughout this process would be remiss without including a few of the challenges we faced. Ironically, some of the harrowing tales came from the very toddlers we were fighting for. The confidence I had as a parent of four children flew out the window on the first day trip into Kampala. First of all, Chris and I were supposed to be together so that we could help each other! Because of the circumstances, I maneuvered through the legal labyrinth without him. Adding my unfamiliarity with the boys' expressions, habits, and potty routines to my lack of enough hands made for hair raising days.

Just as we'd get going on the highway, or as we'd finally make it to the front of the queue on one of our life-critical errands, Joseph would get wiggly and whisper, "*su-su*." Then, with all eyes on me because I was a white woman with two little Ugandan toddlers in tow, I would have to find a bathroom or private spot for him to pee. One time, his urge was so strong as we drove along that I had to call out to the driver to stop along the road as we passed through the jungle. This was a dangerous proposition and highly discouraged because stopping to park on the side of the road made you sitting ducks for the bandits who often waited in the cover of the dense trees and vines.

As he squirmed and became increasingly desperate, I felt like taking a quick risk was our best bet. The only other option was to allow them to soak their clothes which would eventually mean mine would be soiled too as I carried them reeking through a full day of errands in the heat. Finally, most likely because of the panic he could sense coming from behind him, the driver consented, and we pulled over and swung the sliding door of the van open so Joseph could relieve himself. As I stood him on the step and helped him with his pants, another one of the boys said, "Also me!" Before we knew it, there we were with three little boys lined up on the step of the van peeing off into the jungle.

The "Mystery of Urgent Su-Su" was solved when we figured out that the porridge the kids got first thing in the morning was nutritious, but also made them have to pee like crazy. Eliminating that from their morning regimen on town days was helpful but did nothing for Duane's vomiting. Each trip made him limp and miserable. Without warning, in whatever position he found himself in, vomit would escape from him in a violent, vile waterfall and splash over his clothes and the rubber floor of the van. I wasn't sure what made him sick, but I learned soon enough to hold a plastic shopping bag under his chin with one hand every time we traveled in a vehicle.

In keeping with His promises, God provided for our financial needs at just the right time through the generosity of our church family. Within a week of our request, there was enough money for Chris to book travel for himself *and* Julia and Olivia to make the trip. This meant that there were two of us to handle the nerve-racking trips to the capital city, the girls could have a depth of understanding about what we had been through to bring the boys home, and they could begin to bond with their new little brothers. Ironically, with that huge hurdle behind us, adding two children to our family through adoption still brought adjustments and difficulties we had read about, but underestimated.

Once again, head knowledge failed me, and I was back in that vulnerable, groveling position with my Heavenly Father begging Him for help. Our ignorance about the boys' bodily functions was only the beginning of labor pangs. As it turns out, maneuvering through the harrowing legal process in a third world country was also similar to the physical pain of labor and delivery in at least one way. Years of life tend to dull the details in my memory and the excruciating emotional pain of the two and a half year battle have faded into a movie-like drama.

Each legal step has its own perilous story that ends with a miraculous deliverance. After a dramatic, pineapple scented, gut-cleansing vomit from Duane because of his motion sickness, our sons, Joseph Kuteesa Rose Gennaro and Duane Mukisa Rose Gennaro, had their first McDonald's hamburger in the Amsterdam airport and then landed with us at LAX, arriving on U.S. soil for the first time and welcomed by a beloved welcoming committee of friends and family holding balloons. My brief Facebook status updates declared the news:

- December 1, 2007: "... is coming home with her boys!"
- December 3, 2007: "... is a mother of SIX and is with them ALL! Praise God!"
- December 12, 2007: "... is rejoicing that 10 Amani kids are home for Christmas!"

12 | Firsts and Foreshadows

*"Life has many ways of testing a person's will,
either by having nothing happen at all, or by
everything happening at once."*
— Paul Coelho

If God had a supernatural remote during our adjustment to having six children, the pause button was missing. We seemed to live somewhere between play and fast forward with no chance to stop and almost no time to look back. Julia was starting high school, Olivia was finishing junior high, and we had two in elementary school when Joseph and Duane came home. We both had to jump right back into our jobs because we had used up every bit of our vacation time and money. There was no paternity leave and no maternity leave. Our new life felt a lot like we had cannon balled into the deep end. Of course that caused ripple effects for everyone in the household, and beyond.

We had rearranged Jed's room to accommodate a bunk bed and a toddler bed, added some organization shelving in the closet, and literally shifted everything he owned to add two more little bodies. Chris and I always erred on the side of figuring that the big love we had as a family would compensate for wealth and lack of space. Besides, we had passed a home study by a licensed social worker before we were given legal permission to adopt the boys. Living dorm style was totally fine!

Our house was a three-bedroom, two bath house with a built-in room in the back and we made use of every square foot of the property. The three girls shared a room at the end of the hall and slept on a custom, triple-bunk loft set. One was on the top, high up near the ceiling, another was in the middle, and the third rolled under the middle one in an L-shape with a small dresser next to it. That left a little crawl space behind the dresser that they would either use as a hide-out or a place to cram excess stuffed animals. Each girl had their own matching dresser and shared the long closet. The arrangement worked fine most of the time, but it really cramped the older girls' style when they became teenagers. I didn't find out until they were well into adulthood that their arguments would sometimes come to blows. Even in the midst of their cat fights, though, they worked together to stay quiet enough that Chris and I wouldn't hear them.

Life was packed for us in every way. Not only was the house bursting at the seams, but we bustled to and from multiple schools for drop-offs and pick-ups, juggled work and church activities, and participated in the extracurricular activities that came with having a high-schooler. We navigated all of it together as a family, often piling into our big, white, twelve-passenger van with neighbors and friends tagging along.

Julia's high school had a robust theater program, so that meant I dove wholeheartedly into the program as a "Drama Mama," helping with fundraisers, set design, and selling concessions. The rest of the family took on roles, too. Usually, they were all groupies who saw most dress-rehearsals and performances and shouted, "Yay, Julia!" during curtain calls. One time, though, during the production *Wizard of Oz*, the director granted promotions to siblings, and Jed and Silly were cast as soldiers in Munchkinland. Julia played the scariest Wicked Witch and wowed us with her fire-throwing and rap skills.

The description of our life during this time would be incomplete if I didn't stop to clarify that all of the activity happened without leaving Joseph and Duane in the care of anyone else besides Chris and me for an entire year. We had taken parenting classes in preparation for our adjustment to being adoptive parents and knew that the first, most critical focus had to be our attachment to the boys. Even though they came from a loving place, their caregivers were staff and volunteers who rotated in and out throughout the day in shifts. The boys had never had parents. We had to have them with us at all times, deliberately and consistently be the ones to provide their every need, and literally carry them as much as possible.

Thankfully, they were small for their ages! At three years old, Duane wore nine month sized clothes and could still be carried in a baby backpack.

Scrolling through Facebook history plays like a sporadic, skipping slide show for that year. Posts were few and far between, but they still provide an accurate snapshot of those days.

February 10, 2008: "Enjoy these (pictures) of the boys' FIRST field trip with the preschool class I work with at church, to SEA WORLD! Also THE FIRST TIME AT THE OCEAN! If Joseph says he wants to go back to the 'fountain', he means the OCEAN!"

April 22, 2008: There's no caption, but we posted photos from our first family beach camping trip with our friends, the Kirk's.

May 23, 2008: "Rejoicing that in ONE week, Joseph and Duane will FINALLY be ours for GOOD!"

June 13, 2008: "Getting ready to decorate for Olivia's 6th grade promotion! Yikes!"

July 18, 2008: With help from my parents, we had a family vacation in Kauai with extended family. (Note: By this time, Joseph and Duane had big smiles on their faces, a sign that they were at least beginning to adjust.)

Whether documented on social media or not, all of the "firsts" flew by. First time at the ocean, first camping trip, every holiday first, first time to taste our foods, graduations, promotions, birthdays. All of the kids engaged in every celebration with the gusto and verve of explorers in a new land. They had taken turns traveling with us to Africa, endured weeks apart from us while staying with extended family or having family and friends stay with them in our home and waited with us distracted and often grieving through the uncertain process of bringing them home. Because of that, each milestone felt victorious, and we celebrated those firsts together with all of our simple favorites. The older kids eagerly gave us input on what needed to be passed on to their new brothers and joyful smiles frozen in photos are the evidence of a season of wonder.

It would be more accurate to say that it was a season of wonder laced with bewilderment and a steep learning curve. We were navigating attachment and life with two little boys who were learning language and everything else about a vastly different place. They were often shell-shocked, disoriented, destructive, and dangerous. It wasn't all fun and games. One time, I caught Joseph sticking a bobby pin in an electrical outlet, arriving just in time to witness the strong smell of electrical smoke and the unmistakable stain of black soot on the wall above the plastic outlet plate.

There were also times Jed begrudged his new roommates for their lack of experience and respect for toys like Legos. Most of Jed's precious, intricate creations ended up destroyed and scattered throughout the room in a million pieces. We eventually figured out that we had to baby-proof the house even though the boys were far from being babies. Even the snacks had to be moved out of reach in the pantry. At the baby home, the main kitchen was an outdoor area, blocked off from access by the children, and constantly supervised by "Mama Cook." They had never seen an indoor kitchen with doors they could open with immediate access to snacks of all kinds. It must have been after watching the rest of the family grab food from there that they figured they could snatch delicacies like crackers and fruit snacks to gorge on at random times in the day.

There was no doubt that our present circumstances demanded all of our attention and focus, yet there was a persistent longing that gnawed at us in the background. Africa. Bringing the boys home and getting settled into a routine didn't erase the compelling pull we had to move. We prayed and prayed and sought wise counsel from people close to us, some who were in leadership at church, and our families as we wrestled with the prospect of becoming missionaries and leaving all of it behind to take the love of Christ we had experienced to people who didn't yet know Him. The reviews were mixed on this radical idea. Most people expressed that it was too risky, we were too old, we had too many kids, or that we were irresponsible for entertaining such a notion. We listened, but the voice inside of us that pulled at us daily ate at us and beckoned us toward taking steps in that direction. We were fully engaged in life in the suburbs of San Diego while on a trajectory toward a life somewhere far across the world.

13 | Dared to Move

*"A few clear pronouncements on one side and a few honest
questions on the other had, in a matter of minutes,
shown me that life was not going to be as simple,
ever again, as I had thought."*
— Elisabeth Elliot, <u>No Graven Image</u>

The rest of the house was dark, and the TV
room still held a cozy warmth from the heat of day. Soft light
illuminated the room from the large lamp on the desk and a breeze
brought a calming coolness in from the backyard through the open
sliding glass door. Chris and I reclined on the carpet in the family
room and lounged, taking in the stillness of the evening with the
kids all in bed. As we caught each other up on the happenings of the
day, he showed me a DVD he had been holding in his hand. It was
obviously something that had been copied by someone personally
because it had a generic, white sleeve that covered and protected it.

"Ryan sent us this. Wanna watch it?"

Ryan and Heather were our good friends from church. We had
known them from the time they were newly married, hung out with
them in their first house, and even previewed the nursery they had
lovingly prepared when their first baby was on the way. Both of
them are extraordinary teachers, leaders in the field of education,
and have been role models in whatever school they find themselves
in. It was early in their career when their dedication to teaching
intersected with their passion for carrying out Jesus's command to
go and make disciples. Once they saw the opportunity to use their
careers to teach missionary kids so that other team members could
go to remote places with the Gospel, they responded by selling their
house and moving to Kenya where they served as teachers at a
missionary boarding school.

Since they lived in Africa, we saw them as the perfect ones to entrust with what God was stirring in us. We had told them about our travels to Uganda, they had followed our adoption journey with the boys, and they were aware of our growing desire to live and serve somewhere in Africa. Although they were at least ten years younger than us, they had the wisdom of ones who had gone before us into a place we'd never been. They had walked a path we hadn't taken yet and were poised to guide us in very specific ways. As we shared the compelling, consistent, and burning desire God was putting in our hearts to move, they had two main responses.

The first piece of advice was to go with a sending organization. They drove home the importance of having a company behind you for the long haul that would manage donations, provide medical insurance and retirement, prepare us with necessary training, and then giving us the structure and support of a team once we were living in Africa. All of those things were imperatives to our safety and effectiveness in whatever role we held there. They had chosen Africa Inland Missions as their sending organization because they were specifically looking to teach at a missionary school, and it had a long-established school in Kenya. The core values of the company aligned well with theirs and they had confidence that we would also be a good fit with the team they already knew well.

I remember the exact way Ryan said it: "If you're going to move to Africa to serve, you might as well go with the organization we know and trust."

He followed that up with a creative tactic to solidify our decision. He made a video with images from their life in Africa, put it to music, and sent it to us. That was the DVD Chris held in his hand on the quiet night we decided our next step into the future. As he slid the disc into the player, we sat transfixed. Pictures of the land we longed for swept across the screen as the band Switchfoot sang the words that confirmed what we already knew. Whining guitars accompanied our falling tears as we looked at each other and the lyrics reflected the tension we had been feeling and foreshadowed our trajectory into the next season of our lives.

"Welcome to the fallout
Welcome to resistance
The tension is here
Between who you are
And who you could be
Between how it is
And how it should be yeah
I dare you to move
I dare you to lift
Yourself up off by the floor...."[4]

We couldn't shake the compelling charge in our hearts to go. It felt like urgency, and rather than continue to try to resist it, we'd take one step at a time toward what we sensed God was telling us to do. That step became clear, and we knew what we had to do next. We allowed Ryan and Heather to introduce us to key people within their organization, began the application process, and trusted that our Heavenly Father would make the way clear one step at a time.

---

[4] John Fields, Switchfoot. "Dare You to Move." On *Dare You to Move*. Sony BMG Music Entertainment – SWITCH01, 2005, CD, Single, Promo.

14 | Preparing to be Sent

"The 'romance' of a missionary is often made up of monotony and drudgery; there often is no glamor in it; it doesn't stir a man's spirit or blood. So don't come out to be a missionary as an experiment; it is useless and dangerous. Only come if you feel you would rather die than not come. Don't come if you want to make a great name or want to live long. Come if you feel there is no greater honor, after living for Christ, than to die for Him."
— C.T. Studd

The call to "get on board" introduced a tension in my life. Our life was full with living the answers to our prayers for meaningful work, Joseph and Duane being a part of our forever family, and we lived within a couple of hours from family so that we could enjoy holidays and special occasions together. It wasn't discontent that had made us want to shake our fists, throw in the towel, and leave. There was a growing sense that we weren't where we were supposed to be anymore, that there was something urgent we had to do elsewhere. We were firmly grounded in our lives in San Diego but it felt like our wings were bound and we couldn't fly. Thoughts of serving overseas in Africa were always in the back of our minds and in our prayers and we each wrestled with God in a different way.

Chris was confident that we were supposed to move to Africa for a long time; if not forever, at least the rest of our careers. Julia loved Africa, and when she was a preteen girl, visiting every year, used to tell us, "When I grow up, if you want to see me, you'll have to go to Africa." Now that she was approaching the end of high school, she saw the prospect of us moving differently with a bigger dose of reality. She knew that it meant she wouldn't have a childhood home to come back to on Mt. Casas, that her siblings would have a much different childhood than she had, and that very soon her family would be on a separate continent.

The concept of a move seemed to be more of an adventure to the younger the children. Joseph and Duane were still adapting to life in our home and couldn't conceive of what that would mean for them. After all, they were still getting used to being where they were! We lived with an acute awareness of the impact our decisions would have on our children and extended family, but the thought of ignoring what God was clearly compelling us to do left us with a pit in our stomach that felt a lot like a lifetime of regret. As we saw it, we had two choices. Because we were parents, we lived out our faith in front of our kids. They were always watching and observing. We could either obey God and trust Him with whatever happened, or we could model disobedience and live with regret and the consequences of that.

This constant restlessness lingered as a ticking distraction in the background as we navigated the year of "firsts" with Joseph and Duane. Sometimes it was subtle and could be prayed away quickly and other times it rose in crescendo until we had to pause to discuss all of it in depth, praying and talking late into the night until we could make sense of it all. As we wrestled through the details, we also worked through the application process with Africa Inland Mission (AIM) bit by bit. We filled out the long application, had a visit from the regional mobilizer and his wife in our home, a formal interview, hours of psychological tests proctored by our pastor, and took the final step—a week of orientation, training, counseling, and more interviews at the U.S. Headquarters in New York.

We took the three boys with us on that trip because we were still in the year of constant care and attachment, and it was Jed's "turn" to travel with us. We stayed in dorm-like housing with others who were in the same process we were. Each conversation with like-minded people comforted us and made us realize we weren't the only ones living with the stirring to live out this radical idea. It felt so life-altering to me, so much like laying everything familiar aside, that I had a sense I had to sacrifice all of my comforts to make it happen. I was just coming out of the headaches from giving up coffee when we arrived at the campus shaded by dense groves of mature, deep green trees. The landscape was a drastic contrast to the arid, Pacific Southwest scenery we were used to.

As we turned into the drive at the bottom of the property, our insides swelled with feelings that we couldn't push down anymore. There was excitement to be there, relief that the traveling was over, nervousness for what was ahead, trepidation about the enormity of the decisions that were ahead of us, and wonder at all that God had orchestrated to get us to that point. The driver turned left up a sloping hill and parked in front of a long, two story building with broad stairs leading up to a lodge-like entrance. It felt more like we were arriving at a conference center than an office. After being welcomed by name, we were shown to the simple, hotel-like room we would share with our sons for the duration of our time there.

Years have made the details of that time foggy. I don't remember if we were there a week or three weeks, how many hours we sat in meetings, or even the details of every training session, but monumental truths are emblazoned in my brain as markers of God's presence along the way. He showed up in simple, but obviously personal ways beginning at our first meal in the community dining room. Floor to ceiling windows allowed a view into the insides of the woods at the top of the property. The light filtered through the trees and warmed the room with morning sun. We walked in as a family and took in the scene. Our soon-to-be colleagues milled about like confused freshmen students looking for a place to sit among faces they didn't yet know. The smell of fresh coffee caught in my nose and reminded me of my sacrifice. Surely, I would no longer be able to enjoy that luxury in the place God was sending us. I'd resist my temptation and push forward in my commitment to caffeine-free living.

As I got up from the table to make my way to the juice dispenser, I was met with a man my height who was carrying a black, cooler-like bag with a long strap. I filled the plastic cups with orange juice for the family as I watched him from the corner of my eye. He unzipped the bag and began pulling out items one at a time: Ziploc baggie of coffee beans, coffee grinder, and a coffee press. As he stood by the machine that brewed coffee quickly in mass quantities, he proceeded to grind his own freshly roasted beans, precisely scoop the fragrant, rich brown, freshly ground coffee into the press, fill it with the hot water from the machine, and then stood there comfortably to wait while it steeped. He must have noticed my eyes peering at him and he greeted me, "Good morning."

"Good morning," I replied awkwardly.

I knew what I wanted to do. By the looks of it, this guy had been around for a while. It would take a risk of being embarrassed if I asked the question that burned in my mind; but I had to do it. "Are you a missionary?"

His confident smile gave me the answer to my question, and he introduced himself, "I'm Steve. My wife and I are the missionaries in residence this week."

"Tell me about your coffee system there."

"I don't drink that stuff." He motioned toward the tall, standard issue coffee dispenser with the hot water spigot on the front.

"Don't you live in Africa? I thought I'd have to give up my coffee snob life."

Steve chuckled audibly. "You don't have to give up good coffee. The best coffee in the world grows in Africa. All you need is a few tools. If you have a press, you can make good coffee anywhere, even without electricity."

A tingling rose up from the inner child part of me as I realized my assumptions were wrong. I wouldn't have to give up one of my favorite little things. Suddenly, I felt like I could do it. I could move. My Heavenly Father would provide, and I'd even have hot coffee to start the days no matter where I lived. Hallelujah!

We sat through numerous long meetings and emotional sessions about what we could expect when living cross-culturally, leaving and grieving, how to thrive in remote locations without doctors or grocery stores, getting along with teammates of every personality type, and generally drinking of heavy content from a fire hose; we were weary and restless. Both of us took notes in an effort to give ourselves a tool for remembering all we were taking in. The worn pages of that notebook still contain hand-written doodles and notes in most of the unused spaces of each photocopied paper. On the bottom of the first, faded yellow page of the chart with the schedule for the event, in Chris's artistic printing, there's a bold quote that jumps off the page, *"Life always comes out of death."*

In the cool of the evenings, we'd grab the boys from their kid program and lead them down to the meadow for a walk along the trees. The sun was slipping away by then, leaving long shadows and dusky hues of light orange on exposed swaths of grass. We talked about all we were learning and processed what the boys were experiencing too, chatting, and changing subjects along the way with the turning of the path. Suddenly, like a boy who had discovered a hidden treasure, Chris squealed with delight and pointed to a nearby shrub, "Look! See that?! Get closer. Wait for it... It's a lightning bug!"

Released from the intensity of our discussion, we erupted into a frenzy of childlike wonder. Each of us ran and darted from bush to bush, arms extended, hands cupped, waving, and aiming until they were clapped together hopefully. No lightning bug was safe at that point in the hands of that small band of Southern Californians and Ugandans who had never seen them. By the time darkness signaled the end of our quest, we were breathing heavily and giggling, worn out from the full day of heady newness. A sense of truly living washed over me. What was ahead would be difficult, but there would be grace, new discoveries, and joy along the way.

Days ticked by like this until we felt like we belonged in that place. We had forged friendships in the shared intimacy of what we were working through and the common compelling force that was drawing us to Africa. We were exhausted by the hard stuff and full of anticipation for the next steps that we knew would be revealed by the end of our time there. Finally, we were approached by the Candidate Director and asked to meet with him in his office. My heart was suddenly obvious to me, fluttering and bumping in my chest like my babies felt when they moved in my womb. We took our seats silently as we both faced our destiny.

Paul was a tall man who wore khaki pants and a button up, long sleeve business shirt accessorized with a patterned tie. As he leaned in and bent a little lower to look us in the eyes, his stuttered start to what he was about to explain exposed the awkwardness he was feeling. I braced myself for the worst that could happen—rejection. I forced myself to listen despite the dread and found that I was wrong. They saw our hearts and the earnestness of our sense of what God was calling us to do, we were highly qualified and life experience gave us added wisdom that would serve us well, our marriage was clearly solid and steadfast, and the organization desired us to be a part of the greater mission to take the Gospel to the unreached people of Africa. But not yet. We weren't given a "yes, go," or a "no, you're not appointed." We were given a "wait." In the wisdom that came with many years of sending people to the mission field, the ones we had entrusted with the decision about our service saw the needs of our children and the gargantuan task of preparing for such a life-altering change. They appointed us as members of the organization but mandated a two-year wait before we deployed. The time would give Julia a chance to graduate from high school and allow Joseph and Duane to complete their attachment to our family before the upheaval of another cultural change. They also suggested that we have some counseling so that we could work through issues from our past that may be magnified in the pressure cooker of living in a foreign place. There were Bible courses to take, a house to sell, careers to transition out of, and support to raise. Balancing all of that with the rigor of our life would take time, and they wanted us to thrive.

Finally, after years of traveling back and forth, longing, praying, wrestling, and wondering, there was a sign within view on the road ahead, "This way to Africa... Changes ahead... Yield to heightened emotions..."

God used the strategic pause of the waiting time tactically. Our family continued to develop and grow while His messages and lessons hit us from every angle. Milestones did what they do and rolled in like waves, arriving on schedule, but still catching us off guard and slightly unprepared. The kids were growing, developing, moving forward in school, and downright getting older. The big, white van wasn't just the family school bus, but the first vehicle Julia drove on her own. There's a snapshot of her leaving the house on her first solo drive. She's in the driver's seat of a van that most people would have gone through an employee training to drive as an airport shuttle or something. In the picture, a carefree sixteen-year-old waves and smiles confidently, heading out on an errand by herself with enough room for eleven other people.

Looking back, we were also learning about culture acquisition from walking through Joseph and Duane's adjustment to our family and home place. We could only see in hindsight, with the help of

Joseph's teacher, that his grasp of the English language wasn't as developed as we thought. He moved ahead to first grade, but we had him do that grade level for two years, changing teachers but not curriculum. We also allowed Duane more time at home before starting kindergarten. He got to join me wherever I went, to and from work, dropping off and picking up the other kids at three different schools, grocery shopping, and anywhere else life took us during those days. The church preschool was his favorite place during that time, and he seemed to catch up to his peers over time, running and playing, finding his voice, understanding, and speaking English perfectly, and even having a little devious sparkle in his eye for occasional naughtiness.

The other thing that was developing during that time was technology. As the world wide web took over our lives, it became customary to write about personal things and cast them out over an unseen network for the world to see. It would be quite self-centered to believe that God orchestrated the availability of communication for our own personal benefit, but it wasn't coincidental either. As the time approached for us to begin doing our partnership development and raising up prayer and financial support for being missionaries, we had tools to share what God was doing in our lives. With all that God was revealing to us and teaching us, we had plenty of material. We used every technological tool available to us at the time with gusto and even honed our blogging skills. Those writings are time capsules into a time when the rapid succession of transitions and the emotional weight of our imminent move took all of my brain capacity. Where my memory is foggy and time has dulled the sharpness of the details, at least I can look back at these excerpts to get a peek at some of the snapshots.

15 | Look What God Did!

"I don't know about you, but knowing that the CREATOR
OF THE UNIVERSE, the ONE TRUE GOD, thinks of YOU
kind-of makes you feel loved and adored."
– Me

Blog Post by Michelle

One of the things God has done in the last year, is to take a 40-something couple and a six-pack of kids and face them in the direction of the path HE's had for them all along. This has been nothing short of one of His miracles! We're a rag-tag group of sinners who have BIG hearts to love and a bunch of issues like anyone else. It is humbling to realize that God CHOOSES to use me despite myself. AND HE REALLY DOES KNOW MY HEART! How do I know He does, you ask?

On our journey into Africa, Chris and I have gone from having a love for the people of Uganda and a burning desire to go deeper with God and GO, but no clear direction...TO an assignment in a place where we've never been with a purpose that is obviously designed for us! It was opening ourselves to wherever He wanted to send us that made me most vulnerable and yet, I'm realizing now, gave me the most joy and freedom. I had finally come to the place where I believed with all of my heart that my Heavenly Father had a plan that was GOOD and that I should just follow Him – even if I didn't know where He was leading me. Then, He had the mercy to tell us where we are going ahead of time! Isn't that marvelous?! I can't tell you how this has buoyed our whole family into excitement and anticipation! Even the children talk about going with expectation!

I don't know about you, but knowing that the CREATOR OF THE UNIVERSE, the ONE TRUE GOD, thinks of YOU it kind-of makes you feel loved and adored. What's great is, He has that much love for each of us! He's the true King who never ceases to charm, amaze, and cause me to look up in awe at Him! Please continue to pray for those who will partner with us in moving to a rural village in the mountains of Lesotho to share this same hope and truth! The next step is depending on others financially...yikes. That'll be a biggy.

The exuberance we felt as we got our assignment came from a place of wonder and delight at the obvious way our Heavenly Father answered our prayers to match us with the need that existed somewhere on the huge continent of Africa. Remember that Chris was a man who sewed from the time he was ten. What tripped him up for most of his adult life after he received that clear direction as a junior higher that he wanted to be a missionary was the fact that he wasn't a Bible teacher. He wasn't a theologian, didn't have a degree in anything profoundly spiritual, and he didn't think he was a charismatic speaker. He was a dressmaker. How would God use him as a missionary?

Almost a year after we were appointed and given the "wait" by our organization, we were given five assignments to pray about. All five of them needed teachers who would use their vocation to fill a need in the community and build relationships that would eventually be deep enough to share the hope of Christ. Four outlined the opportunities for English teachers and the last felt like our own burning bush experience. It caused us to want to remove our shoes for the holy ground we were standing on. A non-profit organization had donated treadle sewing machines that could run without electricity a number of years previous that were sitting in a vocational school in a remote village in Lesotho. For a few years, up until the time we laid eyes on the paper we were reading, the team in Southern Africa had been praying for someone who could come and teach sewing in order to provide income-generating skills in a place without enough job opportunities.

We couldn't deny that such a task was set aside for Chris, and we knew this was the neon sign pointing us in the direction we were to go. The role we had accepted with AIM was on a volunteer basis and would be a supported job that depended on people praying and donating money monthly for us as we carried out the task. It was a step of faith that was humbling but allowed us to see God at work in our lives and through His people.

With the huge question of *where* we were moving taken care of and answered, we turned our attention toward learning about the place, praying specifically for the people we would eventually know and love, and inviting others to partner with us to make it happen.

16 | Things in Common
Blog Post by Chris

Today, I am so amazed with God's blessings upon our family. I should back up a few days.

Last Saturday, while Michelle and three of the kids were at an AWANA games competition, a friend came over to check out what home improvement projects he could help with (we are getting our house ready to sell). We are so thankful people are willing to help. We have been in this house for 13 years. Eight people in a 3BR/2BTH can get a little tight. I would describe our home like a favorite pair of jeans. We fill out every inch, we rub things a little thin, and we constantly need cleaning. The wear is really showing. Michelle and I chose to have a large family in our small house and do not regret that decision. So, on to the Saturday conversation, which went something like this:

Visitor: (A bit bug-eyed) "This is no small task. The only way we can get all of this finished is to move your family out of the house for at least two months."

Me: (Gulp-trying not to hyperventilate) "There is no way we can do that. We live here, I work part-time out of the house and there is no place where we can relocate."

Note: We are scheduled to depart in 129 days.

Me: "Yikes!"

Needless to say, I was a little overwhelmed for the remainder of the weekend.

So here we are, five days since the conversation. Let me tell you how God has blessed us through His body of believers.

There is not one weed left in our front yard. There are only two plants left on the side yard that was so overgrown, we could not walk along it. In the back yard where there was weeds, and a nice large "divet" to make our "white trash" summer pool deeper, there is now level soil (no weeds) and trenches dug for the repaired sprinkler system. There are new sprinkler valves too! You think that is something!!?? We were planning on just touching up the painted trim on the exterior. This time next week, our entire house exterior will be painted a nice (sell it fast) mocha, with parchment trim and accent color (TBD)!

It doesn't stop there! At the suggestion of our Realtor, we started a pretty involved wall modification that quickly moved way beyond our ability. Today a friend from church came by to look at it. He is a carpenter. He said, "No problem. I'll be here to take care of it on Monday." On his way out, he called another brother in Christ and asked him to come look at some electrical in the wall. That man came right over and said, "No problem, I'll be over Monday to fix it." It's going to be busy here on Monday!

Can you even believe all of this!!! I am feeling amazed, blessed and completely not worthy of such outpouring of skill, hard work and love. I feel like Sally Field at the 1985 Academy Awards!

"...this time I feel it, and I can't deny the fact that you like me, right now, you like me!"

But what is really so much more amazing is that all of these people are doing these incredible works because they LOVE Jesus. It has nothing to do with liking me or not. They are living out what the writer of Acts told about in Acts 2:44 "having all things in common" – meaning voluntary generosity shown by sharing one's skills, labor, or finances with brothers in the faith.

God is once again using His body of believers to confirm His movement in our lives. He is in no way obligated to me or my family. Yet, He lavishes His love upon us daily just as He did when He loved us so much that He sent his Son to die on a cross for us.

He didn't have to do it.
But, I'm so glad He did.

– Chris

17 | "Surely, I Am With You Always."

Blog Post by Michelle

Yesterday I turned 45. I started the day in The Word and was reflecting on the Great Commission because I'm preparing to speak at a Women's Event next week. Jesus' words jumped off the page at me and it was JUST what I needed to hear, "And surely I will be with you always, to the very end of the age." It's what he said immediately after He commanded ALL OF US to GO and make disciples of all Nations, baptizing them and teaching them to obey everything He has commanded us. As you know, that's the command we're responding to. While I have NO regrets for taking this leap of faith, it is a time of trusting God for our daily needs and choosing multiple times a day to remember His character, His mighty acts that He has done in our lives in the past, and TRUSTING Him with our kids, our finances, our house, our future, His timing, and on and on. It was in this frame of mind that I began my birthday.

There's just not enough free time lately. We're still working on getting the house ready to sell. The Body of Christ here has been hard at work helping us and we're still working like mad. TRUST. We can only do what we can do and leave the rest to Him. So, in the spirit of doing what we can, we ran errands.

Finances. God DID change the tax laws just for us this year. I don't know if you heard that! Technically, we can get the rest of our adoption credit in a lump sum. We filed for our taxes and they asked for more documentation in order to receive the credit. The wait...45 days. Within our church family, we have a friend who is licensed to work with the IRS, so we went and signed over a power of attorney for her to look into it for us. Pray for the Expediter she is going to speak to! Meanwhile...

*The clutch went out on the Mini. First, $1400, then $1700...
and, the birthday message, the hydraulic system must be replaced
also...$2000. Needless to say, we don't have that money. However,
Body of Christ again. We can make payments. TRUST. I am with
you ALWAYS.*

*Our kitchen appliances have been out of the kitchen while Chris
installs flooring. (It looks beautiful!) My birthday wish was 1) no camp
cooking 2) no doing dishes in the garage again 3) Souplantation with
the family! Well, even a modest meal like that is a big expense for our
family, so I was trying to get a coupon printed. Did I say our computer
was attacked with a virus, trojan, malware somethingorother and
we can't print anything? TRUST. NOTHING I tried worked. Couldn't
hook the laptop up to the printer, both computers Julia has access to
at school were down, neighbors not at home. Body of Christ. Called
our friend who lives on the way to the restaurant. She printed the
coupon! When we went to pick it up, she realized she had been given
a gift card for us. Guess where it was to? SOUPLANTATION! Coupon
AND gift card!!*

*I decided I should go to AWANA. I haven't been able to go for a
long time and I missed my peeps! Turns out, they were scheming a
blessing! They surprised me with a farewell birthday. The WHOLE club
squeezed into one room and when Demi led me in, they all started
singing. They all had made cards and sweet letters for me. When
I got home and started reading all of them, there were gift cards
galore! There were enough gift cards there to provide restaurant
meals while our house is shown and/or outings for our bucket list
until we leave! TRUST. I am with you always. Your Heavenly Father
knows what you need.*

*Reflecting on the events over the last couple of days and the
truth that God is in control caused me to get lost in my thoughts and
I savored the peace that washed over me. I don't know how all of this
is going to happen, but HE does. I don't have to worry, though. The
joy returned, the burden lightened. Then, suddenly, back to reality...*

*A car sped in front of me abruptly changing lanes with his
middle finger high in the air. Was that for me? This is the truth of
my existence. I'm living IN the world, but am not OF this world. I'm
feeling less and less like I belong in my home, my country, even my
skin. I guess this isn't my home after all.*

"'I tell you the truth,' Jesus replied. 'No one who has left home or brothers or sisters or mother or father or children or fields for me and the gospel will fail to receive a hundred times as much in this present age (homes, brothers, sisters, mothers, children and fields – and with them persecutions) and in the age to come, eternal life.'" Mark 10:29-30

It's all gonna be worth it when I see Him face-to-face. I'm choosing to TRUST. He's in control, trials, middle fingers, and all!

– Michelle

18 | Clearing House

"Do not store up for yourselves treasures on earth,
where moths and vermin destroy, and where thieves break in
and steal. But store up for yourselves treasures in heaven, where
moths and vermin do not destroy, and where thieves do not break
in and steal. For where your treasure is,
there your heart will be also."
— Matthew 6:19-21

Two transitions loomed on the horizon for our family as the calendar pages flipped through the prescribed waiting season—Julia's graduation and moving to another continent. The steps we took one by one to prepare for moving eventually led to us seeing God do things we honestly doubted could be done. While most people our age were preparing their graduates for the transition to college, we were laying the groundwork for a whole-family launch. It was a transition all of us would go through together and, because we hadn't experienced anything like it before, we dug out our notes from our training, sought wise counsel for help, and did our best to navigate the leaving and grieving the best we could.

One of the suggested strategies for the stage we were in was outlined by an acronym that was easy to remember: R.A.F.T. We were instructed to be mindful and deliberate about addressing four things as we got our family ready for saying goodbye and leaving: Reconciliation, Affirmation, Farewell, and Think Destination.

As parents of six kids, there was at least one thing we were pretty good at—multitasking. In order to get anything done around our house, or even in accomplishing more monumental life tasks, we had to have a few things going at the same time. In the normal pace of life, I was usually cooking dinner while helping a couple of kids with homework and keeping an eye on the younger kids playing out in the yard. I could listen for a kitchen timer and the cries of my children simultaneously. Now, we set about the task of traveling to see friends and family, meeting with people to invite them to partner in the work that was ahead of us, and checking all of the "lasts" off of the list we had compiled with the consideration of every family member: last family vacations, last time to favorite restaurants, last sleepovers with favorite people, and finally the last giveaway of our worldly possessions.

After hearing a story about someone who had their adult children put sticky notes on the back of pictures and in inconspicuous places on household pieces, Chris fantasized about the day when he could entertain friends and have them compliment something in our house and shock them with this unexpected move. I can picture his giggle now as his blue eyes sparkled with the anticipation of what he would say in response. "I'll say, 'Oh, you like that? Here, take it!' I'll just take it off of the wall and hand it to them to keep!"

When the time came to let go of all that we had acquired over more than twenty years of marriage, Chris's daydream seemed to make the most sense. Our strategy involved a few stages: clean out every conceivable place in the house, have garage sales to sell the junky, less special things we didn't need anymore, give the usable things to people we knew could use them, and have an open house event for all of our local friends and family we wanted to see before we left. Unlike a housewarming party, guests would leave our party with something special from our home. In that way, we would have the joy of knowing that our favorite pieces were being enjoyed by our favorite people.

We had so much fun surprising our friends with the concept that it added delight to a process that would have otherwise been painful. As the day arrived, we tidied up the house, set out things that we wanted to be visible, prepared snacks and drinks for those who came to visit, and opened every door so that people could mill around and mingle in every corner of our property. Nothing was sacred at that point. Everything was laid bare and fair game.

It's hard to look back at pictures of that day. The images captured our smiles and tears as we wrapped our arms around people who had been a part of our whole adult lives. A trained eye would be able to look at the details and see evidence of the intense season we were in. My hair is clipped back haphazardly and I'm hosting a party without make-up, something completely out of character for me. In the final scenes of the day, the house looks messy in the background, stripped of the wall decor and critical furnishings that made it look like a well-loved home. Lightly faded shapes were all that remained where pictures and carefully collected pieces once hung, shadows of the dust of life the only persisting shadows.

In the end, Chris's daydream to pass on our possessions and empty our house into the homes of our loved ones came true. Our dwelling slowly became less and less our home and more of a launching pad for a destination we were looking toward. Years later, friends and family let us know that they prayed for us every time they looked at or used the things we had given them. The process of leaving and grieving was nearing an end and the day of departure loomed in the not-so-distant future. There aren't enough emotions on the spectrum to describe all that our family was processing on a daily basis and, no matter how we colored it when we talked about our impending move, it was downright debilitating at times.

19 | Pain in Leaving, Peace in Going

"As we cried through those last few days in San Diego,
a few words kept coming to mind:
'HE IS WORTHY.'"

The whole history of our lives culminated in what we were about to do. As a couple with six children, two jobs, a home in San Diego, a church ministry, and close family throughout Southern California, we had a lot to consider. The messages came at us from all directions: "Shouldn't you wait until your kids grow up?" "Why do this at your age?" "Is it safe?" "Don't sell your house!" We asked ourselves similar questions, searching the scriptures for clarity and direction. "Could all of the money be raised for a support target large enough to sustain a family of eight?" "Could we learn another language at our age?"

Each time I tried to find evidence to prove we shouldn't go through with the unfathomably radical plans we were implementing, Bible verses forced themselves to the forefront of my mind and interrupted the arguments I had with myself. On one occasion, my morning quiet time was bamboozled by one of these wrestling sessions as this verse crashed any hopes I had of finding an excuse to change the plans that were overwhelming me:

"If anyone comes to me and does not hate his father and mother,
his wife and children, his brothers and sisters – yes, even his own
life – he cannot be my disciple."
– Luke 14:26

Unable to focus anymore, I slammed my Bible shut and headed to the church office for our weekly staff meeting. Arriving a few minutes late because of my morning cry session, I burst into the room and interrupted the light, pre-meeting chatter of my colleagues. I'm sure they weren't surprised to find out that I had been struggling. My puffy, tear-stained face was the first evidence of the raw emotions I was grappling with. I sat heavily in my chair as I released a deep sigh and declared, "I can't find any reason to stay. Everywhere I look in the Bible says, 'Go.'"

Understanding eyes met mine with compassion and love. I had found the answer to the battle that raged in me for courage enough to face the huge leap of faith we were about to take: it was scary and hard, but it was what God was asking us to do. I'd press on and trust Him despite my fear. As I submitted to the plans I was sure my Heavenly Father had for us, biblical promises replaced the doubts that assailed me.

Matthew 19:29, "Everyone who has left houses or brothers or sisters or father or mother or children or fields for my sake will receive a hundred times as much and will inherit eternal life."

Philippians 4:19, "And my God will meet all your needs according to His glorious riches in Christ Jesus."

Philippians 4:13, "I can do everything through Him who gives me strength."

Verses like these challenged and spurred us toward the most difficult thing we had ever done — leave. Although we moved forward, confident that this was God's plan, the pain was grueling. This wasn't just causing us to hurt; we were causing pain to our children, asking our families to sacrifice and let us go, and leaving our friends and neighbors. Yet we believed then—and I still believe now—that we would rather model obedience to our children and to those around us than keep a white-knuckled grip on all things secure and comfortable.

We celebrated Julia's graduation with joy, pride, and the usual pomp and circumstance. Her milestone event was in the middle of June, and we were scheduled to leave just a couple of weeks later. I remember planning for the party and being torn between two priorities. It was like I had two opposite realities manipulating the thoughts in my head. *We have a grad party to host, so we need to have some of our furniture, plates, and other entertaining accessories to entertain these people. Yet, on the other hand, the house has to be empty and ready to sell before we leave in a couple of weeks.*

This wasn't like packing up belongings into boxes to load into a moving truck; this was touching every single item we owned, making a decision about what to do with it, and then getting it where it needed to go: trash, donation center, friend, or family member's house. Looking back on that time conjures up some shame because of the amount of work that we left for our closest friends to do even after our departure. I know there's still no way to repay them for what they did for us.

Shame wasn't the only feeling that existed in the time and space between our life in San Diego and the vast unknown of our future life in Africa. I'm pretty sure that between the eight of us, we felt every emotion God placed in the human repertoire of feelings. Looking back, those days foreshadowed a life lived in the tension of polarizing opposites. We were so proud of Julia and her accomplishment and were happy for her, full of joy with our family surrounding us; and at the same time filled with a looming dread that we would soon be saying goodbye. Just as soon as excitement welled up at the fulfillment of the dream and vision of a lifetime, doubt would sweep in and cloud it over. Were we doing the right thing? Were we wrecking our kids? How was everything going to play out?

While we didn't have answers to those questions, we took one step at a time toward what we knew God had asked us to do, and He showed us His faithfulness along that unnerving and tumultuous path. As for the details we had been praying about, each need was met just in time. The year of our departure and monumental life change was also a year to remember in our nation's economy. It was in the midst of the housing crisis of 2011 that we prepared our house to sell and listed it to be timed as strategically as possible. We absolutely had to sell our house before we left, and we needed a place for our family of eight to live until we got on the plane.

Thankfully, we had the best of the best in realtors and God on our side. Our friend from church was reaching retirement after a long career in real estate. She trained and coached people who sought to navigate the business as well as she did. Yet, with all of the prayer and all of the expertise, she couldn't make any promises that she could sell our house in the middle of a historically terrible market.

We set about other tasks as the "For Sale" sign stood in the front yard like a beacon of change, and we prayed while we purged everything. One friend bought our van and let us drive it until we left; another friend did car repairs on the Mini and we signed over permission for him to sell it in our absence. Later, Chris admitted that the beloved red Mini Cooper with the black and white checkered top was the hardest material thing for him to let go of. There were so many memories attached to that car and it was a possession he really enjoyed. Friends from every season of our lives came forward and did things like scrub places most people would never see and adopt our old, blind little dog.

Surrounded by family and friends in almost every task, we set out to pack our future lives into twenty-one pieces of luggage that would at least sustain us for the first days in our new, never-before-seen home. The largest room of the house was the combined living room and dining room, and it was void of furniture, so we used that as the hub for the things we would take with us. Thinking through the strategy of such a task kept us up at night, but in the end Chris came up with a plan that made sense to us. Each kid would have their own packing tote to pack what they wanted to take with them. It was a "safe zone." They could choose whatever they wanted to put in there as long as it only weighed seventy-five pounds when the lid was clamped on.

The large room was lined with open totes and brand new, top of the line, name brand luggage that had been given to us by a neighbor. Her father worked for one of the top luggage companies and we had the best of the best. It was one of the many grace-gifts we received along the way.

We packed sentimental things to make our new place feel like "home," winter clothes for the mountains of Lesotho, small kitchen tools that I couldn't live without, made guesses about what clothing we would need, and stocked up on necessities for the long haul. On one occasion, when my mom asked what she could do to help, I sent her to the local megastore to buy a year's worth of three different kinds of tampons. We had to think of everything!

The kids processed through their belongings piece by piece, bringing toys, books, Legos, and stuffed animals to put them in their tote only to remove them and put something else in there the very next day. All of us were figuring out what we couldn't leave behind and the process left us sapped of energy. Once we arrived on the other side, there ended up being many things we forgot and other things we would end up wishing we had. But we learned for ourselves something we were told by others. Things are replaceable. You miss them for a moment and then you move on.

As we cried through those last days in San Diego, three words kept coming to mind: "He is worthy." I reflected on the eternal life that was mine because of Christ's sacrifice. When pain returned, we would press through it, taking one step at a time and asking for His strength to carry us through.

It was the day before our early morning departure that we got a call from our realtor announcing that we had an offer on the house. My parents were over for the last time helping with the last minute packing and soaking up the last minutes with six of their eight grandkids. The chaos of those moments is too much to make sense of. I can't bring every detail back clearly, but the main things are clear. We signed the papers for the sale of our house at 7:30 p.m. the night before we left for good, only nine hours before we pulled away from the curb! Not only that, but we didn't lose the house; we didn't have to foreclose on it like so many people had to do at the time. We made a whole seven hundred and fifty dollars!

It took two SUVs and a trailer to get all eight of us and our twenty-one pieces of luggage to the airport on that dark morning at 4:30. Chris and I hadn't even laid our heads down to sleep that night. Preparations continued through the night until we had every bag shut, sealed, and labeled. There were so many things left undone, but we had to depend on others for that and walk away. Our dear friends came to pick us up that morning, loading our things in and hugging us alternatively. I don't remember who I sat by, nor which vehicle each family member sat in. I know that everybody was clothed, had a backpack, and was present with us. My brain wasn't able to process what we were in the midst of doing.

We got into the trucks and pulled away from it all without looking back. I was in my forties, a wife, a mother of six children, and I had a master's degree, but as I sat in the vehicle with my eyes squeezed shut, I felt like a little girl who just needed her daddy. I couldn't turn my head to look back at what we were leaving behind. It was just too painful. When I felt the vehicle round the second corner and pick up speed, I knew we were on our way and opened my eyes to look ahead. All of the questions had been answered, the money had been raised, our house was sold, and the goodbyes were all said. As our family of eight stood in the check-in line at the airport with tear-stained faces, we must have looked like robots mechanically taking one step at a time toward a place we had never been.

There was evidence of God's presence with us through every goodbye, every security check, every transition, every plane ride, every night when the children would ask, "Where will we sleep tonight?" Our strength came from a power outside of ourselves, and we were able to do the things I never thought I would be able to do. We were received at every airport by someone who had been praying for us and we actually enjoyed laughter along the way. Those things were merciful gifts to us in a time when we didn't know the way.

Leaving San Diego had to be the most painful thing I had ever done up to that point in my life. From the time I had seen the words in Chris's Bible, "I want to be a missionary," my heart had feared moving. Actually doing what my human heart feared, though, opened up a whole new world to me. I learned that the leaving is excruciating. However, following through with what we knew God was asking us to do and actually *going* brought a level of peace I hadn't expected. Everything was foreign, but we had a sense that we were right in the center of His will, and at least we could count on that being eternally consistent.

Part Two |
Lesotho, Africa

"Nothing but breathing the air of Africa and actually walking through it can deliver the indescribable sensations."
– William Burchell

20 | A New Life Far From Home

"First you arrive physically and you are very tired. But only after a while, your soul gets there too. Because the plane is very fast, but the soul takes longer to arrive."
– Marilyn R. Gardner

A lengthy journey across multiple states and borders in planes, vans, and buses with six children and twenty-one pieces of what's left of your worldly possessions tends to accomplish a few things. After the first couple of sleepless nights, our bodies cried out for any horizontal surface. Anything would do at that point. Every leg of the journey made me want to scream, "Lay me down on a rock-hard slab of concrete and let me close my eyes!"

Any choosy, lofty expectation of what our lodging would be like—or even our house at our final destination for that matter—went by the wayside. We were physically and emotionally exhausted and we just wanted to stop moving, set our stuff down, and rest. Our family was used to traveling like that of course; but this time was different. This was a one-way journey. There was no turning back. The weight of it seemed to simmer a punchy silliness out of the vulnerability we found ourselves drowning in. The dizzying magnitude of what we were going through as a family seemed to meld us together into a clumped up heap of giggling confusion. We were disoriented, but we were finding our way together and there was always something to laugh about.

My memories of our arrival come as scenes from a disorganized screenplay with a cast of characters that get thrown into the script from all over the world. We weren't the only ones being trained out of the ignorance and shock from our recent dive into the deep end of culture shock after the biggest leaps of faith of our lives. There were twenty or thirty others who had similar compelling stories that brought them to our current state of disorientation, and day-by-day they became a new kind of family to do life with. We'd all end up going our separate ways to a multitude of different roles in vastly different landscapes all across Africa, but we were part of a greater team and that created a bond that would endure for years following.

Some of those people from our training days are still cemented in my mind, part of the slideshow of pieced-together, random memories that I am able to recall. In scene one, we were deplaning and walking down a crowded, dimly lit jetway. There were many nations represented in the throng that funneled into the cramped space. Pungent whiffs of body odor from days of travel mixed with occasional spicy wafts of unfamiliar, perfumy scents. It was the moment we'd all been waiting for. Our family had awakened to the reality we found ourselves in. We were standing, walking, stretching our legs in the wild air of a new continent we'd laid everything down to enter. The descent and landing of the plane had forced Chris and me into a hyper-alert state that allowed us to corral our children, put their backpacks on their backs, grab hands, and match them up into a spontaneous buddy system that would allow us to navigate whatever awaited us at customs and, beyond that, the long-awaited reunion with our belongings.

As we plodded along slower than our brains wanted to go because of the number of people pressing toward the same goal, a little blonde head caught our attention. Our whole family recognized the three-year-old as the only child of our new friends who would be a part of the aviation team. It must have been her excitement to escape the confines of her airplane seat that led her to slip away from her parents who were walking just behind us. Even our older kids saw the need to spring into action to try to grab her hand and reunite her with her mommy and daddy.

As all of our eyes fixed on her bobbing, golden-haired head and we took in what we saw as if it played out in slow motion. She had her beloved, miniature doll clutched in one hand and held her other hand out to touch every surface she passed with innocent curiosity. She had the childlike trust and witless curiosity we all needed in those moments of immediate adjustment. She wasn't thinking about germs or danger; she was blissfully taking it all in. Then, in a move too quick for any of us to prevent, she turned toward the wall of the well-used jetway, stuck out her tongue, and licked it as she walked. One of us shouted, "Nani!" and lurched forward to stop her from collecting any more bacteria in her mouth while the rest of us burst out laughing. Our nerves were calmed by the random hilarity of the moment, and we let ourselves be shuffled along by the crowd toward customs.

With all of our passports safely stamped and permission granted to stay in Kenya for a while, we stepped onto the descending escalator and caught a view of the task in front of us. A continuous, creaky, well-worn conveyor belt carried luggage, totes, boxes, and awkwardly shaped parcels along an open, expansive lobby-like room like a snake. Bleary-eyed travelers clamored for a spot near the belt to watch for their personal things. We looked at each other as we realized how daunting the task ahead of us would be. As the moving steps set us down on the ground floor, Chris began giving the commands as we pressed through the crowd.

"Big kids, you guys stay over there by that pole while Mom and I pull the luggage off of the belt. We'll bring it over to you and then we'll put it onto carts after that. Jed, see those carts over there? See if you can get a few of those and take them over. Joseph and Duane hold the girls' hands and DON'T MOVE."

As we heaved totes and rolled duffels over to our meeting place, Chris was keeping a count and the older girls were checking his work. Jed had secured a few luggage carts, which allowed us to pile the heaviest totes and bags without wheels first so four of us could push. It took all of us working together to get all of the pieces of our luggage from the belt and out toward the open air. By the time we looked up from our work, the crowd had dispersed, and we were among the last to roll our little caravan out of the open doorway. I have no idea what time of day it was when we arrived, but the sky was dimly lit with an orange hue from either dusk or dawn. It didn't matter. Our bodies were confused from the time travel and solely focused on our next step, finding our transportation.

We stood still for a long pause and took in the sights and smells around us. A look to the right revealed the traffic jam of taxi vans and over-packed cars vying for position for the two lanes that eventually led to the exit. The air was fresh compared to the cramped quarters of the last few spaces but carried smells that confirmed we had landed in a new place. Exhaust from the vehicles that approached, paused, and took off again with more passengers than they were designed to carry reminded me we were no longer in California. There didn't seem to be emissions laws here.

People crowded around with the same goal, bumping past and congregating with less personal space than we were used to. The cacophony of voices calling out greetings in many different tongues blended with honking horns and revving engines. As I continued to scan the arrivals area for familiar faces or signs, the hint of smokiness caught my nostrils. I took in a deep whiff of it. I'd never stepped foot in Kenya before that moment, but the smell took me back to the many arrivals to Uganda and my brain was able to register my location. This was Africa.

Somehow my sleep-deprived brain had gone into a forced mode of instinctual, heightened awareness, and I scanned to the left, catching sight of a huge bus with a large group of white people gathered around. I don't trust my memory here, but I swear one man was on top of that bus and another taller man was passing things up to him. I can look back and use logic and hindsight to fill in the details that must have been truer, but the bottom line was we had arrived, all eight of us, with all that we owned in tow. We were headed to a guest house where there were beds and food. Once we had those things, we could face the next transition.

The next scene jumps precariously forward at this point to a seat on the crowded bus. Although my view of the front window was mostly obscured by the heads of my comrades, I could see we had arrived at the guesthouse where we would be staying for a couple of days before heading out to the Bible College that would host us for our training for the next three weeks. We'd have a chance to get over the jet lag here and store most of our things until it was time to move again.

A tall, white metal gate stood firmly in front of us. It had spikes on the top and a little window in the middle where a guard could look through and see anyone who signaled their desire to enter. The bus driver hit the horn, lightly letting loose two quick honks. Spiraled metal swirls of razor wire topped the high block fence that stood like a tall, armed guard between us and our destination. With a heave and a creaky squeal, the heavy gates were swung wide for us to enter by a guard who waved us in. In front of us a three story, lodge-like Victorian building came into view. It wore a regal, round turret in the front that rose like a crown above the historic property. Huge trees towered over green grass and well-manicured shrubs that filled in the space between the buildings. This was rustic beauty that drew you in with a sacred, welcoming warmth.

We were led to our rooms after being warmly welcomed by the Kenyan staff, each one of them wearing genuine, broad, sparkling white smiles. Deep, singing voices gushed nothing but joy in meeting us, "*Karibu! Karibu sana.*" "Welcome. Very welcome." For a moment, I was swept away with their accents and forgot the weariness and burden of the journey. We were still sojourners, but we were somewhere safe and wonderful.

The old, wooden floors creaked as each individual family filed through the small, modestly furnished sitting rooms in the front of the house. Hunky, wooden-framed couches and chairs sat in clusters, one grouping was arranged in front of a fireplace and a table with aged, well-worn books lying here and there waiting to comfort wandering souls. Every wall held reminders of where we were: a detailed map of Kenya, pictures and paintings of wild animals, tapestries and curios gathered from the countries missionaries from our organization had collected from their homes on the continent for over a hundred years. Each was a reminder of a people group who was loved and introduced to the transforming love of Jesus.

We passed through an open doorway into a small, wood-paneled room with a stairway, almost lost our youngest two to a tiny playroom off to the side, descended three stairs, and jogged left and then right down a narrow hallway. Every step and turn required careful maneuvering as we lugged backpacks, bags, and kids with weary arms. I remember shushing the kids to be quiet at that point. Recalling that long corridor and the darkness has reminded me that it was probably nighttime.

We had to have multiple rooms in order to have enough beds for our family and Chris passed out the metal, skeleton keys and opened each door, pointing out the small rooms across the hall where the toilets and showers were. There weren't enough ensuite bathrooms, so I remember wondering how we would manage the little kids and their middle-of-the night urges and accidents. Once each family member was tucked in, a mosquito net carefully pressed in between each mattress and bedframe, Chris and I found our room and fell onto our own, foam mattress bed. The horizontal softness was glorious.

We heaved deep sighs of relief for having made it that far and my mind wandered back to trying to take it all in. I felt vulnerable and child-like, separated from my babies in the newness of that place. The lingering, low growl of traffic and the occasional, shrill honk of cars outside the gates were the background sounds of the sanctuary we were tucked into, an oasis in the middle of a bustling big city. We were safe, but somehow my soul felt lost in limbo and, despite the sickening weariness I felt in my body, I struggled to drift off to sleep.

There are sweeping gaps in my memory from the time we spent in Kenya for our training. I can go back and count the weeks on a calendar from July to September, but it only creates an outline that I am unable to fill with vivid details that bear repeating. We learned about contingency plans, safety rules, and how to avoid finding ourselves at the mercy of bandits. We were schooled in methods for learning language and securing language helpers in the communities we were preparing to enter and how to treat minor illnesses and injuries in places where there wouldn't be access to doctors. There were other more practical things to learn too, like how to check eggs for freshness to avoid salmonella and E. coli and how to clean fruits and vegetables before consuming them to avoid parasites. It became common knowledge that it was better to eat things well-cooked or soaked in bleach than to risk the consequences. Our new friends quickly learned to understand and enter into our sick humor, coining phrases like, "Better cooked than diarrhea" to help us remember all of the food precautions.

We had outings and visits to local homes where we learned about the culture so we could be exposed to new ways of traveling and eating. I remember watching in wide-eyed wonder as our instructor—a tall, sixty-something gray-haired and rugged missionary who had been in Africa for decades, lightheartedly swerved through traffic and commanded his route through traffic circles in his four-wheel drive Land Rover. Swahili effortlessly tumbled out of his mouth as his wife sat calmly, simultaneously strategizing the best route to our destination and carrying on a conversation with those of us in the back. She pointed out sights to see, explained cultural nuances we would have missed, and coached us in what to do in the next place we were visiting. I wondered if we'd ever feel that comfortable and at home in the place we were moving as they did. In just a couple of weeks we would finally get to fly to our new home to begin the new life we had been anticipating for years. As my mind tried to grasp what that might be like, it was filled with questions that left my insides stirred up in a boiling simmer of tension and anticipation.

21 | Not Quite There Yet

"It's never too late to become who you want to be. I hope you live a life that you're proud of, and if you find that you're not, I hope you have the strength to start over."
– F. Scott Fitzgerald

The mega dose of culture shock and training we received in Kenya must have sizzled my brain because I don't even know how our strategically packed and prayed for belongings made it to our final destination. The stages of our orientation, training, and even the logistics of getting us, and all of our baggage, where we needed to go meant that we had a few stops to make before we would arrive at the village where we would settle. From Kenya, we flew to Johannesburg for a week or so to be oriented by our unit leader, which would be the beginning of more language and culture learning.

Although it was all too much for our brains and psyches to take in, God kept his promise to go before us and carry us through as we trusted Him. We stopped and prayed for every leg of the journey, and when the kids asked us where we'd sleep that night, we just told them what we knew that "Someone will be there to pick us up and they'll take us there."

The first place we landed after leaving Kenya was Johannesburg, South Africa. There was no doubt we had arrived in a different country as we walked down the shiny, modernized jetway toward the wall of tall windows and the automatic, sliding glass doors of the terminal. As the whoosh of the doors welcomed us into a vast, open indoor area, our eyes were drawn upward. All of us took in the towering pillars and rows of windows at the top that let in sunlight from the outside. That place eventually became a hub for numerous reunions and goodbyes over the years, so my mind can picture it vividly. I'm not sure, though, whether it was the light pouring in from those skylight windows that welcomed us that day, or if the sparkle of the lights on the marble floors filled our eyes with wonder. Even the youngest ones in the family were bracing themselves for a new place. Eight-year-old Joseph was the one to speak first: "Are we in America?"

We were picked up from the airport by the leaders of our unit who would be our next hosts and guides. They took us to their home for dinner and then got us tucked into the Baptist guest house for missionaries where we spent the next week. We were able to lay eyes on all of our totes with our belongings that were being stored in a large warehouse on the property, get sleep, and be oriented for the next leg of our journey—our arrival in Lesotho. John, a tall, proper British man with an accent that lured all of us into his calming, encouraging guidance, was our tutor for that phase of our training. He and his family had lived in the house we would eventually live in, were fluent in the Sesotho language, and would be living in a town near us as we navigated our first year of language and culture acquisition.

Each day, John would arrive in the morning dressed in slacks and a button-up shirt, his bright eyes beaming through his round, wire-rimmed glasses with energetic excitement. He would ask us how we were doing, debrief how the night had gone, and then sit with us for the very beginning of our language lessons. Although we had already read the required reading on *how* to learn a language, it was now time to actually begin learning it. We needed at least a few phrases to get ourselves from the airport to the village where we would stay for the next month as we continued to learn. We juggled the instructive conversations with John while the kids played on the small, metal, antiquated playground on the compound and the older kids entertained themselves in the reading room where they had found shelves of familiar books in English and an old TV with video tapes they could push into the player and watch.

There were entertaining conversations along the way where John had to bring up topics that must have been awkward for him. We knew he was feeling nervous because he would hunch down a little and then begin to stutter. This caused us to lean in and listen more carefully as he eventually spit out the next thing he had to caution us about or prepare us for. I'll never forget when he got to the end of our orientation and began to instruct us on what to expect next. His subtle stutter returned, and he lifted his finger to rest on his lips momentarily as he tried to come up with a phrase to describe our team leader, the man we would meet next who would host our family for a whole month in the village where he and his wife and three teenage kids had lived for years.

As he glanced over Chris's tan arms, the silver bracelets on his wrist, and the colorful tattoo that wrapped around his whole wrist, he stammered, "I was initially thinking I would warn you about August, but now I see that you will get on just fine."

A laugh escaped from his lips as he went on to describe August's one-of-a-kind, big personality and his zest for life and adventure. Over the last few days, John had learned enough about us and experienced enough of Chris's quick wit and sarcasm to determine that August and Anita were perfectly suited to be our leaders. Numbed by the many places we had already slept in the last month, we listened as attentively as possible while he described our next steps. We would have a short flight to the capital of Lesotho where one of our team members would pick us up and make sure we had what we needed. After that, we'd pick up our vehicle, drive to August's village and stay for a month, and finally we'd caravan through the mountains with John and his wife to our final destination where we would settle into our new home.

There was one first impression that left the whole family swept off of our feet as we stepped out of the Maseru airport in Lesotho. She was the first thing that caught our eyes as we walked out of the small, rural airport. I'm sure none of us even noticed the mountains surrounding us in the distance, the smell of the crisp mountain air, nor the British accent of the sweet missionary woman who picked us up at the airport. As soon as our eyes landed on the white 1999 Land Rover Defender Dual Cab with the army-green shell on the back and the snorkel adorning her side, we were smitten. We had purchased her ahead of time from August and he had it all equipped and waiting for us so that we could drive ourselves to his village where we would begin our language study and learn the basics of our new country before making the trip into our village.

We didn't know where we were going, we had no idea how to speak the language where we were, and we had so much to learn, but we had a vehicle to take us there. Somehow, the fact that we had one thing to call our own energized us for the next leg of the journey and we loaded up the back of the Landy with new fervor. It felt like we were on a grand adventure again, and we were excited to be in the country we had been praying about for so long. With the boys buckled into their seatbelts, three-in-a-row on the bench seat in the back with the luggage, we moved around the front of the truck to get inside. The three girls piled in the back seat and Chris moved around the left side to get in the driver's seat. As we both climbed into the front seats, our eyes locked as we realized our next hurdle. The steering wheel was on the other side!

Laughter burst from our bellies and the tension melted. We had our own vehicle, but even driving would require learning. Once our bodies were in the correct seats, Chris in the driver's seat on the right side and me sitting as co-pilot in the left, we set out to find our way. Directions to the places we needed to go were printed out from emails we had received from our team on the ground in Lesotho. We followed step-by-step instructions that included landmarks and street names. I'm sure we had at least one cell phone with us, but it was useless without a SIM card. That was on the list of "Things to get when we land." Each leg of the journey was filled with an initial shock as we entered another country, disorientated, and then eyes-wide-open observation as we attempted to navigate everything with somewhat of a sense of adventure and confidence, especially for the kids' sake. Most of the time we were shell-shocked and confused, putting all of our emotional energy into trying to get our bearings. We were so far from home that it was hard to find similarities between where we found ourselves and where we were from.

The whine and hum of the truck engine were the background noises for our three-hour drive from the capital to the village where we would be staying for a month-long "village stay." As the next phase of our training, we would be living in a small, stone house on the compound of a local woman. The two-lane road stretched in front of us as far as my eyes could see, a gray-black ribbon cutting through a tapestry of different tones of green. We drove for long periods of time between communities, and it felt like we were driving to the very end of civilization.

The valley we traveled through seemed largely unsettled and we drove endless kilometers between populated areas. Mountains rose in the distance in every direction. Some looked like they climbed to extremely high altitudes with cracks and crevices slicing their faces in drastic cuts from top to bottom. Other mountains were smaller and seemed to be plunked down in random places in the valley like pointy hats cast aside on a rough green and brown quilt. Later, we would learn that those hills were the inspiration for their traditional straw hats.

The three hour journey was broken up by routine traffic stops with armed police officers standing by make-shift barricades in random, remote locations and a planned stop for supplies. We checked off the landmarks listed on the directions and slowed to look for our final turn. By the time Chris down-shifted into second gear at the sight of the dirt-road we were instructed to watch for, we were exhausted from the hyper-alert brain fog of culture shock. We were looking for someone on a motorcycle at the bottom of a dirt road.

Finally, in the dimming sunlight, we spotted a solo rider waiting on the side of the road with a rugged dirt road rising behind him. He waived and then signaled us to follow him with a sweep of his arm. It was August's eighteen-year-old son, Gustav, who would be our guide on the road that evening and give us our first, harrowing four-wheel-drive adventure to the hut where we would be staying.

The road stretched on for miles and we all hung on as Chris downshifted and lurched over potholes and rocky little ridges that had been carved in the road from water run-off, following Gustav as he sped through the familiar landscape on his dirt bike. These were long, nerve-wracking minutes that droned on while we struggled to keep the motorcycle in our line of sight. Once we had him in our headlights, we'd see him zip around every dip confidently as if he was having the time of his life and then jump off the bigger rides, flying into the air and landing without effort. Clearly, he was in his element, and we were the foreigners in that place. Would living in our new home ever look as effortless as he made this life look?

It was unsettling to wake up after a restless night of sleep and not even know how to make myself a cup of coffee. There was no sink to turn on, no stove, and no switch to flip on for a light; and most importantly, no bathroom to amble into and relieve myself. Chris wandered out of the sleeping room into the small, dark, one-room main area of the cabin-like hut and our eyes met as we got our bearings. There was a chill in the morning air as we opened the door and caught the first sight of the area in the light of the sun. Majestic mountains surrounded us in the distance and a sweeping valley stretched toward them as a river wove through the middle. The small hut was set up against a hill and was slightly higher than the main part of the village, so we had a view of the area. The little compound we were staying on had an outhouse slightly down the narrow dirt road leading up to the cement porch we were standing on and there was a round, raised garden bed immediately in front of us where a healthy, manicured little vegetable garden was growing.

We walked together down to the outhouse and continued our mission to familiarize ourselves with our environment. As we walked down the slight hill, we spotted a big, black pig. It was tethered there and lying in the dust, grunting a morning greeting as we approached, but clearly too lazy to get up. *The kids will have fun with that*, I thought as I opened the wooden door for my turn in the small, odorous compartment.

With our necessary morning bodily functions taken care of, we returned up the small hill and climbed the steps to our temporary house. The sound of a revving motorcycle caught our attention and we turned to look for it before crossing the threshold. Peering down the hill, we could see a rider approaching, bobbing up into view and dipping below the trees out of sight. The rev of the engine whirred louder as a helmet-clad man came into view on the dirt road that led steeply up to the compound. We could see that the rider was different from the young man who guided us the night before. We couldn't see his features clearly yet, but he was less lanky than the young man named Gustav we had met the night before. As he parked the motorcycle near the porch, zipped off his jacket, and removed his helmet, a broad smile greeted us.

This was August, our team leader, and the bounce in his step assured us that he was excited to see us. "Velcome!" His accent made the "w" in welcome sound almost like a "v." "How vas your sleep?!" His Africaaner accent was different that any I had heard before, but it landed on my ears in a song-like, happy rhythm. His tanned arms stuck out of his dark blue, tie-die t-shirt and waved about as he talked. The huge, yellow happy face on his shirt mirrored his countenance and we couldn't help but smile in response. As he continued the customary greetings, my eyes landed on the words that surrounded the happy face: "Smile if you're not wearing underwear."

He must have noticed our eyes resting on the front of his shirt because he blurted out an explanation, "My kids got me this for my birthday! Isn't it funny?! Ooo... you're smiling!"

We knew that instant that this man, our new team leader, would be a trusted friend. All three of us erupted in spontaneous laughter as we shared our first bonding moment as teammates. A little bit of the wary tension faded away as I realized we weren't alone. This family who had been living in the area for many years would teach us what we needed to know before we settled in our own remote village for the long haul.

22 | Long Awaited Arrival

"Life is too short, the world is too big, and God's love
is too great to live ordinary."
— Christine Caine

The month-long village stay held enough lessons and memories to fill volumes of missionary journals and books about learning to live in a new culture, but that was just a step in the direction we were headed, not the final destination. We had to move on. It was finally time to make the ten-hour trek through the mountains to the village we would call home for the next season of our lives. Conflicting emotions filled every member of the family as we packed up the Land Rover again. The weeks we had with our new friends, the things we had learned, and even adjusting to the sound of a new language in our ears had prepared us enough for our next step and the whole family loaded the truck with at least a shred of expectation. It had been months since we had left the curb of our home in San Diego to begin this journey and we were ready to get unpacked. Yet, in order to do that, we had to leave our new friends and say "see you soon" again. That was now a dreaded phrase.

We set out in the early morning down the long, dirt road toward the tarmac highway. It was no longer unfamiliar territory and we anticipated the sights we would see along the way: spigots that dispensed clean, cool spring water could be spotted every once in a while along the way, dark streaks of water pointing the way to a single pipe jutting up from the ground and held up by large rocks at the base, small houses with carefully swept dirt entrances and raised, circular, stone gardens, local animals crowding the road unexpectedly and causing mini traffic jams as humans honked to clear the way. Pointing out the animals in the distance before we happened upon them had become a normal activity and the kids could be heard shouting out their sightings as we drove: "Sheep! There's a donkey! Those people have a pig, too!"

After we passed through the valley we had crossed before, we turned off the main road and began the steep ascent into the mountains. We drove and drove, winding through ravines and turning sharply around the curves of each cliff and crag. The length of the drive made stops inevitable and we watched for signs of civilization and tourist-type destinations. Those places were few and far between, but the wild, isolated frontier of those mountains brought people from far away to experience the vastness of the place, and we joined a handful of those travelers in making a couple of stops to look for toilets and stretch our legs.

We had been told to watch for a small restaurant on the banks of a river and to stop there before heading deep into the mountains for the last leg of the journey. Those were the last available toilets until we reached the town a couple of hours later where we would meet John, our proper British unit leader again. He and his family had gotten settled into a house there where they would live while they looked after and trained us and the rest of the new team living in the general area. They were holding some of our totes from South Africa and would help us pick up more household things in the small town before leading us to our new home.

Both of our Land Rovers were packed with our belongings, but we still had a few more basics to pick up before we could subsist on our own in the house that was mostly empty of furnishings. We pulled up onto the dirt embankment and parked the Land Rover so that we could hop up the high step into the cement entryway of the dark, crowded shop. Once inside, we were greeted by a youthful local man in a tattered uniform with an old rifle slung behind his back. I wondered if the gun was loaded and, more importantly, if he was trained to use it. Turning to scour the large room with haphazardly stocked shelves, I felt the familiar feeling of culture shock bear down on me as I adjusted my eyes to yet another change of location.

My brain was foggy and confused as I looked through each aisle for the things we would need to have to cook, clean, and take care of ourselves for the foreseeable future: a large pot, a frying pan, cheap silverware that felt like camping utensils, some tin cups, tin plates, kerosene lanterns and the fuel to go in them, matches, foam mattresses, and as many food items as we could stuff into the vehicles. We had a cold weather sleeping bag for each member of the family in the totes that we had purchased ahead of time in America to hold us over. It was hard to fathom that we were setting up house and not going on a camping trip.

We couldn't fit the whole family in one vehicle with all of the gear, so some of us went in John's vehicle with him, and his wife Shan rode in our truck with the rest of us. She may have even been driving our Land Rover on that first ride to the village. They wanted to make sure they could talk us through the drive, answer any questions we had, and prepare us for anything they could think of along the way. We had seen pictures of the village many times and had even seen aerial photos of the area because a few team members who had lived in the house, including John and Shan, had been in communication with us.

The road started out as a wide, dirt road with stretches that had traces of gravel. Occasionally, there was a deep rut where water had obviously flowed over the road and cut crevices that required careful planning and skill to cross. After only about fifteen minutes into the hour-long drive, we turned to the right through a small cluster of round huts and then made a sharp left, downshifting onto a narrower road that was cut out of the cliff. We were going down into a narrow valley where a river ran through, watering the only trees that could be seen in the rugged landscape. Both trucks were in their lowest gears by that time, crawling like tractors and clinging to the crude path along the cliff. I diverted my eyes from the side that dropped off toward the river, praying that we'd stay closer to the cliff because there wasn't a guard rail. In the places where the road had washed out, there were cages filled with rocks that were meant to serve as stone dams to keep the road in place; but the forces of nature had overcome a couple of them and they tilted precariously off of the side, ready to fall off in the next storm. It gave me no confidence that we'd stay on the road either.

Eventually, we made it safely to the river valley and crossed a bridge over the glistening, rushing water. I could hear the calming flow and the burbling sounds as it rushed over the rocks. The sound calmed me, and I breathed deeply, calming my nerves, and taking an opportunity to look around. Before I had a chance to enjoy the tranquil scene, we were climbing up a steep hill and taking a sharp left and then right, left, and then right, crawling higher and higher along the mountain that rose sharply from the other side of the river. When we got to the top, the road opened up again and we were driving through a little community. To the left there were bigger buildings built on carved out terraces that looked like a school and a settlement of small houses and huts that spread out from it. Each community was surrounded by fields of different crops. We were getting more and more remote. There were no stores or signs of commerce, and we rarely passed another car. I was thankful for that, because when we did, we'd have to hug the side of the road to let them pass.

The longer we traveled, the narrower the road became until we intentionally veered off to the right and took a rutted, skinny path down toward a creek. There was no bridge at this crossing. As we dipped into the water, lurching with the weight of our load, a young woman looked on from a small pool upstream where she was washing her laundry by hand. Both trucks maintained their low growls, and the engines whined as we made the climb on the other side of the creek. Small houses were built up on the hillside in that place and there were fields growing along the flowing creek. From there, we were driving on more of a well-traveled path than a road, down rocky embankments, and then up steep hills, through valleys with fields of crops growing on either side. The only traffic we saw now were donkeys being guided by young men who followed along with long sticks, tapping one side or the other to direct them along the way. We passed people on horseback occasionally, their colorful blankets wrapped around them, one flap blowing in the wind behind them like a heavy wool cape.

It was easy to understand why there was no electricity out there. How could work trucks of any kind even have access to these places? As we reached the top of a hill, Shan pointed off to the right, "There's your house. Can you see the rectangular shape of it on this side of that next village?"

Her voice was light and excited as if she belonged in this place and was proudly introducing it to visiting family. A nervous feeling like butterflies rose up in my stomach and added to the tension in my back and neck. My jaw seemed to be locked shut in a clenching position as the reality of our circumstances sunk in. We were about to *live* in this place. There was no turning back.

The vehicle with all of the girls in it arrived at the compound first and we piled out of the truck. As Shan climbed the steep, cement steps up to the small porch and unlocked the door, we looked around and tried to take it all in. The girls had one agenda and blurted out, "We're here first! Can we pick our room?!"

The cinder block house had been built by a former missionary who had pioneered the work in that village. He had purposefully designed the house for his wife and son in a more "western" way. The front door opened into a living room with a wall that divided that space from a dining room and "kitchen" area. There was one big counter with a two-burner camp stove on it, which separated the room into two areas. Across from the counter in the kitchen area there was a window that looked out over the village and the mountain in the distance. There were two doors in that room—one that went to the outside and one that led into a storage room lined with shelves.

The floors were smooth, cold cement that needed repair. Cracks here and there revealed higher trafficked areas. There was a wide hallway that led off of the living and dining rooms and gave access to the three bedrooms. The first room on the left was the biggest and the girls decided that was the one they should have since they "needed more space." The room directly across from that one seemed like the one the parents would have since it had two built-in cabinets for closets and a little desk in between. I claimed that one for Chris and me and we continued the rest of the tour as the boys arrived and streamed in. I could hear their voices echoing in the empty rooms. Chris was taking charge, his efficiency-reflex kicking in: "Let's start bringing things in and just set the totes right here."

The boys rushed down the hallway to see their new room. The only one that was left was the room at the end of the hall that was previously used as an office. I wasn't sure how we'd make it work for them, but it had to suffice. We had a girls' room and a boys' room back in San Diego, and we'd have the same set up here. My overwhelmed brain couldn't think ahead or strategize at that point.

I just needed to set our stuff down and figure out what I could feed the family for dinner. With no electricity, no refrigerator, and just a pot and a camp stove, that would take all of the inventiveness I could muster.

There was one more room at the end of the hall across from the boys' room. I'll call it the "bathing room." As far as rooms with toilets go, it was a moderately sized, open room with a toilet, a pedestal sink, and a tiny, square shower enclosure in the corner. The problem with all of those conveniences was that they were just a dream. The sink didn't work without going to fetch the water and pumping it up into the big, green tank outside that sat uphill from the house. Gravity brought it down the hill in a pipe that connected to two other pipes that went in two directions—one toward the "bathing room" and one toward the sink in the kitchen. The toilet had been installed along with a septic tank that sat full to its maximum capacity and was covered with wood-framed, metal covers.

Since the tank was full and there was no truck in the mountains willing or able to navigate the "roads" to our village, the toilet was rendered useless and served only as a low shelf to hold things. A new *long drop* (outhouse) across the yard was the place all eight of us would share to relieve ourselves. With no hot water heater, the shower enclosure became a place to bucket-bathe without splashing water all over the room. A side note is necessary at this point. My good attitude and sacrificial mindset crumbled faster than I'd care to admit as I learned a basic life-lesson in that room: There's one thing worse than not having indoor plumbing, it's *having plumbing and not being able to use it.*

Once everything was unloaded, John and Shan left us to get settled and promised to return the next day to continue our orientation. It felt like we had been abandoned in the middle of nowhere. By that time, the sun was setting, and we had to light the kerosene lanterns we had just purchased, as well as the ones we found in the supply closet to make our beds and eat something. Firewood had already been stacked along the wall in the house for us, so Chris lit a fire in the wood stove in the living room to take the chill off. There was another, bigger "anthracite coal stove" at the end of the hallway, but we had to be taught how to use that one.

The next memory I can coax to the surface happened on the first morning we woke up in our new place. Chris and I were the first to wake and sauntered groggily out to the living room area. The light from the uncovered window drew our eyes in that direction and we were met with a shocking surprise. Little brown faces peered in at us. Children from the village had lined up in the open window to see the new missionaries who had arrived. Life in a fishbowl had begun.

Our first few weeks in the house were more like camping with each of the kids sleeping on foam mattresses on the floor in sleeping bags and Chris and I in a bed left by John and Shan with our sleeping bags zipped together. Of course we had been taught the valuable lesson that window coverings were a major priority. We hung sheets and blankets over the windows until we were able to make our first supply trip out of the village. It would take months to get the house set up with furniture and the necessities of building a life there. Long, four-hour, four-wheel-drive trips out of the mountains took us to a border crossing that led to the highway toward Durban, South Africa.

The seven-hour trip gave us access to a big city with malls, thrift stores, and the friends we had made back in New York during our training. They hosted us for a couple of those "supply trips." Steve stood by directing Chris's every move as they overloaded the Land Rover, strapped whole pieces of furniture to the top, and waved to us as we set off to navigate the treacherous roads to get everything we needed out to our place. Our arrival had been carefully timed for September so that the worst part of winter was over and we didn't have deep snow to contend with.

Looking back, jumping into the unknown was indescribably difficult, but strangely freeing. The fears that had held me back for so many years no longer had a grip on me. It was the actual goodbyes and leaving that was the most heart-wrenching. We missed our loved ones and the comforts of "home," but the prayers of those we had left carried us, and we began to develop a new, more vivid longing for Heaven as we went about adjusting to life in the village. We reminded ourselves frequently that we would be with our loved ones who know Jesus forever and we would never have to say goodbye again. Our purpose for being there was at the forefront of our minds and in our prayers constantly: "Heavenly Father, help our lives reflect your love to our new friends. Show them how much you love them, how completely you provide, and how perfect your healing is."

The three words that we had uttered in the process of leaving everything behind came back to us every difficult step of the way: "He is worthy, He is worthy."

23 | A Teen's Perspective

*"Our homes are not defined by geography or one
particular location, but by memories, events,
and people that span the globe."*
– Marilyn R. Gardner

Our whole job for the first year in the village
was to learn how to live there. The technical term for that segment
of time was "Language and Culture Acquisition," which sounds neat,
tidy, and somewhat academic. The reality of it was all-consuming,
though, and there was no way to categorize it, no way to carve out a
tidy schedule and keep yourself in a safe place for the rest of the day.
Every layer of our lives had been turned upside down and set down
in a place we knew nothing about, and it affected each member of
the family profoundly.

As our country of origin was enjoying the rapid expansion of
the internet, we had plucked our children out of modernity and
brought them along with us as we learned to live in a place that was
altogether opposite of everything we knew. Their perspectives on
the magnitude of the change varied with the span of their ages. It
was right around that time in our parenting that Chris had the kids
paired up in three sets of two so that he could easily refer to them
with humorous, but definitive titles. The two oldest teens, Julia
and Olivia, were dubbed "The Menstruals." This evoked eye-rolling
and whiny complaints from the girls who couldn't help but protest
and laugh simultaneously at their father's knack for normalizing
the awkward things in life. Jed and Silly were the next two, so
they were "The Middles," and Joseph and Duane were "The Littles"
because they were just starting school and still required help with
their bodily functions.

I have a picture in my mind of the day our solar panels were installed on the tin roof of our house. They had been ordered before our arrival, but they didn't actually make it to us until we had been living there for a month or two. Our team banded together for the project that day, August making the day-long drive from his village on the other side of the mountains with the supplies, and John bringing the rest of what we needed and additional manpower in his own vehicle. It was "The Menstruals" who brought the fun to that work visit. Before August's arrival, they gathered craft supplies from the homeschooling box to decorate the outhouse especially for him. On the inside of the door, they had meticulously recreated the logo from the shirt he was wearing the first day we met him. They painted a large, yellow happy face right at eye level with the words, "Smile if you're not wearing underwear" so that he'd see it the first time he sat to take care of his business.

As sisters and friends, they seemed to help each other creatively preserve shreds of their teenage lives, even in their new environment. I can picture them now, perched on the roof of the shell of the Land Rover dressed in sundresses and sunbathing as they worked on cross-stitching and needlework. The men above them worked on the roof, bracing the solar panels in the section of the roof that would get sun for the longest part of the day.

"Normal" teenage things like posting and scrolling on Facebook had to be reserved for planned times that we would pre-purchase sacred data, plug a little flash drive-like stick into the computer's USB drive, and log into the cell-based internet we could sometimes get during small windows of opportunity. One of Julia's posts from that time describes her perspective on our life during those first months.

Facebook Post by Julia 2011

I guess it's time for another one of these. I haven't really felt up to blogging since nothing really spectacular has happened. Upon reflection I have come to the conclusion that the journey TO Lesotho has proved to be more exciting than the journey WITHIN Lesotho (I am speaking for myself, only). I know this may come as a surprise to you.

"Isn't Africa just like when Meryl Streep did that movie 'Out of Africa'"? Or...

"I thought the Wild Thornberrys gave me such an adequate example of life in the wild."

But, alas, I can't talk to animals, and I don't have a pet elephant. Our family doesn't live in a treehouse, and I haven't met any burly jungle men in a loincloth (boo-hoo). We are just a family, who decided to answer God's call to give up our cushy life in America and move to Africa. And everyday it seems like nothing has really gotten done, but in reality, we are just trying to learn how to live here. Trying to figure out how much food to get to last us 2 weeks is a task, driving to town to get the groceries is a huge task, and learning this strange language is an even bigger task! So really, a lot of things are being done. It's just not what we are used to. We are used to the American way, rushing around, filling our schedules until there is no time to even sleep, and constantly finding ways to be NOT BORED.

Well, I will tell you one thing right now, life in Africa is pretty boring sometimes. During the day we do laundry, wash dishes, make breakfast and lunch, clean up our rooms that have mysteriously gotten cluttered even though they were cleaned the day before (isn't that always the way?) and then, my parents go to language lessons, they come back, we have dinner, watch a movie, and go to bed. Mind blowing, isn't it? And with all this incredible amount of nothing going on, I have had a lot of time to think. I have come to terms with the fact that I didn't come here to have my version of

'Pee-wee's Big Adventure,' I came here to be with my family, to see what they are doing here, experience what it's like, meet the people that they meet and so on and so on. This way when I am in America (taking hot showers and driving on paved roads) I will know what they are talking about when they are here (dancing in church and making clicking noises for the letter 'Q').

I hope this has given you a vague idea of what it is like here, I'm sorry if you had expected stories of how I walk down to the river to get water every day and carry it back on my head, or how there was a black mamba in my bed, or how we came to own our new pet cheetah, Spotty. I would love to be able to tell stories like that and have them be true, trust me, I would. But I'm just a city girl, helping my family move into their strange new life in the mountains of Africa. And even though this experience isn't quite what I thought it would be so far, I wouldn't trade it for the world. I have learned so much, and now I know that no matter where I end up in America, I will make it out just fine. If I can live here, I can live anywhere. It's all about perspective.

24 | Motsoalle Oa Rona

"Our Friend"

*"Cultural diversity should not separate us from each other,
but rather cultural diversity brings a collective strength
that can benefit all humanity."*
– Robert Alan

The difficulty of life in the village was often tempered by the joys of a simple life, victories with language or ingenuity with a fix-it job, and sweet signs of friendship. We found that our kids were the best "bridges" to relationships with people wherever we went. Blonde and innocent, our 10-year-old "Silly" seemed to embrace language learning and was quick to warm up to those we were getting to know. She would often walk down to the little one-room "store" and sit with the young woman who worked there so she could have private language lessons. It was her goal to master the clicks that our tongues struggled with. As our neighbors got to know her, she earned a reputation as an animal lover and, although they were perplexed by her compassion for things with feathers that were normally eaten, our new friends rose to the occasion and were generous to share.

Silly's first pet was a scraggly, white "teenage" chick that was given to her by a neighbor as we were walking through the village literally looking for people to get acquainted with. As I remember it, the woman's chickens were kept in handmade cages made out of found wood and wire. They were easily seen from the path we were walking on, so they immediately caught Silly's attention. She stooped down to look at them, poking her finger through the wire and talking to them in a high-pitched voice. It must have been a bit of a shock for the woman to look out of her hut to find the new white strangers had stopped to talk to her little flock, but she welcomed us warmly with the customary greeting, "*Le phela joang?*" (How do you live?)

We all responded individually with the phrase we had the most opportunity to practice, "*Ke phela hantle.*" (I live well.) We continued to fumble through a little conversation in our new language, which was the goal of our errand to begin with. That alone would have earned us a self-proclaimed "A" for the day, but when the woman reached in, picked up a chick, and handed it to Silly, we were dumbfounded with gratitude. In our minds, this was the sweetest welcome we could have received, for our daughter now had an animal to nurture and love. Who cares if we had no cage, no food, no animal supplies, and really no use for it. Silly let us know right away that no matter what other people did with their chickens we would NOT be eating hers!

The grand finale of our language visit that day was the naming of our first pet. As she handed the new family member over to Silly and gently placed it in her hands, her brown eyes met Silly's and she told her, "*Bonga,*" which means "thanks or gift," like a thank you gift. We didn't know whether the chick was male or female, but it didn't matter. That little chick was now a part of our family, and it was the next best excuse to have a number of conversations around the village in order to secure food for the little thing.

Although there was a rundown, small barn-like outbuilding on our property, it was too far away from the house for Silly to feel secure leaving her little pet out there at night, so Bonga's bed was a cardboard box in the supply closet. When it was time for Silly to go to bed, she would get her baby all cozy in there and close the lid loosely until morning when she would eagerly go pick it up to carry it around the compound. As the shaggy chick grew into an even more awkward adolescent chicken, it learned to come when Silly called. As the chicken approached, she would hold her arm down near the ground and the bird would hop up and perch on her arm as she walked all around our yard. During school breaks, Silly would eagerly head out to the sunny porch and sit there with her pet in her lap while it cuddled up and preened its growing feathers.

Bonga had wonky feet that turned in and a growing red cone on its head. As her affections grew for her gawky pet, Silly delighted in recounting stories about their daily adventures. I can hear her high, childlike voice reminiscing about the day she discovered a distinguishing fact about her feathery pal. As she sat with it on the porch in the sunshine, she turned away and heard a strange noise from behind her. It was a squeaking squawk of some kind, but she couldn't figure out where it had come from. Then, as she turned to investigate, her beloved pet seemed to force a sound out that vaguely resembled an attempt to crow. As the connections were made in her mind, she burst into the house and proclaimed, "Bonga's a rooster!"

As Bonga developed into the proud king of our humble village home, there was something missing in his life. This was a favorite subject with my friends each afternoon as I finished homeschooling and headed out to visit and learn language. My first stop was often 'M'e 'MaSamuela's compound where I would sit on the cement ledge of her hut with her and chat about the weather, her garden, or her favorite subject—Silly's pet rooster. Since I was just learning the language, learning phrases, studying the sentence structure of how to put words together, and growing my fledgling vocabulary, our conversations were more like charades. That didn't stop us from huddling together on her stoop, heads leaning in close, and laughter erupting off and on as we understood what the other was trying to communicate. Even with the language barrier, I knew that she found it funny that we would love such an ineffective, wimpy, lonely guy. After all, a rooster's whole job was to "be fruitful and increase in number." We had no hens, so Bonga had a reputation as a useless, spoiled male. In 'M'e MaSamuela's opinion, he needed a wife, and she wasn't afraid to make us an offer.

In our attempts to assimilate into the community, we made every effort to learn what was culturally expected and we didn't want to take from her flock unnecessarily, so we bought a hen from my friend that day. That hen would end up being named "Tsepa," which means something like "Hope." Now that Bonga had a mate, we could do just that. Silly got Bonga and Tsepa all settled into the barn in a proper livestock habitat, and we waited for our new chicken couple to yield fertilized eggs, which in turn she would sit on until they hatched into darling little chicks for our daughter to love.

The fertilization part never happened, though. As it turned out, Bonga must not have known what he was supposed to do and he never "made any moves" on Tsepa, further damaging his reputation in the village as a useless specimen of a rooster. He surely would have been dinner if he had resided on someone else's compound. For us, he was Silly's comfort animal, a living creature for her to focus on and care for; and that was enough, so Bonga lived on and enjoyed his pampered days.

While OUR days were far from falling in the "pampered" category, they were getting to the point where they felt less traumatic. As we got to know people and began to speak more of the language, we slowly started to find a rhythm to life. One of the things we had adjusted to was getting unexpected visitors throughout the day. Living in a village was an amped-up version of small town life. Everyone knew what was going on, they kept their eyes on each other, and although there wasn't electricity or reliable cell service, the rumor mill did the job to communicate *some* version of the latest news from the neighbors: what so-and-so's cow did, the other person is pregnant, someone died, that person is neglecting their fields, the missionaries visited that person over there, and on and on.

It wasn't unusual then to hear a knock at our door with the customary announcement of the visitor's presence, "*Coco*." So, when I heard a soft and understated voice at the door, it didn't come as a surprise. "*Kena!*" I announced, "Enter!" As the door opened, my friend 'M'e' MaSamuela appeared in the doorway. It was cold that day, so she had a few layers under her traditional, wool blanket. The pattern and color of the blanket signified the family line she came from and hers had a rich, dark yellow on the edges and gray and subtle white tones that made up the crest-like pattern.

Traditional Basotho blankets are about the size that would cover a standard twin bed like a bedspread so that they can be wrapped across the body shoulder to shoulder and then one corner pinned with a giant safety pin. Once the blanket is pinned at the shoulder, the corner is draped down making a dignified cowl-like collar. There seemed to be different standards of niceness for blankets, too, so that when there was a special occasion, the colors of the blankets were amped up in a colorful array of pageantry.

On the day of this visit, 'Me 'Masamuela had draped her everyday blanket around her in the customary way, but it was also concealing her secret cargo as she walked across the field from her compound to ours. The rich brown of her skin glowed with the sheen of the hydrating petroleum jelly she had moisturized with, and her graying hair was covered with a knit hat. Her eyes danced with a sparkle that revealed her spunky personality. From the time I met her, the lines in her face and the gray in her hair gave me hints that she had lived enough life to be in her forties like me. There were many reasons I was drawn to her as a friend and had a longing to know her well, so I made an effort to see her daily. The fact that she had knocked on my door caused me to rush to her to see what she needed.

We set down the school assignments we had been working on and I approached her with a couple of my kids trailing behind me. She looked at us and a wide grin spread across her face lighting her eyes up in a bright twinkle. She pointed at Silly and started talking about her chickens. Piecing together about thirty percent of what she said, I realized she was addressing the "problem" Bonga and Tsepa had in producing chicks. She slowly moved her hand toward the folds of her blanket, pulled it open, and reached into a pocket she had made in the fabric of her dress. As she did so, she looked at Silly and said, "*tloho*," "come." Silly came forward and was rewarded with a handful of fertilized eggs for Tsepa to sit on!

I'm not sure we could have received a sign of friendship and blessing that was more beautiful for us. Here was a local person who probably thought we were the weirdest, dumbest people she had ever met, bringing us a gift from her own much-needed flock. These chickens were her livelihood, her main daily source of protein, and she was giving some of them to us out of love. The magnitude and generosity of her offering didn't escape me, and in that moment, I did what was natural to me and awkward for her—I hugged her.

As a family who had become complete through the adoption of our sons, we received eggs that were "adopted" by our hen who immediately took to them and sat faithfully over them, keeping them warm until they hatched. I'm not sure what compelled my friend to show such compassion and love toward our daughter that day, but it communicated to me that she understood and accepted us, even though we were different. Relationships were indeed deepening and now that we had a fledgling flock of feathered friends, we were starting to belong.

25 | Made for This

"I will instruct you and teach you in the way you should go;
I will counsel you with my loving eye on you."
– Psalm 32:8

It didn't take long for me to see evidence of God equipping me over the course of my life for the work He had for us there in the village. Our new rural life drew the mountains out of me as if my core was being awakened with the sights and sounds that surrounded me. Perhaps it was the general ruggedness of life in that place and the daily work required to thrive that took me back. There were four distinguishable seasons just like we had in the tiny mountain community where I grew up, and there were four seasons here, although they presented themselves differently: a warm summer, a bitter, snowy winter, a windy season, and a pouring-down-flash-flooding rainy season. Dirt roads, mountainous views in every direction, dirty feet, the rushing sound of water tumbling over rocks in the rivers, and land to cultivate took my mind back to the days of my childhood and evoked rural reflexes I had forgotten I possessed.

In our village, without a grocery store for miles, we were without a local source of fresh vegetables, but we had plenty of land on our compound to work with. There was even a crude, dilapidated greenhouse, and a fenced garden area. Both were like blank canvases for me to work with. I could picture the harvest and the colorful, fresh meals before I even started working the soil. As soon as weather permitted, I was out there inviting the kids to join me in tilling the soil, bartering for cow manure from our neighbors to fertilize with, and then planting it with seeds of familiar plants that I prayed would grow there: zucchini, lettuce, tomatoes, green beans, and herbs were my first crops.

Breaking through the crusty, unused, first layer of dirt and uncovering the dark, rich ground beneath released the earthy smell that beckoned my inner child to look up to get my bearings. Our neighbor's straggly, bony dog Spotty barked in the distance and the bleating of sheep called from the rocky pen a few huts over. Scanning the horizon, I took in the sweeping fields that were planted with the essential foods our neighbors needed. Each plot brought its own hue of golden yellows and browns or lush greens creating a quilt-like frame for the community of huts and small compounds. Towering mountains rose in every direction, bare of trees, but carved with natural crevices that created shadows and variations of color that invited eyes to linger and stare. Round, stone huts with carefully woven thatched roofs reminded me where I was. This was Africa and I was far from the mountains of Northern California where I grew up. The distinct, sweet, smell of smoke from dung fires rose from the outdoor cooking fires all around the village. As my senses took in the scenes, my mind placed them in a new category: "My New Home."

There were other things that took my mind back to my childhood home in the mountains of California. Bumping and lunging over the rocky dirt path in the Land Rover with my hands and feet working together to shift up and down, up, and down with the rugged terrain also did the trick to shake the memories from my aging mind. Crawling down a rocky ledge in first gear with the engine at a low growl took me back to the plot of land my parents bought when they tired of the rat race and moved from the city.

Both of my parents were born and raised as city people, but my dad had become overwhelmed by the pace of life as a traveling salesman and followed his dream to have land and give us a childhood free of the confines and influences of city living. Dad was a visionary with skilled hands who was fed up with business meetings and being away from his family, so selling their house near the beach in sunny So Cal and buying a couple of acres on the side of the mountain up against the national forest in Concow, California had set him free. He had arrived in the perfect place to raise his little family, and although I'm not sure my mom's enthusiasm matched the pitch of Dad's, she dug deep and adapted.

Our little homestead in the Sierra Nevada mountains became a sanctuary where we learned how to work hard, and "play" meant exploring streams to find pools big enough to swim in and adventuring until the sun went down. My brother Geramy and I can say honestly that we "walked uphill both ways on a dirt road in the snow to get to the bus on school days." We had a menagerie of animals to take care of and each of them were taken in for a purpose. The goats were there to produce milk for my brother who couldn't drink cow's milk; the chickens laid fresh eggs daily; the geese were intimidating guardians of the property, hissing, and chasing unfamiliar animals and humans whenever they got too close; Boss Hog and Miss Piggy were my pets, but destined to be bacon; our Great Pyrenees mountain dogs guarded the rag-tag flock.

I'm not sure if Mom moved willingly or if she dragged her graceful, model-worthy little feet to the dirt of the mountains kicking and screaming, but she had the grit to adapt and overcome. She managed to maintain a certain level of dignity and class despite the hillbilly tendencies of her husband and kids. This balance meant that we learned proper table etiquette from her at the same time we followed her lead in bottle-feeding baby goats *inside* the house because they were too young to be left outside in the pen. My dad spent years building our house with his own hands, coaching my brother and me while we pounded nails and spread drywall mud over the seams in the sheetrock like frosting. My mom did her part to put the finishing touches on our mountain home and chose carpeting the color of corn silk for the main living areas. This became grounds for strict training in removing muddy shoes before entering the house, especially during the snowy, winter months.

Responsible mud handling wasn't the only winter adaptation we had to develop during those growing-up years. Although we had electricity, winter storms often damaged power lines and cut off our service rendering the pump that brought water from the well useless. My resourceful mom would take our biggest pot outside, fill it high with fresh snow, and heat it on our old, gas restaurant stove to *just* the right temperature so that we could still bathe and wash our hair for school. Every season had its challenges and lessons that built a priceless curriculum for life and ingenuity.

As far as we were from town, even medical needs required us to improvise. My parents must have learned how to adapt from the people in the community they built friendships with. I have vivid memories of both of them using native plants for different ailments and emergencies. There was a weed that grew in our area that we could find easily. I'm not sure what the genus and species was for the light green plant with prickly fuzz on the leaves, but we called it "Mugwort." Native Americans from that region dried it and used it as a sleep aid. Once dried, they would use it in the stuffing of pillows and sleep on it to cure bad dreams and bring on restful slumber. As colds came on, or even when we were just short on tea, Mom would send me outside to gather fresh pine needles to boil and drink as a tea rich in Vitamin C. A little sugar made it delicious, and it gave me satisfaction to partake of something I had found and picked myself from our property.

Other remedies for medical emergencies aren't quite as neat and tidy. Without the convenience of having an automotive shop on the nearby corner, Dad usually made at least the first attempt to repair the cars himself. I can picture him now hunkered down with his head buried in the front of our sixty-something Volkswagen beetle. The hood was propped open, and he was trying to fix a spring that was acting up. He had his usual outfit on—cut-off shorts and flip-flops. Without a shirt, his tanned skin revealed the amount of time he spent outside working with his hands. He had escaped the rat race of the city and become one with life in the mountains. I had just wandered over to peek at what he was working on when the hood slammed shut and he screamed like I'd never heard him before. He grabbed his hand and continued to pant and grunt. The sound he made was like sobs without the tears. Gathering his courage, he peeked at his bloody hand. Half of the tip of his pinky had been pinched off in the spring when the hood fell.

Mom ran out of the house when she heard the shouting and moaning. As soon as she saw all of the blood, she begged him to get to a doctor. Someone started searching for the tip of his finger. It may have been my little brother, Dad's constant sidekick and faithful helper. From a young age, Geramy's sensitive spirit and huge heart led him to push aside all fear and squeamishness to help. The three of us hovered around Dad as he wrapped a rag around his hand and headed to the bathtub inside. Mom's desperate imploring continued, "Gerry, please. I'll take you. We need to have that sewn up. That's too big of a wound for us to fix."

"I'll be fine. Just give me a minute. Old Man Ray told me about what he does. It'll keep it from getting infected and heal it up. Someone get me some rags and matches."

"Rags and matches?! Gerry, you need a doctor and stitches!"

As the negotiations continued, Dad rinsed his mangled finger. Blood continued to gush out, mixing with water in the white porcelain tub and flowing toward the drain in streams of red. I felt woozy from the sight of it, but what happened next shocked and captivated me. Our eighty-some-year-old neighbor who was originally born in Mexico and had lived on his own in the mountains for most of his adult life had been tutoring my dad in all he needed to know to be independent from the luxuries we used to know. Now, with half of his finger missing, Dad made a little pile of white gauze-like fabric and lit it on fire. All of us looked on in wonder as concern mounted in our minds.

He didn't let the tiny fire burn very long, just long enough to have a heap of delicate, burned ash-like fibers. He took those and made a poultice, packing it tightly and insisting that my mom wrap it up with strips of the remaining gauze-like kitchen towel. As she wrapped, she continued to try to talk sense into him, but he would have none of it. I'm not sure how long he continued to clean out his wound and then wrap it with ash, but I know he never saw a doctor for it. Eventually, it healed, and his fingernail even grew back in a crooked kind-of way. The only reminder of the harrowing event was the narrow shape of his pinky and a scar along the side where the chunk was sliced off.

That old VW lived on and provided the wheels for adventures for my brother and I much earlier than your average youth. Once I could see over the steering wheel of the bug, we graduated to driving ourselves down the dirt road a mile and a half to "check the mail" and borrow books from the bookmobile. Bumping down the rutted, gravel road, shifting from first to second, and raising my chin to see over the hood became a normal part of my daily existence. When my dad decided to plant a kiwi orchard to grow a cash crop, he acquired a small, "seasoned" rusty tractor to help till the land. My brother and I were eager helpers once that vehicle arrived! Those four knobby wheels and the putt-putt engine became one of my favorite pastimes.

Even before planting the kiwis, my parents cultivated a huge garden that produced vegetables that we enjoyed in every stage of their growth. We learned to make neat sections and rows for each individual kind of plant, long straight rows for corn and large, circular sections for zucchini plants. Watering that patch of agriculture was a task big enough to be a consequence whenever we needed to be disciplined. I remember more than a couple of times when my mom would send me down there with a fiery, frustrated charge, yelling, "Get down there and water the *whole* garden!"

Whether it was a consequence or not, that garden yielded nourishment for our bodies and our souls. As the seasons changed from spring to summer, I remember walking barefoot through the rows of mature plants to look for corn or green beans that were ripe for the picking. Tiptoeing through the shade of the towering plants, I searched every plant for the largest cob. Once I found the perfect specimen, I would peel back the husk just below the silk and inspect the kernels to see if they were plump enough. Next, I would wrench it from the stalk, remove the whole husk, and eat it raw. The snap and crunch of the fresh kernels popped in my mouth delivering a juicy, sweet treat. My mom and I spent hours together over that six-burner stove making homemade blackberry jam from the wild bushes along the stream, canning and preserving the abundance of vegetables from our harvests, and even making a variety of tangy pickles.

There's no doubt my parents had taken a great risk to leave the security of my dad's nine-to-five job and home ownership in Southern California, but in doing so they provided my brother and I with a love of nature, a respect for the land, and life skills that would serve us well no matter where we lived. Without even realizing it, all that we experienced in those rugged, wild mountains of California equipped me for living in what felt like the Middle of Nowhere Africa.

26 | The Boy Who Could Sew

"For you created my inmost being;
you knit me together in my mother's womb.
I praise you because I am fearfully and wonderfully made;
your works are wonderful,
I know that full well.
My frame was not hidden from you
when I was made in the secret place,
when I was woven together in the depths of the earth."
— Psalm 139:13-15

Chris's childhood didn't include life in the backwoods, but it prepared him for living out his purpose at the vocational school, nonetheless. His mom has always told stories of how young he was when she started seeing signs that he had a passion for fashion. My personal favorite goes back to when Chris was about five years old. With permission from his mom and dad, he had invited one of his neighborhood playmates to go to church with them. On the morning of the church outing, young Becky showed up at the door ready for the occasion. She wore a little double breasted overcoat with a cozy hood that hung back over her shoulders. As they invited her inside, Kindergartner Chris asked her the question that burned in his mind, "Can I see your dress?"

In his defense, his parents had always placed a high value on looking nice for church. This wasn't to put on a show for people or to make an appearance, but rather out of respect and reverence for being in "God's house." Little Chris knew that they reserved their best clothes for Sundays, that his dad spent time every Saturday evening making sure everyone's shoes were polished, and that when money was tight, his mom sewed new outfits for all of the kids so they'd have new outfits on holidays. He fully expected that other people did the same thing.

With all of those routines in his mind, Chris waited in anticipation as Neighbor Becky unbuttoned her fashionable overcoat to show him her church outfit. As a five-year-old without a filter, his response still brings an uncomfortable laugh from his mom, Carol: "Awe, that's just an old play dress."

She remembers the beginnings of his fascination with clothes and sewing vividly.

"I made lots of clothes for the boys and Kelly, probably more the boys. When I would be sewing, Chris always showed an interest in what I was making and was excited to see the finished garment.

When he was in 7th grade, on the last day of school, he asked if I would show him how to make a shirt on summer break. We shopped for a pattern and fabric. He did it all. I told him to follow the pattern and I would check each step before he would go to the next step. He really got into it and loved it so much. He was easy to teach. He ended up taking classes in high school. I remember Ms. Miller was his teacher. She had him assist her and one of the girls he helped with was Kisa, who you met at our house and still keeps in touch with us.

Chris took off in his sewing and never stopped. He promised three of the girls that he grew up with that he would make their prom dresses and take them to the prom if they didn't get asked. He made wedding dresses for his two sisters-in-law and of course, wife Michelle and his sister, Kelly. He made me three dresses. He was so full of talent with his sewing. John (Chris's dad) remembers a comment someone who knew the business made at a showing of his garments. She pointed out one particular part of a garment and stated, 'You don't often see this quality in tailoring. No shortcuts.'

He would tell people that his mother taught him to sew. I got him started, but he surpassed me. He was always interested in fabrics. While in high school, he got a job at Beverly Fabrics in downtown Ventura. They made him the evening and weekend manager. His father, John, has always described Chris as a master craftsman."

As John entered his eighties, he took an extended time to write about his own life through an informal autobiography he shared with the family. In it, he recalled similar things about Chris in his reflective piece, *"Looking Back: Seeing Life in the Rear View Mirror."*

"What I saw in Chris was creative genius, talented beyond belief and a champion of the underdog. He was a fighter and had to be to survive all of the things that came his way through his school years. I don't think I understood what a creative person he was early on but saw this time and again in his adult years. He was, as a tailor and designer, a master craftsman who never settled for less than the best. As a family, we saw this in his efforts when there was a family wedding. Debbie, Michelle, and Kelly all wore his creations. For Kelly's wedding, all the female participants also had attire created especially for them.

I was very unsettled about the family going to Africa as missionaries. My misgivings concerned the age of the kids, the location where they would be working, and just the move in general. I had to surrender those feelings to a greater sense of God's moving in their lives, praying, and believing that this was His will for them."

That word, "surrender," was a theme then for all of us, and the posture of surrendering everything to God's Sovereignty in our lives was absolutely critical as we adapted to our new lives. Despite the hardships that cross-cultural living presented, the evidence of God's equipping throughout our lives buoyed our faith and reminded us of God's presence and plan from the very beginning of our lives.

Chris (left) and his big brother Mike welcome Baby Steve to the family. Note their spiffy outfits.

27 | One Verb – One Decision

"If you talk to a man in a language he understands, that goes to his head. If you talk to him in his own language, that goes to his heart."
— Nelson Mandela

Living in a new culture is like being born again; not in a refreshing, renewing spiritual sense, but more like a blank slate, know-nothing, crawling, drooling entrance to a world of others who already have their bearings. It seemed like we found our way one misstep at a time until we could finally navigate the day well enough to tuck ourselves in at night and feel snug in our beds.

The pace of our days was guided by the sun, just as they were for our neighbors who had been born and raised there. The morning began when a strip of sunlight slipped through the crack in the fabric we had hung over the window as a makeshift curtain. What we did next depended on the season. In the summer, around Christmas time, the weather was warm enough that we could just wake up and turn on the gas burner under the kettle to heat the water for coffee without taking the time to light the fires in both stoves. With the water heating, we'd take the long walk out to the outhouse before the kids started waking up.

This began as an inconvenience, but eventually became part of the routine that allowed for a weather check, a scan of the village to see who was out and about, and a general check of the compound. Misty, low hanging clouds usually hung in the valley over the river, so it looked like cotton batting stuffed down into the cracks of the ravines in the distance. Wispy, dancing wisps of smoke rose from each compound as neighbors started their cooking fires and prepared the morning porridge. As I approached the outhouse, I always took a cleansing breath to enjoy the fresh air one last time before entering. For the duration of my time inside, I only breathed out of my mouth as necessary, avoiding the risk of allowing any of that noxious air to pass through my nostrils.

Once the morning walk across the yard was complete, I would saunter back up the cracked, cement steps into the house for my quiet time. There were a few things we had preserved from our normal routine back home in San Diego: morning coffee, our quiet time, and time together as a family at the end of the day. The pace of everything had slowed down, though. We worked hard as long as the sun was up, but there was no commute, no hurrying from one place to another, no hustle and bustle. After a few months of being there, we began to fall into step with the rest of the village and walked at a steady pace, free of Western worry.

Chris and I usually had our coffee and sat at the table for our Bible reading, each of us silently reading, journaling, studying, or praying independently, but stopping along the way to comment on something we had learned or a fresh insight or truth that was encouraging. As we finished, the kids would start to appear from the long hallway, and it was time to make breakfast. The lack of a local grocery store made this process much more basic as well. Sometimes I'd make a pot of porridge similar to the customary one everyone else ate there. It was enough like Cream of Wheat to remind me of my childhood and eventually everyone else would eat it too, sprinkled with sugar and doused in warm long-life milk from tetra-pak boxes.

The lack of electricity removed toast from the menu, but there were usually plenty of eggs, so we could have scrambled eggs with a slab of homemade bread. Anything that we wanted to eat hot had to be either cooked on the stove, baked in the oven, or placed on the wood burning stove. We even had to stock up on propane cylinders in order to have gas for cooking. A tall, metal gas "bomb" sat right behind the stove and had to be turned off and on as it was needed. Eventually, Chris made a red and white decorative cover for it out of the thick, waxy, traditional "Seshoeshoe" fabric he had found in South Africa. Each room of the house had something Chris had made to make the cinder block house our home.

With breakfast complete, we set out to tackle our daily responsibilities. Chris's main task during that time was reaching a conversational level of language so that he could be cleared to teach at the vocational school. He treated language learning like his "day job" and left the house every morning with his man satchel slung across his chest full of notebooks. He usually had a visiting plan each day, strategically stopping to visit the men who had become his language helpers and friends. We'd see him again at lunch time when, as the self-declared principal of our homeschool, he would proclaim it recess and free the kids from my school lessons. He'd enter the house, and with a jolly, hero-like voice call out, "Gosh, Michelle, give these kids a break! Nobody's gonna arrest you for giving them a recess!"

Learning a second language took every part of us, but since it was our top priority, our brains were constantly firing with new connections. The pace of village life usually allowed for time to reflect on what we were learning and some of it was worth sharing with friends, family, and partners back home. On one occasion, it was one verb that sent Chris's brain into a series of firing synapses that pulled together life lessons that begged to be laid down in words.

Blog post by Chris

February 8, 2012

As many of you know, Michelle and I are learning a new language – Sesotho. We have been living in our village for 5 months now. Acquiring a second language is interesting, frustrating, and rewarding all at the same time. Not only do we have to become like children, we also have to put ourselves in the position of saying something wrong – really wrong – like when instead of saying, "I am going to teach students how to design clothing.", I said, "I am going to teach students how to take their clothes off." Not the best thing to be saying.

I came across something interesting this week. In Sesotho, we have a verb, "ho utloa." It is pronounced "hoe oo-tlwah". I first learned that it means to understand. I have learned this week that it is what I would call a contextual verb. I don't know if that is a proper linguistic term but let's just go with it. So, what I mean is that I discovered that not only does it mean "to understand," but it also means to feel, to hear, to taste and to obey. What? This one word means all of these things?

When using the verb while touching, or listening, or eating, or being told or directed, it is understood in each context. When I thought about it – in each context, it made more sense. If someone here asked me to give them the blanket, and I sit still with a smile on my face failing to give the blanket to them, I have not understood. If I pet the horse's coat and can describe how it feels, I have felt or understood the way it feels. If I listen to my neighbor calling a greeting to me from across the valley, and I respond, then I have heard and understood him. If I drink the motoho (soured porridge) but don't wince at the sourness (and fear what will happen inside when I swallow it), then I have not understood or tasted it. If the chief tells me that I must take my animals away from the village to graze in the designated grazing lands and I allow my animals to remain with me in the village grazing on the hills around my home, I have not obeyed or understood what the chief has told me. The more I thought about it, the more it made sense. And as I even talked with God about it, He opened the thought up more clearly.

I can know or know about something – book knowledge- and not have true understanding about it if I haven't actually felt it, heard it, tasted it, or allowed it to change something in me or guide me to a different behavior. Ho utloa – to understand, to feel, to hear, to taste and to obey. Where has God directed me through His word about ho utloa?

<u>To understand</u>: In Ephesians 1:4, Paul tells us that, "even as He chose us in HIM before the foundation of the world, that we should be holy and blameless before Him. In love, He predestined us for adoption as sons through Jesus Christ, according to the purpose of HIS will, to the praise of HIS glorious grace with which He blessed us in the beloved." We can be told over and over again that God chose us and some people will say 'yada yada yada.' But do we UNDERSTAND that GOD CHOSE US BEFORE THE FOUNDATION OF THE WORLD AND ADOPTED US AS SONS?

Creation is a huge thing – a miracle beyond man's understanding – but GOD CHOSE US BEFORE HE EVEN DID THAT! 'In the beginning, God created...' We know those verses but do we UNDERSTAND that even before those words, HE HAD US IN MIND? Do I understand it? How do I know? What does it change in me? Do I tell others about their being chosen?

<u>To feel</u>: God brought to my mind Joseph and the coat of many colors. This may be abstract but stick with me. In Genesis 37 we are told about how Israel loved Joseph so much that he had a beautiful, colorful robe or coat made for him to wear. Most of us know how the story progresses but stop for a minute and put yourself in Joseph's shoes or coat so to speak. As he slipped that colorful coat up onto one arm and then the other, as he adjusted it onto his shoulders and felt the weight of it as it fell down his back skimming his legs, as he grabbed the front and pulled it around himself. What did he feel – what did he understand? Did he feel or understand not only the weight of the physical coat but the weight of what others would see? Did he feel or understand his father's love for him?

When I think of what the colorful coat might point to today, I think of the NATIONS, the many colors of those people not yet reached with the story of Christ. When I slip that coat on, the coat that shows God's abundant love for me, do I understand the weight of it? Do I feel the weight of what God's love calls me to do? Do I buckle under the weight saying, 'Not me!' Or do feel and understand God's love as I pull the coat around me and move to take this love to others?

<u>To hear</u>: In Matthew 13:14ff, Jesus is telling his disciples the purpose of parables. Jesus spoke of Isaiah's prophecy fulfilled when he told his disciples that the people, '...will indeed hear but never understand, you will indeed see but never perceive. For this people's heart has grown dull, and with their ears, they can barely hear, and their eyes have been closed, lest they should see with their eyes and hear with their ears and understand with their heart and turn, and I would heal them.'

The Message version says it even more clearly: "I don't want Isaiah's forecast repeated all over again: Your ears are open but you

*don't hear a thing. Your eyes are awake but you don't see a thing.
The people are blockheads! They stick their fingers in their ears so
they won't have to listen; they screw their eyes shut so they won't
have to look, so they won't have to deal with me face to face and
LET ME HEAL THEM."*

*Do we hear or understand that? God wants to HEAL us. HE, the
CREATOR of the UNIVERSE – HE WANTS TO HEAL US! Search His
word – not only that but He wants to adopt us, bless us, love us, care
for us, provide for us, cleanse us, and SAVE US! Do I, do you, do we
HEAR and UNDERSTAND this? More importantly, Do THEY?*

*To taste: Psalm 34:8 "Taste and see that the Lord is good! Blessed is
the man who takes refuge in HIM!" When we taste something, we
are experiencing it – understanding it. We are having a personal
experience. We can read through all of the wonderful recipes in the
most recent cooking magazine but not until we get up, go to the
store, buy the ingredients, bring them home, follow the directions
and see it through, do we get to actually taste or understand what
we have read in the recipe. It's the same way with our relationship
with Christ. If we don't act on what we've read in HIS word – let it
change something in us or motivate us for HIM, then we really don't
understand or taste that the Lord is good. If we don't take what He
has quietly spoken to us and move on it – call that friend, send that
card, pray for our coworker who doesn't know Christ, hug our child,
then we haven't understood or tasted that He is good.*

*To obey: John 14:15 from the Message translation, Jesus said, 'If you
love me, show it by doing what I've told you.' This is also known as
obedience. This is the verse that knocked me down some time ago
and now is my life verse. If I am told to do something, I can either
obey or not. Even God gives me a choice. But just as Jesus spoke
those words, he followed them with a promise in verse 16, 'I will talk
to the Father, and He will provide you with another friend so that
you will always have someone with you. This friend is the Spirit of
Truth...' Also known as the Holy Spirit.*

*So, it's not like most of our earthly fathers saying, 'It's my way
or the highway!' He's saying that He wants us to do what He has
told us – it is following Him. We can follow any popular human who*

is the current fountain of wisdom and get nothing, or we can follow Christ and He will send us the Holy Spirit to be our friend and guide us through the mountains and valleys of this life.

'Ho utloa' – to understand, to feel, to hear, to taste or to obey.
'Ke khetha ho o utloa.' - I choose to utloa Him.
Chris 4 All 8 G's All Over the World

When the day was done and the sun slipped behind the mountains towering in the distance, it left the village in the pitch black of night. Without electricity to light the darkness, it didn't matter if the daily tasks were finished or not. When there was only a sliver of a moon, dusk turned to a black darkness, so dark that it seemed thick and pasty. Without light to navigate even the simplest outdoor tasks, everyone was forced inside their huts to prepare for sleep.

After a couple of months, we had enough solar power to run a narrow, dometic fridge and charge our devices. Since that was dependent on sunlight, our evening family entertainment was determined by how much energy we had stored in the bank of batteries by the front door. Even the kids knew how to check the little screens to see if we had enough power to watch a recorded show from the flash drive our friends had made of our favorite reality TV shows. We watched them again and again, all of us piled on the couch or the area rug hunched around the twelve-inch computer screen.

When that was done, we bundled up and went out to the outhouse as a family for the last visit of the day. Chris carried the "torch" to light the way over the well-worn, rocky path until we arrived at the tin-sided structure and got in the queue. After a brief discussion about who got to go first, we'd wait in line there with our necks bent back and our eyes locked to the sky overhead. Without a single light for miles and miles, there was nothing to interfere with the brilliance of the stars that lit up the vast, endless atmosphere beyond that seemed enveloped in a vast blackness. Each of us searched the skies for satellites that could be easily spotted as they appeared in the distance and whisked across the glistening sky in their star-like orbit around the earth. "I see a satellite!" one of the kids would shout their discovery as the next one announced a constellation they had spotted.

One by one, we took our turn on the frigid seat and then quickly exited to continue stargazing until all eight of us had done our business. Then, with our nightly reminder of how small we were in the universe, we'd return to the dimly lit house, find our blanket-laden beds, and sleep until the sun signaled the start of a new day.

28 | Battlements

"A battlement in defensive architecture, such as that of city walls or castles, comprises a parapet, in which gaps or indentations, which are often rectangular, occur at intervals to allow for the launch of arrows or other projectiles from within the defenses."

Although life was simple and sometimes mundane, new situations and phenomena found their way into nearly every day of our life in the rural mountain village. We had to deliberately place ourselves in the mindset of being learners and ask questions instead of making assumptions. Our brains seemed to constantly be in overdrive thinking of creative ways to learn about the culture around us. Sometimes we volunteered to help harvest the fields of elderly friends, and other times we asked for help in learning how *they* did things like hanging laundry to dry, grinding dry corn to feed the chickens, and even how to cook the foods we were becoming accustomed to. We prayed that our questions communicated, "We need you and trust you. Teach us your way."

Sometimes in the evenings, just before the sun slipped behind the shadowed mountains, we would hear the bum-bum-ba-bum-bum of rhythmic drumming mount in a steady crescendo toward our property. The first time it happened, we were unaffected and took it in as something else we needed to learn about. As the sound grew louder and approached our dining room window, we moved closer and peered out toward the road that led into the village, watching silently as he passed our house in a trance-like slow walk, with bum-bum-ba-bum-bum beating from the patting of his dark, weathered hands. As a nightly pattern developed, though, we grew increasingly curious about why this man routinely beat his drum around the property.

Stammering through early elementary level Sesotho, Chris and I both set our minds to figuring it out. It wasn't unusual for us to split up for these educational visits through the village; after all, our full-time assignment for the whole first year of our time there was to learn language and culture. The nightly solo parade in question was just one more quiz in our study of this new civilization we now called home. As each of us asked around, the answer eventually developed from pieced-together hints. This man was in training to be a witch doctor and he was practicing his call to the spirits.

It made no difference whether this was true or not. The thought that someone may be calling on evil spirits to descend on our family and our home was unsettling. As Chris and I strategized and considered how to handle this, we knew there was only one thing to do—pray. When we would hear the rhythms of the slow spirit-march begin, we considered it our call to prayer. Sometimes we stopped and prayed aloud, and other times we would just pause and silently cry out to God for protection over our whole property and each of our family members. Living in a place of spiritual darkness was teaching us to do battle on a whole new level.

Our prayers together became like war cries to God. It wasn't unusual for us to huddle together, praying in Jesus' name against any spiritual forces that would attempt to come against us. We had grown exponentially in our faith in this environment and had learned to pray very specifically. Chris was led to ask God to fortify our property against the Enemy. He described a fortress with tall, strong walls and battlements to hold back the forces of darkness. This was his most consistent prayer. We stood on God's promises, and our prayers developed into being reflex responses to anxious thoughts. I too began to whisper that same request even when he wasn't with me, "Battlements in Jesus' name, LORD, battlements around this compound."

We remembered and repeated Scripture back to ourselves, reminding us of truths that dispelled our fears and strengthened us: *"You are from God, little children, and have overcome them; because greater is He who is in you than he who is in the world." (1 John 4:4 NASB)*

Although things like this weighed heavily on us, there were times of refreshment and light that lifted our spirits and kept us going in the battle. Steve (the coffee connoisseur) and his family lived in Durban, South Africa and were running their own non-governmental organization with a number of their friends and colleagues from a church there. Having them a day's drive away was a much-needed sanctuary of American familiarity as we set up house and learned culture. Since they had pioneered the work in the village, were fluent in Sesotho, and had even built the house we were living in, they were like life coaches to us in the very beginning. Every six weeks or so, with the blessing and encouragement of our unit leader, we would pack up the family in the Land Rover and navigate the treacherous roads and passes to cram into their little three-bedroom house and do things like shop at malls, go to church, and stock up on essentials.

Those times in the colorful, bustling, beach city of Durban were life to us. Situated on the Indian Ocean, it felt more wild and dangerous than our hometown of San Diego, but the salt air, traffic, and diverse mix of cultures gave us a sense of home. Adding to that picture of hometown comfort was a warm and vibrant body of believers at a church that immediately welcomed us into their family. When we stepped onto that campus, we were transported from the earth we were struggling to understand to a community that transcended culture and felt like family. Once Steve and Pam introduced us, we were welcomed, embraced, and showered with encouragement and support.

Trips to the mountains were routine for this group. They had become the main network of partnership for our friends as they grew the work in the village, and they would become a life line for us, too. Allowing us time to adapt to life and get settled up there was difficult for them. They were so excited to make the drawn out and death-defying trip up the switchbacks of the notorious Sani Pass and through the dirt roads and mountain passes just to bless us and support what we were doing in any way they could. Our elementary understanding of how things worked in the community limited us in what we could guide them to do, so we suggested a visit that included a walking tour of the vocational school and a prayer walk that would guide them in their prayers for us and the people we were there to get to know and love.

We had never seen a convoy like the one that arrived on our property that day! With the evening light fading into electricity-less, inky darkness, the team rallied together to set up their camp. They insisted on feeding us with the supplies they had packed in and magically grilled coiled South African sausages and meats for that first night's meal. Nine new friends joined our family in our cement floor, rustic home, and our hearts were filled with the warmth of their love, support, and encouragement.

We marveled at the industrious ways they transformed our compound into a functional campground to accommodate their group. As Chris showed them the well-worn, nearly dilapidated garage-like structure, one of the guys leading the group declared it the perfect location for the camp shower. In the far corners of the dark room with the pounded dirt floors, they hung hooks that would hold the thick, black bags of water that had warmed in the heat of the sun during the day. With sheets draped across from one wall to the other, it created a private little triangle for a quick, warm cleansing shower.

During the course of their three-day visit, they went out on visits to other villages where they visited small churches or helped with community projects and then returned for an evening meal with us and times of fellowship before sleeping. We took them on long hikes up and around our own community, past the stone church building, up the path toward the vocational school, up onto the ridge overlooking the fields, and then back down through the center of the village toward the chief's place. As we passed through each location, we shared specific ways they could be covering the community in prayer. Without hesitation, one of the members of the group would start a prayer as we walked to the next place and others would tag on their own appeals to the God who saw and heard even the things we could not see.

When the end of the visit came, they let us know that the last phase of their mission would be to gather around our family to pray. They prayed with power and fervor and their voices joined as an ensemble of passion that cried out to God for us and for God's spirit to descend on the village. As the weight of their prayers built to a crescendo of praise, one of the men began to describe a vision God was showing him in prayer that went something like this: "Thank you, Lord, for your protection over this family. I can see walls like a fortress and strong towers like battlements at every corner."

Chris and I secretly opened our teary eyes and looked at each other. NOBODY else knew what we had been praying for, yet God was showing us that He heard us and was answering! After that, we had no doubt that we were protected by the most powerful force in all of Creation.

29 | Floods, Real and Figurative

"Distance gives us a reason to love harder."
– Unknown

I can't say that the months passed quickly or whether they droned by in a blur of confusion, but time did go by. By the sixth month, we had at least found a routine, knew how to find and prepare food, Chris and Jed were pros at fetching the water and pumping it up to the tank, and we were well on our way to getting to know a few people in the community. All of that was good, but the passing of months meant that it was time to execute the plans we had made during our time of preparation before moving to Africa. We had sought wise counsel about how to navigate all of the transitions with our children and had even gone to a week-long workshop on how to educate them, but it seemed nothing could prepare us for actually implementing that plan.

It all made perfect sense on paper. Julia would take a gap year and come with us so that she would have a sense of place and home, knowing where we lived and being able to picture where her family was. With Joseph and Duane's adoption being pretty recent, we couldn't "abandon" one of our children and leave her behind. To a child their age, it would have been perceived that way even if she had made the decision to do that on her own. No matter how we looked at it, we knew we *all* needed to be together while we adjusted to living in the village. Olivia took a semester off as well and kept up with her core classes with textbooks from home. The plan was for her to stay with us for that time and then go to the boarding school for the second and third terms of her sophomore year.

The dread of being separated from two of my kids was tempered by the sweetness of a visit from home. My mom made the two-day journey to be with us for a few weeks before the girls left so that we could have a long visit and she and Julia could travel back to California together. After that, Julia would live with her and my stepdad while she got her bearings and launched into life as an adult. She was ready to see her friends again and have all of the conveniences Southern California had to offer.

By the time Mom came to stay, we had furniture, and the house was feeling more like we lived there. We hung family pictures, school art, and our Ugandan batik art on the rough, painted, cement walls with whatever worked. Sometimes we used a screw that was already in the wall, and other times we just used sticky tack like one would use in a classroom. The permanence of the decor wasn't the main priority; it was simply meant to make our home personal to us, and it accomplished that well.

There are a few vivid memories of the time my mom was with us. One is really just a comforting, serene scene. In the peaceful, lantern-lit evenings, she would sit with Silly and teach her how to needlepoint. She must have remembered her own time living in the mountains because she had brought along craft supplies. Her goal was to have a dish towel completed before she left for home. I can picture her and eleven-year-old Silly with their heads together, hunched over with their needlework talking in hushed tones. It was comforting to have her there, as if at least one piece of my life as I knew it before still existed. Showing her around, introducing her to our new friends, and having her join us in our life also provided an opportunity for us to observe how far we had come in our adjustment. One day at a time, we had made a life for ourselves in that place.

The next vivid memory is one that is crisply emblazoned in my mind, but my conscious brain chooses not to recall it often. The images stand in sharp contrast to the tranquil, lantern-lit evenings of quiet craft-making. It's worth dredging up at this point, though, because the absence of it would paint an inaccurate picture of what it was like to live in a place where the power of forces beyond our control were obvious. We felt so miniscule as humans in those conditions that humility came naturally.

From where our house sat on the gentle slope of the plateau, we could see the cluster of homes in the village shrinking into the horizon as the land sloped down toward the river. Beyond the towering mountains in the distance, a measureless, clear sky opened up revealing an endless existence elsewhere. That vast view provided us with our own ability to forecast the weather with at least a few minutes' warning. On the day of the storm, dark black clouds seemed to bear down on us in the distance, flying toward us and gathering strength like a squadron of stealth fighter jets bringing forth their deadly force.

We could see the deluge of rain before it hit us, walls of dark sheets suspended from the black clouds all the way to the earth below. Without much effort, we heard the pounding rain like the rushing of a mighty river. As soon as we saw the clouds in the distance, we ran around the yard making sure the doors were closed on the outbuildings before rushing inside. In our haste, we assumed the baby chicks Silly was watching for our neighbor would be safe in the box on the dirt floor of the greenhouse. It had a thick plastic roof and sides and we had latched the door closed with thick wire. Bonga and one other teenage chick were in their homemade cage up on the ledge where the plants should have been planted.

Gusts of wind signaled the imminent lashing of the storm and alerted us to windows we had left open. The curtains blew in violently like warning flags and we all went room-by-room to make sure every window was closed. Before we could catch our breath, a pounding, hammering rain hit the tin roof. The deafening sound brought the whole family out from their rooms to the main room of the house where we could look out of the windows in three directions. There was so much water falling from the sky that we couldn't see anything past our fence. In what seemed like minutes, the dry, rocky ground was saturated and couldn't absorb the sudden onslaught.

The rushing sound of flowing water edged closer until the thunderous pelting made it impossible to hear each other speak. The power of the storm made us feel vulnerable as drips began to show up and puddles grew on the cement floor. We were at the mercy of the storm and there was nothing we could do but wait it out. Everyone was fully engaged in either watching out of the window for a break in the powerful sheets of rain, grabbing buckets and pots to catch water from the leaks in the roof, or mopping up water that was rushing in from the back door in the kitchen. A river had formed as water accumulated up the hill from our house. Its path cut through our yard, rose up on the side of the house above the threshold of the door, and continued down toward the stream at the bottom of the hill.

When the wind finally carried the driving rain on to pummel the next village, the sky opened up, the thundering pounding stopped, and the waters receded. As soon as the new river on the side of the house went down enough that it could be navigated with high, rubber gum boots, Chris braved the outdoors and went to check on things. Silly begged to join him so she could check on her chicken babies, *"Please*, Daddy! Let me go with you! I need to see if they're ok!"

Both of them suited up for their confrontation with the mud and headed outdoors. Chris headed for the garage and Silly ran straight toward the greenhouse where her precious pets were locked up. Although my eyes didn't see what her young eyes saw, the terror in her voice and Chris's description of the scene allow me to picture what my daughter's heart had to withstand in that moment. When she opened the door, the whole bottom of the dug-out greenhouse was filled with water and the dead chicks were floating on top—a wet massacre of feathery death. She turned from the sight, screaming, "Daddy, come! Daddddddyyyyy!!! They're DEAD! They're all DEAD! Help me!!"

I'm sure it was the innate courage of a father protecting his daughter that rose up in Chris and enabled him toward the act of heroism he was forced into that day. Scooping up each chick, he gathered them in a box until they could have a proper burial, and rescued Bonga and the other, larger chick from the shelf above the flood. They were soaked to their bony little bodies, but alive. He handed them over to Silly to wrap up in a towel and bring inside while he dealt with the rest of the mess.

My mom and I both rushed to Silly and gathered her up in our arms as she sobbed. The traumatizing sight had stolen every ounce of sparkle out of her and reduced her to wracking cries. She bawled while she let out the regrets and the questions, "Why didn't we bring them in? I didn't know the greenhouse would leak! Why did God let this happen? What am I going to tell Ntate Mohloki? Those were his last chicks."

Without answers to her questions, we consoled her with as much encouragement as we could muster, pointing out the chickens that were alive in her lap and promising that there would be other chicks to love someday. Grief gripped her as our words fell on deaf ears. She was too upset to hear.

The trauma of that scene lingered for months, clouding the joy of her animal caretaking and ushering in projects and compromises that would prevent future cataclysmic losses. Chris dug a hole down below the greenhouse and we buried the chicks there, placing a lovingly painted rock as a marker for their grave.

There's no way I could have planned or predicted what happened months later as the warm spring sun brought new life to the soil. There, in the very spot where the chicks were buried, a solitary, volunteer stalk of corn grew up. It was Silly who found it first and heralded the arrival of the sprouting plant. Hope seemed to spring from her eyes as she imagined how it had happened. "One of the chicks must have eaten a whole kernel of the corn and then the seed grew to be this plant!"

Her eyes danced at the thought of the miraculous new life and bright signs of hope returned to her glimmering eyes. There was no way for us to predict how powerfully obvious the circle of life and death, destruction and hope, and the contrast of darkness and light would be in the life we were living. All we could do was face each wave of the cycle as it came with the strength that only God could provide.

The circle of life wasn't the only cycle at play at that time. We were stepping into what would be a long season of frequent goodbyes. At the end of my mom's visit, we made the trek to the airport in Johannesburg. After long hugs and tearful "see you laters," my mom, Julia, Olivia, and I flew to Kenya to get Olivia settled in her dorm. It was a special girls' trip with an ending that we were bracing ourselves for. Each of us wrestled through waves of conflicting emotions. Excitement to see our friends at the boarding school and to show my mom around brought the fluttering butterflies of anticipation, only to be overshadowed by the grief of the long separation from family. It would be the longest we'd ever been apart from our kids, Julia for the better part of the year, and Olivia for twelve weeks. The dread and pain of saying goodbye to two of them at once lingered in the back of my mind and squashed down the joy of the journey.

After months off the grid entertaining themselves without screens and connectivity, the girls seemed ready to enter back into civilization. Both of them faced the transition with courage and hope. For me, it felt like I was cutting off a couple of my limbs. Although I knew that the plan was the best thing for the girls, it felt foreign to be leaving Olivia at school and then getting on a plane to leave her in another country. I was comforted to know that we had friends there who would be watching out for her and the fact that she would have the education she needed, peers, and a social life again helped me to push aside my own grief and focus on getting her settled.

Three, twelve-week school terms were broken up by five-week long breaks, so the flow of our life shifted to accommodate the ten-hour trips to and from the airport to pick her up and drop her off. We talked on the phone regularly and she texted occasionally to ask a question, but her life at school was full with the academic rigor of classes and a robust social life. By the second school break, I was able to put my regrets into words for her as she and I rode through a Johannesburg suburb toward a mall to pick up things we would need when we returned home to the village. After I crafted the sentences in my mind, I let them flow out with honest emotion: "I'm sorry we're not there with you to meet your friends, have them hang out at our house, and be a part of all of the activities you are doing. It's weird not to drop you off at school, pick you up, and be a part of your high school days."

She was silent for a long moment, glanced up at the headliner of the truck in thought, and then said, "Hmm, it's funny. I've never thought of it that way."

From that time forward, I was comforted to realize that Olivia was a normal teenager who needed friends and other adults in her life. She had a schedule that kept her so busy that she didn't have time to think of our feelings or our need to be a part of all that she was experiencing in high school. Having her away at boarding school was different from our experience with Julia attending the neighborhood high school back in San Diego; but it worked for this season, and we eventually found comfort in that truth. Our colleagues were navigating the same routine and guided us in how to thrive. Each time we picked her up from the "school plane," we made sure to plan an adventure for a week or so before returning to the village. Those times provided for rich family time, helped us adjust to having five kids in the house again, and gave us something to look forward to when the school terms felt long.

Keeping in touch with family, friends, and supporters back home forced us to process all that we were experiencing and learning. In between school lessons, meal prep, and language lessons, we squeezed in time to keep in touch. After that first, hard goodbye, I sent this update to our loved ones back home.

We're almost six months into our first term in this tiny rural village. In most ways we feel less capable than we ever have. We're learning a new language and are immersed in a culture we don't understand. We're realizing that it's in doing this, the hard stuff, that we're being a light for Him. Our family is now split between three countries and two distant continents. I'm homeschooling our four youngest – 13, 11, 8, and 7. Our first-born is attending university in Southern California. Our second daughter is studying at boarding school in Kenya.

"One thing is for sure; we're not in this alone.
It is only in His strength, through the power of the
Holy Spirit, that we can do this. We know that the
One who called us is faithful.
He will do it."
– (paraphrased from 1 Thessalonians 5:24)

30 | Utter Darkness

"Greater is He who is in us than he who is in the world."
– 1 John 4:4

Hearing people refer to Africa as "The Dark Continent" has always evoked feelings of defensiveness in me, even before I was a resident. The label started in Europe before there was any knowledge or understanding of the interior places outsiders had never been. The truth of the matter is that darkness exists everywhere, not just on the African continent. After living there, I now know that it would be more accurate to say that both the darkness and the beauty are more vibrant there.

We were learning to do battle with the evil forces of spiritual darkness, though, and *that* was new to us. It's not that spiritual darkness is absent in the U.S., it's just that the schemes are subtle and muted, where people seem to go about their lives in a gray stupor, unaware of the enemy prowling around in sheep's clothing. Where we lived, dark was truly dark and light was bright, which didn't make things easier, it just made the battle clear. We had to gear up for it, ask for help, and study up in order to overcome it. The reminder from God's Word became a mantra that we repeated often: "Greater is He who is *in* us, than he who is in the world... greater is He who is in us, than he who is in the world..."

Another thing we were learning about our enemy was that he uses the same tricks over and over. His "M.O." hasn't changed. He spews out lies that we can be our own "gods," that "we surely won't *die* if we disobey," and his goal is to bring division. We were in the village to bring the Truth of the Gospel and to live out the love of Christ. Obviously, our presence was unwelcoming to the spirits of darkness and, although we couldn't see our enemy, there was often a heaviness or tension that was palpable. Add to that the stress of an international move, learning a language, no running water or electricity, scarcity of food, and homeschooling, and you've cooked up a recipe for some pretty fiery trials.

Thankfully, we weren't thrown into the experience alone. We had a structure of leadership watching over us and they checked on us regularly, even working through the training curriculum required for our first year on the field. On one particular occasion, we had a scheduled visit with one of the regional leaders in our organization. We hadn't met him before, but he was doing site visits with our team and checking on the work happening in our country. Our team leader explained that this would be a time of encouragement and that he just wanted to make sure we were adjusting well. Both Chris and I were nervous to have someone we'd never met drop in to see what we perceived to be two fumbling idiots trying to make a life for themselves and their children in a place where they knew nothing.

When the day came, we were in the heat of a battle of some kind. I can't remember what we were arguing about or what had happened, but if we had been in a neighborhood with cell service and accessible roads, we probably would have feigned sick and canceled the visit. There was no doing that without cell service when your guests had to travel for hours on a treacherous dirt road to get to you. So, when their Land Rover was seen edging over the mountain in the distance, Chris went missing. The weight of all he was feeling had overwhelmed him and he couldn't stop crying, so he just left. This wasn't the first time he had done that, so I didn't worry about his safety. The hardest part about the situation was simply that I had no choice but to explain to these men who were in charge of our training and work there that their missionary had literally headed for the hills.

My honesty was met with compassion and grace. They comforted me and told me stories of their own adjustment to life in Africa. It was because they had *lived* it that they knew how to calm my fears. At some point, Chris wandered back to the compound and experienced the same merciful reception I had experienced. Then, over homemade baked treats and tea, we sat for hours and received advice and encouragement from two men who had the love and credibility to be our guides in the hardest season of our lives.

One of the things we were reminded of that day was that the enemy's modus operandi has not changed since the very beginning when he deceived Adam and Eve in the Garden. He is a liar who seeks to bring disunity, fear, doubt, and distrust so that he can keep us from God AND the purposes God has created us for. With the eyes of outside, objective observers, we had help to identify and battle the forces of darkness that were against us. Not only that, but from that day on we continued to be quick to recognize the same schemes and pray against them in the Name of Jesus so that we could move forward with whatever new and difficult challenges we were faced with.

Some of those situations came on subtly as we developed relationships in a culture we weren't familiar with, and others smashed into us suddenly with terrifying force. On this particular night, it was the literal darkness of the sun going down at the same time a thunderstorm rolled into the mountains that brought the unexpected challenge. That would have normally been a routine phenomenon during the rainy season, but this time we were winding through the hairpin turns in the Land Rover trying to get home. There were a couple of "rules" we were instructed to abide by in Africa that came with our training and were meant for our security. One of the most basic was that we were *always* supposed to plan our trips so that we were off the roads before sundown. We believed whole-heartedly in this standard and had planned our day around it, but an unexpected temporary road closure due to an accident on the pass had delayed our drive.

As the dimness of dusk slowly slipped into the uninhibited blackness of the mountains without streetlights or electricity-lit homes, our threat became clear. Our headlights were suddenly out of commission. Nothing Chris did got them to turn on and there was no place to pull over. In the pounding rain and diminishing light, we pressed on. Finally, we turned onto the dirt road that led to our village home. The problem was that the graded road here turned into rocky ledges and river-crossings that would be impossible to cross in darkness. Even without the additional hazard of pounding rain, it was guaranteed that our vehicle would end up careening off of a cliff. We *had* to have light to continue, so we stopped on the side of the road to strategize.

Chris's main idea capitalized on the violent brightness of the lightning that steadily flashed across the rocky landscape every couple of minutes. "Maybe we can just drive forward every time there's lightning." We ruled that out since that would have taken all night and there was no guarantee that the second or two of light would actually allow us to move more than a few feet. Realizing we had cell phones brought a bit of hope. We could call someone to come give us a ride and leave the Land Rover until daylight! Who could we call? As we went through the mental rolodex of our new friends in the area, we only came up with one that owned a vehicle. Our closest friends would have *wanted* to help us but having them come for us on horses was a death sentence.

When Chris dialed the number of our friend with the truck, he answered! Immediately, after the hope of the cell connection, Chris's body slumped in disappointment. Our friend's sincere regret that he couldn't help us reduced the miniscule hope we had to desperation. If *he* knew it wasn't safe for *him* to go out in this weather, we were surely doomed. The stress mounted with each rejected plan, but we continued to brainstorm.

Our next idea was to at least drive far enough to the first cluster of huts and ask for help. As we considered that, though, we realized that we couldn't do that because the closest compound was one we had no familiarity with, and we had just done our shopping. The back of our vehicle was loaded with more provisions than a local store and that made us both uncomfortable. Mind-jolting thunder added fear to the stress and shook the vehicle within seconds of the biggest lightning bolts we had ever seen. The storm was coming closer and closer. We had no choice but to stay in the vehicle where the tires grounded us, but we had no way to move. Trapped in darkness, terror felt like anger.

Chris made one more stab at getting me to drive by the light of the lightning storm and I attacked, "I will NOT further risk the lives of my children by driving them off of a cliff! You can stay here with us, or you can walk this road by yourself, but I CANNOT agree to that plan!"

My voice raised in a crescendo until it was nearly a yell. I was so focused on the intensity of our strategy meeting that I don't even remember what the poor kids were doing in the backseat. As I faced off with the husband I usually adored, eyes bugging with panic and rage, he met me with the same force, "WHAT DO YOU EXPECT ME TO DO, MICHELLE?!"

I'm not sure which of us realized it first, but the recognition of the battle became apparent as suddenly as the flashes of light that bore down on us. We were fighting. We weren't unified. We were on the same team, and yet we were against each other. This was the enemy's doing and we wouldn't stand for it. We knew his schemes and we knew how to fight his little demons.

I can't claim to be the one who suggested it. In fact, I actually don't remember which of us gained enough composure to start the prayer, but as soon as we started, the mood inside our metal cage changed. We both cried out to God in unison, voices raised to the One who made the wild mountains we were captive to. We remembered that even the winds and seas obeyed Him. We asked for His help and admitted that we didn't know what to do. We prayed for a miracle; we prayed every spirit of darkness we could think of out of our presence in Jesus' name. This wasn't hocus pocus, nor was it a test of our theology; it was two tiny children of God crying out to their Heavenly Father because they needed Him. The anger melted into weary humility as we said our "amens."

Raising his head and shifting his weight in the driver's seat, Chris somehow hit the lever on the side of the steering wheel with his elbow. A beam of light flashed from the vehicle! The lights came on!! We looked at each other in shock. This was too good to be true! How could God heal HEADLIGHTS?! We had checked everything before, and there was no way they could suddenly be fixed! Testing each lever and switch confirmed that the headlights still wouldn't come on and stay on; but, if we held the high beam lever in the on position, that held them on and illuminated the whole road in front of us! Our way was clear. As a united team with new focus, we worked together to navigate the treacherous road at a crawl. I hunched over and held the high beams on while Chris drove until, hours later, we inched into our driveway safe from the calamitous storm.

31 | Bare Feet & Butterflies

"I would like to travel the world with you twice. Once, to see the world. Twice, to see how you see the world."
– Unknown

There are many promises throughout Scripture that promise God will carry us, help us, and provide for us, and living at the end of ourselves provided ample opportunities to see those promises in action. It was after Chris started teaching at the vocational school, about a year after our arrival, that our whole team in Lesotho planned the annual prayer retreat that was held at a guest farm in a quaint, rural, historic little town in South Africa. It was just across the border from the border crossing we usually took to get to Johannesburg, so it provided a relatively central location for the team to travel from all of their remote locations for a week of fellowship and renewal.

Our leader announced the need for a speaker and gave everybody the opportunity to invite someone from home to come and encourage all of us in the Word and lead us in the spiritual renewal aspect of our retreat. Others pitched their ideas and began the process of looking for pastors and mentors who were available, and we began praying and scheming hard to make sure one of *our* friends was the one filling that position. It was asking a lot of whomever made the trip because the length of the journey extended the trip well beyond a week. Logistics, expense, and the time commitment narrowed the field of people who could make the trip, and eventually our prayers were answered. Our friends, Eddie and Maggi, agreed to travel to see us in the village and then lead the retreat for our whole team.

Even the thought of having visitors from home lifted our spirits and we were filled with excitement for their arrival. Their visit was a balm for our souls. They helped us with projects around our property that we needed help with like bracing the big water tank that had shifted over time and was precariously edging over the side of the tower it was perched on. It was a joy to introduce them to our neighbors who were becoming friends by that time. Our visit was filled with joy and laughter, long talks well into the night, and time spent with our neighbors who were thrilled to get to know our people from home.

After the team retreat, Chris took the time to share an intimate encounter he had with God during one of the solitary prayer walks Eddie had assigned all of us to do.

Blog post by Chris

We are past due for an update and this one will be interesting. Chris here, being painfully transparent for the remainder of this letter. As I write this, the weather is transitioning. The green we enjoyed for a short time is fleeing and the grass has grown brittle under our feet. Our village seems to have gained some type of magnetism for the cloud cover and we are all beginning to add layers.

The loneliness of winter is imminent.

As many of you know, our family was so excited to receive a visit from Eddie and Maggi. For those of you who don't know, they are friends and fellow "field workers" from our home church in San Diego. Their field of harvest is in Mexico. We had a wonderful time with them and we are confident that even though their visit in the village was short, they got a good picture of what life here is like and the difficulties we face as we traverse these mountains and valleys. They took lots of pictures and videos (including the kids and me driving on our "driveway").

The additional purpose of their visit was to speak words of encouragement to our Lesotho team at our yearly retreat. God prepared Eddie so well for what he presented. Many of the team members have commented after that it was just what they needed.

Thank you, Eddie and Maggi for the blessing you have been! Thank you, to those folks who helped with the financing of their travels. You too are a blessing to us!

That brings me to the moment of transparency and what God has spoken to my heart. On the second day of our team retreat, Eddie had a form of sorts that he asked us to take to a solitary place and have a directed quiet time with God. Two and a half hours were set aside for this time. He encouraged complete silence – no singing or praying out loud – just quiet listening. For the majority of the group, it was a rough start settling into solitude, but in the end it was rewarding. For some, the allotted time proved too short. This was a much needed time for people who are bombarded with needs and wants and visits and everything else that comes with living in another context.

One part of the quiet time was to find an object – a rock, stick, flower or anything and hold it in my hand. This found object was to represent something that I need to say "no" to. I found an interesting rock, part stone on one side and sparkly crystal on the other. It glistened in the sunshine as I pondered what I needed to say no to. I prayed. I considered the last few months and my struggles here in Lesotho.

I asked God. "What is it? What do I need to say "no" to?"

Quietly, He said, "Control."

"I know- huh. Control. Ugh. Control of anything in particular?" I pondered.

"Everything."

"Oh. Everything. Whew! Don't know how this will work, but I know that You are right."

As I contemplated and prayed, I walked far down a rocky dirt road. On this day, I looked nice – very put together – aqua and gray striped v-necked t-shirt with matching gray shorts in my new slimmer size. "Very sharp!" they say here. I walked further and the next step was to get rid of the object. I prayed and asked God, "What do you want me to do with this little shimmering creation?" If I throw it, I am controlling it. If I bury it, I am controlling it. What? Now, this went on for some time. How do I give my control to Him?

"Build an altar." He said.

"What?! I'll get dirty! I look so nice – OK, OK."

So, I stopped and started gathering rocks of various sizes, tossing them to the side of the road. When I had several, I kneeled into the dirt and started stacking the rocks into a mound. Thinking, all the while, "If anybody sees me they will think I am nuts." I continued shifting them so they fit nicely together. When they were stacked, they rose to about fifteen inches above the ground. I was now dirty. I prayed over my little rock and placed it onto the top of the altar.

It sparkled proudly – just like control does.

I turned and began my walk up the rocky road.

"Take off your sandals." He said.

"What? But my feet are clean and I'm already dirty enough." I protested.

"Take them off."

"UGH. I can't do this. It will hurt. This road is too hard and rocky. I've gone too far. Please no."

"Take off your sandals and walk."

I took off my sandals. I walked and it hurt. I never walk barefooted, even inside. My sandals wait for me at my bedside and at the shower edge. My feet don't get dirty. I hobbled up the road and then He said, "This road symbolizes where you live in Lesotho. It will hurt. It will be lonely. It is dirty business and you will get hurt. Be lonely and get dirty."

"But, I look like an idiot. I can't even walk right. UNDIGNIFIED! I cried." Then, I cried because it hurt. It hurt in more ways than you know.

"Be undignified – for ME," He said.

As I continued limping up the road, there in front of me lay a beautiful, but dead butterfly – His creation. I picked it up and held it in my palm. Beautiful yes, but dead.

He whispered, "The Basotho are my beautiful creation. They are dying. Be hurt. Be undignified for them and for me."

Ok, everybody take a deep breath. Let it out slowly. The story continues.

As we ate our last breakfast with the Passmore's before their flights home, Eddie asked, "What do you want the family at home to know?"

"We want you to know that we are doing well but that doing well is still hard and it hurts sometimes. We miss. We hope. We remember. We look forward."

That afternoon, we said, "See you later!" at the airport. Now, they are back with you in North America.

When we returned to the village, there was trouble. Someone had stolen items from our home. They seemed to be somewhat selective in their theft and, adding to the bad situation, it appears to have been an "inside job." The most painful thing taken was trust. I have stewed with sadness, anger, and hurt these last few days. Stewing is not pretty.

Today, I went for my morning run – it's my time to process with God. As I reviewed the last few days, I considered all of the things I could do to control the situation. I have already changed the locks and added additional security but it doesn't feel right. I have reviewed all of the times when people told us this place is safe and that we can leave our doors unlocked, that the Basotho are trustworthy. I have supposed all of the ways I can put folks in their place or bring them to their knees in guilty repentance.

Then, as I ran back toward home, a butterfly flew across my path...

God was speaking to Chris very personally and directly about the posture he needed to have in his relationships with the people we lived among, whether they were friends or others who hurt us. The whole idea of being undignified for God challenged him in new ways and gave him a new boldness in building relationships and taking the risk to have conversations with people in the village, even if it meant he might make mistakes. The more he talked, the more confidence he had, and his influence at the vocational school grew.

After a day of teaching, he would sometimes burst through the door with a new idea: "Michelle! I've got it! Hey, are we out of bread again? You know how there hasn't been bread in town the last few times we went? We could use that so that the students can barter for fabric! I'll get fabric in South Africa, and they can use the things they have to trade with us! You'll have bread to use for the family, and they'll have the fabric they need to make the things we're learning how to sew!"

His whole body seemed to be energized when he was excited. He stood up tall, bounced on his feet as he spoke, and his voice crescendoed as his hands seemed to direct my response, "Yes! What an awesome idea!"

This barter system opened up a whole new economy at the school. Chris taught his students that God loved them and provided for them, too, not just us. He told them to look around and see what could be used as fabric. Soon, the bags that held dry beans were being used to make purses, and women were stopping by the house with freshly-made bread asking to see the supply of fabric that he kept on hand for them. As word got around, he learned that there were older women who crocheted like me! As his enthusiasm bubbled over again, he let me know that I should invite them over for tea and crochet with them.

Ironically, as we both set aside our pride and took risks that often made us feel vulnerable and ignorant, our network of friendships deepened. We were being invited over for meals, helping our friends with harvesting, and we even had people to invite over during the holidays for cookie decorating. Each victory was a sign of life to us, and we sensed that we were finally finding our stride.

32 | Life Lessons

"The LORD HIMSELF goes before you and will be with you;
He will NEVER leave you nor forsake you. DO NOT BE AFRAID,
do not be discouraged."
– Deuteronomy 31:8

Chris's fateful sense that we weren't going to be in the village as long as we thought came in October of 2012. It was just over one year after we moved there, and he was about three months into his teaching at the Skills Training Center. We were finally starting to get into a groove with a daily routine, our house was set up so that we could function, feed ourselves, and sleep without freezing. It had been a long year of trying to find our bearings without our traditional roles and work schedules. On the weekdays, Chris would pack up his backpack, bundle up, and walk down the rocky path toward the creek, cross the trickling water, then head up a rocky bank toward the school where he would spend most of the day teaching in the sewing classroom.

With Olivia at boarding school in Kenya, I was the homeschool teacher to the four younger children. Four grade levels provided more challenge than I had anticipated, so our school days were pretty packed trying to force book-knowledge into brains that were still discombobulated from adapting to our new home. Eventually, though, we were able to eke out a schedule that allowed for recess, a break for lunch, a hard and fast quitting time, and enough learning for the kids to at least be literate.

Sometime in the middle of this life-rhythm, on a day warm enough to wander outside and enjoy the light breeze, Chris and I stood near our fence looking over the now-familiar village. He seemed to have something on his mind and took a long pause. Turning to me, he explained, "I don't know what it is. I can't explain why, but I have a sense we're not going to be here as long as we thought. It just feels like God is about to do something big."

I wasn't sure how to respond; after all we had made a very long-term commitment to being there in that place, and an even longer-term commitment to living in Africa and working for our organization. My mind raced with thoughts and drowned out the rest of what he was saying. I was trying to make sense of his hunch, but I couldn't make it happen. *We had just gotten to the point where we could carry on an elementary conversation in Sesotho, why in the world would Chris be having a sense that we wouldn't be there as long as we thought?!*

Although the random inkling he was having was confusing to both of us, we shrugged it off as just a passing thought or whisper from the Holy Spirit. There was no need to try to interpret it at that point. We just stood there in the moment, he put his arm around me as we soaked in the wondering, and we eventually went about our new routine as if Chris's sense was just a far-off, wayward thought.

There were plenty of thoughts to take captive, after all. As an extroverted mom who had spent most of her married life working outside of the home, it was difficult to adjust to my support role and it took its toll on me. Without running water, the morning wake-up routine was next to impossible, and besides, it didn't seem like I needed to put on make-up or do my hair out in the middle of nowhere. Here, you had to leave your daylight hours to more critical tasks. By God's grace, there was one familiar and significant ingredient that we were able to maintain... COFFEE! I would get up and start heating the huge kettle on the gas stove so that we had enough hot water to make the coffee in the press, wash faces and other parts as necessary, and clean up any dishes that were left from the evening before.

I tried desperately to keep some semblance of a "conventional" flow to our day so that we could feel steady. It felt better to have a time to start school and a time to quit, a time for a break, and a weekend to play. Once I figured this out, I could manage my culture-shock better and make it through most days without breaking down. The weekdays looked something like this: coffee, school, lunch break, finish school, prep dinner, go visiting and have a language lesson out in the community, then finish cooking dinner and eat it together as the sun was setting. As the sun went down, the pent up tension and striving in my body seemed to release and diminish and I was able to take a deep breath. Dusk began to be associated with peace and rest.

Once the sun was down, nothing else happened in the village because the absence of electricity slowed the pace of life. This eventually became something that I appreciated because it meant we would gather in the living room near the heat of the fire, play a game, or huddle around the laptop to (re)watch one of our favorite shows that had been recorded by friends and saved to a flash drive for us. Holding a cup of steaming tea or hot chocolate with the weight and warmth of one of my kids pressing into my side with an arm on my leg gave me new appreciation for the simpleness of life. The woodsy smell of the fire burning and the warm glow of one kerosene lamp in the corner enveloped us in a comforting embrace, and we were able to breathe deeply.

Each day was repeated like this with frequent spikes of excitement or distraction that broke up the routine. Sometimes it was just one of our neighbors dropping by and other times it was a crisis that had erupted. Homeschooling lessons in history gave us additional ways we could describe our remote location. When reading about Ancient Mesopotamia, one of the youngest kids looked outside of the dining room window with an observation. Pointing out to the fields where we could see two men trailing behind two cows connected by a yoke and pulling a homemade, wooden plow, he announced, "Look! They plow their fields like that here, too!"

When we read fiction, it was the Wild West that came alive as school days were halted for anything from an abandoned lamb outside of our fence to a gun-slinging horseback pursuit of robbers who had stolen from the little one-room shop in the center of our village. Each perceived distraction was like an unplanned elective in our school schedule. We'd stop, watch, and sometimes even put the books down to go outside and investigate. Learning was constant, and even the most routine parts of our days forced our brains to take it all in.

There were positive and negative sides to that, of course. Living in that westernish, cinderblock, rectangular house with windows at the top of the gradual hill leading into the village meant that we lived in a fishbowl. Each look outside reminded me how far I was from home and my old life and seeing others looking in at me as they walked on the road made me realize there was nowhere to hide. Snapshots of contrast edged by as remembrances. A man wrapped in a simple, gray wool blanket with worn out gum boots on his feet and a stick walked behind a donkey burdened down with crates hanging on either side of his back, brown beer bottles clinked as it carried empty bottles to be exchanged for full ones. The one, white "taxi van" rode slowly by, with the weight of the crowded passengers causing it to rock as it dipped into the deep ruts in the dirt road. No matter where I looked, my brain was processing, and it was enough to leave me exhausted by the end of the day.

Life droned on like this with the added emotional stress of missing my two oldest daughters, so when I was invited to a women's retreat in the capital city with other expatriate women, I jumped at the chance. My teammate Bekah and I decided we would go together, which was a comfort to me since I had only been there a year and was new to the mountains. Bekah and I both came weighed down with burdens and ready for time with God and each other. She worked in a village even more remote than ours where they were translating the Bible into stories and songs that would eventually be used as a tool to share the Gospel with the least reached shepherds in our country. As we scanned the group of fifty-or-so women, we felt like we didn't fit in there either. Most of the women gathered there lived in proximity and chatted comfortably with the familiarity of a connected community and we would need to work at getting to know people here too if we wanted the benefit of fellowship.

As we found our room for the weekend, we both noted how thankful we were for each other and shared what was on our hearts. The fact that we still felt the tension of feeling out of place where we should have felt comfortable was a sign that our language and culture acquisition had accomplished what we prayed it would. Still, the sense that we didn't belong ANYWHERE anymore weighed heavily on us. We both vowed to soak up the time we had been gifted, open our hearts and minds to what God had for us at that retreat, and lean into whatever God spoke to us.

There was a name to the heavy burden I was carrying: "loneliness." It had been over a year since we had arrived in the village, and I was homesick and desperate for a friend. The stress of adapting to a new culture was teaching me that Chris couldn't be everything for me. While our relationship was solid and we did our best to support each other, we were both still humans with limited power and we couldn't read each other's minds. This was what I would be praying about this weekend as I opened my ears and heart to the messages that would be shared with us.

As it turned out, the weekend was a wonderful change of pace filled with the familiar pamperings of "girl time" at home. The group of American women who came to serve us at the retreat had brought their gifts, talents, and vocations as a blessing to us. We received haircuts, manicures, pedicures, sat in the shade of the trees on comfortable lounges, enjoyed delicious food, and sipped fancy coffee. In addition to the physical indulgences, there was plenty of time to be still, read, reflect, and pray. The combination of all of it allowed me a safe place to hear God. I'll never forget my conversations with Him during that time. They went something like this:

"Lord Jesus, I'm lonely. Please help me learn this language well enough that I can get to know someone and have a deep friendship."

"Michelle, I'll be your friend."

"I know you CAN be that for me, Lord, but I long for a friend my age who can understand me, who I can visit and hang out with," I explained honestly.

"I am with you always. I'll never leave you nor forsake you."

"Chris and I struggle to be all that we need for each other right now and sometimes we even argue. He says it's too much pressure for him to try to be everything to me and that He's not YOU."

"Yes, Michelle. I want to be your ALL IN ALL - your friend, your Savior, even your husband."

Whoa. Now that was perplexing! I knew it was in the Bible, but my mind couldn't fathom how Jesus, who was alive in HEAVEN, but absent from His body could be a husband to me when He had given me this husband. Nevertheless, I left the retreat refreshed and filled with a new comfort from God. He wanted to be my all in all, and He had the power to do that. That was something I could find solace in. Later that month, I was still clinging to that message from Him, and I scratched out this thought in the middle of my language lesson:

"Had a moment today when I realized that I was longing for human friendship when God is right there with me, desiring relationship with me. In these lonely times, I need to cling to HIM and focus on HIS love, acceptance, and presence. AND... embrace the character development which leads to HOPE (in the LORD)!"

33 | What Ifs

"See, I have told you ahead of time." – Jesus
– Matthew 24:25

In the quote above, Jesus was referring to "signs of the end of the age" and warning his disciples about false "Christs" who would attempt to impersonate Him before His second coming. In hindsight, though, I now see that He did that same thing for Chris and me. That sense that Chris had growing in him that we wouldn't be in the village as long as we thought was a whisper from Jesus telling him ahead of time what was to come. It was subtle and compassionate, loud enough to perceive, but not so much that it was distracting to our purpose and calling to be there. It wasn't the only preparation Jesus was doing in our lives, though.

The pace of life in the village moved along with the rising and the setting of the sun. Without electricity, the whole community woke up early and went to bed early, going about the daily work of subsistence and survival. Our neighbors' days were dependent on the seasons and the needs of the fields. The days of the younger children in the mountain communities surrounding us were dictated by the school calendar. They hiked into our village to attend the small primary school down the hill from our house, passing our kitchen window along the way.

With the flow of life in our new home becoming more familiar to us, we felt ready for visitors. One of our colleagues we had gotten to know in the office in Johannesburg wanted to bring her three younger kids out to the mountains to give them the full village "missions" experience, and we were eager to have the company, so we excitedly welcomed them in the beginning of December. We went on hikes, the kids played, we showed them around, and we thoroughly enjoyed the ease of visiting with a fellow teammate.

Both Chris and I were thrilled to have a guest, but I was especially delighted to have a female peer and friend for a few days. While my friendships with women in the community were growing as my Sesotho improved, I really missed my friends at home. Friedrun was a widow with four children, so she also seemed to enjoy the change of scenery and the adventure of being with us. I felt instantly connected with her and comfortable asking her about her journey. Her husband had passed away in a car accident on an African highway after delivering Bible study materials to a neighboring country. In the midst of fulfilling his calling, he was suddenly called home to Jesus. Rather than returning to Germany, Friedrun had chosen to continue serving in our regional office. Needless to say, I was impressed by her strength and resilience and drawn to her story.

Our time together provided a safe place for both of us to connect and share our heart journeys, and I was led to ask her questions I'd never had an opportunity to ask anybody before. I wondered how she had made the decision to stay in South Africa after her husband died. What did she do with his body? How did she tell her kids that their father wasn't coming home? How were they doing now? I was intrigued by this woman who was living with such faithful dignity despite having endured my worst nightmare, the death of my husband.

When she and the kids left, Chris and I were suddenly struck with our own mortality. She was about *our age*... We stood in the kitchen and processed all we had learned about her journey, wondering what we would do in similar circumstances. If one of us died, would we marry again? Our conversation was light-hearted, but flavored with the realization that we weren't immune from experiencing the same thing she had faced. In true Chris-form, though, humor made its way in. He quipped, "If something happened to you, I'd probably make a really dumb decision and get married quickly. We have all of these kids, and you do all of the work. I'd need help!"

After laughing and a quick hug, we both decided that neither of us would want to be alone. We gave each other the awkward blessing to get married again if death parted us. With that, we left the kitchen and joined the kids in the living room for our evening routine of quiet entertainment illuminated by the light of a lantern.

34 | Learning to Trust

"F.E.A.R. = False Evidence Appearing Real"

After a time together with the whole family for a Christmas vacation in South Africa, I returned to Kenya with Olivia. It was finally time to have a bump that was below her chin taken care of. Over many years, it had grown from being the size of a grape when we first noticed it to the size of a tennis ball. With our close friends, Ryan and Heather, still serving at the boarding school in Kenya, Rift Valley Academy, it was a huge blessing to have a place and people that felt like home. The solitude of their downstairs guest room provided the space for me to lean into the Lord and work through my fears about Julia returning to the States on her own and Olivia's upcoming surgery.

As I opened my Bible, the word picture of Noah floating in the ark jumped off the page to me. It said, "God remembered Noah." My brain understood in a new way that God hadn't forgotten Noah and *then* suddenly realized he was floating in the Ark. The word "remember" could also mean "to bear someone in mind and make provision for them." That kind of remembrance meant that God had Noah on His mind the whole time, and that He held him closely in His thoughts the same way I held my daughters in my thoughts throughout the day every day. I connected that truth to my own situation and trusted that God had my precious children in mind, too. My anxious thoughts turned to prayers, and I wrote them down.

"Being apart from Julia and Olivia and trusting You with them is a testing of my faith. It really has taught me how much You remember them. I do a lot of pleading with You to protect and guide them and have found You so faithful. Please help me rest in that."

It was only the tenth of January, ten days into 2013, and the year was already requiring me to take my thoughts captive, turn them to prayers, and then trust God with what I couldn't control.

I knew the dance. In this case, it was one word that sent my brain into the spiral of fear and dread of the worst case scenario. When the doctor came out to meet me as Olivia was waking up, his calm, reassuring voice reported that the surgery had gone well, that they were able to remove all of the tumor from her salivary gland, and they would biopsy the tumor and let us know the results in a few days.

I'm sure my face looked back at him with gratitude and friendly understanding, but my brain wasn't having any of that. He had said the word "biopsy!" What?! We went into this thinking it was just a bump that needed to be taken out. I hadn't even *considered* that it might be cancer! My daughter was only a junior in high school, she couldn't die now! We live so far away... How am I going to leave her here if that was cancer? What if it comes back?

My body was standing next to Olivia's bedside in the small recovery room of the historic Kenyan hospital that was just down the hill from the boarding school, but my brain had already gone somewhere else. By the time the doctor was walking away, I had virtually pictured her rapid decline toward imminent death. Even my ears were muffled with the anxiety of my thought process and sounds were dulled and garbled. *I have to pull myself together*, I thought. I reached down and took my daughter's hand to comfort her as she became more alert. "Are you ready to go back to campus? They have a room all ready for us at the infirmary. Your surgery went well. Your bump is all gone."

One of the nurses from the school came down the hill with a school van, helped me walk Olivia out to the car, and drove us as smoothly as he could up the rocky, rutted dirt road to the infirmary on campus. The long, single story clinic-like building was sandwiched between two, two-story buildings that were used for housing the nurses who lived and worked there together with their families. It was toward the top of the hill and surrounded by lush, green grass, shrubs, and flowering plants. The blades of the grass were thick and sturdy, more related to the jungle than the man-planted turf of golf courses back home. It was much easier to stay on the cement path than to cut through the steep, cushy grass hill that led up to the building. The staff had prepared one of the rooms for us—two twin beds that were covered with homemade quilts that had been comforting missionary kids for generations.

Once I got Olivia settled in and she was resting comfortably, I took advantage of the quiet and pulled out my Bible and journal. I was so thankful to be there with my daughter, but the dream of "what ifs" continued to plague my thoughts. I started with looking up some definitions to gain clarity.

(Dictionary) **FEAR**: *an unpleasant emotion caused by the belief that someone or something is dangerous, likely to cause pain, or a threat.*[5]

Note to self, this is a mis-placed faith, a belief in something that hasn't even come to be. It is dread without evidence, useless pain, and unpleasant emotion.

In the stillness of that small room, as Olivia slept, my mind returned to the passage I had read recently in Genesis about Noah building the Ark: *"Noah did EVERYTHING just as God commanded him."* Genesis 6:22

Then, a quote from the study notes I was using jumped off of the page, *"Noah concerned himself more with GOD'S opinion of him than with the opinions of those around him. So, he started pounding nails."*[6]

Focusing on what I was reading and fixing my brain on things I had read recently was getting my brain focused on the truth and I was making connections quickly. I recognized something familiar about Noah. *"He also walked into the UNKNOWN. At the end of my life, would people, or more importantly, GOD say of me, 'You did everything I asked you to do.'?"*

The nurse who had picked us up from the hospital peeked his head in to check on us. He saw Olivia sleeping and said in a reassuring whisper, "Everything ok in here?"

As I nodded, he continued, "Let me know if you need anything. I'm right next door."

---

[5] *Fear,* n. "Fear, n. 1." OED Online. Oxford University Press, September 2022.

[6] Author Unknown, *Study Notes on Genesis.*

At that moment, I realized we weren't alone, and I remembered a quote I had read recently about walking into the unknown *"with God carrying us and a part of the Body of Christ at each junction."*

My mind wandered to all of the people who had been with us at every single stop along the way, all the way until now. It was a missionary doctor who performed Olivia's surgery, another one was the anesthesiologist; we were being fed and checked-on now, and the list went on.

The next entry in my journal is an actual LIST of people in the Body of Christ who had functioned together and been a part of our lives December 2012 – January 2013. It brought me comfort to look back and see God's promises in action in our lives over the last couple of months. As I walked through Olivia's surgery with her and awaited the results of the biopsy, I was assured that God would continue to provide for us and carry us with the help of our people.

The ten days at the boarding school for Olivia's surgery were evidence of the Body of Christ functioning as He ordained it to work. By the end of my time there, I was really loving it and having a sense of "home" there. One evening, as Heather and I walked up the hill toward their house from the center of campus, I verbalized what I was feeling, and she shared that she had some of the same thoughts. I'll never forget what she told me about how God had spoken to *both* her and Ryan.

"We were both actually talking recently about something similar. Ryan and I can see you serving here someday," she expounded.

My response came from recent confirmations from the Lord that we were where we were supposed to be for that time. "Well, I know we're supposed to be in the village for now. Maybe we'll end up here *someday*."

In answer to our prayers, Olivia's tumor on her salivary gland proved to be benign; she bounced right back from surgery, returned to the dorm, and continued with her school term. As for me, with one fear tackled and my daughter recovering, I set out on the journey home and met up with the next test of my ability to push past my foreboding thoughts and trust God: flying in a small airplane.

35 | Fleshly Fear vs Faith in God's Promises

With Olivia on the mend, my ten days at RVA in Kenya were drawing to an end. Chris and the four younger kids had made their way back to the village and it was time to head back home. But there was *one* thing between here and there that was weighing heavy on me—the last flight into the village in a small mission plane. It made no sense for Chris to make the 10-hour journey *back* to Johannesburg with the kids just to pick me up from the airport, so we had made arrangements for me to take a flight with a mission aviation organization. I would fly from Maseru to Mokhotlong and Chris and the kids would pick me up there. The plan made sense, but flying through the windy, rugged mountains terrified me.

In my defense, this fear wasn't created in a vacuum. When we were newly married, as we were gathered in the kitchen of Chris's parents' home in Ventura, California for Thanksgiving, we heard the sound of an airplane engine that seemed way too close. As we all turned to look out of the window to the sky over the surrounding mountains, the plane careened into the side of the hill and burst into flames. Chris's older brother, without pausing to think about risk, took off to help in any way he could. It was too late. Both the flight instructor and the young aviation student who had been given the gift of learning to fly died in the crash. That was one of those days that lead people to make declarations. I added a new one to my own list that day: "I'll NEVER fly in a small plane."

With the travel day looming, I turned to God and continued to battle my fears.

JOURNAL ENTRY

January 13, 2013

*"For God has not given us a spirit of fear, but of power,
and of love, and OF A SOUND MIND."*
– 2 Timothy 1:7

LORD, despite the ways you have freed me of my fears, they creep in; what-ifs that enter my thoughts. Praise to you, they don't PLAGUE me anymore. They do lead me to prayer, though, and that's where I need to bring you these... and LEAVE them there:

* Julia - her future, safety, housing, and relationship with you.
* Olivia - biopsy and pathology reports
* MAF FLIGHT (with a stressed face doodle)

*"The fear of man brings a snare, but whoever
TRUSTS in the LORD shall be safe."*
– Proverbs 29:25

<u>Promises of God I share with Abraham (from Genesis 12):</u>

The COMMAND: *"Leave your country, your people... and go to a land I will show you."*

* *I will bless you.*
* *You will BE a blessing.*
* *I will bless those who bless you.*

As I wrote each of those promises down, I slowly realized the posture I had to maintain as I continued on in this life that was full of unknowns. It was Abraham's example, from before God changed his name from Abram, which stood out to me, *"Each step Abram took, he built an altar and CALLED ON THE NAME OF THE LORD."*

The direction of my prayers was clear: "Lord, I'm terrified to get in this plane, but you've promised to carry me and be with me. Hold this plane up and get me home."

I took the next step toward the hangar, survived the humility of weighing in with my luggage, boarded the plane, and flew off into the mountains. As we soared over the skyscraping peaks and I looked out over the rugged landscape, I continued my prayers,

"Thank you, Lord, for setting me FREE - not just from my sin, but from FEAR. Help me to conquer this "last frontier" of fear. While I don't want to leave my family and friends on earth YET, I want to live without that yoke of slavery - the fear of dying. After all, You have everything under control!"

36 | Coinciding Anxieties

"HE is WORTHY of all of the stinkiness. ALL of IT. Kaofela (all)!"
– Chris Gennaro

While I was in Kenya helping Olivia through her surgery and recovery and battling my own demons of fear and dread, Chris remained in South Africa with the rest of the kids for a couple of days to get Julia to the airport. It had been a wonderful holiday as a family, and it was time for everybody to go their separate ways. Julia looks back on the send-off with chilling hindsight. Something about Chris just wasn't normal. He had an air of dread that hung over him that gave her spirit the sense of impending doom.

Even though I wasn't with them, I can picture them going through the motions of required departure. They both shared the same tendency to lapse into either humor or anger when feeling intense emotions. They would have had to rustle the other kids to get ready, pull them off the little playground equipment outside of the room, have the younger boys go to the bathroom, and load her luggage into the back of the truck. I can imagine they were either joking about sites they saw on the way from the Baptist guest house to the sprawling airport in Johannesburg, or they sat still and stiff in the cab of the truck, faces frozen in a look of seething melancholy. It was about a twenty minute ride to the airport through a suburb and onto a multi-lane, city freeway. Chris knew the route by then but navigating the traffic and unexpected maneuvers of fellow drivers usually added to any aggravation he was already feeling.

They found a place to park the tall, four-wheel drive beast in the only section of parking structure we knew could accommodate its height and entered the echoey, marble-floored terminal to check her in. The shine off the floor and the sheen of the towering, metal beams couldn't mask the reason they were there. This was another goodbye and, no matter how you looked at it, the pain was almost too much to think about. Julia couldn't put her finger on it, but when her daddy hugged her before she turned to walk toward security and her departure, his hug was longer, and his words felt like they'd need to last her a while. Turning from him, a thought entered her mind like the dread of something unwanted. *Something's wrong with him. He's acting like this is the last time I'll see him.*

Julia has always been freakishly intuitive by nature and this parting was one of her most accurate hunches. Once Chris had made the long journey back over the mountain passes and through the long, winding valleys to the village with the four youngest kids, he took the time to blog about what he was feeling.

Blog post

Posted on January 14, 2013 by Chris

"I'm too young for this."
"I'm too old for this."
"It's not goodbye. It's see you later."
Another trip to O.R. Tambo International Airport in Johannesburg. It's the fifth time in eleven days. It has become our normal but because it seems to mostly mean "Goodbye", it just stinks. I know, some of you will say, "You chose that life – get over it." I know, because I've said it. And you are partly right. We chose to follow God wherever He took us. Here we are in Lesotho but, I will be honest and say as exciting as it seemed it would be (is and can be), this part – the saying goodbye to our kids part – it stinks haholo-holo (very much).
BUT – HE is WORTHY of all of the stinkiness. ALL of IT. Kaofela!
AND – HE knows what we need and what we want AND He loves to take care of us when we don't even know what we want or need. I've been slowly reading through Genesis and this past week, I studied Chapter 12. Famine in the land gives Abram a reason to seek greener pastures in Egypt. Earlier in the chapter, God had promised, "I will bless those who bless you and him who dishonors you, I will curse...and (give) to your offspring this land (Canaan)".

Right there in those two promises alone, he's got protection and a future. That should suffice for a lifetime. Yet as Abram enters Egypt, he fears for his life and for Sarai, his wife, and makes his own plan of protection. I follow this same strategy all too often. When things get uncomfortable and seem uncertain, I want to grab the reins and holler for plan B.

Peter tells us in his first letter, "Humble yourselves, therefore, under THE MIGHTY HAND OF GOD (MIGHTY HAND OF GOD – just in case you didn't catch it) so that at the proper time he may exalt you, casting ALL (ALL) of your anxieties on HIM because HE CARES FOR YOU (HE CARES FOR YOU). Yah yah, I've heard it a million times, sung it even more times-just typed it twice. But it catches me fresh at this time in my life. Yes, it stinks to send Julia to California – away from us, to have Olivia up in Kenya (having the time of her life I might add) and to be so far away from our families/friends. But God did it first SENDING HIS SON and I'm pretty sure being whipped, beaten, spat on and mocked wasn't the "time of His life." They (the Father and Son) did it for you and for me because of OUR sin and still He cares for us and he wants to carry our anxieties.

Lord, I confess that I am anxious. Anxious to have two of my kiddos far away, anxious to have Michelle away in Kenya, to understand this culture more clearly, to learn language more better (-: , to travel these roads, to go away from my house, to teach well and I'm anxious to represent You well. I cast these worries and others onto You and I hold onto "YOU CARE FOR ME." Help me to put myself at your feet as Mary did even when I want to follow in Martha's footsteps – always doing, doing, doing. Thank You for your loving care, your innumerable promises and your MIGHTY HANDS. – Amen

Ntate Thabang (Chris)

37 | Testing

"But (God) knows the way that I take; when he has tested me, I will come forth as gold."
— Job 23:10

With Chris and I both having coinciding anxieties about all of the things we were facing, stressors like pushing myself to face my fears felt bigger than it would have if I had had some sense of normalcy and rest in other areas of my life. As it was, we were faced with a number of hard things in a row and were living with a constant undercurrent of dread. At least these next events are proof of God's generous answers to prayer about one thing—the flight on the small plane through the mountains of Lesotho! If He wouldn't have heard and responded to my prayers for a safe flight, I wouldn't have made it back to the village to begin with!

The pilot was hand-picked by God, not only for his skills in aviation, but because it was time for his annual observation. The flight examiner from his organization ended up sitting in the right seat on our flight and was the defining reason his attention was sharp and free of any shenanigans that his jovial personality would normally have been tempted to enjoy. I'm sure it was God's sovereign plan all along for me to have *multiple* opportunities to lean on Him to deliver me from my fears, so my flight that day included at least *three* more take-offs and landings than were necessary to get to my destination. Due to the need for multiple medical and supply pick-ups and deliveries, we aimed for numerous tiny, dirt airstrips and took off over more cliffs than my courage would have cared to experience.

As we circled the flat, paved airstrip clearly visible in the center of the small town of Mokhotlong, my eyes focused on the white Land Rover and the man with the four children waving. *I MADE it!* I stretched my wobbly legs out of the small plane and was welcomed with hugs and smiles from Chris and the kids. Chris had loaded up on supplies while in South Africa, so we were able to set off on the last leg of the journey home—the hour-long four wheel drive trek over dirt roads, river crossings, and boulders catching up on all of life's events over the last ten days as we traveled.

There's a glaring gap of silence in my journal between my last entry from the school in Kenya and January 28, 2013, as the biggest plot twist of my life began to unfold. Although the evidence of God's presence and foreshadowing hints are obvious now as I sit here looking back, there's one overused phrase that more accurately describes the magnitude of my humanness in those moments: "Nothing could have prepared me for this." As I took my first, shaky, unplanned steps into my own worst case scenario, the only thing I could do was cling to the unseen strength I chose to believe in.

38 | The Exodus

January 23rd or 24th, 2013

*"Fear not, for I have redeemed you; I have summoned you
by name; you are mine. When you pass through the waters,
I will be with you; and when you pass through the rivers, they will
not sweep over you. When you walk through the fire, you will not
be burned; the flames will not set you ablaze."*
— Isaiah 43:1-2

It felt so good to roll up to our compound
after being gone for almost a month. Chris and the kids were all
excited to get me home so I could try Chris's tapioca pudding. Since
he had been caring for the four younger kids on his own for a
couple of weeks, he was eager to show me all he had done. He had
stocked up on the groceries, unpacked them, cooked meals from
scratch for all of them, and had even spoiled them with desserts.
They had worked together to perfect our brownie recipe and had
even mastered tapioca pudding, a family favorite and ode to one
of our favorite movies, *New In Town*. As we rolled up to the side of
the house to unload, Chris allowed the words he had been waiting
to say roll off of his tongue: "Kids, tell Mom what you said about
my tapioca pudding."

Their immediate response was laughter, and then, through
squeals, each of them responded with their unanimous vote,
"Yours is better than Mom's!"

Chris served up heaping portions for all of us and we sat around
the table to catch up on the events of the last ten days. They told
me about saying goodbye to Julia, going shopping for the groceries,
and their journey into the mountains back to the village. I passed
on greetings from our friends in Kenya, told them about Olivia's
life at school and her surgery, and described my harrowing flight

in the sky *over* the mountains. When the conversation waned and the kids shuffled off to their beds, Chris and I went deeper into the details of our time apart.

One of the first things he shared was the unexplainable pain he was having in his legs. He couldn't put his finger on it, but he described it as muscle spasms. There was an urgent medical need for a ride to the hospital in the village and, because the request came from a woman in the village we considered a friend, Chris had acquiesced and agreed to take her and her son to town the next day. When he told me of his plan to go to the chemist for muscle relaxers, I knew his pain must have been off the charts.

Trips to town were an all-day journey that often lacked any hope of achieving that which you set out to accomplish. The ride to the hospital that day was no different. With her son in varying stages of consciousness and no doctor available at the "hospital" in town, Chris and our friend headed back to the village without the medical care her son needed. They made one desperate stop along the way at the rustic Catholic church that was barely visible from the gravel road. Chris described the scene as "creepy" and it haunted his thoughts well into the night, even keeping him awake as he worried about his own symptoms and confronted his fears.

When they were stopped at the Catholic outpost, the priest had approached the vehicle with a crucifix extended in his hands and held it between himself and the young man with the mysterious illness. He mumbled incantations in Sesotho that Chris was unable to make out and seemed to be casting out evil from the patient. Whatever he said, it seemed to bring a cover of darkness over the scene that Chris couldn't shake off. He reached out to friends and family back home in a Facebook post asking for prayer.

FACEBOOK POST

January 22, 2013

Chris here. I haven't quite felt the same since I made the hospital trip. Don't want to cry wolf or go on a witch hunt but please pray that the aches I am feeling all over my body will go away now. Thanks.

The muscle relaxers had been easy to find and were inexpensive, but they didn't touch the pain that continued to move through Chris's body. It was as if he would attempt to describe it as a cramp and then change his mind mid-sentence to a description of a deep pain in his bones. More symptoms began to appear within a day or so. A lack of appetite turned into full-blown nausea, and his lethargy increased until he was bound to the bed with fever and chills.

Neighbors began to notice his absence in the village and stopped by to check on him. He hadn't been out on his "rounds" to have language lessons, to help anyone with their chores, or to carry out any school business in a number of days. A visit from our close friends brought comfort as their concern led them to his bedside to pray for his healing. They mentioned that there were a few others in the village with the flu, so all of us wondered together if this was just a bad virus making its rounds through households in the community.

There seemed to be nothing I could do to bring comfort. I brought him juice, water, and old fashioned hot water bottles filled from the kettle on the wood burning stove to put on his back to relieve his pain. The nights turned sleepless as he tossed and turned with cramp-like convulsions that kept him from being able to calm himself to sleep. I didn't know what to do, but I knew I had to stay calm and try to maintain our routine. The kids and I tried to do school and keep up with the chores, but Chris's symptoms worsened, and our concern grew with every mysterious symptom.

In the middle of one night, I found Chris in the room we referred to as our bathroom. He was trying to figure out how to get a shower working for himself. By that time, gravity fed water from the towering, green tank just up the hill from the back of our house entered the room through small pipes that wound through a wall unit similar to an insta hot. We had seen these work in other places and had just splurged on the gas powered unit for ourselves. Eventually, scalding, hot steamy water dribbled from the shower head onto Chris's body. He shrieked with pain. Every touch of a breeze or liquid that wasn't body temperature seemed to send electrical charges through his body. "AAGH!! I can't. I can't. Help me get out of here. The water hurts. Ugh. Help dry me off. It hurts!"

As he writhed in pain by candlelight, I prayed silently and asked God for help. I wasn't a doctor, but I knew that these symptoms seemed to be signs of an issue with his nervous system. This, together with his inability to swallow, was all the guidance I needed to realize that it was time to get him to a doctor. As I helped him put his clothes back on, I calmly suggested an idea. "Chris, I want to help you, but I don't know what to do. I think we should get you to a hospital for help."

"There aren't even doctors at the hospital here," he winced. "I'm NOT going back there."

"Honey, you can't swallow now, so I can't even keep you hydrated. We *have* to go for help. Please let me take you."

"NO. I AM NOT GOING TO THAT HOSPITAL," his voice came out in breathy gasps as he forced his determined words out between pants. He was in a zone now, every ounce of his strength focused on battling the jarring pain. It was as if he was channeling our Lamaze breathing, sucking in as much air as possible in a long pull of oxygen and then heaving out long sighs as he blew it out through tensed lips.

"Well, ok. I won't take you *there*, but if you aren't any better when the sun comes up, I'm taking you to Bethlehem (South Africa) to the hospital no matter what you say."

I tucked him back into bed as another convulsing whole-body cramp came over him, quietly walked out of the dark room, and started packing our bags. My heart raced with anxiety and my brain struggled to focus enough to get the things we needed for a few days away and prepare the house for us to be gone. The weight of carrying the medical emergency we were in the middle of and guiding the kids through something that felt too terrifying for me to carry out left me with a sense of desperation. I needed help, prayer, anything. Before I took out the bags and started putting things in them, I paused and dug deep for the words in an S.O.S. post.

FACEBOOK POST

January 23, 2013

URGENT. KEEP PRAYING. Chris' pain is still severe. If he hasn't improved by morning, I'm packing and driving out to a doctor.

By the time the sun lit up the vast sky in a peachy, warm glow, I had the Land Rover packed with enough clothes, snacks, and school stuff for the kids to get us through the weekend. I figured we just needed to get him to the hospital where they could get him fluids and help his body recover from this awful flu. We'd be back in a few days. All I had to do was take one step at a time through the contingency training we had had only a year and a half before this. I stood still for a second and forced my brain to recollect what I needed to do. "Step one: notify team leader of emergency and evacuation plans."

With that done, we all made one last stop at the outhouse and locked up the house. Our eighty-four-year-old "village father" who was probably the first one up in the village every morning, noticed me packing up the truck and walked over in his slow, deliberate pace for a last goodbye. Ntate was a pillar of faith in this place, one of the few Christ-followers we knew of. The two friends before Chris climbed into the back of the truck where he insisted he would be more comfortable. There was a proper bench seat welded in back there and a solid shell that would protect him from any watchful eyes that may have caught him in one of his convulsions. Now I know that he was also protecting us from what he was experiencing and preferred suffering in private rather than causing us any more stress than we were already under.

Rain had transformed the dusty, rocky path from the village into a muddy donkey trail that cut through fields of maize in a dangerous and precarious path toward our deliverance. Weakness didn't stop Chris from directing my driving from the bench seat in the covered back of the truck. There were two small slits for windows between us and only one opened, so this only allowed for occasional shouts and thuds from his fists banging to make their way past the whine and grind of the engine and the wrestling of the tires with the mud and mire.

"Don't you have it in low?!"

"Put it in first gear over this part!"

"Now put the diff lock on!"

"Michelle! Gun it!!!"

After the challenge of the route to the tarmac road, there was still a five and a half hour, twisty turny, harrowing drive and a border crossing between our village home and the nearest hospital. Life in the mountains made this a familiar route as we had to pass through this way to get to and from the airport, stock up on groceries, or make our way to government offices for the never-ending process of finalizing licenses and immigration statuses.

As I clenched the steering wheel, my hands were tense and my palms sweaty. I knew I needed to calm the kids and give them some assurance that everything was going to be ok, but I couldn't bring myself to believe it. I needed to focus my brain on the fine motor skills it took to drive the road. I deliberately told my brain what it needed to do— "Look forward. Turn here. Downshift. Almost to the tarmac road. Tell Jed to dial August and tell him we're taking Dad to the hospital in Bethlehem."

I knew that Chris was back there in crippling pain, so my efforts to make the drive smooth for him added to the stress of every bump and every turn. Everything in me wanted to be back there with him, comfort him, and make him better, but I was forced to drive. I had no choice but to buckle down and get there. As we drove along, the whine of the fuel injection and the hum of the engine were the only sounds that interrupted the tense silence in the cab. We couldn't see Chris, so the kids took turns asking questions: "What do you think is wrong with Dad?" "Why is he hurting so bad?" "Will the doctors be able to help him?"

Although I answered every question, I felt like I was lying. The truth was, I had no idea what was wrong with him and everything in me felt seriously hopeless. After five and a half hours of twisting roads and white-knuckled driving, every muscle in my body ached as we arrived at the hospital in Bethlehem. It was late afternoon, and as we pulled into the small parking lot, we received the welcome news that Dudley and Jan, leaders for the Southern Region, were on their way to us from Johannesburg.

Part Three |

The Valley of the Shadow of Death

39 | A Note About Trauma

"Yea, though I walk through the valley of the shadow of death,
I will fear no evil;
For You are with me;
Your rod and Your staff, they comfort me."
— Psalm 23:4 NKJV

I know this will break the flow of the narrative and abruptly shift your brain from the story, but the valley we're about to enter should really have a sign posted at the entrance to it— <u>Warning</u>: Those who travel here will experience changes to their brains which sometimes result in long-lasting damage. If you feel like you have whiplash and your brain has been forced out of the story, you're tracking with me. We were forced out of our life stories and into a Worst Case Scenario we hadn't written for ourselves. Nothing about that time fits into a neat and tidy timeline of describable scenes and experiences.

The trauma of the unforeseen events we lived through was jarring, like being hit with something in the head that you didn't expect. There are sweeping time periods that I literally cannot recall, and sometimes the sequences of the events are difficult to put in place. If you've experienced days like this as well, you know that multiple areas of your brain are in survival mode which renders you hyper-focused on the danger that you're up against. For us, there wasn't one event that threw us into that tense terror, but multiple, gut-wrenching twists and turns through Valley of the Shadow of Death that dulled my senses and stole the vigor out of life.

It's easy for me to understand why the psalmist refers to the depths of despair as the "Valley of the Shadow of Death." Everything is dull, dark, and lifeless there. I couldn't taste anymore, and the world around me took on an out-of-focus, drab color. Even my hearing seemed to be affected, for there were many times I could see that someone was talking to me but their words were garbled and nonsensical. My brain just couldn't track well because it was thinking about Chris every minute of every hour, and I'd have to ask them to repeat what they were saying so that I could force my brain to translate the words.

My prayer in writing these memories down has always been that people who have had their worst nightmares happen will be able to see, as I have, that there is a God who sees us and keeps His promises faithfully no matter what we go through in this broken world. As I've had to revisit memories I never wanted to think about again, I've seen Him. The fact that I remember in shadows, dulled and diluted, is evidence of a loving Creator who knew that it was all too much for me. He made our brains go into shock because He's gracious and merciful. He knew all along that I needed protection from what we were going through. And that, my friends, is a specific answer to His promises in Isaiah 43:2-3.

> *"When you pass through the waters,*
> *I will be with you;*
> *and when you pass through the rivers,*
> *they will not sweep over you.*
> *When you walk through the fire,*
> *you will not be burned;*
> *the flames will not set you ablaze.*
> *For I am the Lord your God,*
> *the Holy One of Israel, your Savior..."*

Come with me but expect the unexpected. I want to be real and honest, so you'll get the real deal, not a contrived and colored-in version of a story that played out in black and white, nail-biting, fear and dread. The color and laughter you'll see along the way is evidence of our Heavenly Father's faithful presence in the middle of it all.

40 | No Help in Sight
January 24th, 2013

"Traveling is a brutality. It forces you to trust strangers and to lose sight of all of the familiar comfort of home and friends. You are constantly off balance. Nothing is yours except the essential things - air, sleep, dreams, the sea, the sky."
— *Cesare Pavese*

Previous drives through the countryside over the last year and a half had been filled with the excitement of new sights and experiences. Crossing the border from Lesotho into South Africa was a sudden, drastic change in topography and culture that we usually associated with time off, plentiful food, and frequent wild animal sightings. Hours of winding through jagged, harsh mountains gradually yielded wider roads and open pastures. The sharpest eyes could look ahead and find ostrich, zebra grazing, or a meerkat standing guard in the vast, groomed farm fields. This drive was vastly different.

This one was all business. It felt like an evacuation, an urgent sprint to somewhere and someone who may be able to help us. By now, I knew my way through the small farming town, past stone buildings and seventies-style storefronts and onto a tree-lined, side street on the edge of town. We had been to the small, private hospital before with Duane a few months earlier when he had an intestinal infection, so I knew vaguely what we'd find when we entered the glass doors into the lobby waiting area. Although it felt more like a clinic by American standards, it was clean, the doctors and nurses were friendly, and they spoke English. In my frazzled mind, this was our best bet.

I pulled the Land Rover into the circular drive and whipped the dirt-covered beast into the first parking spot I saw closest to the entrance. The culture shock side of my brain wondered if this was acceptable, but the traumatized, terrified side won out and I abandoned the cab to continue my quest. It took all of us rallying together to get Chris into the lobby that afternoon. As the glass doors automatically swooshed open, I approached the nearest desk and asked for help.

The memories that remain of these days play in my mind like a stuttering, blurry slide projector, faded snapshots of a time when my brain was set solidly in survival mode. There's no vision for detail in this place, only a search for the basics, the necessities that would carry us through the hopeless desperation of the situation. Chris must have been guided back by a nurse or something while I settled the four kids in a row of chairs in the waiting room with their backpacks of snacks and books. With no clue about what was ahead, we had shifted into auto-drive, following the directions of our contingency plan for the day when the unexpected happened and we needed to pack the essentials and get out.

While Chris was being cared for by the medical staff, I remained in the lobby navigating a health care system I knew nothing about. I sat in a chair facing a person who knew nothing about us either and had never seen the health insurance cards I was handing her. Hands shaking, I grasped for any document I could find that would prove we had coverage in this country. She called over her colleagues to help. Nobody had ever heard of the major American company whose name was plastered in red at the top of the official card with Chris's name on it. With a nine-hour time difference, the offices in America weren't even open for us to call. We were left to handle this situation in the only way they knew how, according to the hospital's policies in the country we were in.

Daylight was fading and shifts were ending, so we had to come up with an immediate plan for the night. With only a few minutes of assessment, the doctors on staff had determined that Chris needed to remain in intensive care for the night to get him stabilized and diagnosed. In this private hospital, it would cost us five thousand U.S. dollars. I didn't have the technology available to me to check my bank balance, but I already knew what I needed to know. We didn't have that amount of money available to us and there was no way to get it.

Torn between comforting and protecting my kids and caring for my husband, I went back and forth between the sterile exam room in the back and the lobby waiting room, now vacant except for the remnant of my own haggard family. Each of the kids had their backpacks and found little things to occupy themselves with, but they shared the same, distracted concern that gripped me. As I approached them and melted into one of the chairs next to Silly, weepy concern furrowed her brow as she asked, "Is Daddy ok? What did they say?"

I was forced to give her a vague answer that would calm her for that moment, the only truth I could muster in that moment without breaking down into sobs. "He has help now. They're trying to figure out what is going on."

The condition and posture of Chris's body wavered drastically, and he shifted and moaned in the narrow hospital bed. One moment he was slumped there, wilted with exhausted limpness and then his body would tense up and his face would morph into a look of frantic stiffness, his eyes opening wide at the apex of the pain and then closing tightly as he braced himself through the paralyzing stiffness that wracked his body with violent cramps. Nothing gave him relief and he begged them to do something for him. "Can't you give me something for the pain?! Don't you see what's happening?! I can't take this anymore!"

Doctors and nurses buzzed around him and took turns asking him questions and examining him.

"When did these symptoms start?"

"Have you been exposed to any rabid dogs?"

"Do you have any infected cuts anywhere on your body?"

"Where do you live?"

He grunted and writhed as he forced the answer to each question. When he couldn't finish a sentence, I added on the rest and filled in the gaps. Sounds of beeps came from adjoining rooms and the air conditioning system blew air into the room to maintain the consistent, chilly temperature characteristic of hospitals. As people rushed into the room, the air would shift and make a little breeze that flowed over Chris. Each slight change of temperature or breeze that grazed his skin sent his nervous system into tense and shocking spasms. I couldn't touch him or hug him for fear of hurting him further, so I hung back and hovered as closely as I could without getting in the way.

There was only one eternal truth obvious to me in this and all other moments: there is a God in Heaven and I could talk to Him. With no time or space to stop and find a posture of prayer, my running dialogue with Him was more like a constant, under my breath, stuttered begging. I'm sure the words were jumbled and came out as nonsensical gibberish. They fell out without restraint: "Lord, help us. Give us someone who can tell us what to do."

Emergencies leave no time to ponder much, and shock prevents organized thought anyway. Well-used reflexes took over as I paced for hours between the hospital room where Chris was and the lobby where the kids were. There must have been a point in the tumultuous trauma when I was able to pull out my foreign made, "Facebook Phone," the Vodafone Blue 555. The simple, chincy gadget allowed me to post updates straight to Facebook with minimal data use. I released a sigh of gratitude as I realized I had stocked up on enough prepaid cell phone minutes in the previous days to hit the little blue button near the one-inch screen and post an update.

FACEBOOK POST

January 24, 2013

Drove out of Lesotho. At hospital in South Africa. Still no answers to symptoms, but in good hands. EKG fine, getting fluids, kids being SO good.

The glass windows all around the waiting room provided a view to the outside world, but the only sight my brain could register was that it was dusk and nighttime would soon arrive. A new shift of medical personnel began arriving, whisking past us with light footed freshness. It was only moments after the changing of the guards that I was beckoned back to the examination room where a new doctor stood by Chris's bedside. She was a white woman with a thick,

Africaaner accent and a commanding presence. A couple of things were clear to her as she listened to our situation and observed Chris's condition: they didn't know what was wrong with him and we didn't have the money for him to stay there.

41 | A Hospital Odyssey

"But a strange man in a strange land, he is no one: men know him not – and to know not is to care not for."
– Jonathan Swift

The bad news the helpful doctor delivered to us that night felt like a blow to the stomach, punching out the tiny shred of hope I had from getting Chris to the hospital. It was clear, however, that God had placed her in that position as a person of help when we needed it. The only other place she had to send us in the small town was the national hospital a few blocks away. Looking back, I understand why she was preparing us for what we were about to face. Her words of advice were delivered with deliberate calm, but her assurances only served to make me more nervous.

She promised that she would advocate for Chris, make sure they received him, and knew what to expect. She gave me her personal cell phone number and told me I could call her around the clock if I had questions. Her last job had been at the hospital we were headed to, so she knew the doctors there, and since she was nearby, she offered to check in on him.

There's an ironic blessing in the fuzziness of my memories from this point on in the story: if I had more vivid memories of every detail, the weight of the trauma would have had even more of a devastating effect on me.

My critically ill husband was discharged from that hospital and into my care for the short drive to the next hospital. All of my senses were in survival mode as I wheeled him out to the Land Rover in a wheelchair and helped him hoist himself in. We had no choice but to press on and follow her directions to what we prayed would be a place he could rest for the upcoming night safely with some relief from his pain.

It was evening when we pulled into the parking lot of a hospital building that rose ominously from the empty lot like a relic from a less-fortunate past. Fearful thoughts rushed in as I searched the dark entrance for a sign of medical staff. Chris's severe pain and increasing neurosis and paranoia meant that I had to convince him to take every step, comforting him with words of hope whether I believed them or not. As we entered the main door, evidence of dusty and disorganized construction could plainly be seen in the dimly lit, dirty room. I knocked on the window to the left and hoped it would bring someone who could give us direction or get a doctor. There weren't enough chairs for our young children to sit while they waited, and the torn feelings of balancing Chris's and helping them navigate this terrifying time ravaged me. Without time to stop and process everything, I was forced to leave them looking worried and scared while I tried to find help.

The next scene that I remember is Chris in a large room with no privacy. A young Mosotho male nurse was the first to attend to him. He spoke English in the familiar accent of our neighbors from our village in Lesotho, so the fact that we were the only foreigners to be found there felt somewhat normal to us. Still, the dramatic shift from the shiny sterility of the private hospital to the dismal and dank conditions at this hospital disturbed me. We were living in the great chasm between the haves and have-nots that still existed in South Africa. Without access to the resources available to us, we were demoted to the same, vulnerable position as the least of the least in that community would have experienced.

Once the doctor was found, he attempted to calm Chris with promises of keeping him comfortable and trying to figure out what was going on with him. We answered the routine list of questions with the same honest, mysterious details we had explained to the last team of doctors: started with flu-like symptoms, fever, muscle pain, maybe it was pain in the bones, convulsions, couldn't swallow, sensitivity to texture and temperature, and the list was growing. Leaving Chris there felt like abandonment, but we had no other option. There was nowhere for us to sit, we weren't offered the chance to stay with him, and we had no choice but to leave and look for somewhere to stay that night. I dug through my backpack for the list of guest houses that the first doctor had given me and started calling them.

The scene changes drastically again here to a quiet, tree-filled, sanctuary-like yard of a woman with a soothing, motherly voice. Something about her felt safe and heavenly. Her helpful reassurance and control of our situation released the floodgates of my emotions. "Let me take care of dinner for you. You must be hungry. This will only take a few minutes and then I'll take you to your room where you can rest."

There was no holding back the tears at that point and I let them flow as she ordered pizza for us and then showed us to the cottage at the other side of the beautifully landscaped backyard of her home. We walked for a short distance on a cobbled path that curved past a single car garage and then turned toward a small structure behind it. Manicured shrubs lined the path, and I could see silhouettes of trees in the distance in the light of the moonlight. She opened a metal security screen similar to the one we had at home and let us in. There was a queen size bed in the main room that immediately caught my attention. Even the sight of it made my body crave the feeling of being horizontal.

As we set our things down and the kids found their beds, my phone rang. It was my colleagues, Dudley and Jan. They had arrived in Bethlehem from Johannesburg and were nearby so they could be with us in whatever way we needed. We confirmed the plan to get some sleep there and then go to the hospital to see Chris and assess his condition and treatment in the morning.

Sleep was impossible. I tossed and turned with the vivid pictures of all we had been through that day playing through my mind. Worry of the unknown consumed me. My body tingled with fear. Being without Chris was foreign to begin with but being separate from him for the night in a strange place transformed my inner self to a child in the fetal position, with covers over my head, afraid of the dark and trembling. I forced my brain into the spiritual discipline of taking my thoughts captive and turned my thoughts into prayers. They lacked profound wording and spiritual finesse. I was pounding on the doors of Heaven and groveling at my Heavenly Father's feet. *"Help us… help us."*

It was sometime in the middle of the night when my phone buzzed and vibrated. The man on the other line introduced himself as a doctor in the hospital where Chris was. He explained that they needed to transfer him to a bigger hospital in Bloemfontein almost three hours away so that he could be diagnosed. Apologizing for the late call and trying to assure me, he said there were more doctors there in the next city and that the infectious disease specialists there would be better able to help him. He would go by ambulance immediately. As I scrambled for a scrap of paper and a pen, he gave me the address and hung up.

Minutes felt like hours as I laid there in the darkness with my worried thoughts attacking me faster than I could capture them. I was reminded of the quick prayer request I had posted on Facebook and prayed that the prayers of our loved ones were standing with us. It was daytime back at home after all.

5:30 a.m. Another buzzing call from my phone jerked me from my anxious nap. It was Chris. I'd never heard him so desperate.

"You HAVE to come now. Get me out of here. I'm dying and they're not helping. Come quick. I don't know where they have me, but I have to get out of here. Hurry."

I told him we would get there as soon as we could and sprung into action. I called Dudley and Jan and woke them up. When I told them about Chris's terrified call, Dudley offered to leave right then. He brought Jan to the place where I was staying so that she could drive the kids and me, and he would go directly to Chris so that he could get there as soon as possible.

The peace of the garden outside was irrelevant as we roused ourselves into evacuation mode again. Waking the kids, we gathered them and our scattered belongings, loaded them in the truck, and took to the highway. The sun was just coming up and we were existing and functioning on emergency adrenaline. My body seemed to be in auto drive, and I did what I had to do to get through one minute at a time. I was a zombie by then, willing my body to move forward despite my fears like I was directing myself with switches on a remote control device. It was a relief to have teammates with me to help carry the burden, and I allowed Jan to drive and to comfort me with her years of experience and wisdom. They had lived in multiple countries in Africa and trained people like us. With her at the wheel, I could focus a little more on the kids and attempt to gear up for the next battle.

Somehow, Chris was able to call again. He was hungry and thirsty. He said there wasn't anything there for him and asked us to stop and get him something. This time, his voice was direct and demanding. I was able to tell him that Dudley was almost there and that we were enroute. We would stop at a nearby petrol station and get him the orange Powerade and biscuits he wanted. It didn't occur to me until after I hung up that one of the reasons I took him to the hospital to begin with was that he couldn't swallow. A question entered my mind: "Is he getting better, or is he even more confused?" I cataloged that detail along with the other mysterious and confusing dynamics of this nightmare and we pushed forward toward the third hospital.

If the previous, construction littered hospital rose ominously like a relic from the past, this one stood as a dominating dinosaur on the outskirts of the large Free State town. An outdated, brick guard station stood between the entrance of the hospital where we needed to be and the world outside. Tension increased as we searched for a parking spot. The ominous, archaic, multi-story building loomed in front of me like a dark foreshadow of what I was about to encounter. Dudley intercepted us before we got out of the car. He already had a plan that would spare the kids from going in. He would stay with them and continue to work with our team leader, August, on a place for us to stay in town while Jan and I went inside to be with Chris.

The processing I was doing in my journal the month previous bears repeating at this point in the odyssey because the truth of it was about to take over our lives as a vast safety net in a foreign place.

"Just as each of us has one body with many members, and these members do not all have the same function, so IN CHRIST we who are many form one body, and each member BELONGS to all the others." WE HAVE DIFFERENT GIFTS... Romans 12:4-8

(Dictionary) **BELONG**: verb, **to be "rightly placed" in a specified position; to fit in a specified place or environment**; to have the right

qualities to be a member of a particular group; to "be a member" of a particular organization or class; to be the PROPERTY OF.[7]

(Dictionary) **MEMBER**: *an individual belonging to a group; A PART OR ORGAN OF THE BODY, especially a LIMB.*[8]

Once Dudley and Jan arrived in Bethlehem on that first night, our team rallied, and we were never alone. Our team leaders and dear friends, August and Anita, were "rightly placed" for us. Being native South Africans serving with our organization in Lesotho, they were well-acquainted with the region where we "happened" to be. Although he was out of town as we arrived in Bloemfontein, August was in constant communication with Dudley, connecting us with resources and people they knew in the area. While I was unaware of it as I left the kids in Dudley's care, they were on their way to August and Anita's friends' house where there was a separate guest cottage and a pool.

Jan and I marched down the dank hallway with purpose, following the rough directions we had been given. We moved in sync like misplaced soldiers down the crowded and depressing hallway. Backless benches lined the walls here and there, each one fully occupied by dark-skinned sick people waiting to be attended to. Some people even sat or laid on the floor, their own blankets wrapped around them. Worn, dingy vinyl-tile floors served as the only overflow seating. Everything was dull and gray to me, and my senses were dulled with anxious dread. My usual, acute sense of smell couldn't perceive any of the familiar, medicinal, bleach smells of other hospitals I had been in before.

Medical staff seemed shockingly absent as helpless people waiting silently and miserably to be seen. Trapped in my own medical emergency, the compassion and empathy I felt for these people was forced to remain inside, adding to the emotions I was already forcing myself to hold at bay.

We entered a small side room where Chris was alone on a gurney-like bed. It felt like a prison room instead of a hospital room.

---

[7] *Belong,* v. "Belong," Oxford English Dictionary, updated September 2022.

[8] *Member,* n. "Member," Oxford English Dictionary, updated September 2022.

The only furnishings were the narrow, metal bed and a small metal sink that hung on the wall in the opposite corner of the room. There were no medical tools or machines anywhere to be found. No nurse welcomed us or asked who we were. There were windows, but no window coverings, so any effort toward creating privacy for the patient was impossible. Outside of the window, another dinosaur-of-a-building rose to block out any view of the compound beyond.

After staying with us to hear an update from Chris and check on him, Jan left the room to give us privacy. Twenty-five years of life together was suddenly reduced to the two of us facing the reality of what we were living in that moment. Chris's emotional and mental state seemed to be deteriorating. One minute he was himself and the next he was tensed up, writhing in pain, begging for help that never came, and planning his escape. His brow was furrowed with a look of anger, but I knew it was a fear more intense than any I had ever seen in him. When I reached out to touch him, he dodged my touch and pulled away. Every sensation triggered his nervous system and sent stabbing sensations throughout his body. His eyes were wild with desperation, wide open and red from lack of sleep. Without any interruptions from medical staff that *should* have been present and attending to him, Chris recounted his traumatic, middle-of-the-night hospital transfer. In one of his only temporary moments of calm, he told how he had gotten there.

"In the middle of the night, a doctor came and told me that they needed to move me to another hospital where they had specialists. He said they had a team of infectious disease specialists here and more resources to diagnose me than they had there in Bethlehem, so they needed to transfer me. I told him that my family was here and that I wanted them with me, but he told me I had to go. He said he would call you and I had no choice.

"They put me in the back of a van on a gurney with a young Mosotho guy who sat by me. Another one drove. They talked loudly back and forth, and I could tell that the van was speeding. It seemed like we were on one of those big highways we have been on that goes through the countryside. Every time the van jerked and swerved to avoid the potholes in the road, my body would have another seizure. The air coming through the vents was right on me and the cold air made my whole body tense up. The change in temperature felt like electric shock, Michelle! I begged them to turn down the air and told them it was hurting me, but they didn't care! They ignored me and acted like they didn't understand me! Can you believe that?! Nobody cares and nobody's helping!!"

He had spent three-hours of torment on the way there and the trauma, anger, and fear of the experience had him feeling attacked and afraid. He told me that he *had* to get out of there. It seemed like nothing I said could convince him to wait any longer. The doctors who had been promised were nowhere to be found and there weren't even any nurses to ask for pain medicine.

Time ticked by as he vented to me about all he had been going through. He would talk for a few minutes and then suddenly go back into a seizure, and I would try to calm him. Confused, disoriented, and consumed by excruciating pain, he was delirious. Every time his body tensed, it seemed like his personality froze and was taken over by paranoia and rage. Without a medical professional to witness it or help him, I did what I could do to restrain him, comfort him, and protect him from himself. From everything I knew, hospitals were a place where you got help and were healed. As the hours played out, the security and hope of that belief faded and I was tempted to slip into the same desperate hopelessness Chris had.

"I'm dying and nobody cares. Nobody is helping me! GET. ME.HELP! I need to get out of here, Michelle. DO SOMETHING!"

Then, the next moment, the husband I knew would return, face softened and tears welling up in his eyes. He told me he loved me and thanked me for being such a faithful wife. He apologized for being a jerk, recounting recent times he had been angry and had reacted harshly. I reassured him that we were doing all we could to help him, that August was calling on those he knew in the area to find doctors and specialists. One of his friends was coming and was going to help. I promised him that I was doing all I could and told him how much I loved him. The truth was, I was weighing the risk of leaving him alone in that room to go *look* for a nurse or a doctor. Finally, a man entered the room with some instruments in his hand.

He explained that they were understaffed and that they were attending other patients. I told him we were brought there because there was a team of infectious disease specialists who could help diagnose Chris's symptoms. His reply droned on with excuses about the team being in a far off city doing something important. All I heard was that they weren't HERE. He told us he had needed to take a biopsy to send to the lab in Pretoria to rule out rabies. They would wait for that to come back and then go from there.

"BUT WHAT ABOUT NOW?!" I begged. "Don't you have something you can give him NOW for his pain?! He hasn't slept, the pain is too much for him. What can you do now?!"

He told us he was just there to do the biopsy. There was no nurse with him, nobody to assist. He asked Chris to lay on his side and I took my place in front of him and held his hand. The procedure was done right there in front of me; a chunk of flesh was cut from the back of his neck and then stitched up with what I perceived as sutures the size of guitar strings. The blood from the procedure trickled down from Chris's neck onto the pillow he had carried with him all the way from the village. It was his only shred of comfort and he had clung to that thing as if it was his last possession.

The doctor stood, told us we would wait for the results, and left the room.

We both froze there, shocked and perplexed. Now what? With no plan or hope for pain medicine, a real hospital room, a team of doctors, or hope of diagnosis, we had no idea what to do. The rational, administrative, missionary-trained, leader side of me knew that I was in a cross-cultural situation and that I had to flex to the way they did things in that part of South Africa, and yet nothing was making sense. I knew there was someone, somewhere, working on the paperwork for Chris's admittance to the hospital. They were trying to figure out our insurance again so that he could be treated there.

Chris didn't care about *any* of that, he just wanted OUT. He told me he was unsafe there, that he had to get out, and that if I didn't help him do it, he'd go on his own. Getting blood on his pillow was the last straw. He was pissed that they had ruined it. I'm sure in that moment the memory of how difficult it was to find the right pillow in the first place was overwhelming to him. Every part of his world was crumbling, and he had to escape.

Jan arrived as we were devising a plan. Without warning, Chris picked up his pillow and stormed from the room. Jan and I looked at each other in panic and had to respond instantly. She would follow

Chris out of the hospital and try to keep him safe and corralled somewhere, and I would search for a doctor or medical staff to try to finesse a transfer and the test results out of them. The first two hospitals had schooled me in the fact that we had to have an official, signed and stamped, approved transfer from one hospital in order to get him admitted into the next. With my husband walking out of the hospital with his blood stained pillow under his arm, I had no choice but to scour the hallways and rooms for someone who could give me what I needed.

I crossed the hall and pushed my way into the double doors in front of me. A long, open room lined with beds and patients stood before me. As I scanned the room looking for a nurse, a tall Afrikaner man came from behind me: "Are you Michelle?"

He introduced himself to me as a friend of August's. He was from the area and would see what he could do to help. His cell phone rang, and he answered. The strength of his voice speaking in Afrikaans comforted me and I no longer felt alone. This was the language of my dear friends, the primary language spoken in this part of the country. This kind man was their comrade. August was on the phone, and we were connected with a lifeline. Help was here!

The cultural dynamics we faced now made it critical to deliver every word with respect and patience. We were the only two pale-skinned people in a public hospital that served the local population. It was as if foreigners had never stepped foot in there. The separateness of South Africa hung in the room, generations of wounds had fractured trust, and we made sure to navigate the situation without being domineering or forceful. There was no way any of these people knew how much love I had for them on the inside. I was stuck in the skin I was made with and didn't have time to get to know any of them. I swallowed the awkwardness and fear like an oversized, dry pill in my throat and thanked the doctor for helping us. We explained that we needed to get Chris to another hospital; it was urgent. We asked delicately for the paperwork for a transfer and the results of the biopsy that had just been taken.

Standing in that room with a stranger advocating for us was like watching my own life play out in a scene from a movie. I stood silently, my thoughts slipping back into prayers, as the two men talked. The hospital man turned to go somewhere. I'm not sure how long he was gone, but he returned with papers in his hand and handed them to me. It seemed he had what we needed! We showered him with reverent gratitude and bolted from the room to find Janice and Chris.

Time must have stood still for our deliverance because the next thing I remember is seeing tiny, petite Jan with her hand on Chris's elbow as he shuffled obstinately out of the double doors of the hospital and into the fresh air and sunshine of the parking lot. Our new friend told us to wait nearby as he went for his car. He knew where to take us and would drive us there himself!

42 | In Good Hands

January 25, 2013

"The Lord your God, who is going before you,
will fight for you... before your very eyes."
– Deuteronomy 1:30

The next hospital was only six kilometers away, but it might as well have been a trip to another country. The closer we got to the center of town, the more modern the buildings were. New, black pavement adorned well-maintained streets lined with trees. Businesses lined sidewalks as their shiny, glass windows reflected the bustling community. Chris seemed to be fixated on the last injustice he had suffered at the previous hospital, his ruined pillow. He hugged it and vented about it, remembering the search for it and griping about how difficult it would be to replace it. I promised to do everything I could to get him a new one as soon as possible. Afterall, this was a town that had more resources available than what we were used to. We turned toward the back of a contemporary, landscaped medical complex where a door was clearly labeled "Emergency" in bold, red letters.

Someone ran inside for a wheelchair while I stayed to get Chris out of the car. He seemed to have a new burst of determination and insisted on opening the door himself and walking into the hospital. As he rose from the back seat, Jan was already there ready to push him in, so he accepted the ride. Our new friend was inside making the first urgent requests for help. With Chris on his way to being admitted, I turned and plucked the bloody pillow from the car. As he turned out of sight, I carried out my secret mission, tossing his precious memory foam pillow into the well placed, nearby dumpster. Replacing that thing was far from being my first priority right then.

219

With a whispered prayer, I entered the doors of the fourth hospital in twenty-four hours, whispering, "Lord, please grant us favor."

The drastic change in the environment jarred my exhausted mind to wake to my surroundings. There was one person waiting in a chair in the waiting room and plenty of clean, new, padded vinyl chairs that lined the walls of the clean, simple room. A young man at a tidy, organized desk with a computer in front of him. *A COMPUTER!!! Yay!* As his hands rested on the keyboard, a flicker of hope rose in me and his kind greeting met my waiting ears, "How can I help you?"

They had already whisked Chris back to a triage room down a short hall. I could see from my vantage point that it only had one bed in it and the walls were equipped with medical equipment and monitors. The walls were glass with curtains to provide privacy if it was needed. They were kept open, so I could see the team of nurses surrounding him. Relief washed over me as I turned back to recount the medical odyssey we had been through over the last twenty-four hours. It was late in the afternoon now, the end of the second day since our exodus from our village home.

He asked for my medical insurance cards and any paperwork I had from the previous hospitals. I retrieved the pile of paperwork I had been guarding and handed it to him. Noting the time, he used his computer to check the time in the U.S. location of the insurance company on the card. "It's early where they are, they may not be open. Let's call just in case."

Gratitude filled me as I sat in front of him waiting to see if our insurance would work there. I wasn't sure what we would do if it didn't, but I was preparing my plea in the event I was faced with more bad news. The battle in my mind continued to rage. As fearful thoughts entered automatically, I headed them off with prayers before the next what-if scenario assailed me. His calm, kind voice interrupted my mental fray, "Your health insurance is international. It will cover his treatment here 100%."

"Excuse me?"

"Your husband can be treated here, and the cost will be covered 100%. I'll take care of the paperwork. You can go be with him."

The relief was overwhelming to me, and I melted into grateful tears. I had to sit there for a minute to regain my composure and then looked at him one last time. There weren't enough words in my vocabulary to express my thanks, but I did my best and did so quickly. I could hear Chris's voice nearby getting louder and my attention was already being drawn toward my next task—getting him calmed down and diagnosed. As I got up from my chair, I told myself that I'd come back later to thank this administrative savior properly.

At least three people were attending to Chris as I entered the well-appointed, sterile room. The raucous tension in the room was a contrast to the familiarity I felt in this medical setting. Even the fact that they spoke English was a comfort to me. While I felt like we had finally arrived where we needed to be, Chris fought them and fired them with accusations: "Nobody's listening to me! Just help me!"

They were trying to get him to lie on the bed, but he was refusing. His frame of mind was still shifting drastically from vulnerable, weak humility to angry, paranoid agitation. Superhuman strength seemed to grip him each time someone tried to touch him because his skin was still so sensitive. The medical staff was adjusting the temperature of the room with every request, using reassuring voices and promising to help him if he could just trust them. Without words, all of us rallied together as one united voice with the same goal—to calm him down enough to give him something for the pain.

It must have been sometime in the evening by the time they got him to lie down and were able to get him settled enough to put in an IV and give him the pain medicine he had been begging for two days. My own nerves calmed as his body rested on the bed, finally covered with a crisp, clean white sheet. They still didn't know what may be wrong with him, and they explained that they had called a doctor who they believed could diagnose him. She was on her way but had requested that he be moved to Intensive Care. Being moved *anywhere* was terrifying for Chris and he lapsed back into a scared frenzy. At this point, his main concern was that people would see him. He didn't want anyone looking at him as they wheeled him through the halls. Every one of his concerns were met with an easy, logical solution. "Chris, you cover your head with the sheet, and we'll get you where you need to go safely. It's just upstairs."

They wheeled him along the echoey, white-washed halls as I walked beside him alternately holding his hand or helping keep the sheet over his head. Each time we passed a double door, the distinct smell of rubbing alcohol wafted into the hall. After the elevator, there was just one more hall to travel before coming to the Intensive Care Unit. Windows lined the right side of the passageway, and I could see that the sun was setting. It seemed as if we were in a time warp, in some surreal reality separate from the outside world. Life looked like it was moving forward out there, but ours hung in the balance.

One of the nurses hit the oversized button on the wall and large, double doors swung open revealing a spacious, round medical unit. Private rooms lined the outside of the ample floor. Some of the rooms had windows to the outside that let in the natural light. Although each room's walls were made of glass, most of them had curtains drawn for privacy and doors that stood open for easy access to the patients. It smelled clean and the crisp, distinct smell of bleach caught in my nostrils. Steady beeps rang out from each room marking heart beats and breaths. Puffs of air from ventilators shushed and whirred from all directions. They rolled Chris into the first room on the left and helped him into the state-of-the-art bed in the center of the room.

It wasn't long after he was settled in the bed that a confident, middle-aged woman entered the room. Stylish, short hair lined her firm, wise face. Her light, grayish-blue eyes found mine and compassion and empathy flowed from her. "Dr. P" was one of the senior doctors in the hospital and, although she wasn't taking any new patients at the time due to her caseload, she had accepted Chris's case because of her expertise in conditions that were hard to diagnose. She exuded kindness and was also direct and business-like. Her attention turned to Chris, and she got right down to it. She introduced herself to him and then moved to the bedside, leaning over to speak directly to him. She had already scanned over his paperwork briefly but had enough information to know where he'd been.

"Chris, I know you've been through a lot, and it's been very difficult for you, but you're in a safe place now. I've treated patients with similar symptoms and I'm going to help you. I just need to ask you a few questions first. Will you answer me honestly?" Her accent only served to increase my growing confidence in her.

"Can you trust me with your care?" she asked.

Looking back at her intently, Chris answered, "Yes."

"More importantly, though, Chris," she continued, "Do you trust GOD?"

"Yes," he responded. "I do."

"Chris, every day I'm going to wake up and ask God to help me treat you. It's HIM you need to trust right now."

As I sat there with tears running down my cheeks in amazement, she went on to explain that he'd been tested for rabies because of some of the symptoms he had been experiencing, but she had a reliable and simple little test that could give her an idea whether or not he had it. The results from the biopsy would still take another couple of days and she wanted to move forward with additional tests to figure out what was going on in his body. "Just stay right there and look straight forward," she instructed.

Rounding his bed, she circled to the back corner of the room. "Tell me if you notice anything, Chris."

As Chris looked forward, behind him and out of his sight, Dr. P placed both hands on the handles of the water faucet and turned them on full blast. Chris didn't move. She turned it off and then asked him if he felt anything. He looked puzzled, but answered no. She did it again more forcefully, leaving it on longer this time and waiting for Chris to react. When he didn't, she turned it off and returned to where he could see her.

"You don't have rabies. Patients with rabies almost always have an intense paranoia of running water. I don't know what's going on yet, but I'm going to figure it out as fast as I can."

She went on to explain that the convulsive episodes that were exhausting him were seizures. It was important that he was able to sleep. The best way to go about the rigorous testing he needed to have in order to find an accurate diagnosis was to have him sleep through it. He would undergo tests on every part of his body, including brain scans, x-rays, MRIs, and a multitude of blood tests, to name a few. In order to accomplish this, she recommended that they induce a coma. They would give him medicine for him to sleep and support his body while they figured out how to treat him.

Every part of him craved sleep, so the idea was welcome to Chris at that point. He joked about the fact that he would take all of the drugs she had if he could only get some rest. The incessant seizures were becoming more and more frequent, and he was desperate to be rid of them. Finally, the hope of having some relief seemed to bring his sense of humor back, and he joked with the nurses as they explained all of the things they'd need to hook him up to. They asked him to remove his jewelry and hand it to me; and I held my hand out to receive his watch, a few silver bracelets, his wedding ring, and another silver ring from the ring finger of his right hand. Even the earrings had to go so he could have all of the scans. One of the young nurses must have picked up on his sense of style and intuitively lowered her voice to warn him of the last thing they'd have to remove, "Sorry, but we have to have you take all of your clothes off too. You're going to have to wear our outfits now," she teased.

Chris chuckled, and with all of his personality present in that moment, sassed right back, "Well, I'm sorry to disappoint. I have my plain black underwear on today."

Hearing Chris's humor calmed me, and I shared the hope that was calming him as they prepared him for sleep. As he listened to the doctor, two nurses were connecting him to IVs and leads that would deliver medicine and fluids to his body and even breathe for him while he drifted off in the drug-induced coma. He allowed them to pick up his hands as needed and submitted to their care as they adjusted his body in the bed. As they pulled a sheet up to his shoulders, I stood to say goodnight. The motion came naturally to me, and I leaned in to kiss his forehead. It was cool and clammy on my lips, but I was so glad to finally be able to touch him. As my lips grazed his skin, I whispered, "Goodnight. I love you."

"Love you too."

One of the nurses placed her hand gently on my shoulder and guided me toward the door. With Chris in good hands, Dr. P encouraged me to go get some food and rest. In a motherly tone, she told me to take good care of myself. The concept seemed foreign and impossible to me. It was as if I was barely present in my own life, dull to the outside world, and no longer one with my body. With blind obedience, I took one more glance back at Chris, told him I would see him first thing in the morning, and walked out of the room.

An hour later, as Chris drifted off into the deep sleep of coma back at the hospital, I laid awake in a borrowed bed. I was reunited with my kids in another backyard guest house, physically safe but emotionally fragile. It was as if I couldn't feel my body anymore and I was suspended in some kind of twilight zone I had never experienced. As I grasped for any sense of normal, I found my phone and updated the prayer warriors back home.

FACEBOOK POST

January 25, 2013

"Thank you for your prayers. Wow. This will take a while to share, but Chris is FINALLY resting and is going to be just fine. More details to follow."

43 | Long Wait for Healing

"There (in the wilderness) you saw how the LORD your God carried you, as a father carries his son, all the way you went until you reached this place."
– Deuteronomy 1:31

It had only been a few weeks since I had been away from Chris during Olivia's surgery, but all that God had spoken to me during that time seemed remarkably applicable to all that we were experiencing in the present. Shock gripped me, reducing my capabilities to walking like a zombie, responding to whomever was right in front of me, and making medical decisions. Nighttime meant lying in a bed that wasn't my own, comforting my kids to sleep, and then wrestling with the anxious thoughts that plagued my mind until the soft light of dawn stole through the sheer curtains. By this time, I was well-accustomed to the routine. One-by-one I would mull the thoughts over, catch myself in fear, and then transform them to prayers. Writing in my journal became a sacred space where I cataloged the insights from God that came to me as whispers in my mind, responses to my scattered and desperate conversations with my Heavenly Father who promised to be with me.

Our team had dropped everything to come to "Bloem" to help us and they took on the bulk of the care of the kids. I was driven everywhere I needed to go, which was really just back and forth to the hospital from August's friend's place across town. As I sat by Chris's side in ICU, our team was looking for a longer-term place for us to stay. Without a diagnosis yet, we were praying for healing, but preparing for a long wait.

FACEBOOK POST

January 26, 2013

Prayers still needed for Chris, but God is in control, ever PRESENT and faithful to provide for our every need (even beyond my expectations)! Chris promised to write a book about this leg of our journey! Stay tuned...

> *"Yesterday, I faced my FEAR OF DEATH __head on__."*
> – Me

The reflection was penned in my journal to process one of the many heart-wrenching days we had as Chris laid in a comatose sleep at the hospital and we were painfully apart from him waiting. It must have been a few days after we left him there that my cell phone vibrated and woke me from my trance. I was supposed to be sleeping but was just lying there in a traumatized stupor, as still as I could be so that I didn't wake Silly who was sleeping beside me in the small bed. We were still crammed in the granny flat of our new friends awaiting any news about Chris's diagnosis. My emotions still wouldn't allow me to rest. They assailed me whether I was awake or asleep, so I usually lay frozen, eyes on my cell phone poised for a call from the hospital.

Although I was subconsciously waiting for that device to come alive with any news from the hospital, the sudden buzz of the call made me jump and I sprung from the bed. "Hello? This is Michelle."

It was a social worker from the hospital. In her thick, Africaaner accent, she let me know, "We need you to come to the hospital as soon as possible."

How I made it from the bedside to the front seat of the small sedan with Dudley driving and Jan in the seat behind me wasn't laid down in my memory. The weight of the events that were unfolding must have been too terrorizing to store trivial details. The scene inside the car is as vivid as if I lived it yesterday, though. Dudley was at the wheel to my right driving as fast as he could through the early morning traffic in the center part of town. Normal life whirred past in a blur; nothing out there was relevant to what we were experiencing inside the moving capsule.

The tension and fear that had gripped me over the previous week seemed to burst forth in volcanic sobs as I allowed myself to let the truth of my terror out. I had been praying and trusting God every step of the way, but this one felt like more than I was willing to handle. I couldn't hold it back anymore, and my prayers to my powerful, Heavenly Father flowed out of me loudly in brutally honest, raw emotion: "I gave You everything I owned to follow You here! We left everything we knew at home to come and serve You! I laid it all down because You told me to and now Chris is dying?! God, I sacrificed all of that for You, but YOU CAN'T HAVE HIM!!! Please don't take him from me, God, PLEASE! Don't let him die. I don't want him to die, Lord! Nooo... no... Don't take Chris from me!"

As I wrestled with the God of the universe, Jan's hands massaged my shoulders from behind me and stroked the sides of my arms as I cried. I'm not sure how long I wailed, but the next thing I remember is trying to walk into the hospital, legs too limp and weak to hold me up, my drive and will dissolved and absent. Somehow I went from being held up by Dudley and Jan to sitting outside a little meeting room with August and Anita. Well, maybe all four of my friends were there at that point. Whatever the case, I was only a shell of myself. My friends were speaking for me, holding me up as I walked, and gently guiding me everywhere I needed to be to make decisions I never thought I would have to make.

The woman who called me earlier appeared. Her dark, short hair was colored with purple lowlights, and she blazed onto the scene with the determination of a drill sergeant. I recognized the harsh, all-business voice that had broken the silence of the early morning, "Come, let's talk in here."

We filed into a narrow, interior room that was the shape of a long closet. There were chairs lining the far wall and a couple of chairs on either end. Either the lights were too harsh and bright in there, or anxiety had intensified my senses and I had to shield myself from the brightness of the room. I hunched over and held my face in my hands. I didn't want to be there, didn't want to hear what she had to say. I just wanted to be rescued from the circumstances and wake up to normalcy.

She introduced herself as the child social worker for the hospital or something like that. Her official title didn't register, but the only thing I gathered was that she was wanting to talk to my children. Whatever she was saying sounded garbled to me. Her lips were moving, but I could barely comprehend her message. The only thing I was thinking was, *Nobody is going to talk to my children. You're not going to put any ideas into their minds about what COULD happen. We have people around us who love us, and your mean voice won't come near my family.*

My friends were my eyes and ears during the meeting. I must have stared at that woman with the look of a mother bear as she spoke to me, eyes bulging and muscles ready to pounce. She may have been a nice woman only doing her job to give families the worst case scenario about the prognosis of their loved ones. I'm not sure who she really was. In my mind she resides like the Wicked Witch of the Hospital, purple hair flaming and coming for my kids. Only bad news registered with me, and sentence fragments made it through: "Your husband's illness is serious... could be fatal... might die... prepare your children..."

As I turned from her and buried my face in my hands, August took over. My charismatic, kind, jovial friend had morphed into a superhero of some kind. He stood up, suddenly lifting me by my forearm as he rose. The rest of our group stood with us, and he let her know our decision. "We'll take care of the family. Please don't call Michelle's phone again. If you need anything, you can call me."

He pulled me from the room and someone behind me whispered his phone number to her as the rest of us escaped her presence. We didn't want to talk about what *might* happen to Chris! We wanted to talk to a doctor about what was actually going on in his body! My fears already told me enough about the potential of him dying. I didn't need a person who lacked empathy to tell my children that their dad wasn't going to make it through.

In a final act of valor, August reached over and took my cell phone. The Vodafone 555 was pried from my hand as he explained what would happen from that day forward. "We'll take all of your calls from now on. You don't need to be answering the phone and going through this unnecessarily."

There weren't many places I could find comfort during that time, but when I had time late at night, it was the Bible that had the words and promises I needed, and I clung to the promises I found there. My face-to-face confrontation with death was processed the next day and I found the hope I needed to face another day.

JOURNAL ENTRY

God's Word for my Heart TODAY:

> *"Do not be afraid (of them); the LORD your God will fight for you... O Sovereign Lord, you have begun to show to your servant your greatness and your STRONG HAND. For what god in heaven or on earth can do the deeds and MIGHTY WORKS you do?*
> *– Deuteronomy 3:22-24*

"The LORD gives strength to his people;
the LORD blesses His people with peace."
– Psalm 29:11

LORD, how I praise you for revealing your GREATNESS and your
STRONG HAND to us yesterday. I cling to that power and ask that
you give us ALL your peace. Minister especially to Jed's heart today
as he struggles to trust you with his dad. The waiting is so hard.
    There is NO BEING who can do the works that You do and I know
and trust that You are working on Chris' behalf. I pray as Chris goes
in for this test that it will a) be conclusive and b) reveal NO long-term
damage that will stop Him from doing your work.

With Chris lying in a coma, the other half of me was absent, suddenly cut off, and silent. Conversations that would have been had in the evenings after the kids had gone to bed were nonexistent and the stillness was deafening. I had been walking through life with this man by my side for over twenty years, and now I couldn't stay with him, hear his voice, depend on him to help make decisions, or even just tell him about my day. Without that, I felt lost and alone, and my mind spun so fast trying to make sense of the events swirling around me that I couldn't ground myself. It felt like I was constantly disoriented and confused. Yet, it was that brain that I still had to depend on to make decisions about my kids. I'm sure that's why I talked to God so much in my journal. At least He was there all the time, even if I couldn't see Him, and the physical act of pen to paper forced my brain to focus on that one thing.

I was praying for Jed that night because time was passing and plans we had made previously were now approaching. Olivia was still at school and was preparing for the big junior/senior banquet, which was an event that carried more magnitude than Cinderella attending prom. The hype for the event was electrifying for the students because it also involved a chance for junior parents to come and participate in the decorating process. Our family plans to travel there included a chance for Jed to be on campus again because he was nearing the end of his eighth grade year and would start as a freshman in the fall. Now, with Chris out of the picture for the time being, we had to recalibrate our plans. None of us had any idea how long Chris would be lying in that unconscious state, what the outcome of his illness would be, nor where we would be in the future, so we had to make one decision at a time.

The rest of our team had teenagers at the school too, so they knew the nuance of that season on campus and were well-suited to help us decide what to do. In the end, Jed really looked forward to the chance to see the school, get shown around by his big sister, and "represent" the family, so we all decided it would be ok if he went to Kenya. Everything fell into place for the trip. One of the other parents was already traveling up there, so he had someone to fly with, and he would stay with our friends Ryan and Heather who would care for him as their own for the week. The hardest part of the decision for Jed was leaving his dad. He was only a couple of months away from turning thirteen, but he seemed to carry the weight of his family on his shoulders. The kid in him wanted to go, but the adult that prematurely rose up in him nagged him with the responsibility of staying with me. Besides, as hard as it was, he wanted to be there for his dad.

With the reassurance from me and the rest of the team, he made the trip. Roll call was much shorter with Julia in California and two of the kids in Kenya, but I reasoned that at least their minds could be occupied with life outside of the hospital. My teammates continued to help care for the three younger kids so that I could spend my days at the hospital. The days ticked by, but I had no sense of time, nor knowledge of what date it was. For me, life had come to a screeching halt, and we were suspended in time in a place that was fuzzy and gray. We were somehow stuck between life on earth and life in Heaven.

Although most of my other senses were dulled and useless, the fact that my partner in life was so sick had unleashed an innate drive and courage in me to fight for him. My Mama Bear instinct was hyper-focused on my husband as he laid there in that high-tech ICU bed. With leads coming out of his body from what seemed like every orifice, a ventilator to help him breathe, and monitors to watch his heart rate and oxygen levels, I felt like I needed to be with him every waking minute. As I stood watch, his physical body was being supported while a team of doctors from all over the country raced to figure out what their medical enemy was.

August officially took his place as the commander for the support of our family after the meeting with the social worker at the hospital, and Anita stood by at their farm in Lesotho, which was a three-hour drive from where we were in "Bloem." They were tag-teaming the care of their farm and ministry and supporting the kids and me while Chris was being cared for at the hospital. Dudley and August's fervor in coordinating our team to care for us matched the intensity of military commanders. They made sure we were never alone and that there was always someone taking care of the kids and someone at my side.

As more of our team gathered around us, it became clear that we needed to call upon as many prayer warriors as possible and beat down the doors of Heaven for Chris's healing. On February 3rd, we all sent out an urgent request:

"Calling for unified prayers for Chris's healing at 3:00 pm our time (South Africa) - that God would totally eradicate the powers of darkness in Jesus' name. NO FEAR."

"Is any one of you sick? He should call the elders of the church to pray over him and anoint him with oil in the name of the LORD. And the prayer offered in faith will make the sick person well; THE LORD WILL RAISE HIM UP."
— James 5:14-15

As his brothers and sisters in Christ, we had the sense that there was a war being waged in the heavenly realm. We had been living in darkness after all, in a place where witchcraft and curses were real and not just fantasies you read about in novels. This felt like the Olympics of faith. All of the other times I had girded up my strength, taken a deep breath, remembered the promises of Scripture, and trusted a God I couldn't see were just practices for what I was living at that time in that hospital room. The outside world rarely entered my mind or even came into focus in my vision when I entered into it briefly. Praying for Chris, supporting him in making decisions on his behalf, comforting my children, and doing battle were my only tasks. Thankfully, I was not alone in any of it.

There was one evening when August brought together church leaders from around the world on a conference call at Chris's bedside. A few of us who were there in Bloemfontein gathered in person, hovered over Chris with hands linked in power and unity, and joined those on the other line for a time of prayer. We took Jesus' words seriously and literally, calling on His power to heal Chris. We rebuked any spirit that would come against his healing, called on God to work in his body through the power of the resurrected Jesus, and entrusted him into God's powerful hands. Taking a tiny vial of oil from his pocket, Dudley anointed Chris's forehead with oil, swiping a thick line of the shiny liquid across his resting brow.

Voices raised together and increased in volume as prayers went up from that room. Although I couldn't *see* God's presence as we clung to each other in those moments, it was as if the air in the room was heavy, my skin crawled with goosebumps, and the rest of the world faded further from my consciousness. Here at God's feet, there was a bright and powerful sense of comfort and peace. As one of my comrades whispered "Amen," I stood there in awe with an assurance that Chris was being held there by His Heavenly Father and safe from any other lesser power. This was sacred ground and God was truly with us.

In addition to being surrounded by our team and the medical team of doctors and nurses at the hospital, friends and family were glued to Facebook and posting prayers there for us to see. Our call for united prayers had unleashed a global prayer network and the written prayers of the saints gave the kids and me a sense that we weren't alone. When I wrote a post, hundreds of people would comment with prayers and well-wishes, and I would scroll through them on the computer when I should have been sleeping. Julia was also keeping a constant watch on the feed because it was her lifeline from California.

As the days droned on and a new month began, we plodded through our limbo life like grieving zombies waiting for signs of life: lay down, toss and turn, battle the what-if thoughts, pray, get up, gag down some form of food that I could no longer taste, go to the hospital, sit by Chris as nurses came and went, go back to the guest house, update the kids and our parents, force myself to bathe, and repeat.

44 | Grace for the Journey

*"'They will fight against you but will not overcome you, for
I am with you and will rescue you,' declares the Lord."*
– Jeremiah 1:19

We were living out our worst nightmare,
confronting our fears of death, and vacillating between looking
for signs of hope, believing that God could heal Chris, and bracing
ourselves for the possibility of losing him. Our lives were eclipsed
with the magnitude of our circumstances, and we dragged ourselves
through each day in a fog of confusion—our bodies present, but our
minds elsewhere. Despite the grayness and gnawing grief of that
time, God was giving us grace to buoy us along. Beautiful moments
of joy would spring up, and as I noticed them, I allowed the little
sparks to help me breathe.

We were away from our village home, staying in borrowed
rooms, and depending on others for our meals; but there were
little signs that God saw each of us right where we were. On one
particular day, we must have set out on errands to pick up personal
things we needed since our stay was extending so far past the few
days I had anticipated we'd be away from home. We needed extra
clothes, our toiletries were running out, and the normalcy of a little
retail therapy sounded good. There were enough friends in town by
that time to encourage us to have a break from the hospital. "We'll
go hang out with Chris today. You guys go get what you need."

As we headed out in the Land Rover, it felt strange to be driving
through town toward the mall without Chris in the car. It had only
been a few months since he and I had celebrated our anniversary
in this same place and now he lay in a coma in a hospital we hadn't
even noticed. The town bustled with signs of life that were foreign

in the halls of the intensive care unit where I spent most of my days. We allowed our customary sense of adventure to take over as we navigated through the streets of the busy town. The kids called out things they noticed as we passed by, and we kept a virtual list of places we'd want to go back to: "Look! There's a McDonald's right across from the hospital! We can get special drinks!"

We had a family custom of getting treats "for the road" and had continued that tradition as we lived our new life in Africa. It was an investment to buy treats for the whole family, so we reserved that splurge for road trips and vacations. As it turned out, we had trained our kids to have an eye for every opportunity to cease the moment and get a milkshake, Slurpee, or ice cream cone along the way. Pulling my brain back into the moment, I engaged my tactical driving to figure out how I could turn into that drive-through on the right side of the street from where I was driving on the left side of the road. I took a quick left in an effort to go around the block and give myself another opportunity to turn in.

"Where are we going?" one of the kids called out from the back seat. "Are we lost?"

That wouldn't have been unusual. It seemed we were always trying to find our way. This time, though, I was determined to provide my kids with a good memory to soothe their stress, if only for a few minutes. As the golden arches came back into view, I spotted the entrance on the back side of the restaurant and navigated toward it. "Oooo! Are we going in?!"

As I downshifted and cranked the wheel toward the drive-through lane, I revealed my surprise: "Think about what you want! We're getting special drinks!"

Squeals of delight mingled with the usual banter about who wanted what and siblings correcting each other about prices and sizes while they called out to each other like treasure hunters picking through a new discovery. "Look! They have McFlurries!"

The familiar taste of the vanilla soft serve and the soothing coolness of the ice cream in my mouth took me back to the carefree days of summer back in San Diego and I was reminded of what it felt like to be alive. The kids ooed and awed about how good their treats tasted as we made our way through town toward the mall on the other side of town. As a manmade lake appeared in view, we marveled at the fountains that sprung from the little lake, the outside patios where people sat eating leisurely along the water, and the towering size of the indoor mall. My favorite thing about malls in the cities of South Africa was that there was always a well-appointed grocery store right in the mall. This one was no different. There, in large letters on the top of the building was the name of my favorite South African grocery store! A cacophony of voices shouted out what they hoped to find there, and I allowed my spirits to lift in response to the excitement.

As we walked through the expansive mall, the ceilings rose at least three stories high, and the gleaming tile reflected the light that came in from the skylights. The voices of expectant shoppers echoed as we passed shops of every kind, some familiar and some I had never heard of. Still, the concept of an indoor mall with inventory displayed attractively in store windows and the smell of coffee and food gave us a sense of familiarity and calmed us. A store caught our eye as we took a sweeping turn down a new wing. *The Body Shop* read clearly above the entrance. Silly let her wishes out, "Oooo! Can we go in?!"

Anytime we could find products that took our senses back to a time and place when we felt like we knew what to expect and belonged, the stress melted away. As my eyes scanned the merchandise, the order of the colors and products lured me in. Each color of the rainbow was matched to a luscious fragrance, and I couldn't resist reaching for each tester, opening the lid, and lifting it to my nose to draw the smell in with deep, relaxed breaths. We had dispersed throughout the store by that point and as I scanned the room to count the kids, they all looked like happy samplers calling out their product reviews. "This one smells *just* like coconut! Smell it! Oh, I like this one! Mom, smell it!"

It had been a long time since I had heard delight in their voices, and I allowed for a moment of joy as I took it in. I moved toward Silly as she picked up a round, disk shaped container of strawberry scented body butter and brought it in for a deep sniff. "This one is my favorite. Can I get it?"

As she asked the question, it jarred my mind back to reality. Chris wasn't there to consult about prices, or budget, or whether or not we should buy them something now or wait. We usually consulted each other on purchases like these to make sure we were staying on track with our money and pacing ourselves on luxuries. It suddenly dawned on me that the decision to buy things rested on me. The thought was neither painful, nor revolutionary; it just resonated in my inner being and I felt an unfamiliar sense of control as I let my decision be known. "We're all picking a treat today. Is that what you would like yours to be?"

"*I can get it*?!" she responded excitedly.

"Yep. You can get that and I'm going to get some body wash."

That moment seems insignificant here, but it was an education for me. I learned something about myself and my daughter in the classroom of a toiletry store that would carry us into our next season of life. Fragrance ministered to us and took our brains to calming places. With everything else in our lives spinning out of control, we could twist off the cap of those fancy bath products and be swept away to another time and place. That was priceless.

We ended our shopping spree by boarding a tall escalator that delivered us to the top story of one of the taller buildings in the mall and entered the grocery store. This time it was a culinary adventure, and we explored the shelves for foods to take back to the guest house. New fruits like gooseberries made the cut and landed in the cart with a variety of "crisps," which we had learned were potato chips, and we tossed in easy breakfast pastries that we could warm in the microwave too. Somewhere in the expedition, Silly spotted a little plant that had a personality that intrigued her. It was a baby Venus Fly Trap with a skinny stem that stood tall like a body that held a head with an open mouth and sharp little teeth lined up neatly around the edges.

I had gotten the hang of swiping my debit card by that time and saw no harm in adding a plant to the few belongings we had with us. My Facebook post the next day was proof that our shopping day had been an effective distraction, and we had even learned from it.

Silly wants you all to know that she got a Venus Fly Trap today. Now she has to catch flies AND rain for it. She informed me that there are too many minerals in the tap water for it. Nurturing helps her. This'll be good. 😮

Holy Coffee

It may sound trivial to mention coffee as I describe the hardest days of my life, but it is another piece of evidence that God was with us and that He not only provides what we need exceedingly well, but He also knows how to give great gifts. Somewhere along the way, someone in our growing network there in Bloemfontein recommended a Christian cafe to us that eventually became a safe haven for all of us. It was conveniently located in the area of town between the guest house and the hospital, so it made it easy to drop in at various times of the day to grab a bite to eat, gather for a meeting, or even pray together.

Nestled back a couple of streets from the main road in a quieter part of the neighborhood, the compound opened up like an oasis beyond tall, stuccoed, vine-covered walls. The path to the main entrance led through a tranquil courtyard that was manicured with green plants and lush, shady trees. As soon as the door was opened, the welcoming smell of fresh baking bread overwhelmed eager nostrils and spiked a hunger response powerful enough to win over my grief-soured stomach. Entering into the large room with groupings of tables was a feast in itself. To the left, racks of fresh-baked bread were displayed on wooden shelves and a blazing fire could be seen glowing from an open, wood burning oven. Weathered bricks lined the walls on either side of the oven, and rustic, sturdy, black iron fixtures outlined the oven above and below the hearth.

Bible verses tastefully accented the warm, tan-painted walls. The mission of the restaurant was evident in the powerful scripts and the loving greetings from the staff and servers. It was even customary for the servers to offer the opportunity to take communion as a group at the conclusion of each meal. Groups who accepted the generosity of the suggestion were brought a section of the homemade bread and small, individual cups of grape juice. On more than a couple of occasions, we seized those special moments as another chance to pray through our specific prayer needs and lift Chris to God's throne again.

Eventually, we were such regulars that we knew the servers by name, and they knew our circumstances. It was as if God increased our network and extended our family to include the phenomenal, loving staff of that place. They were so kind to us that they went out of their way to make sure we had exactly what sounded good to us at the time. They even named a custom coffee drink with our kids in mind after repeated special orders.

God made His grace so clear that I was able to notice it, even with my reduced emotional and mental capacity. Good smells, coffee, and having a place where we were known were added to our list of happy places.

45 | All Kids Present

"I am getting so weary of waiting. God's Words for me today are to REJOICE IN HIS NAME ALL DAY LONG. So, for today I will focus on GOD, seek HIS face, and rejoice in HIM and His Sovereignty."
Journal entry, February 3, 2013

Two worlds existed for both Chris and me
during this time. Chris laid in an ICU hospital bed hooked up to life on this earth, but clearly catching a glimpse of Heaven. I found myself in a precarious balance also; bound with him in the traumatic space of intensive care but experiencing life with the kids on the outside. For this reason, the timing of when things happened in the real world is vague to me. I'm not sure when these "grace breaks" took place in relation to what was going on with Chris at the hospital, but the important thing to remember is that they HAPPENED.

I'll go ahead and insert a shameless plug for my sending organization who kept their word to support us while we were on the field. During this time, we were supported by both the home office *and* the leadership on the field. While I muddled through my weary days bewildered and haggard, they gently guided me toward decisions that would benefit our whole family. On one particular day pretty early in the hospitalization, their guidance led us to a counseling session with a child psychologist. Again, I don't remember how many of the kids were present on that day. I hadn't even made the appointment myself, yet despite the trauma fog, we rolled up to a small complex of office buildings, found the counselor's name on the door, and sat in the chairs outside ready for anything.

Cross-cultural living had prepared us for the unexpected and unfamiliar, so, as usual, we braced ourselves for the new experience with trepidation and humor. We waited in a small, tidy waiting room until my name was called and then we all piled into the small, shelf-lined room. There weren't enough chairs for all of us, so I remember sitting on the floor with my legs crossed. The kids sat in silence while they built their emotional walls up for protection. The counselor's accent was so thick that she was hard to understand. She was a small woman with sharp features and a short, stylish hairstyle. Although she was well groomed and nice enough, her serious demeanor didn't woo any of us to naturally open up to her.

She started her line of questioning as we all stared blankly at her. A short child's indoor sandbox separated her from the kids and held their attention. Despite the silence, she persisted. Eventually, she shifted her tactic. Waving her hand toward the shelf behind her, she pointed to small figurines of all kinds. There were tiny plastic superheroes, cartoon characters, Disney princesses, dinosaurs, and other familiar animals and figures jumbled in a disorganized mass. One at a time, she invited the kids to choose a character. They were quick to accept the invitation and jumped to choose their favorites. Then, she had them sit around the sandbox with their toys.

This is where things get blurry. I had never experienced play therapy before and my mind was elsewhere, distracted, and focused on what may be going on with Chris at the hospital. My attention drifted in and out of the scene as if I was watching a movie and dozing off to sleep intermittently. During one, miraculous minute of attentiveness, I engaged myself in the exercise. She was asking the kids a question that went something like this: "If there was something really scary going on, where would you go to feel safe and happy?"

One at a time they went around and answered.

"In a pool."

"The ocean."

"Swimming."

"The water."

Their answers to her question gave me valuable information to help them through this scary time. This *one* insight was worth whatever we paid for the session and all of the awkwardness we endured trying to understand the foreign feeling of it all. My San Diego babies, whether they were born in the U.S. or Uganda, all felt safe and happy in the water! I logged that piece of valuable information into my mind for future reference and tolerated the rest of the session until we politely said thank you and left to find our obligatory reward treat.

Each day seemed to hold a combination of medical decisions at the hospital and preparations of tasks that we hoped would contribute to our wellness in the unforeseen future. For example, the longer Chris went without a diagnosis, the clearer it became that we would need a place to stay that would accommodate the whole family *and* our teammates who were tag-teaming their time with us. Because August and Anita's village in Lesotho was only a couple of hours drive to Bloemfontein, they had a pretty wide network in that town. According to Anita, "August is an extreme extrovert and makes friends quickly wherever he goes." Thank God for that! This paid off in dividends as the storm of Chris's illness pressed on.

Arriving at the guest house of August's friends was like dropping anchor at your best friend's place. A crafty, hanging sign hung near the mailbox just off of the suburban road and I noticed it had the word "*Shalom*" in the name. Peace was at hand. A delightful, cheery couple welcomed us with open arms, literally hugging each of us as we piled out of the Land Rover. We were shown to a two-room suite upstairs that had beds for four of us. There was a double bed that Silly and I could share and two twins for Joseph and Duane in an adjoining room. Our hosts spoke in the familiar Afrikaner accent we had grown to love. "Please make yourself at home here. Don't worry about a thing. You can have this room for as long as you need it. Let us show you around."

The cozy, upstairs suite was nestled among full, green shade trees so that it felt like we were in a treehouse. Looking out over the sizable backyard gave me an immediate sense of tranquility and peace. To the right, closest to us, there was a rectangular, in-ground trampoline. It was unlike any I had seen at home. The bouncy part was level to the ground and a huge hole had been dug underneath to accommodate deep jumps. When the kids saw it, they squealed with delight and immediately tried it out.

In the center of the outdoor sanctuary, there was a covered gathering place. Conveniently located right outside the door to the kitchen, it was furnished with a couple of tables and chairs, a barbeque, and even an outdoor fireplace. Potted plants and quirky yard ornaments made it a comforting and relaxing place to sit by yourself or share a meal with a group. This would end up being our main refuge and the place where we all met together for meals, updates, prayer, and long periods of waiting.

Within view of the outdoor BBQ area was a kidney-shaped pool. At the time we were introduced to the place it was empty, but our hostess didn't miss a beat with the kids. She promised that she would have it filled up for them within a few days. Then, she proceeded to offer them something that I'm sure every child dreams of at some point in their life. She told them the pool was almost finished being repaired and that they were about to start filling it. As long as they were careful, and with my permission, she said they could play in the water *as* the pool filled up. The opportunity even made the child inside of me jump up and down with eager anticipation! The kids all looked at each other and then back to me asking, "Can we do it?! Can we do it?!"

The anticipation of getting to play in the water interrupted our tour, and we made an executive decision to shift our focus from the lush green of the yard to finding the room where we could set down our bags. We turned from the pool and faced the long, ranch-style building. Individually decorated, homey guest rooms lined each side of the main part of the house so that they all had a view of the backyard. There were enough rooms for our whole family, our team members who were in and out staying with us, and eventually for our extended family who joined us there.

The kids couldn't pay attention to anything but the deep, empty pool after the invitation was spoken, so I allowed them to change into their bathing suits right away. Once changed, they bolted back outside to the pool where our new friend was waiting and stood lined up all in a row, on the edge of the pool listening to her instructions. She held the hose and let the full stream of cool water pour into the deep end of the pool. As the water cascaded in, swooshing and burbling with hopeful, watery pleasure, I stood in the middle of the perfectly planned property and took in the scene. The sound of the water bubbled like a relaxing waterfall and the warmth of the sun enveloped me. Birds sang and darted from one tall tree to the next going about their worry-free lives. I scanned the whole place and marveled at the fact that evey one of our needs had been provided for, *including* unlimited access to a pool for my water babies! God had provided for us beyond what I had asked for or imagined and this was truly our Shalom, a place of peace.

As Chris's condition continued to decline, Dr. P. pulled me to the side and suggested that it was time for all of the kids to come. I'm not sure what day that happened nor the details of how the international travel for all three of them was arranged, but it must have been miraculous because I don't remember making any of the arrangements. What I *do* know is that Julia got back *on* a plane to return to South Africa less than a month after returning to the States following our post-holiday family vacation. Since they were there together at the boarding school, Olivia and Jed flew from Kenya to South Africa to join us, accompanied by one of our colleagues who was also making the commute.

While it was a relief to me to have all of my kids there with us, it was excruciating for me to see them hurting. I didn't want to force them to go see Chris in the hospital because it was so hard to see him on life support. Twenty-one leads were connected to his body and ran from head to toe, routing out of the sheet that covered his body and ending up connected to various beeping monitors and machines. It was around this time in his coma that he had to have a tracheotomy. The doctor explained that after ten days on a ventilator, it is normal for the throat and mouth to become irritated with the ventilator and a tracheotomy is less painful than having a tube down your throat. The thought of Chris having a hole in his throat unnerved me and gave me a sense of finality and hopelessness. This felt like a sign that he was getting worse, not better. I couldn't imagine him being whole and well like he had been with a huge scar in the middle of his throat.

When the doctors explained the medical necessity of it, I remember asking about the healing process of the actual hole in his neck. I knew Chris would care about that, but I was also sure he'd be able to design a tattoo placement or a fashionable accessory to cover it. As a family, one thing that Chris led the way in was having a sense of humor about *everything*. Laughing together was still one of our strong suits, so we adjusted to yet another change in Chris's physical condition by picturing him modeling his new designs.

As Chris continued on in his lingering coma, our days of waiting began to feel like a routine work commute. I would rise early from my fitful "rest," greet the family and have coffee, and then leave for the hospital. Sometimes, there were others who joined me for the vigil; but no matter what, I was lovingly chauffeured to and from by one of my teammates and was never alone. Back at the guesthouse, others from the team stayed with the kids and had them do a little homework before taking them on fun outings around town. At the end of the day, we'd all gather around for a dinner someone else had prepared and debrief the events of the day.

During those evenings, as we drew into the outdoor patio area with our friends, I could almost bring back what it felt like to be normal again. Chris's absence felt more temporary in those times, as if he was away on a business trip or something. That sense comforted us enough that we were able to play a game or two of Dutch Blitz and laugh a little.

By the tenth day of Chris's coma, I felt like God was giving me signs of His healing work in his body and reassuring me that Chris was safe in His hands. Passages of Scripture reminded me that God had supreme power over all that was happening and that He had Chris's eternal best interests in mind. The promise that God's faithful love was with him and that he would be held up in God's name gave me peace. It felt so personal to me because we had indeed anointed Chris with oil days before and begged God to rebuke each and every unclean spirit that opposed the healing of his physical body. The verses jumped off the page to me as if God's finger was pointing to it on the page.

"I have found (Chris) my servant; with my sacred oil I have anointed him. My hand will sustain him; surely my arm will strengthen him. No enemy will subject him to tribute; no wicked man will oppress him. I will crush his foes before him and strike down his adversaries. My faithful love will be with him, and THROUGH MY NAME his horn will be exalted."
— Psalm 89:20-24

On the day after I read those verses in Psalm 89, I perceived physical signs about Chris that seemed like healing was taking place in his body. He opened his eyes, followed me around the room, and even smiled when I told him not to be embarrassed about the lipstick kisses I had left on his forehead. As I lingered there, just inches away from his face, there were clear messages that God was whispering to me.

- ♦ "SEEK MY FACE."
- ♦ "I want to be your ALL in ALL (family, friend, AND husband)."
- ♦ "There are purposes I am working in the Heavenlies that are GREATER than what you see and want. THESE purposes are worth waiting for."
- ♦ "I am ALIVE, ACTIVE, REAL, AND PRESENT with you."
- ♦ "I have always had a PLAN and this doesn't take me (God) by surprise."

We had been taking the verse in James literally and being consistent in obeying it — *"Is any of you sick? He should call the elders of the church to pray over him and anoint him with oil in the name of the Lord. And the prayer offered in faith will make the sick person well; THE LORD WILL RAISE HIM UP."*

I believed most assuredly that God *could* raise Chris up and heal Him instantly if that was His will. The problem was that I didn't know God's will. It was that fact that lingered in my mind and argued with my solid belief in the healing power of God. There were days when believing in God's sovereignty was a comfort that released me from the burden of making the right decisions on Chris's behalf and trying to comfort each of my children with the last remaining shreds of strength I had left. Then, there were other, darker days when I still believed in God's sovereignty but knew that He saw the big picture of our whole lives into eternity and that He may not have plans to heal Chris on this side of Heaven. That was the truth that kept me up at night and left me raw and disheveled.

It was one of those wrestling nights that I had a dream that Chris was well, even stronger than ever. As I stood in front of him and gazed up at him, a feeling of wonder washed over me. God had healed him so well that he was tall and muscular. Don't get me wrong, Chris had always been strong, but he was a little shorter than me in real life. My emotions were swept up in his countenance and I felt the butterflies of new love as I stared into the blue of his bright eyes. I asked him to hold me, and he wrapped strong arms around me, enveloping me in healthy warmth.

When my eyes opened to the beginnings of wakefulness, I saw that I was in a darkened room and rolled over to check the bed next to me. My hand fell on cold sheets and the chill of the empty bed brought back the looming dread of reality. Chris was still across town lingering between this life and Heaven, and I didn't know which way he was heading.

Disappointment filled me and my empty arms ached for my husband's presence. Since I had awakened to the despair of a new day, I wasn't able to return to the sleep that brought the comforting feeling of him holding me. The only reflex I knew in my hopelessness was to open my Bible and search for hope. Since I didn't know where to turn, I used my concordance to look up words that came to mind. "Fear" and "afraid" were at the top of the list, so I turned to every verse in God's Word where those words were found. It was a passage in Isaiah 54 that brought my message from my Heavenly Father that morning and I took them as personal promises for us.

For CHRIS: *"Do not be afraid; you will not suffer shame.*
Do not fear disgrace; you will not be humiliated.

For ME: *"For your Maker is your husband –*
The LORD Almighty is his name –
The Holy One of Israel is your Redeemer;
He is called the God of all the earth.

For Chris: *"'... with deep compassion I will bring you back...*
With everlasting kindness I will have compassion on you,'
Says the LORD your Redeemer."

Those were beautiful promises for Chris and me; words I could cling to. There was also a verse that assured me that, eventually, everything would be ok, and that God would "expand our territory."

The passage began with, "Enlarge the place of your tent, stretch your tent curtains wide, do not hold back…" I took that to mean that God would continue to give us influence and use us for His glory and that I shouldn't give up. Only one verse in that passage perplexed me, "For your maker is your husband." I had a husband and I still wanted to keep him.

46 | Diagnosis

*"Courage doesn't always roar. Sometimes courage
is the little voice at the end of the day that says
'I'll try again tomorrow.'"*
– Mary Anne Radmacher

Day #13

My daily routine continued to start with solitude, hunched over my Bible and journal in a corner of the dimly lit room as the kids continued to sleep, or out in the backyard with the morning sun easing its way into a new day and casting a warm glow over the plants that surrounded me. I opened the well-worn book that was held together with animal print duct tape, desperate to find the hope I needed to face another day. The promises I found there might as well have been lit up like neon signs. They beckoned to me and reminded me of the character of the God I believed in.

*"The LORD is GOOD, a refuge in times of trouble.
He cares for those who trust in Him."*
– Nahum 1:7

God knows our hearts and cares about our innermost being. He is a good Father who even wants us to have our desires, not just our needs.

*"Cast ALL your anxiety on HIM because
He cares for you."*
– 1 Peter 5:7

Although I started each day with hope, clinging to those promises, it seemed like I ended every day with fear and doubt heavy on my heart. Each new "lead" into what was going on in Chris's body brought the promise of possible treatments, but also new potential outcomes. His heart showed signs that he had suffered a mild heart attack at some point along the way. Had that been related to his pain and trauma, or was that part of the whole picture of his catastrophic illness? Would the neurological symptoms cause permanent damage to his brain and affect his ability to function?

I couldn't help but wonder what our life was going to be like in the days to come, let alone in the near future. It was hard to imagine that Chris would possibly never be whole again. The mystery lingered. I knew that I had to cling to God's promises at all times because He was the only one who could see our lives both in those terrifying moments *and* into the unseen future. There were a few things that I knew for sure, and I often repeated them to myself throughout the long days.

- ◆ God is with me.
- ◆ His plans are greater than my plans.
- ◆ He is in control.
- ◆ He is working all things for the good. (from Romans 8:28)
- ◆ He has promised to be compassionate to Chris.

I knew I had no choice but to take the negative, doubtful, fearful thoughts captive and throw them out so that I could focus on those truths that I was searching for and that I was constantly being reminded of. I had a supernatural sense of God's presence with me that felt a bit like morning mist at the beginning of a spring day. It enabled me to walk along with just enough sight to take a couple of steps at a time. I had never prayed that fervently nor called on God more desperately. I urged myself to move forward in faith, knowing that God had been with me as I had walked into other unknowns. Surely, He would be with me through what we were being faced with as we waited to hear a conclusive answer to what was happening in Chris's failing body.

There's no definitive timing for when, in the course of Chris's hospitalization, we got a diagnosis. I'm pretty sure it was about a week into his induced coma. The timing is insignificant. What mattered was that after numerous brain scans, blood tests, biopsies, research, consultations with specialists from around the country, and prayers from around the world, we were given a name for the infection Chris was fighting.

It was in one of the many meetings I was called to where Dr. P would meet me at the foot of Chris's bed and speak to me, her head pressed in close to mine, her brow slightly furrowed with compassion, and her voice soft and gentle. That morning, as she cradled the growing volume of Chris's medical record in the crook of her arm, she let me know the purpose of the consultation we were about to have: "We have a diagnosis for Chris, and I'd like to tell you about it."

She went on to describe the basics about the illness that wracked Chris's body. "He has an infection called encephalitis. It is an inflammation of the brain. A few things could cause such an infection, but the most common cause is a virus. Sometimes it causes only mild flu-like signs and symptoms like a fever or headache, but other times it can cause confused thinking, seizures, or problems with movement and senses like sight or hearing. In some cases, encephalitis can be life threatening. Chris has been fighting this for some time now, but we're going to do everything we can to treat him. We'll need to continue to support his body so that the medicine can do its work in his brain."

While the diagnosis wasn't necessarily good news, it explained a lot and allowed the doctors to begin treatment. It also explained Chris's behavior over the last couple of weeks. The swelling in the brain had been the culprit of everything he'd been suffering: confusion, agitation, hallucinations, seizures, muscle weakness, loss of consciousness (including coma). We didn't know how he had contracted whatever initially caused the infection, but we knew the enemy.

Now that the doctors knew what they were fighting, they could administer the appropriate treatment. The team of doctors and nurses God assembled for Chris's care were beyond remarkable. They were personal, dedicated, highly trained, and compassionate. I was often summoned to their offices for personal consultations, either for fact-finding sessions that would help them figure out what was going on with him or for them to simply explain what their strategies were on any given day.

It was decided that Chris would have a "cocktail" of antibiotics and antifungal drugs administered through his IV. Ironically, this same treatment had worked for my uncle when he had the same infection a few years previous. Chris remained on life support so that his body could be supported while his brain was receiving the powerful drugs that we prayed would eradicate the infection and inflammation in Chris's brain once and for all.

As we entered into a new phase of waiting, a real sense of three potential outcomes plagued my thoughts, and I continued to end my days praying through Scripture. Chris could be healed and fully recover, the infection could be cured but leave him with permanent physical challenges, or he would be healed in Heaven and be gone from this earth. When it was difficult for me to focus and I didn't know what to pray for, the Word of God proved itself alive and active for me and put the words to my prayers that I couldn't even voice. I continued to write out my prayers to God in my journal, documenting each one so that I could go back and pray it again and again.

Day #16, February 10

"Hear my cry, O God;
Listen to my prayer.
From the ends of the earth I call to you,
I call as my heart grows faint..."
– Psalm 61:1-2

"Find rest, O my soul, in God alone;
My hope comes from him.
...One thing God has spoken,
Two things have I heard:
That you, O God are STRONG,
And that you, O Lord, are LOVING."
– Psalm 62:1-2, 11

Those quiet moments in prayer were the only way I could calm my spirit, and I grounded myself on the truths I found there. I played

253

the last two over and over in my mind as we continued our daily routine and vigil: "God is strong... God is loving... God is strong... God is loving." All we could do was wait and pray.

47 | Behind the Scenes

"Whether you turn to the right or to the left, your ears will hear a voice behind you, saying, 'This is the way; walk in it.'"
– Isaiah 30:21

As the weeks dragged on, our team seemed to form a routine for our care and the support crew in Bloemfontein grew. I remember at least one long weekend when August and Anita took the kids out to their farm in Lesotho to let them have respite and play a little. Their place was a child's haven with dogs, horses, a river, vast open spaces, and narrow mountain paths to discover. It gave me comfort to know they were safe and distracted in such a wonderful way. This freed me up to be at the hospital as much as I needed to be without the additional emotional stress of feeling like I needed to care for the kids; but it left me needy for company. I didn't know how to be alone very well, and I was painfully lonely in the quiet times.

God didn't skimp in providing help and comfort. When my teammate Bekah swooped in for her shift with me, it was evidence that God knew my heart and what I needed most. She and I had enjoyed the retreat together months before and she was already a comforting presence for me. The kids were out at the farm with August and Anita when she arrived, and I had been at the hospital all day. Her gentle, smiling face welcomed me back to my temporary home at the guest house. Her hugs were further evidence of the fact that God had arranged the parts of the Body of Christ just as they needed to be at the exact time they were needed. The truth of the passage came to life as Bekah's nurturing spirit ministered to my broken, exhausted soul.

"But in fact God has placed the parts in the body, every one of them, just as he wanted them to be."
– 1 Corinthians 12:18

After squeezing me for a bit, she turned her attention toward checking on my felt needs. She asked if I had eaten, reminded me that I needed to sleep, and reassured me that she would be nearby in the adjoining room. "Oh, no you won't," I clarified, "I need you to be right here in the same room!"

She acquiesced and we bunked in the smaller room with the twin beds so that I didn't have to be alone. That wasn't the only rescue plan God had prepared for me. Around that same time, about two weeks into Chris's hospital stay, I received a call from my cousin from Australia. "Hey, Cuz. My mom and dad told me about Chris. I can't imagine what you're going through. You need family with you and I want to come. I've been to South Africa before, so don't worry about me getting there. I'll make a way."

He and his wife were church planters there, and with a similar faith and ministry background and cross-cultural living experience, he was well suited to enter into the deeply personal trial we were going through. All of the kids trusted him implicitly and Chris had a deep respect for him, so whether he was swimming in the pool with the kids or sitting by Chris's bedside during the hardest watches during the wee hours of the morning, Jason became our ministering angel.

By the third week, my mom's presence brought a comforting completeness to our support crew. With her there, it felt like I had an extension of myself for my kids and a shoulder to cry on no matter what. When Jason and I picked her up from the airport, an old familiar sense of familiarity and comfort washed over me. We had been wandering from place to place in towns we were unfamiliar with for a long time, but now I had two people who had known me my whole life by my side. I knew I wouldn't have to give instructions to them, nor tell them how to care for the kids. They had known them from the time they were born.

It was evening when Mom arrived, and as the sun slipped away, the parking lot lights at the small airport had taken over and cast a covering of light over the place where we stood. As we opened the trunk to put Mom's bags in, we turned and embraced each other in a tight group hug. Words weren't necessary. They felt the pain with us and were entering in. There, locked in their arms, I allowed myself to breathe.

On one warm afternoon, some of us gathered in a poolside room to brainstorm about the future. I remember Olivia being there next to me on the couch, and I think it was August who sat across from us, his cell phone in hand connecting him to other members of our extended missionary family in Kenya. The neurologist had been preparing me for potential outcomes if Chris was able to recover from the infection, so we were mulling over this information and pondering what our next steps might be. We knew that even the best case scenario would require us to leave the village for a time. Our family had to be in a place where we would have access to schooling for the kids and medical care for Chris's recovery. At best, he would require rehabilitation and a high level of care to recover from this. Getting him back to the States with physical challenges would also make that possibility next to impossible.

With the shaky voice of a teenager facing an unknown future, Olivia voiced her desire to stay at Rift Valley Academy. She explained that we had promised her she could graduate from there and begged me to consider letting her stick to that original plan. Her determination didn't stop there; she let it be known that she had heard there was a teaching position open at the high school and then reminded me, "Mom, that's what you do. You could teach there, and we could go to school."

It never occurred to me when my friend Heather shared their vision of seeing us being there at RVA that I would actually be talking about the possibility of *doing* it just weeks after she had mentioned it. Yet, I couldn't deny the providential truth that it might be meant to be. The school was strategically positioned in a community that was a ministry hub for our organization. There were hospitals in nearby Nairobi and doctors on staff in town who would be accessible if Chris needed ongoing care. We had a counseling center in Nairobi staffed with a team of counselors and psychologists who could provide emotional support. Most importantly, the remaining five school-age kids would have a viable and strong school option while I continued to serve in a support role. While the possibility perplexed me, seeing a potential direction for our future was comforting. We all logged it in our long list of prayer requests and August and Dudley promised to look into it.

48 | Dreams and Reality

"The hardest part of dreaming about someone you love,
is waking up to see that person gone."
– Unknown

Being still has never come easy for me, but I was trapped in a time when I had no choice. There was nothing physically I could do to fight this battle. It was as if Chris hovered between our reality and Heaven. Our physical needs were met through the generous outpouring of love from our team and the Body of Christ there in Bloemfontein. The owners of the guest house accommodated every "crew change" as our friends took turns staying there to care for us. The kids' days were filled with outings to the movies, bowling, swimming, jumping on the trampoline, and sporadic worksheets and lessons from the homeschool materials I had brought from the village. There wasn't much capacity to think during that time, but some sense of "normalcy" was comforting as it brought a sense of routine.

I was exhausted in every sense of my being. My thoughts raced with what-ifs and the burden of life-and-death decisions and trying to be strong for the kids. It seemed my emotions were the most consistent dynamic at play at all times. Shock, grief, and despair hung on me like a heavy cloak, weighing me down and then overwhelming me in long spells of crying that I couldn't stop. Physically, I was depleted and exhausted but couldn't feel anything. Hunger felt more like nausea, and nothing tasted good. I subsisted on the miraculous, intensely seasoned, American Snyder's pretzels I had found in the nearby store, coffee, and the over-the-counter sleep aid that the nurses made me take. Despite the all-consuming tiredness and the medicine, sleep eluded me.

Cousin Jason's presence continued to be a profound help because I felt even more free to leave the kids with him. Somehow knowing they were with family released me from feeling like I was inconveniencing people. It had been weeks of pulling my teammates away from their work to depend on them, and although they were all doing it willingly out of love and not obligation, it was difficult for me to rest knowing that others were taking care of my children around the clock.

One night in particular, it must have been obvious that I needed to sleep. I don't remember who made me do it nor which of the adults present with us arranged for me to have a room by myself that night, but I ended up in one of the guest rooms all alone. The bed was comfortable and the furnishings were pleasing to the eye. I remember there being deep reds, room-darkening curtains, and heavy, soft blankets. It felt strange and foreign to be getting ready for bed with nobody else in the room. The kids were all the way on the other end of the property sleeping in a room together and there I was in silence, staring at the walls and feeling like a part of me was missing.

I forced myself into the bed and laid there awkwardly. Even after drinking down a couple of the sleep aids, my mind raced and sleep wouldn't come. Shifting in the bed, I tried everything I knew to force my body to sleep. Taking every thought captive and turning it into prayers, I cried out to God. He was the unseen power I believed was present even though I couldn't see or feel Him there in the darkness. One thought at a time rolled into drowsy pleas as I drifted into restless sleep.

Chris appeared lying peacefully on a sterile, gurney-like table. His body was the only illuminated figure in a formless, darkened space. He was asleep just like I was used to him being now—in the Intensive Care Unit, still and nearly lifeless. As my subconscious scanned the scene, a transformation appearing as a subtle, changing orb of pulsing light began to take place near his feet. Glowing, dim twinkles caressed his feet and seemed to bring them to life, warming and waking up his tissues as they moved slowly up his body. Little by little, light overtook his body until he was healed and standing before me. He looked alive and well again, healed from the tips of his toes to the top of his head.

Harsh light fell on my eyes, and I woke to find myself in the guestroom still alone. Turning my head to avoid the sliver of sunlight,

I scanned the stuffy room. Reality set in. Nothing had changed. The vision of Chris being healed was just a dream and I had to force my body to face my usual daily drill: check on the kids, drive to the hospital, blankly push the button on the elevator, walk out into the corridor that led me to my unconscious husband, and take my place by his side to wait. The only thing different about that morning in particular was that my thoughts kept returning to the vision of his body surging with the light of life and the tiny flickers of hope that had crept in.

JOURNAL ENTRY

February 13, 2013
Day #19

This is the Valley of the Shadow of Death... I never pictured having to tell my kids that their daddy was on the edge of life and death. Yet, I know you are with us, God.

Chris has been in my dreams. In the wee hours of the morning, I had a dream. Chris was well and strong, stubborn as ever. He was working and lifting too much. I said, "Be careful, you need to get strong again." He said, "I'm ok. It's not what they think." He took me in his arms and held me.

Oh, how I want to cling to HOPE, to Your promises, God. Yet, I teeter on the precipice of living my worst nightmare. This is the journey I didn't want to walk. Lord, carry me. Take away my anxious thoughts. You spoke to me yesterday, 'I will/am fighting for you. You need only be still.' Teach me how to do that.

LOVE'S LAST WORDS

Existing in the time warp between life and death blurs a person's sense of time and removes the value of the earthly calendar that marks the passing of days. Although I was usually unaware of the date, the small gift shop in the lobby of the hospital clued me in that it was February. Valentine's Day was approaching. Thankfully, Bloemfontein lacked the commercial fervor and capitalistic merchandising gusto I was used to in Southern California and there were no heralding banners that assaulted me throughout town. Only a few hearts and cheesy stuffed animals adorned the windows of the shop tipped me off to the impending celebration of human love.

Awareness of a holiday looming hit me like a slap in the face and reminded me of two main things that gripped me with pain and fear: I was far from home and my husband was lying comatose hooked up to a machine to stay alive.

Seeing Chris like that was gut-wrenching. His normal self was so full of life, vibrant, funny, sassy, and fully present. In a coma, he was still and lifeless, and people had to move him and care for every physical need. Tubes, wires, and hoses protruded from every part of his body that was visible.

I wanted to be near him, comfort him, encourage him, protect him, and be a part of every decision they made for his care; but seeing him like that was so traumatizing for me that I felt like my own life was wasting away too. There was no way I was going to *force* the kids to visit if it was too hard for them. I allowed them to decide when they wanted to see him and how long they wanted to stay. Once Julia arrived, I remember her coming most days. She did a lot of singing and talking to him, which even drew a detectable smile to his face occasionally. As her rich, full voice sang low for him on one particular day, our eyes met as we both noticed a tear stream from his eye.

However, by February fourteenth, Dr. P was encouraging me to have all of the kids see Chris to give them an opportunity to say what they felt like saying to him. Pain that deep is all-consuming and felt in every part of your body, casting darkness over your soul, deadening every one of your senses, and lasting for years. Shock takes over and the life that's left shuffles and stumbles ashen and insensate through commands given by trusted guardians. That's all I remember about getting the kids to Chris's bedside on Valentine's Day. I was told it was what I should do, and I brought them there. The rest of the day is foggy, harder to retrieve than a dream in the night that you can't quite bring back.

The room comes back to me in a kind of sterile, green-white blur. Chris was the same as he was every day—clean and groomed, still and ashen, leads coming from under the sheet that covered him and returning to their machines. Oxygen hissed and pumped rhythmically, the heart monitor beeped his heart rate, and the rest of the world fell away into silence. The kids gathered around. I know I was doing my best to hold back the tears, but I was failing. Their faces were tense and taut with the effort it took to look at their dad without crying. They had mustered the courage to walk in there, and they stood there determined to obey. I don't remember which of them spoke; some of them weren't able to force out any words. There weren't any in my own vast repertoire that I could force out, either.

With all of my kids gathered around the bed with me, we shared moments we didn't want to live, and then Silly moved to the head of the bed and leaned into Chris's ear. "I love you, Daddy. Thank you for being the best dad ever."

No matter how hard I try, I can't bring back anything else from that ICU room that day. My next memory is returning to our upstairs, two-room suite at the guest house. I wandered to the back room as I normally did, aimlessly wilting onto one of the beds in a droopy pile of exhaustion. As I entered, an unfamiliar sight caught my attention. There on the small table catching the light from the window was a giant flower arrangement. It was huge, more lavishly arranged than any I could remember receiving. Long-stemmed red roses caught my attention: *This is for ME, it's personal and intimately made with our family in mind. Who knew that all of my kids bear the name 'Rose?'*

It was my long-standing tradition to make Valentine's Day a FAMILY day, a time to express our love to each other, and I always surprised the kids with small gifts, candy, and love notes on this day. Here in the Valley of the Shadow of Death, I wasn't able to even keep track of the days, let alone know it was a holiday; but someone else had done for us what I would have done at home. I received the gift of flowers, candy, and snacks for all of us as a gift from God, the only One who knew my heart and saw my intimate needs. Reaching for the small card tucked in among the blooms, I opened the card. All of it was from the couple who was *already* generously pouring out love on our family. The owners of the guest house had put all of this together for us, knowing that the day would be taking its toll on us. Stunned and frozen in the abyss of our circumstances, I sat and soaked in the gift of grace. Somehow, it gave me a sense that no matter what happened, we'd still have living to do.

Who's in Control Here?

"It is not length of life, but depth of life."
– Ralph Waldo Emerson

Rising from bed on Friday had me mindful that this long wait with him on life support was totally against what Chris had always instructed me. As someone who wasn't afraid to die, he would often tell me exactly how he wanted things to be if he died before me. Those conversations had happened throughout our twenty-three year marriage, so there was one particular mandate he had given me that was haunting me as he lay there in that hospital bed: "If something happens to me, don't hook me up to life support and leave me hanging there, just let me go."

It was much easier to take that when he was his normal, alive and vibrant, snarky self. Now, after lying there asleep for almost three weeks, still and unmoving with a machine helping him breathe, I could just imagine what he would say to me if he could speak. As I carried out my dazed, daily commute to the hospital, I became more and more determined to find Dr. P and ask her the question I had been too afraid to ask.

Dr. P. was a highly sought after and trusted specialist who cared deeply for her patients. It didn't matter if I met with her in her office or by Chris's bedside; there were always people waiting to see her. Without an actual appointment, I wasn't sure how I'd get a word with her, so I prayed she would make the rounds at some point that day.

My answer came at a time when the lights were dim and the whole ICU ward was quiet. I'm not sure what time of day it was, but I remember looking out of the glass door into the common area where the nurse's station was and seeing her familiar and confident frame buzz by our door and enter the unit. There was just enough light in the corridor of the Intensive Care Unit to make out her short, wispy, feminine hair style and her bangs that swept across her middle-aged forehead. As she came closer, I seized the moment and caught her there before anybody else had an opportunity to interrupt my mission. The light from the doorway of Chris's room fell on her face as she turned toward me so that I could see her gray-blue eyes peering intentionally into mine.

"May I ask you a question, Dr. P?"

"Of course, what is it?" she answered in the accent I associated with help and love.

I paused, took a deep breath, and forced the words out through tears: "Chris never wanted to be on life support... how long... I mean, when..." I stuttered and stammered, not knowing how to ask the thing I never wanted to ask. Finally, I pushed through and just spit it out. "When do I have to make a decision about life support?"

She looked at me confused; my vague question didn't register with her and she was forced to ask for clarity. "What do you mean, 'make a decision'?"

"Well, I know Chris never wanted to be on life support, but he's been on there so long. When will I have to decide to take him off?" I couldn't be strong anymore. My emotions escaped and my head bowed to cry in earnest. My American self remembered long debates and political seasons of wrestling through end of life decisions like the one I felt bearing down on me now and there was no part of me that could possibly make a choice.

"Oh, Michelle. That isn't something you have to decide. We will support Chris's body with the machines while we treat his brain until he is either healed or Home. Only God controls when a person dies."

Peace and relief washed over me. I wouldn't have to "pull the plug" or tell our children and family that I had "given up." I rested in knowing that Chris was in God's hands and not mine. While it didn't give me any new answers, it set me free to trust God's plan for Chris. As I sat with him and studied his face and his eyes, it seemed like he and his Heavenly Father were already working through the same thing. He was still asleep, his body completely unstirring except for the rise and fall of his chest as the ventilator breathed steadily for him. Although his eyes were closed and he was clearly not awake, his eyes moved under his eyelids and knowing expressions occasionally made him appear to be listening to someone.

My last task of the evening before heading back to the guest house to have dinner with the kids was to talk to my in-laws on the phone. With the time difference, they were just rising to a new day as we were ending it. I don't remember the whole conversation with them, only the last moments of the call will stay with me forever. Placing my phone on speaker, I held it up to Chris's ear for his dad to talk to him.

"Chris, it's Dad. Hey, I want you to know I love you and I'm so proud of you. We're praying for you and wish we were there with you...."

There was no doubt Chris heard those words that every son longed to hear from his father. He couldn't answer back verbally, but a tear fell from his eye and rolled down his cheek.

49 | The Biggest Plot Twist of All

"If the LORD had not been my help, my soul would soon have lived in the land of silence. When I thought, 'My foot slips,' your steadfast love, O LORD, held me up."
– Psalm 94:17-18 ESV

It's hard to imagine that Chris WON'T be whole again. I had been mulling that thought over in my head for weeks, and increasingly after the most recent neurologist's updates on Chris's condition. Brain scans showed extensive damage to his brain from the infection. They weren't able to tell if his brain stem had been affected, whether or not Chris would ever walk, talk, or care for himself again. We had already been told he was blind. Doctors could tell by routine tests and checks of his eyes. As much as I wanted my dream to come true and have Chris stand before me alive and whole, my spirit knew that he was teetering between this life and the next.

Saturday dawned the same way all of the other days did. This time, though, my mom was there and able to go to the hospital with me. Dudley and Jan were resting back at the guest house and would be there in case we needed them later in the day. Cousin Jason would return to the guest house, rest for a bit, and then be with the kids for the day once we relieved him at the hospital. He usually took the most difficult shift by Chris's side, sitting with him through the night, reading and praying. That was often when his body was the most unstable, so it was stressful and intense. Jason stood in for me, bearing the weight of the "witching hours," as the nurses called them.

Our favorite nurses were on duty when we got there. Only a couple of them had seen Chris when he had been admitted and knew his sense of humor. Although the whole staff gave him very personal care, these were his champions. Mom and I spent the day catching up, alternating normal conversations about things at home with peeks at Chris's vital signs and chats with the nurses who came in to care for him. He was having a pretty good day in the beginning. His body seemed to rally, and his facial expressions even appeared to respond to us a couple of times. The machines faithfully breathed and beeped: air in, air out, whoosh, click, puff, whoosh, click, puff.

Around five o'clock in the evening, Mom and I were getting hungry and started telling the nurses we'd probably go have dinner with the kids and come back. Standing by the monitor by Chris's bedside, the nurse who had been there when Chris was admitted was making notes on her notepad and pushing buttons. In a calm voice, she let us know what her gut and the numbers told her. "I don't think you should go now. His blood pressure is dropping. Let's wait and see what happens."

It was at that point that I had to make one last decision. With Chris's blood pressure dropping rapidly, the doctors gave me an option. We could try taking him off of the seizure or pain medicine which tended to lower blood pressure. Maybe that would help his blood pressure go up. Of course, there were risks involved in this decision. The seizures that wracked his body with tense pain and brought back the earliest trauma of his illness may return without the medicine. Still, I knew I had to do everything in my power to help him. We had to try.

Dudley and Jan rushed over to the hospital and joined us in the room. I'm not sure what time they got there, but it was as if they brought the heavenly choir. The four of us stooped over Chris's bed, them on one side and my mom and me on the other. We rubbed his arms, prayed, and sang. When we forgot the words to the songs, Dudley would whip out his iPad and find the lyrics that he had saved. Jan, who had survived a near death experience while giving birth, leaned in and whispered in his ear, alternately singing and then thinking of something else to say to him: "You're probably seeing Jesus by now... isn't it beautiful? You're almost there..."

Nurses came and went to check on us, joining us at times and sometimes even offering to pray for us. Peace reigned...until the seizures began to return.

As his body began to tense up and shudder again, I struggled to stay by his side. Fear gripped me every time his muscles tightened and forced his body into awkward, rigid positions, and it was as if my own body was consumed with his physical pain. I cried out to God to help him, to bring relief, to hear our cries. Time and reality were blurred in that space, and all I was aware of was what we were experiencing in that room. At some point, one of the nurses suggested we turn the sound from the monitors down so we didn't have to hear the beeps anymore. Yet, the ventilator kept breathing on. The machines that held Chris's physical body continued to do their job; but they weren't in control. We knew the One who was.

As we prayed, I noticed a coming stillness. It was subtle, but unmistakable. Chris's feet slowly relaxed, then his legs. Before long, his body was softening and resting. The room was filled with a heavy presence, voices without restraint sang out songs of praise. I was on his left side holding his hand and lightly rubbing his forearm in the familiar way I always did when one of the nurses appeared by my side and wrapped her arms around my shoulders. She was praying into my ear in a whisper.

Then, out of the serenity, I sensed it. Everything was still. Only light puffs of air came from the ventilator. I turned to the nurse who held me there. "Is he gone?" I asked.

"No, he's Home."

The way the kids tell it, they knew when the car returned from the hospital with me in it. Looking out over the balcony, they saw us arrive, and the security light from one of the eaves of the house illuminated my face and revealed the truth of the update I was about to give them. We had talked about the potential of this outcome, but it was our worst case scenario. Still, I had to tell them. Every step felt heavy. My stomach felt sick with the burden of it. I climbed the steps to our room, entered, and collapsed on the bed with all six of them. I don't even remember the first words I forced out, but it was something like, "Dad is in Heaven."

We lingered there for a long time. Our world had forever changed, and time didn't matter anymore. As we were piled on that bed in a heap of tears, memories would overcome the grief and one of us would tell a story about Chris and we'd all crack up. It was in this strange space of sorrow and enduring love that a promise welled up in me that I shared with the kids. I prayed that this would be our mission in the years to come: "We're not victims. We're victorious. Your dad received his 'well done' and he would want us to LIVE."

It was the beginning of a new, long season, and the lessons about humility, trust, and surrender started that first night. One of my teammates gently coaxed me from the kids for a bit while my mom and Jason stayed with them, and then I took the time to update those around the world who were praying.

Email Blast

February 16, 2013 8:10 p.m.

"To all of you all over the world who have been praying fervently for us through this time, this is Michelle. I am letting you know that Chris is now whole, healed, and safely in the arms of his loving, gracious Savior. Chris was actually pretty stable today, but has been having "tremors" or "seizures" over the last few days. These were extremely painful for me to watch him endure. Throughout these weeks, as we have had knowledge of Chris's brain being involved, I have been asking his heavenly Father to heal Chris completely, make him whole, and not give him more than he could handle if there WERE outcomes that involved blindness, seizures, or brain damage of any kind.

Chris has always been VERY specific with me that QUALITY of life is a priority for him. As his "tremors" increased this afternoon, they had to reduce the medicine he was getting for pain because it was causing his blood pressure to fall pretty rapidly. It was at that time that I knew what God had so mercifully decided for my beloved.

Present at Chris's bedside were me, my mom who had just arrived from California two nights previous, Dudley and Jan, and a number of the nurses who had so faithfully and lovingly ministered to Chris. We shared the most intimate, deep, immensely moving worship time that I have ever experienced. We prayed over Chris, Dudley kept up a continuous prompting of beautiful hymns and songs that we sang together, Jan read passages from the Word about Heaven, and at different times, nurses would come in and pray with us, embrace me, and personally pray for me.

God freed me from my fear of death so that I could be at Chris's side, embrace him, and assure him as he entered Heaven. I sensed an incredible strength and peace. I can testify that God has taken my BIGGEST fear, the ONE JOURNEY I had told God I was unwilling to take, and made beauty from the ashes. In addition, the hardest thing I have EVER had to tell my kids was also like being on holy ground.

All of your prayers for us have been answered. We will have hard days, we will miss Chris deeply. He has been my best friend, my constant companion, and my PERFECT partner for more than half of my life. However, he has left a legacy in his kids and they were already laughing about stories about Dad as we sat and talked about him being in Heaven.

My prayer is that you will also see CHRIST high and lifted up, glorified, sovereign, and GOOD as you have walked this journey with us. Your prayers that Chris would be healed completely for wholeness and fullness of life have been answered. We got to witness it happen before our eyes as the striving and tremors ceased and he calmly rested.

Please pray that the seeds that Chris has planted throughout his life will bear much fruit. That God would be glorified among the NATIONS and through our family as we testify to His presence and goodness in the midst of our suffering. Pray that Chris's life - and Homecoming - would bring revival in Lesotho, the mountain kingdom that we have grown to love so much. That they would know the ONE TRUE GOD, Sovereign over all spirits, the One who has known Chris from when he was knit together in his mother's womb to this evening when he received his Heavenly reward.

Words cannot express my gratitude and the sense that God has already used Chris's life to unite the Body of Christ for something powerful. We covet your prayers for this next season of our lives.

Finally at peace, Michelle"

50 | Siblings Forever

*"A person without a sense of humor is like a wagon without springs.
It's jolted by every pebble on the road."*
– Henry Ward Beecher

Although it was always profoundly evident that we were far away from home, the distance felt more vast and impossible in the midst of a medical crisis. When it became evident that Chris's illness may be fatal, his family did their best to get to us, but many of them didn't have the documents required to travel. Our organization came alongside and helped with the process as best as they could while the family tried every possible way to expedite the process. Chris's siblings dropped everything, expedited passports, made emergency travel arrangements, and rushed through two full days of international flights to make it to say goodbye, but arrived about a day after his departure to Heaven. Still, their presence there with us as we grieved through those first few days was a comfort to us.

Since Chris and I had met when we were twenty and twenty-one, his family felt like an extension of my nuclear family rather than just distant in-laws set aside for the holidays. My relationship with my sister-in-law, Kelly, was especially close. She was thirteen or fourteen when Chris and I met, so she was still at home with her parents and present for our frequent visits. It seemed the timing of our time together coincided with developmental milestones in her life, so our sisterhood was sealed with the firsts of her womanhood. Leaving the personal details aside, I'll say she has always been a little sister to me. She and I could have a conversation without words, so that came in handy when she and Chris's brothers, Mike and Steve, arrived at the guest house.

As the uncles caught up with the kids, I pulled Kelly to the side and had her follow me to the downstairs room where she would be staying. The room was small and cozy, and the dark, rich colors of the decor seemed to draw us in. We sat side-by-side on the bed, looked at each other, and let the pent up tears flow freely. The truth of why they were there hit both of us and there were no words for what we felt in that moment. We lingered there, clinging to each other. There was so much to catch up on, but only one thought overwhelmed us. The outcome we had dreaded had happened and Chris was gone.

The heaviness of the truth was paralyzing, but I had a mission that had come to me as a sudden gift idea. I wanted Chris's beloved baby sister to have something from him to cling to, a piece of him to hold onto in his absence. It was as if I knew he would want me to communicate to her that he loved her, and I held something precious to both of us that would remind her of that. Reaching in my pocket, I pulled out the silver cuff, custom made ring that matched the one I wore on my wedding finger. We had them made for our twentieth anniversary as a confirmation of our vows and enduring love for each other. They reflected our growth in our love for Jesus, too; a reminder of the song we had chosen for our wedding day, "You and Me and Jesus." Our names were engraved on the wide silver ring with a cross in the middle.

Taking Kelly's hand in mine, I explained that I wanted to give that to her as a reminder that her brother and I both love her. She had been part of our courtship and we would remain close always, no matter what. I can see us huddled there in that dark room, sisters embracing in an eternal moment, but there aren't words to recall. All that we needed to know was communicated in that room. We'd still be sisters, and we'd always have Chris with us.

This was the very beginning of the process of reframing our lives without our husband, brother, father, and son. He was a part of our daily existence in this life. His soul was woven into our identities, and we needed to learn how to live without him. Walking through the final milestones of Chris's life on earth with his siblings was our first journey together without him, and the first step into a long, painful process. The four of us went together for a last goodbye, entering into a small, plain side-room of an antiquated mortuary to see his earthly body one last time. Even in that space, we were still who God made us to be. Death couldn't take away our humor, the weaknesses we had that made the situation scary and awkward, nor our laughter that erupted as a release for all that we were feeling. We shared intimate moments only the four of us know about, laughed, cried, and said goodbye.

Each day of that week required us to run errands that we never pictured ourselves doing. On one warm day, my brothers-in-law went with me to pick up Chris's ashes from the mortuary. I drove the Land Rover and navigated the streets of "Bloem", driving on the left side, which was familiar to me by then. We all rode along in heavy silence to the outdated mortuary building that looked like a relic from a by-gone era. When we arrived, I couldn't make myself go in. This seemed like such a final step. With Chris's soul gone from this earth, seeing a little box that contained his body sounded like more than I could take. My brothers offered to go in on my behalf.

They were inside for a long time, and I started to feel restless. What could the problem be? After what seemed like an hour, they emerged from the swinging door and walked down a ramp toward me. Mike held a small, wooden box in both of his hands and walked slowly, with respect that neared pageantry. It was as if pomp and circumstance was playing in a score behind him. The love and care his body spoke as he carried the remains of his brother were evident.

As they approached me, humor returned, and they began to describe the scene inside. Chris's name was misspelled on the plaque, and they had to request that a new one be made. After all, this was a final remembrance. We wanted his name to be spelled correctly! Their familiar banter melted the tension and my focus returned. Looking at the hands of both brothers, another error came to my attention. "Is that the only box they gave you?"

"Yea," they both replied as a puzzled look of dread fell over them.

"That's only half of Chris. I asked for him in two separate boxes."

"Oh, no... You're saying we have to go back in there?"

The reaction was the same for all three of us. We couldn't help but be reduced to a physical response that was a weird combination of groans, tears, and laughter. Dreading what may be the outcome inside, my valiant brothers turned to retrieve the second half of our precious cargo. The wait for the resolution of that next gargantuan mistake was even longer. The guys returned to the car, and we waited together, weaving together macabre scenarios about what may have happened in the recesses of that place. Laughter calmed us as we reasoned what the truth was. Chris wanted to be left in Africa if something happened to him. This would surely guarantee that his wishes were carried out, at least halfway, no matter what the second box contained when we finally received it.

The presence of family provided more than just closure for all of us. Sharing some of our lives in Africa with them was a bond that loss could never take away. I remember joy welling up in me as we crossed over the border from South Africa into Lesotho as the landscape opened up to that vast, wild wilderness.

"This is Lesotho," I declared.

As the words left my lips, I was filled with the deep, warm sense of pride that comes when you welcome someone into your home. All of the hard memories slipped to the back of my mind to be replaced by accomplishment and purpose. I wanted them to see the people we had grown to love, to travel back in time with us to the place that had become our second home. A deep satisfaction welled up in me as I watched Chris's big brother attempt jovial greetings in Sesotho to strangers at the gas station. Joy came effortlessly as the kids and I let loose of the stories that flooded our minds.

Our final destination that day was the home of our beloved South African team leaders, August and Anita, who had grown their farming ministry in a remote village. It was a full circle experience for us as this was the place we did our home stay and entered into the culture for the first time. We didn't have time to take them all the way to our own village on the other side of the mountains, but this was a wonderful opportunity for them to meet our friends and at least get a snapshot of what our lives had been like for the last couple of years.

Enjoying a proper South African *Braai* (barbeque) on the veranda looking out over the river and the mountains in the distance was the perfect way for Chris's siblings to end their week in Africa with us. This was the life we had been living. We had taken the biggest leap of faith of our lives to do the hardest things we had ever done. Yet, the beauty, majesty, and eternal significance of our experiences had ushered in a depth and purpose to our lives that we hadn't had up to that point. Sharing that meal felt like a sacred communion, a blending of my blood family, my family in love, and the team that had become a family to us in that remote place. Surely we were experiencing a tiny taste of what Chris was now experiencing in Heaven.

51 | Quick Answers, Hard Goodbyes

"The only cure for grief is to grieve."
– Earl Grollman, writer

Although my faith didn't waver, Chris's death seemed to render my weary brain nearly useless, with little ability to think. The world was blurry and dull and the best I could do was to go through the motions of each day, one at a time, taking care of the needs of the kids and responding like a lifeless robot to the requests of those around me who needed me to make decisions and move forward. My memory is foggy when I look back at this time and the whole year following, but there are records of what God was doing around the world in the pages of my journal and in the cloud of Facebook's memory. With all of the potential for harm and evil social media has, it was a powerful tool of encouragement and prayer as we navigated the hardest days of our lives.

My colleagues continued to be my main communications team, keeping me updated on critical information and decisions as others swooped in to guide us along toward the next steps we would take as a family. In the days that followed my email announcement of Chris's death, they received reports back from churches all around the world. Since Chris had entered his heavenly home on a Saturday night, my message had landed in the inboxes of pastors who were waking up on Sunday morning. This meant that they met their praying congregations with the news that Chris had passed from this earth. Many of them read my email update and whole churches lifted us in prayer that morning. Not only that, but a few pastors were led to give an invitation to salvation in Christ and we were receiving reports back that many were coming to faith as a result of our testimony!

I didn't put it together at the time, but stories like those were the beginning of the answers to my very personal prayers to God asking Him to bring purpose to our suffering, that He would continue to use Chris's life and death in the lives of others, and that God would continue to be glorified in our journey.

A South African Farewell

The irony that Chris and I had enjoyed a romantic long weekend in Bloemfontein for our twenty-third wedding anniversary only six months previous didn't escape me. As we drove to a small church near the outskirts of town for our first memorial service for Chris, I struggled to orient myself to the reality of where I was going. I recognized the road we were traveling on and a flash-back assailed me. I could picture myself present with Chris in the cab of the Land Rover, bags of specialty foods stowed in the back seat for a special meal we were going to barbeque at our rented cottage for two, carefree smiles on our faces as we chatted about what it was like to enjoy free time away together. We were just beginning to feel at home enough in the region to breathe deeply, and we relaxed and explored, got massages at a local spa, and went about our celebratory weekend with no idea a life-storm was brewing.

As I was driven along that same road to Chris's memorial service, the pain was so intense that I was afraid to let any tears fall. I knew that if I did, I may never stop. As we navigated the curving streets through sleepy neighborhoods to the tidy, brick church, I forced myself to breathe through the thoughts. I had to be strong for the kids. I had to be composed for all of the guests who were coming to say their farewells and give us their condolences. As thankful as I was for the support and care we were receiving, I didn't want to be doing any of it. I just wanted my husband back. I wasn't ready to stop counting years of anniversaries and celebrating milestones with him. He was supposed to raise the kids with me, and we were going to be old together. Yet, here I was, still young and without him. I wasn't denying that he was gone and in Heaven; I just couldn't believe it was true.

I remained in that same mental state as I got out of the car and entered through a glass door into a dimly lit corridor and followed the group into an intimate, side room of the small, understated church. Wooden pews rose like bleachers on two sides of the room and looked over an open area in the center. To the left of the open area, a piano or raised table of some kind held a framed picture of Chris. The picture had been taken at my stepsister's wedding before we moved, and he was being silly, lying on a ledge posing and laughing at his own joke. He was fully alive and vibrant in the picture, decked out in a stylish, muted green dress shirt. His blue eyes sparkled through his trendy, black-rimmed glasses. I diverted my eyes. I couldn't look at him.

Our family lined the first and second rows, and I remember thinking how remarkable it was that there were so many of us in Africa at one time. My mom, Cousin Jason, Mike, Steve, Kelly, and all of the kids filed in, carefully preventing their gaze from falling on Chris's picture, and found seats together near the front. Normally, we would be filled with joy to be surrounded by grandparents, aunts, uncles, cousins, and teammates, but we didn't want to be doing this. It was a foreign emotion to feel sadness when there would normally have been excitement and joy.

As the guests entered the small room, heads bowed in sorrow and respect, my emotions swelled with each person who had made the trip to come. Friends like family from our organization had driven long distances to come, and our Basotho "sisters" had even gone to great lengths to bring their beloved father, who was in his late eighties, all the way from the village to Bloemfontein for the occasion. Each precious one who entered heaped deeper sentiments upon the ones I was already attempting to squash and the pain in my chest grew to a point that I could barely hold myself together. Then, just when I thought everyone had assembled, one more woman entered alone and moved toward the back. It was the nurse who had been with us when Chris was put into a coma; the one who knew him and remembered him alive. I couldn't hold it in anymore and bowed my head in my hands and cried.

The familiar sound of August's accent snapped me to attention, and I found my composure. Raising my head, I dabbed my eyes and prepared to listen. Still reeling from my struggle to find my bearings and accept where I was, I pointed my eyes to the front and looked at each person standing there; but most of their words made it to my ears as if they were garbled and nonsensical. I couldn't focus. My only thoughts were, *Get me out of here. Please, can't this nightmare be over? This isn't how it was supposed to go. Take the pain away, Lord, take the pain away. I don't want my kids to have to do this. I don't want my kids to have to do this...*

Toward the end of the brief service, someone stood to read a letter written by our unit leader, John, who was unable to make it that day. One line from the letter made it to my awareness in crisp detail: "Looking back, it's as if Chris was working in fast forward all along. He learned language quickly, he worked tirelessly to understand the culture where he lived, and he made deep friendships in a very short amount of time."

That statement would remain in my mind as a reminder that none of this took God by surprise. The thought was comforting even though I didn't like the outcome we were living, and I left the service with a sense of gratitude that Chris had been able to live out his purpose to be a missionary and had finished in one, big, two-year grand finale. I didn't want him to be gone, but I sure was proud of him.

The next scene of that first farewell happened at the cafe we had come to love. When the owner found out that the loved one we had been praying for so intently for the last few weeks had passed away, he was overcome with compassion for our family and offered the restaurant for the gathering following the service. When we walked through the familiar cafe and out to the patio, a beautiful table full of delicious home-baked breads, gourmet cheeses and meats, and other irresistible finger foods awaited us. The staff had provided their best for us and my heart received it gratefully. Our worlds seemed to collide in an oasis of love as our family from home got to meet our village family and all of the people they had only read about in posts and newsletters. Pictures were snapped and hugs were exchanged as we all shared memories that united us in the grief-bond we now shared.

We lingered there for a while until the glowing light of dusk signaled that it was getting late. Hugs were tighter that evening with most of our team because I wasn't sure what our future held, nor when we'd see them again. When we hugged Ntate, our village father, though, we were able to say, "See you in a few days." Our next step was to make the winding journey through the mountains to the village to pack our house and say goodbye.

My insides were tight, and my back was tense with anxious exhaustion as I made my way through the restaurant to the exit. But a strong hand touched my shoulder and intercepted my escape. The rotund, seventy-something, gray-haired, jolly, and generous owner of the restaurant stood in my path and placed both of his hands on my shoulders. His determination drew my eyes to his and he expressed the message that He said God had placed on his heart for me. As his words took form, his discourse felt awkward and too personal in that space and time, but he spoke with the urgency of someone who knew he wouldn't have another chance to communicate an important message. He went on to say that he knew I was young and that, Lord willing, I had a lot of life left to live. What tumbled confidently out of his mouth next made me want to run away: "Someday, God will give you another husband."

I didn't hear anything else he said and my eyes were on the door. All I could think was, "I want *Chris*, I want *my* husband back. Too soon. *Too soon.*"

His words were spoken in love and may have indeed come from God in a prophetic message as he prayed for me, but the thought felt like a blow to my stomach. How could I begin to think about another husband when I couldn't even fathom that Chris was gone for good? All of this processing got piled up on the thoughts that already polluted my mind with wrestling thoughts, and I couldn't get out of there fast enough.

Later, in the stillness of the night when everyone went to bed, I was left in solitude with my thoughts again and paused to update those I knew were praying for us.

FACEBOOK POST

February 20, 2013

"Our friends and family here in Southern Africa celebrated Chris's life today. Praising God for the life he led and the fruit God has allowed us to see. Still feels like he'll walk in the door any minute... We covet your prayers as we seek God's peace and move forward in FAITH."

Village Memorial

On our last day in Bloemfontein, as I anticipated our return to the village to pack up and have a memorial service there, I penned this prayer in my journal:

JOURNAL ENTRY

February 23, 2013

"Lord, as we prepare to go to the village for closure, prepare our hearts. But, more than that, Lord, I pray you will prepare the hearts of the people to receive your salvation. May the tragedy, loss, and anger that is there for Chris's death till the soil of their hearts to receive the Gospel. Oh, LORD, that the people of (the village) would be the beginning of a powerful revival in the mountains of Lesotho!"

After teary farewells to the Gennaro siblings and Cousin Jason, we set out on the winding trek through the mountains and arrived at the village in a convoy of Land Rovers. The kids and I were accompanied by my mom and our closest friends and team leaders, August and Anita. They were our constant guides through decisions and tasks that were too big for me to face. We dismantled the home we had *just* made for ourselves there and, once again, had to get rid of most of the furniture and other belongings we had painstakingly accumulated to set up in that cinder block house for the long haul.

The heaviness that pressed down on me when we pulled into our compound threatened to pin me to my seat. Something like fear gripped me as I faced the house we had finally come to love as our own. I had to force myself to walk toward it and climb the concrete steps to the rough, wooden door. August unlocked it and entered before me, which gave me my first peek of the inside that I had buttoned up a month previous for what I thought would be a weekend trip for medical treatment. As I crossed the threshold, the weight of my grief overcame me, and I couldn't hold myself up any longer. My legs gave way and I shrunk to the floor sobbing. My mom was right there to comfort me as I finally let the wails of my sorrow flow out of me.

For some reason, when I think of returning to the village for the final goodbye, one of the most vivid scenes that pops into my mind is a vision of myself sitting on the bone-chilling plastic toilet seat in the outhouse. The cement "throne" that the seat rested on was too tall so that my feet dangled off the edge as if I was a potty-training child again. It seemed that every time my bare skin met with the icy seat, it triggered every primal struggle that simmered in me as we adapted to life in that remote place. My biggest tantrums were thrown in the privacy of that little, stinky, fly-ridden, windswept outhouse. Somehow, not even two years later, those homesick cries to God had turned into sobs at the thought of having to leave that place. The irony of my feelings kept me frozen there for far too long as I attempted to come to grips with the next transition we were preparing to make.

Furniture was passed on to new missionaries who had arrived to work in the nearby town, clothing was passed on to our closest friends in the village, and our most personal belongings were packed in totes to be stored in the garage of our new friends in Johannesburg until we knew where they would be shipped. Without a clue about what our future would look like, the kids and I each packed one bag that would go with us to America for our Compassionate Leave.

There was one last task to be done in the village that had become our home. We had to provide some closure to our time there, a time to say goodbye to "Ntate Thabang" (Chris) and to honor him. Thankfully, none of them asked where his body was. They wouldn't understand why I had carried out Chris's wishes to be cremated. There was no way we could contextualize a funeral and burial when we were so far from our home place and family. This memorial service would have to go on without the vigil of the body lying in state so that the community could pay their last respects. Since August was fluent in Sesotho and had spent enough years in the culture, he was able to work with the village elders to plan a little service that would be appropriate and relevant. Arrangements were made to have a gathering in the church building near our compound.

The physiological fog of shock and trauma lingered and acted like a protective veil for me through the few days we spent tearing ourselves from the village. Our loved ones must have been doing the majority of the work as the rest of us followed directions and answered questions in a semi-alert state. I was going through the motions, but my mind hadn't yet caught up to the reality of what we were doing, and I plodded along feeling confused. Only one eternal, life-giving, peace-engulfing conversation remains in my memories of that day. As the service was dismissed and I turned to leave the echoey, cinder block church building, I filed past familiar faces and thanked them for coming. *"Kea leboha haholo, 'M'e. Kea leboha, Ntate. Kea u rata. Kea u rata."* ("Thank you so much. Thank you, sir. I love you. I love you.")

As I turned toward the alcove and headed for the door, a strong hand touched my arm and I turned to meet the warm, brown eyes of a young man who wasn't familiar to me. He spoke with familiarity, and I wondered if he might have been a student at the vocational school. He spoke perfect English, so I understood every word of what he said to me. Grasping my hand in a lasting handshake, he said something like, "We know what you had in America and what you left to come live with us. You came and stayed, and now Ntate Thabang has died for us."

That phrase didn't sound right. We came to bring Jesus, not Chris. I wanted that to be clear and understood because that detail was of eternal significance. I took a breath and clarified, "Jesus died for you."

"Yes, but I've never seen anybody love like Ntate Thabang, and then he died."

I was speechless. Memories of Chris with his students and the neighbors we loved forced their way to the forefront of my mind and I stood frozen... Chris leading our whole family in harvesting the fields of our village grandfather when he was unable to... piling into the taxi with his village friends to go to town even though he had a perfectly good Land Rover... transporting the casket of our dear friend to his burial site...trudging through the snow and then spending hours setting up his classroom... trading bread for fabric... teaching his students to make useful things out of grain-storage bags... teaching the young women in his class to make a beautiful wedding dress for their friend...sitting by the side of his beloved student who had betrayed us and robbed us so that he wouldn't be beaten to a bloody pulp until he confessed...

There was nothing profound that came to me as the emotions took over. Only the most familiar phrase escaped my lips: *"Kea leboha haholo."* (Thank you a lot.)

It would be months before I made the connection that God was trying to tell me through that man the truth about the fruit of our time there.

John 15:12-13, *"My command is this: Love each other as I have loved you. **Greater love has no one than this: to lay down one's life for one's friends.**"*
— Jesus

Chris had literally laid down his life for his friends there and they had NOTICED! Putting this together gave me the peace I needed to walk out the aftermath of our obedience. The one sentence I repeated as we left the curb to board the plane to Africa came back to me as I prepared to uproot our family again, "Jesus, you are worthy. You are worthy."

Another Leaving

The weather was growing cool and crisp as we sorted and packed our belongings and said our goodbyes. A steady stream of neighbors and friends trickled into our yard to pay their respects and say goodbye. I had grown to notice and appreciate their gentle, friendly demeanor. Walking was more of a saunter than a brisk, task-oriented rushing. It was as if walking slowly allowed them to take in their surroundings as they approached a person or destination. Whether it was danger or welcome, scanning eyes were searching. Each blanket clad smiling face that entered our compound with eyes set on our home was a reminder of how many of them we had come to love. They were friends now, not foreign, mysterious neighbors.

Chris's colleagues from the Skills Training Center came together to visit us at our house to pay their respects and say goodbye. One by one, the three leaders of the school filed into the living room shaking hands with each of us. They wore the clothes they usually wore to the school when it was in session. They had on uniform-like slacks with collared shirts and the women had blankets wrapped around their waists over their dresses to resemble a wrap-like skirt. The woman who taught the catering class had on a bucket hat that topped off her outfit with the rural flare we had become accustomed to. One of them gently touched my shoulder and guided me so that I was standing in front of them. The family gathered around, and I anticipated them saying a few words to us in parting. But rather than the customary pleasantries and condolences I expected to hear, their voices joined in song and filled the room with joyful harmonies. With hands clapping, loving smiles, and tearful expressions, they sang over us. We all stood in awe and let their voices wash over us as we cried grateful tears. Clearly, in that short amount of time, they had grown to love and respect Ntate Thabang, their colleague and friend.

The last, most emotional goodbye was to our village father. At the age of eighty four, he wasn't only one of the eldest in the village, but he was one of a handful of Christ-surrendered, Bible believing souls we had known there. He was Chris's most trusted friend, language helper, and guide. His daughters who lived in the capital city and in Bloemfontein had become my friends and sisters in the Lord. Our true and deep friendships had culminated in our family Christmas celebration just weeks before as they returned home to the village and gathered in our home. On this day, Ntate shuffled into the driveway, his body weary from so many years of living in that physically demanding place. Every part of him exuded honor and respect. He had a suit on as if he was on his way to church with his traditional blanket draped over his shoulder that gave him a regal air, wrapped in a cape-like shield from the biting wind.

I saw him approaching and met him in the driveway. Our friendship was real now, there was no need for formality. I hugged him without reservation, and when our embrace was released, his soft, brown, creased face was streaked with tears. His eyes were unique, different than any I had seen there. They were more of a hazel color, rather than pure, brown-black, and they peered into my soul in that moment. After a long pause, he spoke, "This isn't goodbye. I know that my God has made me a house big enough for all of us in Heaven. I will see Ntate Thabang soon and we'll share our mansion."

He had lived a full life and was ready to go Home. With his wife in Heaven and his adult children living in other cities, Ntate often spoke about the hope of Heaven. His readiness to die felt uncomfortable for me in those moments, so I encouraged him to stay well for a while longer until his time came. We both stood there paused in the heaviness of the moment. There was really no doubt in either of our minds that we wouldn't see each other again on this side of eternity. My broken heart ached from too many goodbyes like this, and I wanted to cry out, "Don't make me leave!!"

That thought came to mind as a sudden self-awareness. It was evidence that God had taken my fearful, change-resistant heart and changed it over the course of the last ten years. He had taken my soul from "Don't make me stay" to "Don't make me leave," and now I stood face-to-face with the consequences of loving the very people we had asked God to help us love. Yet, I had to leave them. It made no sense to me, and I had to dig deep into my reserves for the physical strength to give my village father one more hug and turn to walk away.

With our convoy of Land Rovers loaded to the snorkels, it was time to leave. We had made a commitment to be there for the rest of our careers, at least ten to twelve years. Now, it was profoundly confusing for me to go through the motions of leaving, and yet it would have been impossible to stay. How could I physically homeschool four kids, fetch the water, maintain our rural home, and carry on the ministry? After all, I didn't even know how to sew! How could I teach them?! The suddenness of our circumstances had placed us in the loving hands of those who had long-term answers when I couldn't even take another step. Wise decisions were being made on our behalf and all I could do was allow myself to be carried along through them.

Shock had wrapped a protective cloak around our traumatized brains and, despite being the adult in charge of our family, I hadn't escaped the frozen confusion of it. Only one more memory remains of that day; it's the only scene left that I can bring back. I'm sitting in the back seat of my own Land Rover, unable to drive and hunched over wracked with sobs. Although my memory may be failing me, I picture my friend Anita in the driver's seat. She's talking me through each step of the leaving process in her low, calm voice. Her Afrikaner accent is assuring me that we're doing the right thing. "Everything will be ok, we're all here with you."

Questions overwhelmed me. "God, why is this happening? Why did you bring us here only to make us leave? We finally know how to live here! We have friends and we love them! Why did we do all of that work just to leave?! What will I do now? I can't do this. I can't start over again. I just got my brain around being here, how can I just leave them? We left everything to be here and I have nothing left to return to. This isn't how it was supposed to go!"

I'm not sure if that can be called prayer, but if prayer is talking to God unceasingly, I was now a pro at it. Without my partner in life with me, my soul seemed to know the One who could hear me. Questions and heart cries flew out of my mouth and mind in gushes, and in this space of profound brokenness, it was as if God gave me a direct line to Him. The Bible came to life in a new way, like there was a tin can held to my ear, connected by a string with my Heavenly Father on the other end whispering into His own Heavenly vessel. The written Word of God slowly brought the answers to my questions as I plodded through the days I never wanted to live.

These flashbacks of leaving the village are now evidence that God had marked out the appointed time we'd be there, and that He was in control. I had to lean into His Sovereignty and trust Him to provide the next place where we'd live.

"The God who made the world and everything in it is the Lord of heaven and earth and does not live in temples built by hands. And he is not served by human hands, as if he needed anything. Rather, He himself gives everyone life and breath and everything else. From one man he made all the nations, that they should inhabit the whole earth; and He marked out their appointed times in history and the boundaries of their lands."
— Acts 17:24-26

Author's Note: *Now, years later, I'm not even sure if it was Anita in the driver's seat that day. She's the one whose friendship still has a comforting effect on my soul, though, so perhaps she remains there for purposes beyond my understanding. Family members will be able to correct this, but I'll choose to leave her there in her rightful place. She was my rugged, passionate, direct, fiercely competent, courageous friend from the first day we stepped into the country, and she'll remain in my memories as the one who carried me out.*

Part Four |
Navigating Life Without Chris

52 | Out of Africa

"He gives strength to the weary and increases the power of the weak. Even youths grow tired and weary, and young men stumble and fall; but those who hope in the Lord will renew their strength. They will soar on wings like eagles; they will run and not grow weary, they will walk and not be faint."
— Isaiah 40:29-31

There's really no honest way to describe our departure from Africa back to America for our Compassionate Leave. I know that Olivia and I flew to Kenya to pack up her belongings and that we flew from there to meet my mom and the rest of the kids in Johannesburg where they were staying with our friends. Julia may have traveled with us. I question whether that's true or not. One very brief scene pops into my memory like a frame in a brief video reel. I can see my mom and me sitting at the dining room table in our friends' tasteful, suburban home on the outskirts of the sprawling city.

Cushy, tan carpet pads our feet, and we have bags and documents spread out over the expansive, glass top of the table. She was helping me to think and pack, making sure I didn't forget anything and helping me choose what we should take with us to California. We had no idea where we would live after this and no certainty about what we should do with our worldly belongings. They sat stacked in a corner of our friends' garage packed in totes and waiting as if shipment on a pallet was imminent.

I understood why we had to go back to America for a time. It made logical sense to return to our home country to be with family, heal, and process Chris's death; but the term "Compassionate Leave" just didn't fit what I was feeling. My emotions weren't predictable and washed over me in waves of despair, longing, and something that felt like desperate anger. I was numb to my surroundings, and I couldn't put my finger on what I needed or where I wanted to be. Nothing felt comforting or compassionate. I was lost in the world without Chris, longing for him with no way to bring him back, and the thought of going to America felt like I was somehow leaving him behind. I wanted to stay and just continue my life with him in it, continue what we had started, and stay in the place that had become home to us. I was unexpectedly back in the same place I had been when we left the curb of our old house in San Diego and left for the airport. My life was packed up, and I was dragging my kids along with me to a destination and an itinerary I didn't feel capable of preparing them for.

Our bodies arrived in California safely, but I have no recollection of getting there. All thirty-six hours or so of travel are non-existent in my memory, washed out in an empty space like a chronic, profound case of Highway Hypnosis. I know in my intellect that we somehow got from Johannesburg, South Africa, to an airport in Southern California and that we slept at my mom and step dad's home, but nothing exists in my mind from the journey. Only a couple of recollections return when I try to make sense of the blank spaces. I'm thankful for people who were there for us and took care of us. Some were family and others had entered into our lives like angels in bodily form, providentially placed in a space and time when we needed them. Others were strangers along the way who showed compassion as I broke down and cried in hopelessness at checkpoints and government offices.

There's another spiritual explanation that comes to mind; one that I can't deny. A passage in Scripture I had written down and claimed as a promise from God to us while Chris was in the hospital describes what was going on supernaturally during the months that my brain was elsewhere. He had carried the Israelites through the wilderness in keeping with His promise, and He was carrying me just like He said He would in that familiar verse.

"The Lord your God, who is going before you, will fight for you, as he did for you in Egypt, before your very eyes, and in the wilderness. There you saw how the Lord your God carried you, as a father carries his son, all the way you went until you reached this place."
– Deuteronomy 1:30-31

53 | A Hero's Memorial

"A good character is the best tombstone. Those who loved you and were helped by you will remember you when forget-me-nots have withered. Carve your name on hearts, not on marble."
— *Charles Spurgeon*

I woke up in a hotel room in San Diego on the morning of my husband's funeral to the ironic truth that I was homeless in my hometown. The realization left me feeling lost and vulnerable. Some of the kids were piled into a room with two queen beds with me and a few others were next door with my mom and stepdad. Sandwiched between people who loved me, with four of my high school girlfriends sleeping in the room on the other side, I still felt desperately lonely. Somehow this funeral felt different than the other two memorial services we had already had in South Africa and the village. Soon, I would be face-to-face with people who had known us since our honeymoon, supported us in every major milestone of our lives together, and sent us to Africa.

The thought of looking into their faces felt so intense that it made me want to cry and I wasn't even there yet. I dreaded walking into the church that he helped decorate to sit in chairs he had picked out and hear the songs he had noted in his Bible that he wanted someone to sing "someday at his funeral." How could it be that I was already walking out this journey when we had a whole lifetime of plans?

Flashes of scenes from the day bring enough scattered images to pull together a whole memory of a day I never wanted to live but made it through better than I ever dreamed that we could. The first is sometime early in the morning. As my eyes opened and I was reminded where I was, I focused on each of the kids still sleeping and decided they would be ok if I snuck out and went next door to see my friends. I crept out of the door of my room, eased it closed behind me as quietly as possible, took the two or three steps to the next door, and tapped quietly. As the door opened, my heart was comforted to see four of my lifelong friends opening drowsy eyes to greet me.

"Oh, Meesh! Come here! How are you? What can we do?"

I randomly chose a bed and collapsed into their arms. It wasn't unusual for us to have sleepovers as adults since we had been getting together as much as we could annually since we had graduated from college. That morning, our souls were ageless piled on that bed that was too small to hold all of us, and I felt safe and loved in their presence. They had known me since I was a young teenager, even before I had come to know Christ, and we had been there for each other through many transitions in life. They listened as I poured out my fears for the day. At some point, one of them realized it was time to get ready and said, "I'll help you get the kids up then we can all get ready together. Come on. We can do this!"

Having my tribe with me seemed to snap me into awareness and I was able to rally the strength I needed to get myself dressed and get the kids out the door. It literally took a whole team of people to get us to the church that day and there was an ironic familiarity to the preparations. The fact that people from every season of life were gathered for a special occasion where we were getting ready together made it feel like a wedding, but every step of the process reminded me that this was an event I never wanted to plan, let alone speak at. Each step that I took revealed that I was walking out of my absolute worst case scenario. Before our nightmare had unfolded, I had imagined what it would be like if Chris died; and I never thought I would be able to physically walk, let alone give one of the eulogies. Yet, there we were dressing up and putting on make-up to attend the event we knew we had no choice but to make it through.

The one thing I had no trouble deciding on for that day was my outfit choice. I wore the bright pink, two piece, traditional Basotho dress that he had just made me for Christmas. Each design element of the dress echoed styles we had admired on other local women, and he had picked every detail to flatter my figure. It had been meticulously sewn with a "manual" sewing machine. What that meant practically was that he had to crank a gear with his right hand while guiding the fabric through the presser foot and needle with the other. Every line was precise, and the carefully sewn trim accentuated the tiny print of the fabric that had a cheery orange color that I loved. The combination of colors was one of my favorite combinations, and our friends in the village had been so excited to see me wear a dress so similar to theirs.

In the twilight awareness of shock, a team of people had helped me plan the service, publicize the specifics about where and when it was going to be, and even made the arrangements for the whole thing to be livestreamed for our friends around the world to watch. I think it was Chris's sister who had the idea to invite people to wear garments he had made for them, or bring items he had sewn to be on display in Fellowship Hall for the gathering after the service.

Our church is built on a hill with buildings on seven different levels, so I couldn't see the main sanctuary from where we parked on the top level. We were early, but the parking lot was nearly full. As I walked toward the first set of stairs, the patio came into view, and I had to stop to take in the sight. Every inch of space was taken up with people as they filed into the church or found seats in the overflow chairs outside. Taking a deep breath, I forced myself to enter the throng. I'm thankful for the number of family members and friends that surrounded me, for the magnitude of what I was feeling took every bit of strength and focus that I had. No matter how hard I try, I can't recollect where my kids were in this scene. Were they clinging to me and hiding behind me as we navigated the throng of compassionate friends, or had they been whisked into the front row inside through a side door so that they were shielded from greetings from people they didn't remember?

It was difficult to move forward past people who had been praying for us while we suffered on the other side of the world. Each one was anxious to hug me and express their deep concern for us. Eventually, I made it to the foyer where we had a guest book for people to sign and family members were greeting people as they arrived. Many people in attendance pointed out their outfit choices, dresses, tops, and purses Chris had designed and made for them over the years. With tears in their eyes, they reminded me of special times with him as he had created their special garments. Others pointed out that they were wearing the silver necklace another friend had designed and had manufactured as a fundraiser for the family. The circular, silver pendant had a cut-out of the continent of Africa and was engraved with the words "G8, Victorious, Psalm 91." Many of our friends had been wearing them as a reminder to pray for us.

It must have taken someone else to guide me to the front row to join the kids where they were sitting. Each of us braced ourselves as the service began. By that time, we were well acquainted with the surges of emotions and pain that would wash over us in the next couple of hours. I looked down the line of drawn faces and wished I could take it all away. Just as I was wishing, our pastor began the service. Joseph remembers there being a slide show of our life in Africa and that our friend and worship pastor, Nathan, sang the songs that we had chosen for him to sing. I'll trust him on that, although I have no solid evidence to back it up.

Once the songs concluded, a steady procession of loved ones from all stages of Chris's life came to the podium to describe what he meant to them, to tell stories of experiences they had shared, and to honor him. Without having planned anything together, each person recollected how Chris had made them feel like they were special, how he had accepted them and loved them unconditionally. "He was a one-on-one kind of guy," one of his college friends said.

His older brother, Mike, stepped onto the stage and up to the microphone to briefly describe what he was wearing. He proudly wore the jeans and dress shirt Chris had recently made for himself and they fit him pretty well, despite the pants being a little short. Before moving on with his message, he stepped out where the whole audience could see and did a spin like a model and a little shake of his backside to feature the pocket details on the back pockets. Chris had used the tan thread traditionally used in mass produced jeans to stitch a big "N" in the left pocket and a "T" in the right pocket for his Sesotho initials, "Ntate Thabang." His humor evoked a welcome laugh from the crowd and lightened the mood.

By the time a few people had spoken, it was obvious how much Chris was respected and loved. The standing-room only congregation either sat or stood in silence, tearfully riveted to every word. Nobody mentioned anything negative about him, and at one point one of our kids turned to me and whispered, "Dad wasn't a saint or anything. He wasn't perfect."

As my turn to speak approached, I processed the truth of that statement. Chris was a human just like each of us. There were people in that room who didn't yet know Jesus and the last thing I wanted them to take away from the service was that you had to clean yourself up and achieve a certain level of greatness in order to be loved and saved by God. Thinking intently about what I was going to say engaged my brain and woke me up to the task in front of me. After hearing my name, I stood and stepped up the few stairs to take my place as the last person who would speak. Turning to face the overflowing sanctuary, I scanned the crowd in silence for a long moment. There was one thing my reverse culture-shocked brain couldn't miss, and my filter must have been broken that day, for the first thing out of my mouth was, "Wow. There sure are a lot of white people here."

Thankfully, my comment was met with laughter. These were friends and family who knew we were fresh off the plane from Africa. With the ice broken, I continued with the introductory comments I had just pieced together in my mind before I approached the microphone: "All of the things that were shared today about Chris are true, but the kids and I want you to know that he wasn't perfect. As a matter of fact, he said some bad words... sometimes really bad."

The crowd erupted in laughter. It was important for me to explain to people how they could be forgiven and have a relationship with Jesus like Chris did so that they could have the hope of Heaven. The middle of the eulogy is a blur, but as I remembered my husband, thanked God for him, and honored him as the father of my children and an obedient child of God, I was filled with a sense of gratitude that I had been his wife. The words flowed easily as I read the heartfelt words I had put together for the first testimony of God's faithfulness in my life without Chris. I concluded by asking for prayer for the new season we were walking into,

> *"Please continue to pray for us as we learn to trust God in new ways and learn to live life without Chris. Pray that I will be 'fruitful in the land of my suffering' and, as I continue to serve God in new ways in Africa, that our testimony would be for 'the saving of many lives.'"*

54 | Lonely in Familiar Places

*"We understand death only after it has placed its
hands on someone we love."*
– Anne L. De Staël

By the time we had carried out three
memorial services for Chris in three different countries, the kids and
I were absolutely depleted; but there was one more commemorative
event to carry out in his hometown of Ventura. There were many
people who couldn't make the trip to San Diego, so his family wanted
to have a get-together for the people he grew up with. I was so eager
to be with Chris's parents, to debrief with them, and to be able to
answer all of their questions and simply *be* together, but the idea of
being around a lot of people again was overwhelming. My thoughts
and feelings were all over the place; one moment thankful for the
man I married and the love so many people had for him and the next
just wanting to crawl in a hole and escape everything about the life
I found myself in. I felt like a rag doll being handed from one person
to another until my stuffing was lumpy and my button eyes were
hanging on by a thread.

The gathering was planned more as a reunion than a memorial
service and was held in the backyard garden of his brother's house.
Mike and Debbie's backyard looked out over the hills and a mature,
shady oak tree sat on the north side of the property as a dignified
frame for the edge of the property. The afternoon was planned as
a luncheon, so there was food set out for the guests and a variety
of beverages to choose from. As each person arrived, they greeted
each one of us with a warm embrace, expressed their condolences,
and exchanged the customary questions about how we were doing
and what our plans were. The steady stream of love was heartfelt but

talking about our loss and being reminded of what had happened and the fact that I didn't know our plans felt more like being punched in the gut over and over again. Surrounded by Chris's people in the places where he was most at home made his absence even more glaring. These were his friends and family, the stories and memories were familiar to me, but I was used to hearing them with Chris by my side. When he was there with me where he was supposed to be, and the story would reach the climax, he would turn and put his hand on my arm to make sure he had my attention, and then add an extra detail to drive the hilarity of the story up a notch, and then erupt in laughter, his blue eyes dancing and sparkling. Now, as I looked around, it was the same people, but without the one who connected me to them; I felt lost and confused.

Once everyone had arrived and found their cluster of friends to catch up with, I ended up attempting to shield myself behind the drink table exchanging real feelings with my brother-in-law, Steve, to wait out the night.

One of the deepest joys of my life has been belonging to the Gennaro family, and in Chris's absence, the way they continue to embrace me as their daughter has been a profound comfort. I had been returning to their home for visits for more than half of my life by then, so staying with them felt normal and routine. My relationship with them went beyond that of "in-laws." They were another set of parents to me, confidants, spiritual mentors, models of what a godly marriage that stands the test of time looks like, and a source of unconditional love. That was present as we walked through the doors to stay with them for a week or so to reconnect, grieve together, and debrief all that had transpired over the last couple of years.

The road curves up and around to the edge of their neighborhood before their house comes into view on the left. Looking to the north on the front side of their house, the landscape feels like a life-size diorama, an orchard of mature avocado trees in the foreground, and towering, rolling mountains in the distance. This house was their "retirement downsize" decision, a medium-sized, recently remodeled, three-bedroom ranch-style house with a backyard that was small enough to be manageable.

As we arrived, welcoming lacquered oak double-entry doors with etched glass beckoned us to enter and reminded me that this was one of our safe places. There was no need to knock; we knew we simply had to enter. All it took was a crack in the door and a step over the threshold to alert me to how drastically different this visit would be. Every wall was decorated with family pictures, large-framed wedding photos, collages of each of the families that had grown from their own children. My eyes fell on a new addition to the wall directly adjacent to the entryway—an eleven-by-fourteen print of the picture I had used for Chris's first memorial service in South Africa was blown up to a grainy, super-sized version and framed for prominent display. Seeing his face took the wind out of me and shook me back to weakness. I wasn't sure how I could stay there with his face on every wall. Glancing behind me, I wondered how the kids would respond.

We moved through the living room and down the hallway to find the rooms where we were staying, each of us handling the presence of the pictures differently. I diverted my gaze and walked with my eyes forward fixed on my destination, while others peeked briefly as they took one step at a time down the passageway. The boys peeled off and put their bags down in the first room and I continued to the room at the end of the hall, saying, "Girls, why don't you bring your things in here. Let's have a girls' room and a boys' room. We'll figure out where everyone's sleeping later."

Another blow hit me as I walked into the guestroom. The whole bedroom set that Chris and I had decided to store there was set up and arranged as the room's main furnishings. Even the quilt was the one I had selected for our bed in the house on Mt. Casas. As the only new furniture we had ever invested in, we kept it for both sentimental and practical purposes. We wondered if maybe one of the kids would want it someday. The dark, mahogany colored, shaker style bed, matching dresser, and nightstands stood as a blatant reminder that our someday had arrived in the most unexpected, devastating kind of way. I would never sleep with Chris in that bed again and I couldn't bear the thought of sleeping in it alone. Choking back tears, I uttered the invitation, "Who wants to sleep with me?"

We were all walking into a season of survival, taking one grueling step at a time through a journey we didn't want to take and decisions like those became necessary habits. In many ways, I felt like a terrified child again, shaken and unsure of my surroundings; but I couldn't act on that. I was the mom and I had to keep moving, comfort my kids, have an answer for their questions, and make sure they were safe and fed even though I longed for someone to hold me and comfort me. Emotions filled me like I was going to burst, but I knew there were two people who must have been feeling the same just down the hall. I turned from the room and entered into the time I had set aside to process with my in-laws, the parents who had raised the man I was grieving. It was excruciating to face, but I knew there was no other way to move forward. We fell into the pattern of our normal visits, "Mommars" in the kitchen offering comfort food from scratch, and Papa in the living room perched in a cozy chair where he could view the TV and engage with whichever kids plunked down in the room with him. Everyone knew that Papa would be asking questions like a well-seasoned interviewer, but his genuine interest inevitably drew each one in.

Sleep continued to be impossible no matter where I lay my head, but each day the warm glow of the sun brought welcome permission to rise from a horizontal position in the bed and relocate. My favorite spot at the Gennaro's was either in the backyard or at the breakfast bar where I could look out over the mountains in the distance on the other side of the agricultural valley. I carried my trusty morning companions with me to the spot—my well-worn Bible with notes in the margins and highlights on the passages that had jumped off the page at me, and the journal that was its necessary counterpart. Together, they were my link to God who had promised to be with me no matter where I went.

During the month of many memorials, I was actively processing what it meant to grieve and beginning the overwhelming odyssey of navigating who I was without my husband and learning to live without him. I opened my journal and wrote out my prayer to God.

JOURNAL ENTRY

March 12, 2013

*"Oh, Lord, how I still long for Chris even now that he is in heaven! Teach me how to long for You, Lord. Search my heart, O God, and reveal those parts that I have not surrendered to you. It seems to be the PHYSICAL comfort and companionship that I have always had with Chris that I miss so intensely. In those times, I must cry out to **you** to be my comfort, companion, and "ever-present help."*

As I prayed through my feelings, God responded with clear instructions and a promise that I took to heart. Writing it down so that I wouldn't forget it, I took the words of His promise seriously and realized that this needed to be my posture as I found a new identity and figured out what our life was to look like moving forward.

ENTRY CONTINUED

"These words have shown me where my heart must be focused and WHOM I must seek. (Jeremiah 29: 12-14) 'Then you will call upon me and come and pray to me, and I will listen to you. You will seek me and find me when you seek me with all your heart. I will be found by you, declares the Lord, and will bring you back from captivity.'"

Not only did I have the hope and strength I needed to get through that day, but I had clear direction on how I needed to move forward every day of my new life. And, I had clear promises I could claim from the God who knew my heart: He listens to me, I would indeed find Him when I sought Him with my whole heart, and He would bring me back from this captivity someday.

55 | Moving Forward in Baby Steps

"God's plans and His ways of working out His plans are frequently beyond our ability to fathom and understand.
We must learn to TRUST when we don't understand."
– Jerry Bridges

I had lived with the fear of Chris dying for most of our married life. It wasn't that he was sickly or took unnecessary risks in life-threatening adventures or anything, but rather I simply couldn't picture life without him. His love had always been a firm place to stand, a constant steadiness in a world that presented intense challenges and unexpected tragedies. Logically, then, if he was gone, wouldn't I then be rendered helpless, vulnerable, and unable to function? The answer in my mind was, "Yes, and I would probably just quit everything, pack up, and move to my mommy's."

Logistically, the "packing up everything" had happened and, because we were living on the other side of the world when our worst case scenario unfolded, we *did* end up landing at my mom's house for a time. Julia was living there too, so our time with my mom and stepdad provided the safe landing we needed. I had help with the kids' daily needs, we got to be with Julia, and we had focused time with family. Eventually, though, my days began to feel aimless. Living out of suitcases made me feel like I didn't have my footing and accentuated the fact that we didn't have a home. I began to pray, reached out to my church family, and waited for direction.

I continued my daily, early morning, routine coffee date with my Bible and journal, working out my emotions, fears, and all-consuming feelings by writing them down and praying. The physical exercise of writing things down calmed my brain and helped me process what I was going through more rationally. I was learning my way one little, shaky step at a time.

JOURNAL ENTRY

March 21, 2013

"I am remembering the way I depended on you, LORD, every step of the way while Chris was in the hospital. This discipline, or really "reflex," helped me focus and depend on you. This is a practice that I need to continue in my life – committing every step to you and asking you for strength, not 'wasting' my focus on 'fighting fear.'

One eternal blessing and perspective that I'm seeing is that I am on a 'journey with Christ toward heaven' too! What a comfort to know that I'm headed to the same peace and rest! Now, I must focus on You and take one step at a time on the paths You lead me down."

By the time Easter season rolled around, a unit in our church's mission house opened up. The multilevel property overlooking Mission Bay included a three story, historical home that was converted into two separate living areas. The bottom floor was a two-bedroom, one bath unit, and the two stories above contained a second, three-bedroom unit that was set up for an average-sized family. We weren't average-sized, but it was still somewhere we could unpack our bags in our hometown city. All of the resources we needed to accomplish what we had to do and our main support network were there, so it made the most sense to have that as our base camp until we knew where we were going next.

The fact that the rent was minimal and affordable on the salary I was still receiving as a supported missionary and the use of a minivan was included made the decision easy. As we lugged our bags and totes through the squeaky door of the back porch and into the linoleum-floored kitchen, it was like stepping back in time. Since the house was on the same property as the church, every window looked out to a view packed with memories. I was assaulted with flashbacks from the first glance out of the small kitchen window where the gigantic, two-story fellowship hall building was the only sight. We had just had Chris's memorial service reception there and immediately under that level was the children's area where I had worked for nine years and our kids had gone to preschool, AWANA, and Sunday School.

As I scanned the kitchen to take inventory of where I would be cooking meals and storing food, I noted the gas range, the square tiled countertops, and a large basket of bread items. It was the first sign that someone had already stocked the house with the necessities. Not only would we have running water and indoor bathrooms, but a double-door refrigerator sat near the door of the room. Opening both doors to get a glimpse of the inside, I took in the magnitude of what our friends on our support team had done. The refrigerator, freezer, and pantry were all stocked with food fit for a large family. Warm gratitude eased my spirit and a sense of home and love mingled with the wave of melancholy sadness.

Turning away from that sight, I continued into the small, separate dining room. Since the house was over a hundred years old, each room was a separate compartment that had been modestly updated little by little over the years. Two small bathrooms were added to modernize the house at some point. One was awkwardly situated right off of the dining room, and the other a tiny, closet-sized bathroom with a camp-sized shower off of one of the upstairs bedrooms—the one with the bunk beds. Logistics swirled in my mind as I attempted to assimilate to my new surroundings. The showstopper in the dining room was a large, floor-to-ceiling picture window that looked out to the west. Mission Bay was just across the freeway from where we were, and the expanse of beach communities and the Pacific Ocean spread out in the distance beyond that. The view was stunning, but my emotions tainted the joy as memories of long, early runs with Chris flashed without effort into the forefront of my mind.

There was an L-shaped, living room on two levels with blue, cushy, padded carpet which was furnished with second-hand furniture that had been donated from church members through the years. Paned windows lined every wall of that space, looking out onto the yard and the church parking lot above, allowing a view of the steep hill that went down on the south side of the house, and an expansive panoramic view toward the bay and the ocean to the west.

Climbing the narrow stairs, one creaky step at a time and wrestling my heavy duffle around the turn near the top, I entered the short, narrow hallway that separated three small rooms on the top level. Pausing, I took in the set-up of each room. There were twin beds in the small room to the left, a double bed in the room next to that one, and a king-sized bed in the larger room to the right. And just like that, another reminder of my circumstances slapped me in my face. This house was set up for an in-tact, nuclear family, and I didn't have that anymore. The realization hit me like a powerful jab, but I had to continue to strategize so that I could tell the kids where to put their things.

I had no husband to sleep with me in that bed. There was only one parent in our family now, so I'd have one of my daughters as a bed partner. With two daughters and three sons to squeeze in there, I was having difficulty figuring out how to assign the rooms. It was a puzzle I didn't have the capacity to solve with the wave of grief that had washed over me, and the details are buried in the confusing storm of culture shock, memories, grief, and stress. Somehow, we all had a horizontal surface to sleep on, food to eat, and even gift baskets in every room to temper the whole experience with love and joy. The last scene I can bring back from that first entrance into the mission house is a vision of the kids attacking their personalized gift baskets with the wonder and excitement of Christmas morning.

Later, as I reflected on where we had landed, a sense of gratitude prevailed.

JOURNAL ENTRY

"81" is written at the top of the page. I was keeping track of the number of days I had lived through without Chris.

2 Samuel 7:18-29 "Who am I, O Sovereign Lord, and what is my family, that you have brought me this far?"

I have been overwhelmed, awed really, with how you have "lifted us out of the pit," given us dignity, and allowed our testimony to bring glory to you. That has been my prayer, "For your glory, Lord."
The provision you have given us through the Body of Christ is also beyond my wildest imagination. Truly, you keep your promises! I didn't allow myself to worry, but I was thinking, wondering how we would manage on support in this higher cost of living area. Thank you for placing us on the hearts of your children.

THE TRUTH THAT BROUGHT ME PEACE

"All the days ordained for me were written in your book before one of them came to be."
– Psalm 139:16

If there's one truth about the nature of life on this planet to count on, it's that time just keeps on moving forward. Days don't wait on hurting people to heal before they just press on with their milestones and blaze ahead at lightning speed. Although I wished I could step off of the spinning world and escape all that I was going through, the responsibilities I had kept me accountable to force my body into getting up, getting dressed, and carrying out my motherly duties as best as I could. Before I knew it, our first family birthday arrived. Sicilia turned twelve.

We were in America, the land of commercial wonder, so I figured we should make the most of it. Another benefit of being in San Diego for this in-between time was that I had a network of friends to call on. My "BFF" from church, Lisa, continued to be on the short list of people I felt comfortable calling on no matter what, so I asked her to help me pull off a sleepover and trip to American Girl Place in Los Angeles for the day. Five of Silly's friends who she still kept in touch with joined us at my mom's for a fancy tea party and stopping place between San Diego and Los Angeles. Pictures from the day are graced with big smiles and girly, pink wonder. The celebratory focus of the day brought welcome joy to our heavy hearts, and I carried that perspective into my quiet time in the morning after.

JOURNAL ENTRY

Today, I have been given the greatest gift by God! This truth from His Word that has set me free from thinking I could have changed the timing and/or outcome of Chris's Home-going.

(According to Psalm 139:16), even before Chris was born, God had ordained the number of Chris's days. I didn't know how many he would get to have on this earth when I committed to be with him for the rest of his life, but we fulfilled that promise.

Now, I can look at those days, his last ones, with new eyes. I can be thankful for the meaning and guidance from God that each contained. And, while I can't see the purpose of the traumatic, disturbing days at that scary national hospital, I know God had some purpose that I may never see, and that He is even working that one for the good. I know that a battle was fought there and that Chris and I were victorious – GOD was victorious!

And, what an awesome privilege it was to share Chris's life with him, even helping him through those last days and committing him to the loving God who made him and numbered his days.

56 | Discerning Next Steps

*"When our days become dreary with low-hovering clouds of despair,
and when our nights become darker than a thousand midnights,
let us remember that there is a
creative force in this universe, working to pull down the gigantic
mountains of evil, a power that is able to
make a way out of no way and transform
dark yesterdays into bright tomorrows."*
– *Martin Luther King Jr.*

The melding of that very specific desire to continue to do good and the prayer I was praying for God to lead me where HE would have me go eventually drew my mind back to that warm, poolside room in South Africa. The brainstorming session where Olivia offered up the news of an English position open at the boarding school wasn't just a memory; I now knew that it was a stepping stone in the new path God was marking out for us. Ryan and Heather's dream-like vision of us living and serving at the school with them had been more of a providential peak than just a random, passing thought. As we lived out our days in a new limbo of grief, disoriented transition, and the confusing reality that we were back in San Diego when we were supposed to be in Lesotho still made me feel like the only thing that made sense was returning to Africa.

When we pulled away from the curb of our family home in San Diego in 2011, we had left for the rest of our careers. Although we didn't know exactly how long that would be, we had committed to serve in Lesotho until the work was done. We would be "finishers" as they call it, giving the rest of our careers to make sure the Gospel took root in that place. Now, only two years later, it didn't make any sense to quit. My spirit was still sold out for the call we had responded to, "Go! Get on board!"

Thankfully, I wasn't in a place where I had the freedom to just frivolously drop everything and switch countries on a whim of my own. I was still accountable to the requirements of the organization, my trusted church leadership, and our families who were doing their best to support me and give me freedom to find my way in this new normal. All seven of us had to have counseling and I willingly allowed for communication between our counselors and those who were walking with me to determine if and when we may be ready to move again. The four older kids and I saw one counselor that was just down the hill on the edge of the nearest beach community, and Joseph and Duane saw a child psychologist almost thirty minutes to the east.

If that would have been our only focus during that time, it would have been grueling by itself. We were trying to fit in weekly sessions for all of us and most of the kids felt more comfortable if I was with them. That meant that we were facing our trauma and grief head on in emotionally exhausting counseling sessions on nearly every day of the week. Then, with no capacity to curl up in a ball anywhere, we'd reward ourselves with a special drink from the nearby 7-Eleven, McDonald's, or Starbucks if it was a really hard day, and press on to the next responsibility.

Although Julia was living with my mom and stepdad, she and I worked together on her next move, applying for college after almost two years off. Later, she would tell people that "she took a gap year *and* a sabbatical" after high school. It may have been unconventional, but it was consistent with our plot-twist-filled life. We had to go back in time to get her transcript and navigate federal forms we'd never filled out with bits and pieces of information because we'd been out of the country for two years and didn't even have a real address to report. As we filled out the college application, I prayed that God would miraculously pull all of that together into a plan and direction for her next few years. Her acceptance to a Christian university in Southern California revealed the next steps for my first-born and we chalked that up as a huge answer to prayer.

As I navigated life insurance forms, the FAFSA, a college application, international forms to get Chris's death certificate, and changing the primary account holder on every single account, there seemed to be no end in sight to the trail of legal forms I had to fill out. By the end of March, I declared in a Facebook Post,

"I think my new job is 'paperwork do-er.' Whew."

An aerial photo of our lives during that time would have probably looked like a jigsaw puzzle that had fallen to the floor and broken into thousands of pieces. I would wake up every day bleary-eyed from lack of sleep, creep down the squeaky stairs, strategically missing the spot with the loudest creak so that I wouldn't wake up the kids, and face a new day of trying to put a couple of those pieces back together. It seemed like each necessary step required more documentation, another office visit, or a piece of paperwork that I couldn't locate. With my life divided between continents, it felt impossible to make all of those decisions on my own.

Providentially, I had a close friend who was ahead of me on the journey. She had joined the "Club Nobody Ever Wants to Be a Part Of" when her beloved husband, and father to her four children, passed away instantly in his early forties. At Chris's San Diego memorial service, she handed me a book titled *From One Widow to Another*. She had caught me up in a huge hug after the service, taken my shoulders in her hands, looked me in the eyes, and said, "You'll be given a lot of books to read. Most of them are for people much older than us. Read this one first."

I tucked it into my bag that day and placed it on the top of the stack of books I was quickly acquiring. I was in no mood to read anything but my Bible during that time. My thoughts and emotions were so intense that it seemed like I had to re-read paragraphs three or four times to comprehend anything. I'd start the book, read the first couple of pages a few times, and then set it down in frustration. As the decisions mounted, though, I was desperate for help navigating everything, and I picked up the book to see if it would offer anything helpful. I couldn't put it down. It was as if the author was in my head. She got it. She had done what I was

313

doing, and she knew what it felt like. I knew I could trust what she was advising to women in our situation.

She contrasted decision-making with a husband to the process of making decisions as a new widow. When you have a whole life to run by yourself, you need people for wise counsel that you can trust and go to for advice in each area of your life. "Think of it as your board of directors," she suggested. "Picture yourself in a boardroom with a large table of empty chairs to fill. Who, besides family, do you trust to help you in all of the areas of your life where your husband used to function?"

It wasn't that family couldn't be a part of your support network, she explained, but those relationships should be protected from the business of finances and other things that may cause conflict. As I pondered her suggestion, it made sense to me. I scratched out on paper the people I wanted to contact to fill those chairs and began to assemble my board of directors. The man in my life was gone and it was a relief to think of having trusted men and women who I knew I could count on ready and willing to help me in the ways they were most gifted. Once they were all in place, I was better able to garner the strength for one decision at a time.

With the supernatural strength I was promised, I plodded through each list with methodical prayers and hesitant determination. It felt foreign to navigate decisions and government offices by myself, but I knew that I had to leave no stone unturned in the process of forging ahead. Every little jigsaw piece of my life that lay broken on the floor had to be put back in its place: finances, job, ministry, education for the kids, where we would live, transportation, and even communication. The cell phones we were using in Africa weren't even working properly where we were in California. Then, to top it all off, Chris was listed as the primary account holder on most of our accounts and I had to have an *original* death certificate in order to get access. Since he had died in another country that meant international phone calls finding the right person to talk to in the American consulate in South Africa, and waiting.

One gargantuan saving grace came in the form of a distant recollection of a piece of mail that showed up every year in the form of a Social Security statement. One line kept coming back to me. Now that our life had taken this unexpected turn, I was compelled to pursue it: "Death benefits for your family if you were to die this year."

As a woman in her early forties, I remember opening that, scanning through the numbers, and thinking toward retirement benefits. The notice about death got skipped over as if it wasn't even possible; but as a widow with six kids, the line flew through my mind like one of those huge banners that flies behind the planes over the beach in the height of summer. I had to investigate.

I made an appointment at the office on the ground floor of a tall office building in downtown San Diego and took a break from homeschooling to meet with someone there. I had one question for them on that day: "Are there any benefits for us that I should know about?"

By this time in my life I wasn't a stranger to federal offices and knew what my role should be. Take a number, be polite, sit down, and wait. I had no doubt in my mind that once I was called in for my chance to get answers to my questions that the next steps would be to expect delays, fill out more paperwork, and wait some more. I was terribly wrong. That statement I had disregarded every year of our adult lives was completely accurate. My children were entitled to survivor benefits until they graduated from high school! The number sounded too good to be true. It would double my missionary salary and allow me to afford what we needed to live!

A couple of days after that paperwork Facebook post, I was able to declare the fruits of my labor and the answer to many prayers,

"Counting blessings: Mission House, awesome partnership team, and tax return! I am now TOTALLY DEBT FREE!"

"So then, those who suffer according to God's will should commit themselves to their faithful Creator and continue to do good."
– 1 Peter 4:19

On the same day that I received "the truth that brought me peace" from Psalm 139:16, I had prayed this very specific prayer,

"LORD, I do commit myself and my future to you. I want to continue to do good and to participate in your work for the Nations. Lead me to where YOU would have me and be able to work most effectively for YOUR glory. I trust you to match it with what is best for all of us.

I say YES to you and what you are doing in my life. Help me to focus on you and what You have for me today... For your glory."

I had said "yes" to what God was doing in my life and He was showing up in *big* ways. Opportunities to speak were pouring in and I had a hard time saying no to them. After all, I had penned my heart's desires to God and asked Him to help me steward our testimony well. When people asked me to do that, I saw it as an open door and walked straight into it without hesitation. As I worked through all of the counseling, spent mornings in the Word, and added speaking preparation to my brain "exercises," it was as if I could almost begin to see God writing our story.

Unfortunately, I couldn't linger in those moments. Five of my kids were still legally obligated to be working on their education. Olivia was midway through her high school term and had to prove she was completing competencies in order to fulfill requirements for graduation the very next year. Other people who had to be away from the boarding school for a term had used an on-line high school, so the same thing was recommended to us. It took both of us working together to try to navigate three different time zones and a new program to turn in her work. Then, there were huge delays in hearing back from the teacher, delayed responses to our questions, and more calls to administrators I didn't know to advocate for my stressed out daughter. With limited emotional capacity, it was too much for us to bear.

At the same time Olivia and I were fighting that educational battle, there were four other kids who should have been learning something. I had the notebook of my carefully planned out homeschooling lessons that we tried to follow and work through, but it seemed that each of us took turns melting down when we all sat down at the table to try to focus. I was attempting to hold my children accountable to learn things that I myself felt were trivial in light of all we were going through. In the grand scheme of eternal, life-shattering events, who cared about a math problem? Eventually, together with the counseling department at the boarding school, we came up with a Plan B that allowed Olivia to quit the on-line learning platform and finish up basic requirements for her junior year. Summer was approaching and we were all desperate to tap out of the educational battle and breathe. In a unilaterally unanimous decision, we declared that the kids had learned all they needed to know that year and I pronounced the school year *over*.

We threw ourselves into youth activities, beach days, time with family, and maintained our emotionally heavy therapy sessions while I continued to pray that God would direct me to the place that was best for *all* of us. It must have been around that same time that the desire and idea to teach at the boarding school moved to the forefront of my mind and emerged as an answer to that prayer, becoming a tentative plan rather than just a vision. Yet, there were things that had to happen before we were cleared to go. We all had to have the "green light" from our counselors, and my support had to be sufficient to maintain us for at least two more years in Africa.

The top of the pages of my journal read more like a travel diary as we hit the road to spend time with family and friends, to connect with supporters, and to fulfill the requests to speak at different locations: Santa Cruz, Palo Alto, Mexico, Peachtree City, Santa Paula... Getting everything done each day made me feel like I was running an eternal marathon and sleep continued to elude me. Still, time passed, and milestones came and went. Jed's birthday, my birthday, Mother's day, and eventually Chris's birthday arrived. It would be the first one of his special days that we would have to navigate without him. I continued to find my footing in the Word and journaling my thoughts and prayers.

JOURNAL ENTRY

June 9, 2013

The first of Chris's birthdays in Heaven

LORD, ever since Chris entered my life, our love was such a primary focus. That's a good thing, I know. What a blessing to have loved AND been loved like that. I realize, though, in Chris's absence, that I'm sure there were many seasons when my love for Chris took the forefront. Teach me how to put You in that place. You are teaching me that as I commit each day to you. I do want to be "radiant with YOUR presence, nothing of my own, but only You on the throne."

57 | Direction

"But you, O God, do see trouble and grief; you consider it to take it in hand. The victim commits himself to you; you are a helper of the fatherless. You hear, O Lord, the desire of the afflicted; you encourage them, and you listen to their cry, defending the fatherless and the oppressed, in order that man, who is of the earth, may terrify no more."
– Psalm 10:14

I had walked through other seasons of waiting and discerning before, but this one felt so different. Navigating the transition we were in and living in limbo without my partner in life required me to trust God, and others, in ways that were uncomfortable and foreign to me. When the next step in the process of decision-making came in the form of a trip to our home office in Georgia, I knew I couldn't do it alone. I just didn't have the courage or emotional fortitude to get on a plane by myself and return to our organization's home office to process Chris's death without back-up.

The first person I thought of was my BFF from church, Lisa. We had always been a dynamic duo, especially in serving, parenting, and praying together, and we were used to walking through tough things together. Her steady, predictable ways brought stability when my own emotions were swirling all over the place. Lisa was always willing to go with me. She'd sit contentedly crocheting or knitting the time away while listening and observing. At the end of the day, she was a patient, listening ear for my overabundant, emotionally charged words.

It was my first time to the offices in Georgia because the organization had moved while we were in Africa. The drive from the airport in Atlanta to the hotel near the office was beautiful, with lush, green, tree-lined highways all along the way. As we arrived at the hotel and walked toward the wall of glass doors, the two center ones automatically swooshed open to welcome us in, and a deep voice called out, "Welcome in!"

Lisa and I noticed a couple of golf carts parked outside as we exited the taxi, and in a rush of sudden spontaneity, I blurted out my question like a kid in a toy store, "Hi! Are those golf carts for guests to use? Can we drive one?!"

"Yep, they sure are! Let's get you checked in and I'll tell you what you can do."

Once we dropped our bags in the room and freshened up, we took advantage of the guest golf carts and headed out on an adventure to get the lay of the land and find something to eat. Somehow, as I drove that little vehicle, my inner child awakened, and a latent feeling of joy rose up in me. We traveled the winding cart paths through the dignified neighborhoods marveling at their resemblance to Wisteria Lane, the neighborhood from the popular TV drama, *Desperate Housewives*. Narrow little roads connected the whole city and outlined lakes and streams. The cart paths backed up to houses three times bigger than the ones we were used to in our middle class, Southern California neighborhood. Whisking through the woods with the wind in my hair and giggling with my friend felt rejuvenating and prepared my spirit for the upcoming meetings.

The next morning, we were shuttled to the office by the hotel shuttle and dropped off at the two-story office building nestled in a business loop of professional buildings with distinguished, stately columns in the front and woodsy backgrounds of mature, green trees all around. I hit the button to request entrance and, as we were buzzed in, I took a deep breath to summon my courage. These people knew my story, for they had known Chris and me from the beginning of our missions journey and had walked with me through the worst of my days from a distance. "Michelle! Come in! We've been praying for you!"

My prayers had been specific: "MAKE THE WAY CLEAR." As I found myself sitting in a corner office across from the U.S. director of our organization to discuss the official decision, my insides felt squirmy and nauseous. This was the conversation that would determine our next season of life and I felt the weight of it tingling in every extremity. My hands were clasped in my lap and the clamminess built as we went through the usual pleasantries before getting to the heart of it. Wade had been appointed to his position while we were living in Africa, so I hadn't had an opportunity to meet him in person yet. Still, his soothing, deep voice expressed his interest in slow, intentional phrases that I could focus on easily. "It's so good to finally meet you, Michelle. Tell me, how are each of your kids? You have six, right?"

I went down the list for him and gave a brief update on each one. I was used to answering that question for others, so I started off by stating the disclaimer, "Each one of them is unique, as you know. They process their grief differently."

"Julia has been accepted to a Christian university in Southern California where she has good friends. She'll be moving into the dorms soon. Olivia has finished her requirements for her junior year and has gotten quite good at playing the ukulele. The four younger kids were homeschooling, but we finished that for the year, and they've been enjoying time with family and friends this summer. Jed is a young man now. He turned fourteen in April. He's been spending time with friends, and has learned how to play the guitar. Sicilia is twelve and is finding joy in our baby monarch butterflies. Each of them has had an opportunity to go to camps and retreats with our church. Joseph and Duane were old enough to attend a small, Christian summer camp in the local mountains with other kids from our church. It's been a busy summer."

The conversation flowed through all of the key areas of our life without feeling like I was being grilled. His genuine care and interest calmed me as we came to the part I was waiting for—the final confirmation about our plans for Kenya. It was clear that we had already been prayed for faithfully, for each aspect of our future had already been considered in detail. As I let out a deep breath of release, I summed up the direction I perceived was from God.

As the summer days had ticked by, our monthly financial support had continued to increase until the amount we needed to be sustainable on the field exceeded one hundred percent. Our counselors had also confirmed that they believed we were processing our grief in a healthy way and had the capacity to move and thrive with a plan that would include a move to Kenya where I would teach, and the five kids would go to school. Our organization had counselors both at the school site and at the full-service counseling center we had in Nairobi. It was staffed with psychologists and professional marriage and family counselors who would be nearby to support us if necessary. Julia would already be living in the dorms and adapting to her new life at her university. The rest of our possessions that were being stored in Johannesburg would be shipped to us in Kenya. The way seemed clear to me, but the decision ultimately didn't rest in my hands. Before we moved to Lesotho, we had placed our trust in the leadership there and they were a critical part of the safety net God had provided for me.

Once we had weighed each consideration, there was a long pause as Wade's head calmly tilted to the side as his compassion-filled eyes rested on me. Eventually, he agreed that it seemed evident that God was making a way for us to return to Africa, but that he would continue to check on all of us along the way. He reminded me that the organization cared about the whole family, and if even one member was having difficulty, we would reconsider.

My physical response was a feeling of relief and exuberance. I had been living in the tension of feeling disoriented and unsettled, and this was the clear direction I had been praying for. I can picture Lisa and I reclining on our own queen beds in the hotel room later that night talking through each minute detail of the conversation. Her hands moved rhythmically as she listened, her knitting needles clicking and clacking as the colorful yarn magically found its place in the design. I didn't have Chris with me, but God had kept His promise to go before me, guide me, and provide for me. I had a friend by my side and our way was clear.

With my new assignment confirmed and a departure date set, I set about preparing the family for more international travel and another gargantuan cross-country move. There were still way too many things to be done for one person to handle, so my focus on grounding myself in the Word in the morning and asking for more of God's presence in the midst of all of it continued. I was so afraid to be still and sit in the truth and pain of Chris being gone forever. Going back to Africa where we had planned on being for the next long season of our lives gave me a sense that I was continuing with the plans we had made together and that made me feel closer to him.

JOURNAL ENTRY

July 21, 2013
Mission House, San Diego

"Trust in the LORD with ALL your heart and lean not on your own understanding. IN ALL your ways acknowledge Him, and HE will make your paths straight."
— Proverbs 3:5

This season of compassionate leave has been so busy and hectic. The doing, doing, doing has kept me busy and given me purpose, though. As things start to wind down and we finish up here, I have been thinking about a slower pace and bracing myself for a new wave of grief to hit.

So, Lord, I want to commit that to you and claim this verse from Isaiah. I am taking note (once again) that the rest and quietness must be focused on you and quieting myself in your Presence. If the down times are committed to You and 'relaxing in Your company,' it won't be painful, but it will renew my strength. May it be so, LORD, in Jesus' name.

"In repentance and rest is your salvation.
In quietness and trust is your strength."
— Isaiah 30:15

58 | All Systems Go

"When He allows us to get to the very end of what is humanly possible and then works in and through us, he takes us, or allows us, 'crises of belief' and then shows up powerful and glorious."
– (from a sermon study on John 11)

Although I had been reminded by God numerous times to be still and quiet, I continued to live with a voracious "seize the day" mentality. I'm sure there were a number of dynamics at play that kept me going from one event to another, cramming visits in with people from every season of life, and squeezing in time with family as much as we could. Having plans and being with people helped with the loneliness and gave us all something to look forward to.

Languishing indoors in a house that wasn't ours brought little comfort and time spent with friends and family was more effective at boosting our spirits, so I continued to pack our social calendar. Besides that, now that we had a solid departure date to move to Kenya, I felt like a short timer. My brain shifted into a mode of preparedness and the doing gave my brain something productive to focus on. My camera roll is filled with pictures of me with college friends, Joseph and Duane with friends who had also been adopted from the same orphanage, a group of us at a wedding, and all of us lying on a beach at a lake in the mountains with the Gennaro family.

I documented updates on social media for those who were keeping track of our journey, praying, and supporting us as we took steps moving forward.

FACEBOOK POST

July 26, 2013

"Said goodbye to sweet friends who have been with us this week, travel vaccines, positive TB test (Joseph - because of a vaccine as an infant), chest x-ray for him, last Wal-Mart stock-up, picked up prescriptions for the next year, pack for mini-vac with Gennaro's AND be ready to pack up for Africa in one day. Yikes."

That "pack up for Africa in one day" part sounds crazy, but at the time I was just thinking that we needed to put all of our clothes back in our luggage. We had only been bunking in the mission house for four months and it still felt temporary, like we were living out of our suitcases. With no household items or furniture to contend with, I just thought, "We'll throw everything back in the bags and head out."

As the sun came up on our last day in San Diego, there were still people on my list that I hadn't seen, and I felt constrained to see as many of our supporters and prayer warriors as possible before we moved again. The plan I came up with accomplished that, but my foggy trauma brain had grossly underestimated the task before me. Thankfully, just like the last time we left San Diego for Africa, I had faithful back up. My mom and my loyal sidekick, Lisa, jumped in as extensions of myself and took it upon themselves to do what they saw needed to be done.

The mood in the house felt like a going away party. As I hovered in the kitchen and dining room cleaning my way out of the pantry, refrigerator, and the drawers we had been storing school supplies in, friends entered through the back door. Each time a new person crossed the threshold, it was a mini reunion, so I would stop what I was doing, embrace whomever had stopped by, show them around a little, and then get back to what I was doing. If someone asked if they could help, I pushed back any discomfort I had about the mess and gave them something to accomplish. The kids were fluttering in and out, too, going back and forth between taking last spins on their scooters and packing up their belongings from the rooms upstairs.

Occasionally, I'd call out a reminder, "Don't forget that whatever you leave behind will stay here and you won't have it in Kenya!"

Eventually, when the storm of activity calmed and only the kids and I remained with my mom and stepdad, our belongings were safely tucked into various closed containers and stowed in the back of the truck for the hour-long drive to my mom's house. I knew I'd have a few days there to organize each bag and re-evaluate what needed to go and what could be left behind. The creaky, aged house was quiet again and I did one last walk-through to make sure we had everything. As I entered each furnished room and looked around, memories of the summer returned to me, and as the reflective thoughts flooded in, I talked to God about all that I was processing:

"What a CRAZY idea to have an open house on my last day in San Diego! It WAS good to have a chance to connect with all of those people, though. What wonderful, amazing supporters, senders, and friends they are! How I praise you for the way you have designed your Bride, the church.

Even with the chaos, I can't say I regret it. I would probably not try to mix the work and the good-byes, but it WAS wonderful that people were able to help. All of the tasks were completed! That was so wonderful.

It is still pretty awe-inspiring for me to experience being held and carried by You. Thank you that I don't have any nervousness or anxiety, but just excitement for what you have ahead for us. I have this wonderful sense that something really special awaits us at the school in Kenya."

My parents' house served as a launching pad for us during those times of transition. Without a home to go back and forth to, it added at least a little bit of stability to the chaotic, nomadic life we were living. As we arrived there with our cargo, their two-story, professionally cleaned, well-appointed suburban So-Cal home for two transformed into a temporary camp for travelers. Every room upstairs had open duffles and suitcases in it with their guts spread out across the creamy white carpeting. With our travel date days away, I went from room to room checking bags, touching every item to determine if it was needed enough to be placed back in the bag to be weighed. Each piece of luggage had to be precisely forty-nine pounds to allow for any difference in the scales between the airport's and mine. I used the handle scale to weigh each one before I closed and zip-tied them. Running my hand across the closure in a gesture of finality, I double-checked that each piece was labeled with our future address in Kenya.

Those last couple of nights were late ones as I pushed myself to be ready for our impending travel. The three boys were sleeping in Joe's "man cave" across the hall and the adjacent room. My mom and I tucked Joseph and Duane into the cozy beds she had made for them on the floor with cushions from the patio furniture and puffy comforters she had pulled from the hall cabinets as additional padding and covers. Jed's bed was in the room next to theirs, his growing teenage frame spread out on the mattress of the pull-out couch-bed. As we said our goodnights and left them to sleep through their last night in California, I heaved the unfinished bags out of the rooms into the hallway to continue my task after they had gone to sleep.

There were rooms enough for all of the girls to have a bed, so they retired for the evening to their own spaces and, eventually, I was left by myself to finish up. There in the darkness, the truth of my reality was obvious. It was just me and the kids now. At the end of the day, the responsibility of all of this was on me. As I sat on the floor surrounded by bags, thoughts of Chris flooded my mind, and I couldn't hold back silent tears. Life without him felt twice as hard, but I didn't want to be stuck in the sadness of it. I was ready to step into my next job and pour myself into something purposeful. Stacks of zip-locked supplies and unfolded clothes reminded me that there were things to be done and sleep had to wait. With one last push, I finished the packing puzzle and sealed everything up. The next day was the day I'd been praying for.

The travel nerves that woke me early were familiar. I'd been feeling those since I was a kid. On nights before we went on vacation or drove to Disneyland, I wrestled with sleep and laid awake with anticipation. My mom and the kids were gathered in the kitchen putting together breakfast, so I went around the room throwing one arm around each person's shoulder for a good morning squeeze. When I got to my mom, I whispered, "Thanks, Mom."

With my steaming cup of morning coffee in hand, I left them to make breakfast together and found my usual seat in the dining room for one last quiet time.

JOURNAL ENTRY

Lord, thank you for the healing work you have done in our hearts these last five months. To come to this day and not feel sorrowful to leave, but excited. No nervousness. No anxiety in leaving. That's totally YOU, a confirmation that we are headed exactly where you want us to be.

Prepare the hearts of our parents to do this again.

Thank you for the way you have blessed these times I have had with you. You TRULY have been powerfully present in these quiet times. I have sensed you calling to me in the mornings and You have met me here in such special ways. This time with you is so precious. Continue to help me to find this hour in the mornings – even with our new schedule.

"Surely you have granted me ETERNAL blessings and made me glad with the JOY of your presence."
– Psalm 21:6

The very last blank page of my journal from that year has a providential idea prominently written in the very middle of the page like it's the cover of a book. The idea I wrote there popped into my mind in the summer of 2013 and then lay dormant for eight years until I FINALLY quieted myself, rested, and began to write. Uncovering it in the process of actually writing this memoir makes me realize that when it was noted there, I had no idea what chapters God would write in the days ahead.

A New Surrender

Finding God faithful in my worst-case scenario
(integrate e-mails, posts, etc.)

59 | Landing in Kenya

*"Not quite understanding how. He knew what he
needed to do. He didn't get it. The feeling - the epiphany - was
a strange one. Foreign and familiar at the same time. But it
felt... RIGHT."*
— James Dashner

The miracle of God's creative design for
our brains has clouded the details of arriving in Nairobi that morning
so that, considering the circumstances I am about to describe, the
snapshots that remain are strangely calm and positive. With the
help of hindsight, I can attribute that to our missionary training that
included courses and books about language and culture acquisition
and contingency planning. We had digested lessons about how
to assimilate to a new culture and thrive and what to do in an
emergency. Living in Lesotho had been the lab for those studies,
and it was as if we were entering the next seminar.

In the first scene of memory, we're still on the plane circling over
Mount Kilimanjaro but not quite to Nairobi. As the pilot gave the first
announcement over the speaker, the title to one of the books from
our training came to mind, *Foreign to Familiar*. It must have been
either a certain level of preparedness or the desensitization of years
of travel back and forth to Africa that made me shrug off concern as
the pilot voiced the delay, "There are delays on the ground at Jomo
Kenyatta International Airport in Nairobi. We'll need to circle here
in a holding pattern and may need to land at Kilimanjaro for fuel.
Please stay in your seats with your seatbelts fastened."

In the end, we didn't need to land in Tanzania for fuel and were
able to touch down in Nairobi safely. The plane was parked at a
different part of the airport and, after deplaning in the open air,
all of the passengers were guided through an alternate route that
eventually landed us in a temporary, make-shift arrival area where

they could check our documents. I have no idea how late we were by this time, but I know that the kids and I were methodically moving through each step with routine deliberateness.

As all six of us approached the immigration agent, Jed volunteered to go first. I handed over the yellow form and his passport, opened it to the page with his picture, and it was checked and stamped. Once that stamp slammed onto the page, he handed it over to me and said, "I'll go look for our luggage."

Up to this day, Jed would describe himself as someone who doesn't like to travel. He has always gotten anxious about potential delays and long, exhausting stretches of time without sleep. It must have been the honorable necessity of his mom needing help that pushed all of that to the side as we arrived in Kenya. As soon as we hit the line for immigration, he transformed into a strong, valiant luggage rustler. By the time the rest of us found him by the baggage carousel, he had started a pile of our bags and was calling out instructions to his siblings. As Olivia stood by the belt nearby waiting to muscle totes and suitcases over to us, I could hear Jed's adolescent voice above the crowd: "Someone grab some more of those luggage carts. There's another one of our bags! Silly can you get that one?"

With our maximum allotment of twelve bags loaded up on multiple luggage carts and Joseph and Duane each clinging to one of the carts, we navigated the crowds toward the exit. The next scene that immediately shows up in my mind is a vision of the five younger kids and I crowded into the taxi van from our organization's guesthouse, chatting joyfully with George, our driver and friend at the wheel. His huge smile had welcomed us with the familiar sign, and in those first minutes in the van, his deep voice and cheery accent welcomed us back to Africa. He cared enough about us to have kept track of our journey up to this point and asked about our time in America. As we took that first, long curve away from the terminal, I looked off to the left toward the open grasslands and spotted a giraffe grazing in the distance. Smoky air wafted in through the cracked windows and the chill of the early morning reminded me where we were.

My involuntary reaction to that reminder is what I remember most from that morning. As I looked out at the billboards that advertised a myriad of products available that weren't "Made in the USA," my spirit rose with a realization: "I'm home." Although that sense would rise and fall with our circumstances over the next couple of years, that first feeling gave me the confidence that we were where we were meant to be for that season. A new home we had never seen awaited us and we were filled with anticipation.

Another miracle was at play with this move to the boarding school and our new season of life: the generous love of friends. Ryan and Heather had pictured us living and serving in Kijabe less than a year previously and had sprung into action to help us settle once the vision came to pass. As other families transitioned out of life there for various reasons, our sweet friends had purchased used furniture and arranged for rented furniture from the surplus on station to set up our basic household. Throughout the last month or so, Heather had been working tirelessly to search for just the right pieces, send me photos of her finds, and then they had moved everything in for us. By the end of that first day, we had settled into our own house with full bellies. News updates explained the delays we had experienced at the airport that morning. Headlines in international newspapers around the world reported:

"Nairobi airport evacuated due to 'severe' fire"

Huge fire destroys Nairobi airport terminal

Jomo Kenyatta International airport reopens for some flights, after fire engulfs arrivals hall.

Kenya airport fire: 'arrivals hall and offices destroyed', minister says

A remarkable combination of emotions flooded me as I entered each room and helped the kids settle into their new rooms for their first bedtime in Kenya. There was gratitude for our safety and the abundant, generous provision of the home that was already set up for us. Each of us had beds to sleep on that very first night: a queen-sized bed for me in the upstairs master room, bunk beds for Joseph and Duane across the hall, another set of bunk beds in Silly's room with drawers for storage underneath, and private rooms for both Olivia and Jed on the ground floor. It was the largest home I had ever lived in, and my mind swirled with the irony and wonder of it. It wasn't fancy or updated; it was a stone house with dark brown, parquet, hardwood floors, a musty smell from the dampness of the jungle right above us, and an outdated kitchen, but it was safe and comfortable. Just as my mind wandered toward the fact that I had my own room and would be alone in it in the unfamiliar newness of the place, Silly approached me with a tentative question: "Can I sleep with you? I don't want to sleep alone."

"Of course. I think I'd like that too."

"Those who sow in tears will reap with songs of joy.
He who goes out weeping, carrying seed to sow, will return with
songs of joy, carrying sheaves with him/her."
– Psalm 126:5-6

Our adjustment to life at RVA was quick. We had close friends there already, so it felt like we had family with us. Olivia was where she wanted to be and could have her senior year of high school with her friends. She admitted that it wasn't as fun being a "station kid" as it was being in the dorm, but she was glad to be back in so many ways. She also had to tolerate having her mom as her English 12 teacher. She recommended me for the job after all!

Besides the intensity of my grief, it's clear in looking back that my next greatest burden was being away from Julia. Day after day, I prayed for her transitions to life in college, her roommate situation, her healing, her spiritual life, and every single other thing that came to mind whether she had shared it with me or not. Having Chris in Heaven and Julia in California made it feel like we had lost our sense of family. Life at home felt weird and forced without two of our family members. They were always on our minds and my family members who were so far away were the main ones in my prayers.

As with any other cross-cultural move, there were new things to experience. We had moved onto a 90-acre campus with other staff members and their families and were awaiting the arrival of hundreds of students who would fill the dorms and bring the campus to life. The school was over a hundred years old, so there were signs of its history wherever you looked, even in our home. One afternoon, after running through the kitchen from the backyard, Joseph and Duane were stopped in their tracks by a strange ringing sound. It was coming from a clunky, tan-colored device on the narrow kitchen counter on the far end of the room. They slowed their steps as the ringing continued. Entertained by their curiosity, I let it ring and watched as they inched closer. "Do you know what that is?"

Both of them replied quickly as their eyes remained on the source of the repeating sound, "No."

"It's a phone! Watch."

"Hello. This is Michelle Gennaro."

They stood staring at me as I listened to my colleague who was checking to see if we needed anything. We said goodbye and I hung up the receiver to continue my lesson on how to use a landline phone. It was hard to believe my young sons had never seen one and I couldn't hold back my smile as I showed them how to use it. "Look! You can use this list to find the number and then push these buttons to call their house. Always make sure to tell them who you are and say please and thank you. If you ever hear it ringing, you always answer like this 'Gennaro's, this is Joseph,' or 'Gennaro's, this is Duane.'"

Besides the usual chances to adapt and orient ourselves to our surroundings, living on the school campus provided plenty of opportunities to pour ourselves into activities, both academically and socially. Lesson planning, teaching, grading countless essays, parenting, adapting to the culture and way of life in Kenya, hiring help and getting to know them, becoming acquainted with our neighbors and community, and the seemingly endless social opportunities kept our days full of purpose and distracted by busyness. At the end of the day, though, when the sun went down over our house tucked up against the forest, silence haunted me, and my pain resurfaced. Sleep didn't come without taking the over the counter sleep aids that the nurses had prescribed months before when Chris was still in the hospital. Silly continued to sleep with me as a comfort to both of us. We were broken but hobbling forward in a safe place.

It wasn't difficult to have extended quiet times in the morning. I couldn't sleep most nights anyway. The comfort and guidance that came from that time was often the thing that roused me from bed and helped me face getting up to more solitude. The house was dark and quiet early in the morning as the sun's light hadn't yet risen over the distant mountains. A soft, gray glow illuminated the curtains just enough to see my way from the room without turning on a light to wake Silly. Creeping down the hall, I could now anticipate the three stairs down to the main level and turned right with my hand on the wall to guide me. My left hand turned on the harsh, fluorescent light in the kitchen and my eyes automatically shut with the brightness of it. As I put the kettle on, I glanced out of the window and out toward the jungle. Dark silhouettes of giant trees and dense vines were the city-free view I looked at every day. Even the monkeys were asleep as I went through my coffee press routine.

Our belongings had arrived from Johannesburg, and I held one of my favorite mugs in my hand as I made my way through the open doorway to the dining room and sat at the head of the table facing the living room and the huge picture window that opened to the Great Rift Valley. From where I sat, I could watch the landscape change as the sun warmed the valley in a rich glow, gradually brightening each element of the view as the burning orb's light ascended. First, the yellow grass glowed like carpet in the lowlands until the light creeped gradually up the mountain toward us, beckoning creatures and humans to rise with the new day. With a steaming mug of coffee, I opened my devotional book, followed it with my Bible reading, and picked up my pen to write my prayers to God—the only One who was *always* present. I sat there alone on the milestone of our wedding anniversary processing the magnitude of my new life and all that had transpired to bring me to that point.

JOURNAL ENTRY

August 26, 2013

Another milestone... with peace!

Last night was the first night since February that I slept without help! My "peace meter" is reading "PEACE." A great day for the LORD to remind me that "HIS peace is sufficient for me."

Thank you, LORD, for removing the dread of this day and giving me an eternal perspective. I am believing - and being thankful - for the way my story reads from YOUR perspective:

You led me to Point Loma, following Rhonda, whose family had pointed me toward you. You LITERALLY redeemed my life from the pit, protecting me from consequences too serious for me to even fathom. You forgave me and gave me a fresh start.

Then, you brought me Chris. His love and forgiveness was an earthly picture of YOUR forgiveness, "That is not the person I know. You are forgiven and new."

You continued to bless our marriage and our relationship, drawing us both closer to you individually and as a couple... through CEBC, BSF, Beth Moore Bible Studies, Kay Arthur inductive studies, BAPTISM, trips to Uganda, and more until we were BOTH ready to follow You into missions to be a part of Your story for the Nations.

We struggled through leaving, getting rid of our "earthly baggage," trusting you more and more and finding You utterly faithful. And still, You were drawing us both - ALL - closer to You.

Each of our children, the last being Duane, has found You as their personal Savior.

As Chris's "ordained day" to go Home approached, You prepared us and spoke to us until, in your Mercy, You ushered Him Home to receive his reward and - instantaneously, renewed my purpose to follow You and serve You wherever you lead me.

*THAT is a beautiful story of redemption, salvation, sanctification, and GRACE. A LOT to be thankful for! And THAT is the story I will **choose** to remember on this day every year.*

60 | Adjustment and Heart Cramps

"I am the Lord, the God of all mankind.
Is anything too hard for me?"
– Jeremiah 32:17-19; 27

Adjusting to living in a new African country

moved forward like a great migration. We moved from valleys of despair to high peaks of joy and confirmation that we were in the right place. There were times of longing and emptiness with a growling hunger for the family we had left at home. Then, a time of refreshing would appear like a cool watering hole after days of dusty dryness and we would bask in it, feel renewed, and press on. I had good days, was developing good relationships, and there were times of laughter; but in the midst of all of that, it was as if my heart always had a "cramp" in it. There were outward signs that all of us were adjusting well—we were making it to class, my lessons seemed well-received, the kids were meeting friends and asking to go to their houses for spontaneous play dates, and everyone was eating, sleeping, and finding their way around.

Even with the good things that were happening, our grief was the dark-hooded downer that reared its head at unexpected times, triggered by unexpected things. It looked different for each of us, and I learned to watch for signs of sadness in each of the kids. For Jed, it looked like quiet melancholy. He'd hole up in his room in the darkness for long periods of time until the cloud passed. Silly was active in her grief and asked me to look at pictures with her and talk about her daddy for a while. Olivia tended to disappear and find her friends at the dorm where she had friendships deep enough to provide a safe place for her sorrow. Joseph and Duane threw themselves into the freedom of outdoor play, spending most days outside exploring the playground, yielding sticks as swords, and exhausting themselves in the wonder of huge grassy fields and playgrounds without fences.

Occasionally, I'd find a little note on my desk or in the margin of a homework paper that would snap me out of the feelings that threatened to distract and derail me. As I read the words of encouragement, joy and purpose warmed me at the core and I had enough strength to keep going.

"To my dearest Mrs. Gennaro,

We love you so much and are so thankful for your teaching and devotionals every day! Your class is a perfect start to all of our days! God is doing amazing things with you and your kids! My goal is to someday be like you. Love flows out of you even when you are tired or stressed. You make learning fun and interesting. I am so happy that you are here right now."

The days were full from early morning to late in the evening when the sun went down, and I'd have to locate all of the kids, round them up, and beckon them home to get ready for bed. Life in that community was a chance for my children to experience a childhood similar to the one I had experienced in the mountains of Northern California. Within the gates of that 90-acre campus on the mountain, they could roam with their friends, explore, and play until darkness forced them home. It wasn't unusual for me to get a call on our landline phone from a fellow staff member and friend: "We have (insert kid's name here), would you mind if he/she stayed for dinner and then we'll send him/her home?"

Relief was usually my first emotional response to that question. It meant that I didn't have to get dinner on the table, and I could breathe for a bit. Stacks of essays were my most devoted daily companions, but the quiet was welcome. Besides the help of my colleagues, I also had the welcome favor of a cultural expectation to hire local people for help in the house and even outside as groundskeepers. Culturally, it was understood that if someone had the means to pay for help, then they should literally "share" it and hire someone who needed the work. Both local people and expatriates with the means to do so brought people in to help.

Based on the recommendations of friends, I interviewed and selected a few people to help me with the running of the house while I taught full time. Fridah and Ann each came to help inside the house and shared a part-time schedule, divvying up household tasks based on what their strengths were. They washed the endless piles of laundry, hanging it to dry on the clothesline outside, snatching it off when the rain came, and then re-hanging it. They dusted, prepped meals, cleaned the floors, and kept the bathrooms clean from the constant dirt that made its way in from outside play.

Joel, my outside worker who helped me two days a week, did the yard work and maintained the property surrounding our house that sat at the tippy-top of the campus up against the forest. That task alone would have kept one person busy enough, but he also took it upon himself to keep me stocked with firewood and split it perfectly into uniform sticks for kindling. It was his last task of the day that spoiled me the most. After sweeping the ashes out of the fireplace and tidying up the area, he would build the perfect fire so that all I had to do was light a match to it. The glorious layers were carefully crafted: paper first, then the split kindling stacked like waffle squares, and finally split logs of increasing size.

Simple, gracious acts of kindness from the people around me buoyed me through my days until they had been checked off the calendar and we found ourselves nearing the end of another twelve-week school term and the opportunity for a break. When the students returned to their families who were spread out all over the huge continent, life on the bustling campus screeched to a halt and turned to a ghost town. Families pulled in and couples used the time to spend time together, lavishing the free time that was absent during school terms.

The contrast of whole families and blissful couples highlighted the finality of my circumstances and, as the truth sunk in, my prayers began to focus on the unseen future. It had only been a year since that fateful conversation that Chris and I had shared in our kitchen in the village and the providence of it seemed to give me permission to peek into what God could possibly do someday. When I was alone with my thoughts and wondered what my days would look like, I whispered silent prayers to God:

"I commit my dreams to You - whatever they are: that if there is someone out there to share life with again in Your timing, that he would be a man of faith, a spiritual leader, yet humble enough to respect and appreciate our love for and memories of Chris. Provide and direct me to where You want us to be to DO what You would have me do. LORD, strengthen my faith for the day-to-day, trusting You with the future and KNOWING that You are working on my behalf, that You have plans and a purpose for me, and that You WILL bring joy again; You WILL bring fruit from our suffering "for the saving of many lives."

The fact that I was already focusing on being tired of waiting for a new season after only nine months reveals the magnitude of the journey. I was navigating life with a burden on my back that I couldn't shoulder by myself, and my communication with God seemed to be the most consistent coping strategy that I depended on. There was encouragement and strength for the new challenges that each day brought, and I got through them one at a time until the end of the hardest year of my life was upon me.

December brought milestones that I couldn't face alone, so I came up with a strategy that would give us something to look forward to and also provide a companion who could walk through them with me. We made plans to travel to Uganda to spend a good part of the break with our good friend, Cassandra, who had gone through training with us and felt like a little sister to me and an auntie to the kids. Being with her in Uganda felt a bit like returning home, so it seemed like the best way to face our first Christmas without Chris or family.

Besides time with a dear friend and visits to landmark places of our past, a visit from Julia provided the next dose of grace that lured us back to Kenya. Her presence filled the house with new energy and made the house feel fuller. With most of our nuclear family unit together, we eased right back into old roles and family jokes with ease. As we squeezed around the little breakfast table in the kitchen snacking, she tutored us on pop-culture back in America. Without her help, we would have never known what a fox says or how wrecked Miley was. Besides the gift of having all of my kids under the same roof for a time, we added pets to the family. Silly's Christmas gift was two baby bunnies that we adopted from a family down the hill. With little animals to nurture, she was busy caring for them and had furry things to snuggle.

As the year of my worst-case scenario ended, I couldn't help but pause to remember all that we had been through.

JOURNAL ENTRY

Last day of 2013!

How I praise you, LORD, that You speak to me, prepare me, guide me. I look back at the end of last year when You were calling me to allow YOU to be my all-in-all. I had no idea what you were preparing me for, but you were preparing me for the most difficult year of my life when I really had to depend on You – and YOU ALONE.

Even the devotionals I started had to do with overcoming fear. In hindsight, only weeks after starting those devotionals, I would be faced with my GREATEST fear of all – losing Chris. Most days I still can't even fathom that I am on the other side of that, having faced it, survived, and now live victorious despite that profound loss. I give you the praise for the strength to get through 2013.

61 | Milestones

"Sorrow becomes the expositor of the mysteries of God that joy leaves unexplained."

By the time our first year in Kenya passed, we had adapted to life in the community pretty well and had the support of friends and even pets to love on. Despite Chris laying down the law in 2012 after our Mosotho puppy died, we had acquired a menagerie of pets. A couple of chickens, a duck, and a fluffle of bunnies occupied our spare time and gave Silly creatures to nurture. Their tendency to reproduce, and sometimes die, gave us plenty of material for talks about the circle of life.

Our own lives continued to move forward before my heart could catch up. June brought Chris's second birthday without him and Father's Day, both of which brought a heaviness and dread for a few days before and a lot of reflection. God's merciful provision continued to carry us through those days by bringing us friends at just the right time.

Our school campus tended to be a hub for missionaries from our organization who lived and served in the far reaches of the continent, and one of the benefits was running into people we knew from other countries. It was always a blessing, but on the day before Chris's birthday, it was a comfort and gift to us that ministered to our grieving hearts. A scheduled conference for people who worked in agriculture had brought most of our former team to gather on our campus and we got to drink deep of their fellowship for an evening of catching up. The last time we had seen them was at Chris's memorial service in Bloemfontein and we had a lot to talk about.

As the fire roared in the fireplace, we all gathered around our living room and chatted as three different accents filled the room. One couple from the UK, August from South Africa, and Jonathan and my family from America recounted events over the last year.

Each of them knew Chris personally, so it was an indescribable gift to be surrounded by memories of him and sense the love that these people had for him. As my gaze wandered from one smiling face to the next, I couldn't help but reflect on the fact that we were all alive and continuing in our service while Chris was already in Heaven.

It was dusk when we were forced to say our goodbyes. The fading light was barely enough to illuminate the grassy area of our front yard for a group picture. We all lined up, threw our arms around each other, and brought the kids in as a neighbor snapped the shot. We're looking at each other and laughing with the familiar joy of family and the kids are laughing. At the end of the night, when silence descended on the house once again, a cloud of sadness brought questions for God about why Chris had to leave, and we were all left here without him. In His mercy, an answer came within moments with a truth that brought sustaining perspective: "*Chris was finished with his work; you all are not. It's not a bad thing for a believer to be called home, you just miss him.*"

I flipped off the light and stepped up the stairs to my room as I whispered my melancholy response, "Yes, I do."

The next milestone was Olivia's graduation from high school. I anticipated how difficult it would be to go through that day without loved ones and the familiar traditions of home: extended families in attendance, lavish parties, new clothes, and the anticipation of generous gifts. Every celebration was a reminder of the one we were missing, so I quickly learned to counter that by investing the resources necessary to have a nice "Plan B." Since we were in Kenya, there was no way I could recreate a graduation day like Julia had in San Diego. Extended family and friends had gathered in our home, we had special food, and she had a special dress we shopped for to wear under her gown. Graduation was a rite of passage in America and I was unable to recreate it in Kenya. After much prayer, we came up with a plan to make it special.

I made arrangements for Julia to travel to Kenya for a visit so she could be there for graduation and then accompany us on the trip back to California for the school break. We also brought Olivia's best friend to stay with us so she could join in the celebration and see her class graduate. Her family had served on our team in Lesotho and had returned to the States by that time, so she was eager to be a part of the day somehow as well. Because Ellen was a part of both our time in the village and Olivia's time at boarding school, they had a special bond.

I woke up on graduation day with Chris on my mind. This was one of those days families went through together. Without him, I felt like I was alone on an island. My mind wandered back to the village, leaving there that fateful morning, and what it would be like to go back. Longing filled me as I remembered what it was like to have a complete family unit and a partner in life. I prayed for God to fill me up and strengthen me for the day and for the upcoming transition of Olivia being gone too. It was time to celebrate the good, so I turned my prayers toward praise before rolling out of bed.

Excitement and gratitude rose in me as I reflected on the past year. I was excited for Olivia's achievement; thankful she had the opportunity to return to RVA as she wanted to do, and so blessed to have had the year with her and her classmates. It was such a privilege to have been a part of all of the traditions, to know her friends, and to be a part of her life.

Later that morning, as we zipped up the black graduation gown over her dress and put the traditional red and black buffalo check scarf around her neck, anticipation began to build. Families had come from all over the continent for the occasion and were making their way to the large chapel for the ceremony. The campus grounds were groomed to perfection and the air was filled with buzzing energy. As we found our seats, I could not help but be caught up in the moment. There was a sense that we were a part of something special as decades of tradition went into the planning of this hour-long segment of time.

Pomp and circumstance started to play and the rush of emotion and love for my daughter drew me into the present. My chest rose with the fullness of life and the flood of feelings rose with the crescendo of the music. There was a moving choir piece, speeches, and an address to the class by one of the teachers before they were declared graduates and reached their hands up to switch their tassels to the other side of their caps. After the ceremony, the audience turned their eyes toward the open doors at the back of the auditorium as the graduates filed out and took their turn at attempting to jump high enough to hit the top of the door frame. The custom was so long-standing that the whole crowd was enraptured by it. Like a crowd at a basketball game waiting for a slam dunk, the voices of the crowd lulled when the shorter classmates fell short, burst into laughter when one of them over-exaggerated their efforts, and then erupted in cheers when a loud, victorious whack was heard.

After hugs and photos with their friends and the expected group pictures, the graduates gathered on the steps outside of the cafeteria, counted to three, and then threw their graduation caps in the air in victory. Their high school years were finished!

I stood in wonder at the vision of it. Another one of my children was growing up and time was moving forward.

With the year over, we weren't the only ones reflecting on our lives and the transitions we were about to walk through. Notes from students came with little gifts and spontaneous envelopes dropped on my desk. They were a balm to my lonely, searching soul, and a confirmation that I was exactly where I was supposed to be for that season.

Dear Mrs. Gennaro,

Thank you so much for being my awesome English teacher! You were always there to encourage and teach us more about God's grace and his Power than English! Thank you so much! You have come alongside all of the seniors and carried our burdens. Laughter, joy, and tears together. God has blessed us, the school community and the class of 2014 with a godly teacher like you!

You will be in our hearts! Thank you for your support and willingness to help and edit my college essays!

I will miss you, Mrs. Gennaro! You are one of my role models in life. You have taught me courage and strength to fight hardships and know that everything goes the way He planned it! Through your testimony and daily devotions, they encouraged me to speak last Sunday!

Your loving and tender heart has changed so many lives! Through Christ, I see a change here! May God bless you as you step into a new chapter of life here! Keep shining for Jesus and pursue the spread of His Gospel.

Sincerely, your student
Jin Soo, South Korea

> *"If we decide not to opt out in fear or cave to constant*
> *self-comfort, others following below us may see how we imitate*
> *lives of great faith. They may muster the strength*
> *to reach a little higher."*
> *— Unknown*

After graduation, we spent the summer in California with family and I got Olivia settled in Maui for vocational school. She would study Aesthetics and live within a mile of my dad. The thought of her having at least one family member nearby was a comfort to me, but with two of my kids on separate land masses thousands of miles away, my thoughts and prayers for them consumed me.

Our family unit was now the four younger children and me. Our household felt significantly smaller and much quieter. Olivia's absence left me without an adult in the house and I was acutely aware that my life was different. It felt strange to think about there being only five of us in Kenya and two of my kids so far from me. As I pictured it, I couldn't help wondering if I was doing the right thing. We had achieved the goal of Olivia's graduation, I was thriving in my role as a teacher and was receiving so much good feedback, and the kids seemed to be doing well. Still, my loneliness became more obvious and intense as our numbers dwindled. With all of the changes, I begged God for direction for the future and questioned my purpose and call. Where should I be? What should I do for Him? Was I doing the right thing? Should I be staying in San Diego or staying in Kenya longer?

As I wrestled internally over the details, I wrote them out in my prayer journal so that I could process them and have visual evidence when the answers came. Before we got back on the plane to return for our second year at the school, I jotted down praises for the confirmations God had given me over the course of the visit. In hindsight, they jumped off the pages as foreshadows of what was to come.

JOURNAL ENTRY

July 30, 2014

Thank you for the confirmations You gave me while in San Diego: "NOT YET," staying in Kenya for a while longer is the right timing; a short Home Assignment is a good idea; maybe not church ministry in the future, maybe it's speaking, mobilizing, and training that you are preparing me for?

62 | Immeasurably More

February 2015

"I (have been) under great pressure, far beyond my ability to endure, so that I despaired even of life. Indeed, in my heart I felt the sentence of death. BUT this happened that I might not rely on myself (or even other people) but on GOD, who raises the dead."
– 2 Corinthians 1:9-10

My time in prayer leading up to the second year anniversary of Chris's death reflected a heaviness of heart and the weariness that came from life without him. I was longing for peace from the sorrow and comfort in new ways. On February 13th, I wrote, *"Jesus said, 'Peace be with you!' and 'Do not let your heart be troubled – and DO NOT BE AFRAID.'"*

> *"Lord, my heart was troubled last night. I was just sad and discouraged. How I was longing for my old life back; for the security of having Chris by my side. LORD Jesus, fill that gap with MORE of Yourself. Comfort my heart and show me the ways you are working in my life. Continue to use my life, my waiting, my tears, my loneliness, my testimony for YOUR glory. How I long to see You in my life."*

Somewhere along the way, I was given advice to anticipate the milestones and have a plan so that we had something to look forward to rather than a heavy day to dread. As it turned out, the plan never erased the dread, but it *did* give us something to look forward to. We called the actual anniversary of his home going "Heaven Day."

It was hard to deny the evidence of God's generous provision for us in the dreaming up of such "grief getaways." Since we lived simply, I usually had money set aside to dream up something special with the kids and then make it a reality. On this occasion, I had a sense of what I needed: friends like family and a safe, comfortable, beautiful place... with water! The kids' comfort came in the form of water play and the presence of either a pool or the ocean meant rest and refreshment for me too. With this detailed list of needs, I contacted our special friends whom we knew from the beginning of our time in Africa to invite them to join us and began the search for a place that would be big enough for all of us.

I was unprepared for the answer to my prayer for God to *"show me the ways He was working in my life"* through the setting He provided for our time away. I had seen pictures of Leleshwa House online, but our journey and destination were better than I could have imagined. Without a car to my name, even the transportation was a miracle. Having friends close enough to loan me their Land Rover was just the beginning of His goodness! This didn't come without risk, though. With my recently issued Kenyan driver's license, this meant that I had the responsibility of driving on the unfamiliar, unpredictable, and sometimes treacherous Kenyan roads to get to our blissful retreat location. In addition, it was clear in the directions to get there that once we left the tarmac, cell service would be spotty at best. We most likely wouldn't have the security of working cell phones.

It was the four youngest kids and my spunky, go-getter "mission sister" Cassandra who set out with me on this quest for rest, peace, fun, and adventure. We were all looking forward to time away, especially since it meant we got to have time with a family we all adored. Remember the ones with the little daughter who licked the walls of the airport when we first arrived in Kenya?

Driving the highway proved to be less terrifying than I anticipated, and as usual, our expectations for excitement weren't disappointed. Kenya delivered! We left the paved road with a bump and squeals of delight to find the densest dust we had ever experienced. Swiping, swishing wiper blades were no match for the fine piles of light brown powder that billowed through the air and settled on the windshield from unexpected road crews and gusts of wind. We slowed to a crawl, closed the vents to prevent breathing it in, and prayed that there weren't oncoming cars or trucks that suddenly materialized out of the earthly clouds.

Once past the work zone, we adjusted our eyes to find towering acacia trees on either side of the road and sweeping fields of grass that promised sights of wild animals. These landscapes always reminded me that life in Africa had its adventurous perks. Climbing slowly on the rutted, gravel road, the dirt turned redder and cliffs rose on either side. Just as we reached the top of the ravine, one of the kids shouted, "Look ahead!"

We all turned our peering eyes to the right of the vehicle to see the huge, intimidating form of a male baboon. He sat boldly and firmly on his muscular haunches staring us down as if to say, "I belong here. Don't even THINK of making me move so you can intrude on my territory any further." We paused to study him in greater detail and then thought better of getting eye contact with him. As our knobby tires ground their way up the rest of the hill, his harem of female followers and spindly offspring could be seen passing through the area at a safe distance behind him.

Anticipation grew for what our place would be like as we entered a more inhabited and groomed community surrounding a golf course. A golf course?! We should have had more of a clue after passing through the large security gate with guards who checked our destination and names. Shady trees lined the dirt road and unique, custom gates stood as wooden or metal sentries for comfortable country homes. Looking both ways, we made one last, unfamiliar crossing over a small airstrip before taking a sharp left up a small, private drive.

All of the features of the property were concealed by trees, flowering shrubs, rustic landscaping, and stone walls that blended in with the native scenery we were now a part of for the weekend escape. As we parked, we were welcomed by the jovial, beaming smiles of the staff who helped us get our things and carry them down into the house. Paul the cook and Salome the housekeeper would become our familiar friends, the irresistible icing on the cake of this magical place. Their own personal stories equipped them to be our ministering angels every time we visited.

The massive, two-story walls of stone and custom, wood-framed windows didn't prepare me for all my eyes would strain to take in as we crossed the threshold. Everywhere I looked, wood from the trees and shrubs from outside had been painstakingly carved, smoothed, and varnished to create the curving banister and one-of-a-kind wild trims to shelves and lighting features everywhere you looked. My spirit soared, and my inner child took over. The house was named for the shrub-sized trees in that area and gnarled, lacquered pieces of it were used in every room of the house. I dropped my bags in the entry and bounded up the stairs to allow my curiosity to explore every room and corner of wild workmanship.

Our whole road-weary, life-heavy group split off to lay claim to where we would sleep. There were plenty of rooms to choose from, but we had to be strategic as we were expecting the Koski's any minute and they were a family of four. With my inner child, Little Michelle, in charge, I didn't hesitate to stake my own claim: "I get the queen's quarters!"

Transported to this little piece of heaven, my soul found rest and the heaviness in my heart eased slightly to allow joy to seep in. With Chef Paul making breakfast and dinner, and Salome caring for the cleaning, I was able to rest in the safe shelter of the hideaway. The kids had the whole, chilly pool to themselves, and we went whenever they had a craving for play. We popped old videos into the VCR to watch movies in the evenings with a crackling fire. We had true fellowship with our friends, lingering over delicious homemade meals and sitting out on verandas looking out over the African bush, steaming coffee and morning mist in the morning, and the cadence of pounding rain taking over in the evenings.

The whole weekend was the calm oasis I needed, but the MOST memorable and meaningful gift from my Heavenly Father was the sweet and generous sign He gave me in answer to my prayer: "*LORD Jesus, fill that gap with MORE of Yourself. Comfort my heart and show me the ways you are working in my life.*" My first exploration of the outdoors revealed it. As I wandered through the garden, my feet meandering on soft, mowed grass and my eyes darting from plant to plant, flower to flower, I nearly crashed into it. There, in the middle of Kenya, far from home, was my favorite plant of all time, a blooming plumeria bush. Tears welled up as I leaned in to smell the tropical bloom.

Memories of visits with my dad in Maui and vacations as a family filled my thoughts as I remembered my daughter Olivia being in that place at that very moment. In that space and time, I had the comfort my heart needed. I leaned in to smell the crisp, sweet fragrance of the flowers and breathed in the sense that God was with me working out every detail that seemed scary and out of my control, and that He was with my daughters, too, even when I couldn't see them.

During my contemplative times in the serenity of that place, I could hear God clearly. He was speaking to me through His Word, and I let it sink in. Some of the words came through louder than the others and helped me refocus my heart and increase my courage for the unseen future.

"FIX YOUR EYES ON ME."

"For nothing is impossible with God."
— Luke 1:37

"He is able to do IMMEASURABLY MORE than
we ask or imagine."
— Ephesians 3:20

"His divine power has given us everything
we need in life and godliness."
— 2 Peter 1:3

"And GOD IS ABLE to make all grace abound to me,
so that IN ALL THINGS at all times, having ALL THAT YOU NEED,
you will abound in every good work."
— 2 Corinthians 9:8

63 | Transitional Living

"'God's success might be as much what He is doing IN you as what He is doing THROUGH you.' Don't underestimate the part you play and remember that loving HIM with all of our heart, soul, mind, and strength is His number one commandment for all of us!"
— Tim Hall

As the third and final term of our second school year started, my seniors began to realize the nearness of their next transition. Their graduation was beginning to feel imminent, and they would be leaving Africa, the home they had known for most of their lives, to live in places that were unfamiliar to them. I felt their pain and trepidation and was often a sounding board for their fears. Even though I was in my forties at the time, my emotional self felt like I was eighteen again, trying to figure out who I was and a little fearful about what my future would hold. As I mindlessly scrolled through Facebook one evening, a post from one of my students caught my eye and got me thinking.

"Said goodbye to my home for the final time. Only God knows how long until I return. Lived here for about 7 years-gonna miss everything, especially my dog and our workers. Prayers for our 4 day drive would be greatly appreciated."

Since I taught seniors, it meant that ALL of them were going through transitions similar to what she was experiencing. I never thought that, through all of my own experiences in change, goodbyes, and grief, God was preparing me to pour into young people who would be struggling through feelings I was having. Their circumstances were different but our hearts understood one another. Teaching at the boarding school wasn't on my radar and far from my plans, but as I lived it out, I realized it was an answer to my prayers in 2013 when Chris was lying in ICU. At that time, I had prayed two key prayers repeatedly: "Lord, prepare us for whatever testimony you have for us" and "Lord, don't let my suffering be in vain."

As soon as I made that connection in my mind, I realized that I had been writing a lot in my newsletters and blogs about my journey through grief and toward Jesus, but not as much about my daily life. The start of that term in particular was the beginning of a huge transition for my students and their families and it led me to reflect on my own life leading up to that assignment. It was as if looking at their lives awakened me to our own family journey and the truth of it forced a timeline out of me. My eyes were opened to the fact that our family's life had been in transition since about 2007—*nearly eight years*! It had gone something like this:

July 2007 – We traveled to Uganda for Joseph and Duane's adoption court date, but had to leave them behind because the judge didn't write his ruling.

December 2007 – Our family grew by TWO! They had to adjust to a new family, new culture, new food, and all things American. We adjusted to all of the above too and didn't allow them to leave our sides for about a year in order to bond with them.

Fall 2008 – We applied, attended Candidate Week, and were appointed as missionaries with Africa Inland Mission.

There were a couple of job changes for Chris somewhere in there…

January 2010 – Started support raising and "simplifying" to prepare for our move to Africa.

June 2011 – Our first born, Julia, graduated from high school.

July 2011 – We sold (or gave) our house, cars, and possessions away and moved to Lesotho, Africa – with a *lot* of help from our friends and family!

September 2011 – August 2012 – We took on new "identities" in the village and did the hard work of language and culture learning – and I homeschooled the kids on four different grade levels.

January 2012 – BOTH Julia and Olivia left the house – Julia to California and Olivia to boarding school in Kenya (hmmm...foreshadow?).

August 2012 – Chris started teaching at the Vocational Skills Training Center.

February 2013 – Our lives changed forever when Chris went Home.

March 2013 – We moved out of our house in the village and went to San Diego for Compassionate Leave.

August 2013 – We moved to Rift Valley Academy in Kenya, leaving Julia to start university in Southern California.

July 2014 – Olivia graduated from high school and moved to Maui to attend Esthetics School.

December 2014 – Olivia became a certified Esthetician and moved BACK to California.

If your head is swimming from just *reading* that, then you have been given an overview of my "training" to work with missionary kids at a boarding school. You see, my students lived lives of transition as well and God was using my perspective and experience in order to understand, mentor, love, teach, equip, and disciple them. Most of them were kids of missionaries, but some of them lived "cross-cultural lives" because of their parents' jobs or ministries outside of missions. I was living an answer to one of God's most difficult-to-grasp promises to "use all things for the good for those who love Him and are called according to His purpose."

355

Every day, I had the privilege of using my gifts and my experience with students whose lives clearly intersected with my journey. That brought purpose to my suffering and spurred me on. Yet, watching them was like looking in the mirror at the next upheaval of our own family life—a Home Assignment in San Diego. I updated my friends and family back home and asked for prayer support for the unknown future.

"Please pray that God uses that time to prepare us for our NEXT transitions: what will probably be our last year and a half in Kenya, another yet to be announced one, Jed's graduation from high school in July 2017, and only God knows what ELSE! I'll be speaking a lot, will have the privilege of being the "Missionary in Residence" at AIM Headquarters for their new candidates, will meet with supporters, will especially enjoy time with family, friends, and our church family, and will be praying that God will give me a sneak peak into my next role in His Kingdom work. What's crazy is that God has changed my heart and made it more flexible to what HE has planned for me. I have a strange sense of anticipation for what He is working behind the scenes on our behalf!"

64 | Burdens Shared

"The LORD said, 'I have indeed seen the misery of my people...
I have heard them crying out... and I am concerned
about their suffering."
— Exodus 3:7

The three people who I hired to work for me
were the key players behind the scenes who made my life in Kenya
possible. Ann became my confidant and sister, walking with me
through long days of loneliness and repeated loss, guiding me through
culture as I adjusted to life in Kijabe. Fridah was also a widow, linking
arms with me and understanding me on levels most people couldn't.
Her journey constantly reminded me that I was not alone, and that no
matter what, there was always someone whose burden was heavier
than the one you were carrying. Joel, my outside worker, continued to
meticulously groom our landscaping, trimming the lush trees, cutting
the grass that grew with gusto on the edge of the forest, and helping
us manage the pets I hadn't had the strength to say no to. The animals
were a furry and feathery distraction, cuddles and hope in our sorrow.
It was Joel who was there for every unfortunate, traumatic end that
our bunnies and chickens endured living on the edge of the jungle.

In the mornings, before she walked to class, Silly fed her flock
and let them out to scratch and peck around our yard. They tended
to stay close to the house, grazing on the bugs in the grass and
feasting on little delicacies they would find under the bushes. It was
a normal practice for chickens and ducks in the daytime because
they didn't tend to wander. All was well. For a while.

My classes ended before the kids', so I had some time in the
afternoon to grade papers and plan before they came home. As
I huffed it up the hill, memories of the last few hours with my
students and tasks for the afternoon filled my mind. I climbed the
first set of stairs, flowering dahlia bushes on either side, past the

357

rope swing Joel had made for the kids in the giant, shady tree to the right, passed over the narrow, dirt easement between my house and my neighbors', and started up the curving, gradual steps up to my front door. A feather caught my eye on the ground to my left, then another, and another. Immediately, my body knew something wasn't right. I quickly took attendance: duck, chicken... wait, there was one missing! I began the search for what I feared and found it under the bush. One of Silly's beloved chickens was lying there, still limp and warm, but dead. I froze. My thoughts raced through my head in anxious panic as I looked at the body.

"She's DEAD! What do I tell Silly?"

"I don't want to touch it!"

"I need a man to help me!"

"Chris is gone. I don't have a husband." The tears built to angry sobs as I remembered.

"My neighbors are all in class."

"It's Joel's day off here... WAIT! He's working at Ryan and Heather's today!"

I burst into the house, the realization of a plan giving me resolve. I was out of breath. This was an unexpected death again and I wasn't ready for it. I don't remember ever having one thought about that limp carcass being "just a chicken." She was Silly's pet, and I didn't want my daughter to have to grieve again. I grabbed a plastic grocery bag, raced back out the door, and scooped up our hen friend like a pile of fresh dog poop, never letting any part of her limpness touch my hands. I took off running down the dirt road to my friends' house where I thought Joel might be. I couldn't breathe. The altitude was against me as silent wailing seemed to steal oxygen from my lungs. I tried to call for him, but my voice only came out in squeaks: "Joel! Joel!"

With the bag of tragedy in my hands, I rounded the corner of the house and found Joel raking cut grass, his calm demeanor changing as he laid eyes on me. I can't imagine what he must have been thinking, as these were times the differences in our life experiences left us wondering. I showed him the dead chicken and told him where I had found her. He wasn't sure what to say or how to comfort me, but I could see in his eyes that he wanted to help. It was in that moment, as I stood there trusting him, that I knew we had made our way to friendship. The weird mystery of the family who had chickens for pets and not to eat had been replaced with compassion for the fact that another loss was happening, and our sweet Silly was about to be wrecked. His face showed the shared dread, and I could tell he was sorry at the thought of it.

"I don't know what to do. I can't touch her. Will you PLEASE take care of her? I don't want Silly to see it. Maybe you can take it home and..."

I couldn't finish my sentence, but Joel knew what I meant. I didn't want her life wasted by this untimely death. He put the bag on the back of his *piki* (motorcycle) and walked with me back down the dirt road toward the house. Then, in one final act of love for my kid, he cleaned up as many of the feathers as he could while the breeze carried the rest of the evidence away.

The next morning, Jed walked with me down the rutted, dirt road to class. With his backpack on his back, he looked the part of a high school student, and his growing body made him eye level with me. In the privacy of the moment, with the other kids heading to their own section of the campus for school, he took the opportunity to tell me how he felt about the previous day's loss: "Mom, why do you keep saying yes to pets?! Dad said 'no more pets' for a reason when we were in the village. You have to stop! Can't you see? They always die!"

I had no response to his rebuke. He was absolutely right, and his tone was like a voice from Heaven coming out of his mouth. Having pets opened our hearts to caring for the creatures and, eventually, it was inevitable that we would have to say goodbye to them in some form. Either we'd have to leave them, or they would die. As I listened to him, I pondered whether the circle of life lessons and the cuddles balanced out the grief. As the oldest kid in the house at that time, my son was doing his best to be an advocate for his siblings, and as he peeled off toward his classroom, I couldn't help but be thankful.

"Thanks, Jed," I called out with a little chuckle at the realization that he had sounded just like his dad in those moments. "I love you."

He turned his head toward me as he continued walking to acknowledge me and raised his hand in the air to wave his response.

65 | Unexpected Belonging

"For my thoughts are not your thoughts, neither are your ways my ways," declares the Lord. "As the heavens are higher than the earth, so are my ways higher than your ways and my thoughts than your thoughts."
— Isaiah 55:8-9

We pressed on with the rest of the term as our Home Assignment drew near. We juggled school, preparations for travel, I had a successful laser eye correction, Joseph had an elective surgery to remove preauricular sinuses on both ears, and I worked on packing our belongings every chance I could get. It seemed there was no getting away from the intensity of life, and the deep life lessons continued right up to our departure.

No matter where I looked, it seemed like there was a responsibility to carry. The four kids were capable and helpful when I asked them to do something, but I was the captain of the ship now, the only one guiding and directing our lives. The pressure of it often left me drained and lonely. In my loneliness, all I could see were couples and intact families who were looking forward to the next thing together. Where did I fit in?

As I shuffled totes and went through our storage room to make room for our personal household things we were leaving behind while we were away for a year, my thoughts matched the gloominess of the room. The cinder block, bottom floor of the house backed up to the bank of the hill and dampness hung in the air. One lightbulb in the center of the ceiling lit the room, but the light was harsh and unnatural and barely reached the corners of the small room. I felt gloomy as I carried out my task, thoughts passing through the darkness of my mind:

"I'm so needed as a mom right now; how will I do all of this on my own?"

"Still, I'm often called upon to help others who are going through hard things, too."

"I'm without Chris, but still being used."

"I don't have a partner, but I still fit in somewhere…"

As the thought passed through the shadows in my mind, a realization flickered like a hopeful beam of light: "I fit in with my Kenyan friends."

The recognition of that profound truth led me to pray for my friend in the circumstances he was facing: "Be with Joel and his wife and new baby. Thank you for a safe delivery. Keep the baby and his wife safe as they recover today and go home from the clinic. Give Joel wisdom to be a good father and husband and grow him in his knowledge and relationship with You."

I never expected to find myself at the edge of a grave just twenty-four hours after whispering that simple prayer for safety, but there I was standing among the small group of mourners with my colleague, Steve, the campus chaplain. My body, mind, and emotions seemed on separate planets as I tried to hold myself together. Joel and a group of burden-bearing men from his family and community were finishing the chasm where their new baby son would be laid to rest, tucked into the soil in a far-off place on their property rather than bundled in their arms where he belonged.

Once they finished, someone said something that seemed like a prayer, the mini casket was lowered in, and mourners took turns placing one scoop of dirt at a time over it. There wasn't time to learn the cultural implications of such a tradition, but I'm pretty sure that their thoughts were the same as anyone else's in the world at that point: "Our baby won't grow up with us like we thought he would."

A time of sharing was next, so the whole group quietly moved to another part of the property where there was a line of about five chairs set up, just enough for the members of the immediate family to sit in. Grasping for something familiar, I imagined the rest of us standing behind the family for a message of some kind. Steve and I moved silently toward the back of the gathering, seeking a place to be with them, but not the center of attention. That wasn't ok with Joel. Scanning the faces of his friends and family, he landed on ours and motioned us to the front. We awkwardly made signs to him that we were ok. We'd stay there.

Nope.

With a newly acquired, bold assertiveness, Joel commanded us to move forward. As a man, Steve was at an advantage right then. He insisted on leaving the chairs for the women and headed to the side, remaining closer to the front than he was before at least. With everyone still and in their places, there I sat next to Joel's wife in the very front. My emotions couldn't make sense of the honor, so my reflexes took over. Sitting next to my grieving friend, knowing her arms were aching with emptiness and that her tears must have been held back by a dam of strong-willed dignity. I put my arm around her and left it there every chance I got as I continued my duty to document the event with pictures.

It was close to sunset by the time a select, smaller group of us was invited into the house. Big kettles of chai had been prepared and there was a meal that was about to be served. Steve and I knew we weren't supposed to be driving on these roads past dark, so the ticking timers we had in our minds prohibited us from accepting the meal. That would mean a couple more hours there, and that would make our journey home on the dark, rural roads risky.

What little cultural prowess we remembered at this point spared us the consequences of resisting the gift of shared fellowship. We knew that saying "no, thank you" to the chai that was being offered would send the wrong message to our friends. This was one of those moments of cultural contrast that challenged our western values. Our time constraints had found their way back into the forefront of our minds while the very people we were trying to build relationships with were inviting us to stay. I noted the sinking sun and was thankful to have someone to drive back with.

All eyes were on us as we received the steaming cups of milky, sweet tea. The gesture and smell of it was familiar and it comforted me. I had grown to love the custom of pausing a couple of times a day to be still with those around me and share a cup of chai. I lifted the tin cup to my face and took a long, deep whiff of the steam. Then, blowing delicately along the rim, I cooled it and took my first sip. Friendly chatter filled the room as the conversations got going. My ears perked up as I heard some English being spoken. It was a relief to be able to introduce ourselves and give an explanation for our presence. We were met with kind words and generous compliments for our work at the school and in the community. Without realizing it, I had sipped all of my tea in a matter of minutes. One of the men on the couch near me loudly declared, "Look! She's one of us! She can drink chai better than me!"

That one sentence brought my whole life in Africa into focus, and I sat there looking over it with what seemed like an aerial view: The hard living in the village. Chris's traumatic and sudden death. The depth and weight of my daily sorrow. Dead bunnies and chickens. Long hours with my beloved friends who started as my helpers over steaming cups of chai and all of the questions I asked them about their lives in this place. Pushing past my fears to be there for an event I never wanted to happen. All of this had prepared me for this moment and my reward was clear: to the ones in that room, I belonged.

66 | Back to America

"His pleasure is not in the strength of the horse, nor his delight in the legs of a man; the LORD delights in those who fear HIM, who put their hope in His unfailing love."
− Psalm 147:10-11

Finishing out our second year in Kenya felt a lot like watching a movie on a VHS stuck on fast forward. Navigating the harrowing highs and lows of the circle of life with my friends and balancing teaching and parenting kept my eyes off myself for most of the long days, which was a welcome respite from my own thoughts that raced with sorrow and uncertainty when I was still. God continued to heap on measures of grace to counter the heaviness of life and that felt miraculous. A visit from a friend for my birthday and a dream trip to the Maasai Mara for safari had shown me God's love on a new level. My take away from that time was that I needed to "relax in the knowledge that the One who controls my life is totally trustworthy."

Picnicking in the middle of the Savannah within sight of a trio of lions resting under a tree and watching my kids squeal with delight as they spotted elephants, giraffes, and other animals that most people only see on documentaries had reminded me of God's limitless provision. As far as I could see, sweeping plains of tall, toasted butter-colored grass spread out toward the horizon. Towering acacia trees, perfectly created in the shape of arching umbrellas, dotted the landscape. As we stood in the safari van with our heads sticking out of the top and the warm wind blowing the hair out of our eyes, I couldn't help being caught up in the wonder and abundance of life. There, in the wildness of God's creation, I breathed a prayer: *"Oh, LORD, help me relax in the knowledge that you control my life. I know there is nothing I need that you cannot provide. Help me to relax in that truth. I am so thankful for all you have done in my life. Forgive me for not trusting your plans and your timing. Work out your will in my life, LORD."*

The lessons I jotted down and the prayers I had spoken after those days of lavish amazement at God's power and goodness were the ones I had to tap into as we faced another transition.

Inevitably, the day of our departure for Home Assignment showed up whether I was prepared or not and, after nearly 36 hours of travel, we arrived at John Wayne Airport in Orange County, California. My body was present with all of the children, all of our travel documents, and even every piece of our luggage. The kids were so excited to see their grandparents that they bounded off with Papa Joe and Nammy to find the truck while I waited at the curb with all of the bags. The warm Southern California sun made me too warm in my sweatshirt and I peeled it off to adjust to my new surroundings. Palm trees lined the busy street in front of me and honking horns tooted close by and then in the distance. The scene was familiar, but feelings of confusion swirled around with conflicting sighs of relief for having arrived. Leaving the school was difficult and I didn't feel ready for it, but I had a sense that I just needed to keep waiting on God.

As I flagged down my stepdad's white truck, I reminded myself of the mantra God had given me during my last time in the States:

"Make new memories; cherish the old; proclaim what God has done; seek HIM for our future."

My prayers the next morning were focused on Acts 17:26-28. It was the same passage that had become real to me as we left the village for the last time. The fact that those exact verses were part of the *scheduled* devotion that morning brought a smile to my face, and the reminders from it comforted me:

(verse 26) *"HE determined the TIMES set for (me) and the EXACT places where (I) should live."*

I let my conversation flow with the One who promised to be with me, and my pen flew over the page of my journal as I realized His Word playing out in my life.

JOURNAL ENTRY

Lord, on this FIRST day of this season here in California, I commit my times to you. Use this year for your glory and to speak to me about YOUR plan and purpose for my life. Give me peace about the many unknowns and help me to simply rest in you and bask in Your presence and this time you have blessed me with.

(verse 27) "God did this so that (I) would seek him and perhaps reach out for him and find Him, though He is not far from (me)."

Lord, this is a time to be seeking hard after you and reaching out for you. Thank you for the very personal reminder that you are right here with me and not far from us.

"You will never feel completely at home again,
because part of your heart will always be elsewhere.
That is the price you pay for the richness of loving and knowing people in more than one place."
— Miriam Adney

Finally achieving a sense that I belonged in Kenya while drinking chai with Joel's family filled me with purpose and wholeness—a feeling that I was exactly where I was supposed to be. There was a problem with that, though. We weren't there anymore. All of us hovered in a twilight zone of confusion, gone from our home, but back where we *used* to belong. Even though memories surrounded us, we felt like strangers in a place that should feel familiar. We were reeling with reverse culture shock and the disorienting sense that we didn't belong in our own home place.

Besides the question of where I belonged, I was constantly overshadowed with another question: to whom do I belong? Every time I turned around, my psyche remembered that Chris was missing. Since we had gone to college in San Diego, started our married life there, and raised our kids there (well, Julia at least), every street held a memory with him. Without him, I felt incomplete, lost in a culture that idolized marriage and family, and desperately alone.

Situations frequently came up that reminded me that my kids felt the same way—unsettled, confused, and insecure. I guess they had been with me one too many times when I would confidently set out on an errand and then pull up to the store only to find out that it didn't exist anymore. Eventually, after we had settled back into the mission house, Joseph took matters into his own hands. My mom called with a question, "What size shorts does Joseph wear?"

I gave her my estimate and then asked her why she needed to know. He had called her to ask if she would buy him some basketball shorts because he needed them for the church team he was practicing with. I apologized for such a direct ask. It seemed so rude that he would just ask her for something so directly! Why didn't he just ask his own mother?!

When I followed up with him that same day, I wisely worked up all of the patience and empathy I could muster and asked, "Joseph, why did you ask Nammy to buy you basketball shorts instead of just telling me you needed them?"

His response illuminated the truth of where he was in his adjustment to being in America: "I didn't think you would know where to get them."

There it was. My own child had culture shock in the city where I had lived for my whole adult life. It wasn't just me who was struggling. Later, it would be those feelings of inadequacy that would be my undoing and lead me to burn out. All of this was more than one person could handle. How could I help my kids feel secure when my whole life was upside down?

67 | Beloved
September 2015

"The heavens praise your wonders, O LORD,
your faithfulness too, in the assembly of the holy ones. For who
in the skies above can compare with the LORD? Who is like the
LORD among the heavenly beings? O LORD God Almighty, who is
like you? You are mighty, O LORD, and your faithfulness surrounds
you. You rule over the surging sea; when its waves mount up, you
still them."
— Psalm 89:5-9

Back in 2014, as I had prayed and pondered
what God's will and direction was for my future, I received a thought
that was like a silent voice. I recorded it in my journal to remind
myself, *"maybe it's speaking, mobilizing, and training that you are*
preparing me for?"

I had also received numerous affirmations that I was to *proclaim*
what God had done for us. When I put all of those pieces of guidance
together, I couldn't help but discern that they were answers to my
prayers for direction and purpose. Without other sources of earthly
security, I learned to depend on the Word of God, literally. I was
living out the evidence of God's promises and seeing them real
in my life.

"Whether you turn to the right or to the left, your ears will hear a
voice behind you, saying, 'This is the way; walk in it.'"
— Isaiah 30:21

It was the sincere conviction that God was directing me to speak
that influenced my decisions to say yes to nearly every opportunity
He brought my way. Doors were opening for me to give my testimony

and share our story and I prayerfully considered each opportunity. Besides opening the doors, He also provided for the kids in my absence. If my mom wasn't available to come and stay, He brought in back-ups. Renewed friendship with Chris's good friend, Lyle, from college provided another church family for us. Each of them were uniquely gifted and poised to be extended family to all of us; another local uncle to the kids, a trusted man for my boys, single women who were godly and capable for being my "sub mom," and prayer warriors who willingly prayed and "held my arms up" as I navigated the chaos of that season.

With the help and support of a small army, I said yes to as many speaking engagements I could fit in during our Home Assignment. Each time I went, God's presence and voice were obvious to me, and I felt fully alive. Although my loneliness and the longings of my flesh continued to rage inside of me, God mercifully directed me toward purposeful ways to share all that I was learning. For me, grief felt like an intense longing, and it was a constant thorn in my side unless I focused on something that pointed me outside of myself. Being the main speaker for a women's retreat in Maui led to one of the most supernatural messages from God I have ever received.

My emotions and feelings surged inside of me like a raging sea, even as I sat looking out at the powerful waves breaking on the black, volcanic rocks of a remote cove on the island of Maui. No matter where I was, I often awoke with thoughts of humans rather than God. In order to quiet my thoughts, I prayed for God to forgive me for my fickle heart and for my longings that always threatened to distract me. Then, I found an activity that would redirect my focus. Finishing my notes for speaking that weekend was the timely obvious choice, so I found a private place and settled in for a study session on the veranda of the cottage I was staying in.

It wasn't difficult to feel like I was immersed in the presence of the Creator when I sat with my Bible and journal on a covered porch perched on the cliffs overlooking the ocean. I took in the scene of the powerful, crashing, foaming waves with every sense built into me. Darkened hues of lush green cowered in the darkness of early morning, waiting in stillness for the battering of rhythmic waves. With a mighty roar, each wave would roll toward towering onyx rocks and then explode in thunder over its target. Foamy, white froth hissed out to sea as the steady rhythm of the tide lunged forward in succession.

Breathing was easy here and each deep breath into my lungs brought the cool moisture of morning and the delightful, salty, tropical fragrance I craved. Maui had become one of my sacred places because it held so many precious memories of time with my dad. He still lived there as a *"kamaaina,"* or local. He found sanctuary in this place when my parent's marriage suddenly ended in divorce. The island and surrounding Pacific had been a comfort to him, and I sat there calmed with the power of God's creation.

There were four speaking sessions that I was prepared to deliver, so I found this spot before each meeting to pray, pull my thoughts together, and prepare myself to be used in the lives of the women there. Even after the first day of the retreat, my prayers reflected the way God was opening my eyes to the fact that I wasn't the only woman on the planet who was struggling.

JOURNAL ENTRY

September 27, 2015

"Be strong. Take heart. Wait patiently for the LORD."
– Psalm 27:14 (It was the "Psalm of the day"
- #27 on the 27th)

Thank you for showing me that I am not alone. Many women live with the same longings I have for MANY years. This weekend I met a 70-year old woman who was divorced very young and has been single all of this time and a fifty-nine year old, beautiful woman who has never been married even though she longed for it. I can't begin to understand your ways or Your timing, Lord, but I DO know of Your goodness.

Help me to live more intently focused on the light of your presence. How I praise You for showing up this weekend! Speak through me in this last session and leave these women with an embrace from You that will fill them to overflowing in this community.

As the women gathered in the meeting room for the very last session of the weekend, I took a few minutes on the balcony to pray and focus. Looking out over the jungle of green and the dark ocean beyond, I continued to ask God to speak through me so that the women at the retreat would be filled. I asked Him to give them a vision for how they could allow that to overflow on the people who needed Jesus and to open their hearts for the Nations. With one last deep breath of the ocean air, I turned and entered the long dining hall where we would have our last meeting.

Clusters of friends gathered on the far end of the room where we had chairs set up and a small podium where I would sit to speak. Since it was a group of only twenty-five or so women, I usually sat on the edge of the platform or stood in the small space in front of them when I got a little more passionate in whatever I was saying. The listeners in the front were in the splash zone, for my suffering and joy still intermingled inside like two fronts of a storm that met unexpectedly and exploded into squalls of tears and watery snot. Those unexpected waterworks shows had trained me to ask for tissue in advance of events like these.

I looked at my watch to see that only five minutes remained before we sang a prelude of worship songs. Looking up, I noticed a woman motioning for me to meet her at the back of the room near one of the tables. Ayme had been one of the women I was drawn to from the time I met her. She was close to my age, and she seemed to carry the depth and afflictions of her life in a countenance of warm compassion. As we got acquainted during one of the weekend meals, her eyes met mine in a bond of pain that said, "I understand. I've been to the darkness of pain and loss where you have been."

That familiarity with suffering had bonded us in that single, late-night conversation so that we greeted each other with a hug of new friendship on the last morning of the retreat. She took my hand in hers. Although we had just met, it was as if she could see into my soul and anticipate my innate inner turmoil when I was in a position of receiving rather than giving. Her sincerity was humbling as she warned me, "Don't stop me or tell me no. God told me to do this."

As I sat obediently, tears already falling from my eyes, she removed the ornately carved, silver traditional heirloom Hawaiian bracelet from her wrist. I knew what it meant because of repeated visits to the island to visit my dad. Hawaiian culture took this seriously and the deep sentiment of receiving such a gift had been passed down for generations. It was against their tradition to buy this jewelry for yourself; it was historically only worn as a gift received in love. For that reason, I had silently longed for the beautiful, hand-crafted jewelry but never owned it.

Now, I sat with my arm out to receive this gift from a new friend who had been given an assignment from her Heavenly Father. She didn't even know that I was about to speak about being obedient to the prompting of the Holy Spirit! As she removed the bracelet from her own wrist to put it on mine, she said, "God wants you to know that you are His beloved. My name is Ayme, which means 'beloved.'" As she ran her finger over the black engraved script on the bracelet, she continued, "In Hawaiian, that would be translated, 'Mea Aloha.'"

"Michelle, God loves you and wants you to always remember that you are not alone. You are His beloved. Please have this as a constant reminder."

I sat in shock. To begin with, there wasn't a living being in all the earth who knew how badly I wanted a piece of this jewelry, but jewelry is just a material thing! God had taken a tangible, human desire and used it as a sign that this gift was directly from Him. He moved in Ayme's heart to give it to me and then used it to get my attention so that I would hear what He wanted to speak over me that day!

It wasn't easy for her to give me the token of love, though. As the clock ticked away the remaining minutes before I was to speak and the worship leader began to strum, Ayme struggled to force the bangle over my big hand and onto my wrist. She had to call in a back-up who eventually ran to the kitchen for a disposable plastic glove. Placing that over my hand, both of them shoved the bracelet over my hand, leaving streaks of swollen redness in the wake of the loving gift. Needless to say, the bracelet has remained on my wrist for all of these years as a reminder that God is with me and that He calls me His beloved.

68 | He Sees and Hears

*"A father to the fatherless, a defender of widows,
is God in his holy dwelling."*
— Psalm 68:5

After returning from the trip to Maui, the fall continued on with a schedule that onlookers would have assumed was normalcy. Julia was studying at university and Olivia had finished her Aesthetics program and returned to California to spend some time with the family and get her bearings before figuring out where she would go and what she would do next. The four younger kids were enrolled in the local public school district and attending weekly classes at an independent studies site. The flexible schedule allowed them to do their schoolwork whether they were in San Diego or staying with grandparents when I had to travel.

Before the end of our last term in Kenya, I had journaled that I was feeling a "strange sense of anticipation" about whatever awaited us in America. By the fall of that same year, a trip to our organization's headquarters revealed that the "strange sense" wasn't a fabricated feeling or a fortune cookie prediction of what was to come. I had packed up our house at the school and put things in storage with every intention of returning after a yearlong hiatus, working there until Jed graduated, and *then* asking God what His plans were for me. I had no idea that my tidy little timeline wasn't what God had in mind. He was about to blow my mind with another surprise.

The trip to Georgia to serve as the "missionary in residence" at an orientation week came a couple of short months after Ayme shoved the silver bangle onto my wrist as a constant reminder that I was beloved by the God of the universe. Without any way of removing it, I passed through TSA for my trip and, as the alarm

374

on the metal detector beeped, I felt a sense of joy rather than embarrassment. With a little smile, I remembered Ayme's message from God: "I AM LOVED."

This time, when I arrived in Peachtree City, Georgia for meetings at our home office, I slid the hotel card key in the magic slot that unlocked the room and entered the modern, corporately clean hotel room. Crossing the threshold, I breathed in the sterilized smell of the crisp, fresh towels and bedding and was immediately confronted with a new me. I had traveled there solo. For the first time in my adult life, I faced that empty room with a sense of independence and even energizing anticipation for the time of solitude I would have for that week. The opportunity to share all that God had done so far in our journey had given me an overview of His purposes in my life.

God's work behind the scenes on our behalf wasn't revealed until mid-week when Wade, the U.S. director, suggested meeting with me to hear another update on the whole family. The opportunity was an example of the love and care I continually received from the organization, and I was moved by his interest. As I unpacked the last year and a half or so of our trauma, transitions, and progress, *including* the ways I was seeing God use Chris's life and death, his countenance became pensive. By the end of the second meeting, he was asking me to pray about moving back to San Diego to recruit and send people to work in Africa rather than be the one to go.

Immediately, the idea of serving in a new capacity as a mobilizer and living in the States became the "lab" for the lessons God had been teaching me *months* before. Looking back, I was less of a willing student than I would have hoped to be. While I could clearly see God's preparation and leading in this direction, my heart and spirit protested with the thought of another move and more transitions for the kids. I returned to San Diego seeking wise counsel and prayers from my family, church family, and faithful prayer warriors. Within a few months, the reason for my earlier anticipation appeared as clearly as a brightly lit runway: "WE ARE TO RETURN TO AMERICA."

69 | Persistent Widow

"My present circumstances that are pressing hard against me are the tool God is using to shape me for eternity. So TRUST HIM and stop pushing away the instrument..."

The irony of belonging in Kenya and being directed back to San Diego seemed to poke at me like a thorn in my side, although every voice in my life, including God's, confirmed that accepting the role of Southwest Mobilizer and settling back in our SoCal hometown was what we were supposed to do. With our personal belongings packed in storage in Kenya and a whole household to sell, I returned to the school with the three younger kids to sort our things, get rid of what we could, and move again. They were the ones who had expressed a need to say goodbye and I knew that would help them process the next move. Even though I was confident I was doing the right thing at the time, my heart pushed back because of the pain of wrenching ourselves away from a place and people we loved again.

Stepping back into life in America after living in Kenya for only two years stirred me up in a myriad of ways. Although family and friends were much closer geographically, life was busy and much less focused on community. There were no house helpers or friends who came daily to help me nor sit and have chai with me. The kids' learning felt like a ball and chain to all of us. Everything felt so different and hard. How could they retain anything when their whole world was spinning?

It often felt like it was too much to bear and the pit of loneliness I found myself in often left me discouraged and depleted. I knew where to go for hope and strength, so I begged for it. My fiftieth birthday approached, and I felt like there was no way I could face a future alone. There was no way my kids could understand my longings for companionship and touch. They were kids. The isolation of my inner struggles made the emotions even more intense, and with two of my widow friends getting married within weeks of each other, my desires felt magnified. It seemed like everyone else in the world had a partner, someone to share their life with, someone who would think of them and celebrate them. The fact that nobody was initiating a plan for my big milestone birthday made me feel isolated and hopeless in my grief.

My written prayers revealed the darker side of my thought life. Three years after Chris's death, my body moved through the motions of my busy life, but inside I was the modern version of the persistent widow.

JOURNAL ENTRY

April 28, 2016

> *"But when they cried out to the Lord,*
> *He raised up for them a deliverer..."*
> *— Judges 3:9*

Today, you have reminded me that *You hear my cries and you are in the process of raising up a deliverer.* You are never late! In that passage, when Othniel was raised up by you, the Spirit of the Lord came on him and he *knew* what he was called to do AND he was *ready* to become the man they needed.

Lord, YOU are my Deliverer, my very present help. I know that. Would you be raising up a man to be my helper, my companion, a stepfather to my kids. Through your Holy Spirit, will you prepare and equip him to be exactly what each of us needs. And, will you work in him so loudly that he will *know* what you are calling him to; that he would quite literally *become* a husband and father-figure to us (just like Othniel *became* Israel's judge and went to war).

While I was praying for one helper in the form of a man with skin, God was working behind the scenes answering my prayers in ways I hadn't asked for. My help came in the form of a few people at church who were well equipped to help me navigate the real estate market in San Diego. We were going to settle in, and we needed a place of our own. Although I was confident that the decision I had made to accept the role of mobilizer, which would have me working remotely from home and traveling a bit, I still had an inner dialogue going on that must have seemed like a rebellious five-year-old who was being made to do something she didn't want to do.

Even as my milestone birthday was approaching, so was the new school year. We needed a place to live so that I could enroll the kids in school and be ready when the first day of school came. The deadline gave me the urgency I needed to push through my hesitations and grumblings, but I still didn't want to *buy* a house and put my roots down in America. In my mind, being in San Diego was only temporary. Wasn't I supposed to be in Africa?

Those thoughts and questions plagued my mind and distracted me no matter what I was doing. On this particular Sunday, my prayers were more like begging and wrestling and distracted me from the sermon. It wasn't until Pastor Kenny stood up and gave the benediction that I awoke to my surroundings. I surveyed the scene as people stood to their feet and started the customary end-of-church greetings and introductions. My eyes caught Justin, an acquaintance who I somehow knew was in the real estate business. I took in a deep breath, squashed my pride, and tapped him on the arm.

"Hey, Justin. How are you? You're in real estate, right? Do you know anything about renting houses in this area?"

His towering frame made him approachable and jolly and, as he looked down slightly at me, a deep chuckle escaped with his response, "Yea, you can say that. I actually manage rentals in the area, but that's not what you need. It would be better to buy."

"Oh, I don't need to buy a house," I explained. "I don't plan on being here long-term. I want to be available and ready when God tells me to go somewhere else... like back to Africa."

"Well, here's the thing about buying versus renting. Renting's going to cost you a lot more in this area and I'm not sure you can afford that. Do you have any money set aside to put a deposit down and buy a house?"

I didn't want to think about why I had money set aside. It was life insurance money from Chris and I didn't want to touch it. It felt sacred and I didn't want to spend it haphazardly. Pushing back tears, I spit out my honest answer, "Well, I have life insurance money, but that would be a lot of money to spend out of there."

It was Justin's next response that God used to point me in the direction I needed to go: "Michelle, putting a down payment on a house to purchase it is an investment. It's not wasting the money; it's diversifying your portfolio. And besides, just because you own a house doesn't mean you have to *live* in it. My whole business is managing other people's properties for them while they live elsewhere."

With that nudge in the right direction, I had what I needed. Humbling myself further, I reached out to more friends to help me with the house hunt. Our administrator from church was a trusted friend and agreed to join me in the search. He even looked at houses for me when I had to be out of town for work. Then, I called on our same hero realtor friend, Ann, who had sold our other house to act as my agent. My college friend, Lyle, brought the other set of eyes to scope out the aesthetics and neighborhoods. Together, we all set out to find the house that would shelter us through our next season.

I had a serious list of what I was looking for. It had to have four bedrooms, turnkey ready to move-in, located in a "safe" area, big enough to fit four kids and me. Yet, I wanted it to be small enough that I wouldn't be knocking around in it if I ended up living there alone and gray when the kids grew up. It also needed to sit within the boundary lines of the neighborhood schools I wanted the kids to go to. Oh, and I didn't want to look out my window and see houses on every side. I had been living in places surrounded by mountains, open spaces, views as far as the eyes could see, and had just come from the edge of the jungle where I greeted monkeys in the morning. How could I live in a neighborhood again?

We didn't have to look at very many houses as there was a limited number of them on the market during that time. Besides, once we approached the house with the red door, I knew we had found it. Ann's husband, Hal, was the one to turn the key and open the door that day. He carried his camp chair in, set it down in the empty living room, and took a seat while we walked around. As I went room to room, I checked off the mental list in my mind: park across the street, only a few houses on the cul-de-sac, one-two-three-four bedrooms, two bathrooms. The hall bath had ugly, yellow paint, but I could paint well! There were restored, original wood floors, appliances, a two-car garage with a washer and dryer, and a backyard with a lovely curly willow tree that shaded most of the grass. Something on the far side of the yard caught my eye. There, next to a garden box, was something I had always wanted…. a real, multi-layer, Smith & Hawken compost bin!

It probably isn't wise to base a decision to buy a home on things that weren't even on the list of needs, but three things served as signs for me that day: the red door, the wood-burning fireplace, and the compost bin. Those features of the house showed me that God knew my heart and He wasn't just providing what I needed, but He was giving me things that I wanted and hadn't even prayed for. The compost bin was just the beginning. We were about to move into a house of our own and we had nothing to fill it with.

Our move into the house by the park was like our move *out* of our house in 2011, but in reverse. This time, friends from church and family members pooled their resources to bring furniture *into* the house rather than moving it out. I bought a few things from garage sales and consignment stores, one of my mom's Bible study friends was downsizing, moving, and selling a whole household of designer furniture, and my mom and stepdad were ready to get rid of their couch. By the time the kids and I stood in the kitchen together eating hot n ready pizza in our new house, we each had a bed to sleep on and a table to use. We could finally unpack our totes and luggage after eleven months of staying in the mission house!

There was no time to rest, though. The first day of school was imminent and four of my kids still needed schools to attend. As another summer passed with warm days of outdoor activities and home projects to make our house our own, I set my mind to navigating the school system. As it turned out, our new house sat right *on* the line that divided the feeding patterns for the neighborhood schools. I would have to pray for a miracle and ask for favor from the district to get my kids into the schools where they had peers and some familiarity. We had missed the deadline for the "school choice application" because we were still out of the country, but I filled out the necessary paperwork and headed to the district office to make my plea.

The labyrinth of bungalows didn't provide the grace and favor that I had prayed for. As I stood there with a file folder of paperwork and a string of plot twists to explain the reason we had missed the choice deadline for enrollment in the schools I wanted for my children, I was met with a very firm, final answer. "No, ma'am. We cannot make exceptions. There are waitlists at these schools and the site administrators make those decisions. They'll have to go to the schools according to the zoning map."

"But those schools aren't even the ones closest to our house..."

"I'm sorry. No exceptions."

Indignation rose in me, and it felt like bile rose in my throat as I turned to walk away. My shoulders hung in exasperation and tears streamed down my face. With no other plan or idea in sight, I voiced my plea to the One who promised to be with me wherever I went: "Lord, I need help. I can't send my kids to those schools. They won't be safe, and they can't walk that far when I'm unable to pick them up. They need to be close to our friends so they have somewhere to go when I'm working. *Please*, make a way."

A few weeks passed and the first day of school arrived. Both Jed and Silly were able to attend our high school of choice because they had a "grandfather clause" that allowed seniors to stay at the school even if they moved out of the neighborhood. Since Jed was going into his senior year and Silly was an incoming freshman, I was able to get her enrolled based on Jed's attendance at the school. With two down and two to go, I packed lunches for Joseph and Duane, dressed them in their new school outfits, and drove them to the same middle school Olivia had gone to years before. While I wasn't promising them anything, I told them that we were going to pray for God's favor and do our best.

The drop off zone in front of the school was crowded with cars dropping off students of a variety of sizes. Some looked too young to be attending middle school and slowly approached the open gate hesitantly with trepidation, and others looked like they belonged at the high school across town. The vast majority of the kids, whether they walked with confidence or with dreadful hesitation, all sported crisp, bright new outfits, and clean shoes. As I approached the driveway that led to the administration building, Joseph and Duane's eyes scanned the crowd with curious interest.

I turned into the parking space in front of the office, took a deep breath, and calmed my inner "mama bear" so that I could present myself in the most patient and kind way possible. I squashed down the fear of what I would have to do if this plan failed and opened the back door for the boys. "Ok, boys, put your backpacks on and follow me. I'll answer all of your questions after I talk to the secretary at the desk."

The warm summer sun still lingered outside, so entering the cool office felt refreshing and promising. A businesslike voice greeted us before I could even get the lay of the land. "Good morning. How can I help you?"

I noted that she would need some buttering up and poured on the sweetness. "We've just recently moved back to the neighborhood, and I am hoping to enroll the boys for school. I'm sorry. I know today is a crazy one for you."

She paused, shifting her eyes toward the two dark-skinned boys who had entered with me. There was another quick pause as her mind caught up to our curious lack of family resemblance. "I'll need to check our numbers, but I'm pretty sure we still have openings. Just one second."

My prayers started as soon as she stood and walked toward the back of the office and through a doorway to an adjacent office. Time stood still. The clock hanging over the door ticked its seconds and there was a buzz as the first bell of the day signaled the impending start of the school day. "Lord, please make a way."

She returned, and my heart raced as a lump formed in my throat. I waited as she approached with papers in her hand. "Here's the paperwork you'll need to fill out for them to start today. Let's get them to class and then you can finish the forms and bring them back later."

"They're in?" My voice was breathless as I asked in wonder.

"Yep. We still had a few spots and we're still finalizing enrollment numbers for the district. Welcome to iMiddle."

"Oh, wow. How can I thank you? God used you to answer our prayers today!"

"You're so welcome. Just doing my job."

She arranged for a student aid to show Joseph and Duane to class, and I stood staring after them as they walked toward the school building. There was no way to know how their junior high experience would be, but I breathed deeply and rested in the knowledge that God had clearly led us there. I knew in my head that God was providing for us, teaching me, refining me, and making me stronger than ever; but my heart still cried out. The pages of my journal that summer reflect the tension that I lived with, a desire to be content and dependent on God, but an aching longing for someone to love.

JOURNAL ENTRY

Summer, 2016

Thank you for this house, a home base that allows us to "enjoy safe pastures." You knew exactly what we needed for this time. We needed the freedom to put things on the wall, make it our own, and "DWELL" in the land.

Thank you for showing me that I can be ok and have a good life without a man. Do I still want to be married? YES! Yet, I see that you are using this season of suffering and grief to refine me, to grow me, to show me who I am in You and standing alone before You. You are showing me that I can do all things through You, that You are my helper and my very great reward.

I still want to beg you to let me have someone to love, to beg you to bring an end to the waiting, but I will "drink this cup" you have given me. It's not going to be a guzzling mess with my nose plugged, but rather a steady drink that allows me to taste it and glean all that you would have me learn from this time. You delight me, Lord. Thank you for this picture that has helped me understand what you are doing.

70 | Crying Out

"He is ABLE to do IMMEASURABLY MORE than all we ask or imagine, according to HIS POWER that is at work within us."
— Ephesians 3:20

With a stateside position with AIM, a roof over our heads, and all of the kids settling into a new normal in San Diego, my life as a widowed mom continued with a new and heavy sense of finality. I battled against the continued shock of having a routine that was similar to the one Chris and I shared when we were raising the kids in the same neighborhood before we moved to Africa. I drove the same streets, dropped the kids off at school in the mornings, and picked them up in the afternoons. We were involved in the same church and the rhythm of our life started feeling similar to what it was before. But it wasn't at all what it was supposed to be. Chris's absence felt even more obvious as I lived out the days that had been determined for me.

Holidays and milestones were still the most difficult to bear, and my loneliness often bore down on me with more of the same struggles. When my lone, widowed friend remarried, I felt like the reality of my life was downright disheartening. I had to develop little tricks and tools that brought me comfort and purpose when the darkness of my pain set in. My goal was to replace the hopeless thoughts that plagued me with specific words from God that would refocus my mind and heart on HIS eternal plans for me. Above all, I knew I had to stop comparing my life with those around me and focus on eternal truths.

One helpful trick I did every year was to ask God to give me a word or phrase to meditate on. Sometimes the process felt downright superstitious, but it was better than focusing inward at the torrent of misery that boiled under the surface of my emotional life. As 2016 ended, the kids and I had made it through another year by simply living one day at a time and it was time to choose a truth to live by. Each day, as I read during my quiet times and listened to an unending stream of worship music on K-Love, I watched and listened for a consistent message. My prayers went something like this:

"Give me the kind of faith that would write my name next to a promise in your Word and *claim it*. I remember your promise of peace. Help me to leave things in your hands, and be THANKFUL. Strengthen my resolve to trust in *your* plan and BE STILL."

It was a turn of the page that landed me on two words in 2 Corinthians 1:6, "patient endurance."

Yes! I thought, *patient endurance is mine in Jesus! I can do this with His help!*

As I started the fourth year without Chris, I chose to navigate another year with this prayer: "Lord, give me patient endurance as I wait for the fulfillment of Your promises in my life!"

Without the power to see the future, I had no idea what He was up to behind the scenes.

71 | The Promised Land

"LORD, You have heard the desire of the humble;
You will prepare (her) heart;
You will cause Your ear to hear..."
— Psalm 10:17

New Year's Day fell on a Sunday in 2017, and since the kids and I had already returned to San Diego after celebrating the holidays with extended family, we rolled into the second service a bit late, road weary from our road trip through Southern California. I had been attending the church for so many years that it wasn't difficult to find a friend to sit with; but no matter who I chose, it was a reminder that Chris was gone, and I was no longer a part of a couple. Now, it was normal for the kids and me to approach the double doors of the sanctuary as a family; but then the kids scanned the congregation for their friends and went to sit with them. I looked for a place where I wouldn't be noticed, and I could just focus on the service. Loneliness still lingered from Christmas, leaving me sensitive and solemn, so I slipped into a chair in the side section during the opening prayer while everyone had their heads bowed.

I hate to admit that I don't remember much now about the service. What happened next hijacked any other memories I have from that day. Once the closing song finished and the "amen" of the closing prayer was spoken, I stood and turned to greet my fellow attendees as the pastor suggested. Before I made it two steps, a familiar looking man approached me. I had seen him often but didn't yet know him personally. He was older than me and not yet elderly, but he was using a walker.

As he introduced himself to me, he sounded frazzled and nervous. "Hi, Michelle. I couldn't help notice you. When you walked in late and sat down, it was like the Holy Spirit spoke to me... I know this sounds really weird, but I have to ask you. I've been praying for an answer from God, and I think I just got it. I booked a dream trip to Israel to take my mom for her 80th birthday. It's always been a dream of hers to go, but now my health won't allow me to travel... I know it's short notice and you are a very busy person, but will you please consider accompanying her on the trip? Of course all of your expenses will be taken care of. Like I said, the Holy Spirit told me that you're the one who is to go with her."

I'm sure my face reflected my shock. WHAT DO YOU SAY TO THAT?! I was stunned. I felt like I needed to look around to see if someone had exposed the fact that I had a long-time, unrealized dream to go to Israel. This wasn't just a tour; this was a biblical archaeology tour to places most other tourists don't get to see! I'm still absolutely sure that God and Chris are the only ones who knew how badly I wanted to go to the Holy Land, and they were both in Heaven! When you're in shock, logic seems to take extra thought. Knowing that Chris couldn't have told Dave about the fact that I even envied people who got to go on such a trip and struggled with jealousy over it, I had to believe that he had told me the truth of the matter! The Holy Spirit had directed this man who barely knew me to send me on the trip of a lifetime with his mother who was also a widow. I couldn't have even *dreamed* this opportunity up and definitely hadn't even asked God for it!

While I absolutely *wanted* to go, there were a few things in the way of me giving him an immediate and definitive answer. I was a widowed mother who still had four kids at home, a full-time job, *and* I was scheduled to be the main speaker at a youth camp in Pennsylvania the very day we were supposed to return to LAX. I did the only two things I knew I could do: I turned my plans over to God and took one step at a time to ask people for help.

Moving forward with such a bold plan to ask for help and permission for me to be out of the country *for over two weeks* seemed like too big of an ask, yet there were tell-tale signs that God was in it. This was one of those "Jordan River moments" when my circumstance felt like a river at flood stage. Like the priests in the book of Joshua, I had to stick my feet in to see the miracle happen. My first step was to ask for permission to leave work for two weeks. That request was met with generous and excited encouragement to go and consider it a gift from the Lord. My boss saw it as an opportunity for growth that would benefit me in my position. My mom and my "substitute mom friends" were available to come stay with the kids. Then, when I got word that the itinerary could be changed slightly without additional expense and I could fly directly from Istanbul to the East coast rather than LAX on the return, I knew God had answered my prayers and made a way. HE HAD DROPPED ONE OF MY HEART'S DESIRES IN MY LAP WITHOUT ME EVEN ASKING FOR IT!

If there was one way to instill patient endurance in me, it was to show me in a tangible, supernatural way that He knew my heart. I was going to Israel! Not only that, but I would depart on the four year anniversary of Chris's death. Only a loving Father would know how perfect that timing was! There was plenty to process, but *this* time it was for something unfathomably good!

"THE LORD HEARS WHEN I CALL TO HIM." Psalm 4:3

It seems completely selfish and blind in light of the huge gift God had just handed me that I still found myself feeling like I was living out my existence in a dry, deserted desert. My life as a widowed mom had extended into another year and the milestone of the fourth anniversary of Chris's death loomed in my subconscious. By this time, even I was growing weary hearing my own prayers. In my heart of hearts, I knew there was a God in Heaven who was real, who loved me, heard my prayers, and cared about what happened to me. After all, look what He had just done in my life! The truth was, though, that at the end of the day, when the house was quiet and I sat alone dreading going to bed, my sorrow would grow overwhelming and I'd have to force my mind to believe God's presence was with me and search for it, even when I didn't *feel* Him.

Thankfully, by this time I had tried and true things I knew I could *do* that would turn my thoughts away from myself and back to trusting that God saw me. With the house darkened, I would turn the TV off, put down my phone, light a beautifully scented candle, and put worship music on. Closing my eyes, I allowed myself to focus on the music of hope and truth. Eventually, I'd coax myself to crawl into bed and pray myself to sleep.

"Here I am again, Lord, in this place of longing that drives me crazy. You are doing huge things in my life - beyond my wildest imagination - and I still can't shake my thoughts from wandering to my desire for a human companion. Fill me now, Jesus. You are my joy. You have the power and presence to NEVER leave me or forsake me... when I call, you listen... When I want to spend time with you, you never say no. I love you, Jesus, fill me up to the point today that I see afresh that I can have contentment without a man by my side. Show me your presence, LORD.

Have I discerned a promise from you that I won't always be alone? Are you telling me, 'It's not NO, it's just not NOW?' Speak to me clearly about this so that my heart can 'wait expectantly' on your promise. I don't want to wait for something YOU haven't promised.

How long, Lord?! Turn! Deliver me! Either set me free from these longings or bring forth 'the appointed time!'"

WALKING WHERE JESUS WALKED!

There was a lot to process and plan in order to get ready for the trip of a lifetime, and there was even required homework to do. I was jumping in at the last minute to take Dave's place on the trip, so that meant I had to cram and catch up. After all, I didn't want to miss *anything!* All of the preparation served as a healthy distraction for my wrestling and longings and took my eyes off myself.

From our homes in separate states, each member of the tour group watched videos about some of the archaeological digs we were going to visit, poured over historical accounts about the region, and worked through a Bible study that highlighted the biblical history of the places we would visit. I searched for just the right journal to use for all of these things and planned to take detailed notes throughout the journey. The front of the vibrant, pistachio-colored blank book was inscribed with Psalm 46:10: *"Be still and know that I am GOD."*

Making this journal my own brought me tremendous joy, and so I penned quotes, verses, and notes with purpose. The inside title page displays my excitement. Right above *"Michelle"* in cursive is this inscription, "Israel, 2017 because 'He is able to do *immeasurably more* than all we ask or imagine, according to His power that is at work within us.'" Ephesians 3:20

My notes on the first few pages are haphazard and unorganized, just like my thoughts during that time. I had lists scratched on one-page and journal entries on the next. Prayer requests interrupt the content on other pages as communication among the tour group increased. Right above a list of prayer requests, there's a written goal: "Choose something special to buy and wear 'as a memorial to the LORD' for what He has done." We had been reading in the book of Exodus about the priestly garments and I was inspired by verses eleven, and twelve, *"Engrave the names of the sons of Israel on the two stones the way a gem cutter engraves a seal. Then mount the stones in gold filigree settings and fasten them on the shoulder pieces of the ephod AS MEMORIAL STONES for the sons of Israel."*

Meeting my traveling companion, Rachel, was a sweet comfort and confirmation. Dave, her son who obeyed the Spirit's prompting to charge me with accompanying his beloved mom, invited us both to meet for lunch at a local restaurant. As soon as I stepped into the lobby and met Rachel for the first time, I knew we'd be compatible. When our eyes met, we both seemed to breathe in a deep sigh of relief. Her warm smile told me that we were already friends and I reached down to give her a side-hug. She was shorter than me and stood with a certain unsteadiness as if she needed to have her hand on something secure in order to feel strong. When I looked down to glance at her hand on my forearm, there on the tips of her fingers was the only sign I needed to confirm that this was indeed an arrangement made by God Himself: she had glittery, silver nails! It was a choice I would have made!

Getting acquainted with Rachel was like meeting up with a dear relative I hadn't seen in a long time. Her skin glowed with sunshine, and she had sparkly eyes that grew brighter when she spoke of her late husband. Although he had passed away ten years before our trip, she still lived with his lingering presence through her vivid memories. Turning eighty was stirring up a restlessness in her because she just didn't *feel* that old! Her styled gray hair and denim jeans gave her a dignity and spunk that drew me to her, and I detected a stubbornness in her that would give her what she needed to hike through the Promised Land with her little shuffling feet.

A couple of short weeks later that milestone day arrived. It was February 16, 2017, four years after Chris's death and the first day of my God-given dream trip. After a memorial lunch with my kids at our favorite local burger joint, Dave and Rachel picked me up, the kids sent us off with waves, and air kisses from the whole family. While Rachel was a bundle of nerves to make her first international trip, I was full of excitement and anticipation to board a plane and leave U.S. soil for a destination where I'd never been. There were few things that took my mind off of my current circumstances like getting on a plane, and I had a sense that there was a treasure of some kind waiting for me there on that holy ground.

As it turned out, there were so many deeply personal connections to the history I encountered there, that it was difficult to catalog each of them in the pages of my journal. It's not an exaggeration to say that there's enough to tell about that trip to fill another book. I can already picture the title: *Beloved: A Persistent Widow's Journey Through the Promised Land*. Every day held more lessons, beauty, and visual evidence than I could possibly retain or record. There are places in my journal where the writing trails off in wiggly squiggles because I was attempting to write, listen, and hike around an archaeological site at the same time. I saw evidence of the One True God I had placed my trust in way back when I was twenty years old. I stood in places and looked out over the same mountains that Abram saw before God renamed him Abraham. Many nights I struggled to sleep because my mind was racing in an attempt to file the sights that exceeded my wildest dreams into logical categories in my memory.

Our days were filled with traveling from archaeological sites to major places of interests and landmarks all over Israel and the West Bank. There was so much to see that either our guide or the biblical archaeologist who was with us even gave instruction as we rode along in the tour bus. Those were times of clarification when we could ask questions and get added insight on places we had just seen, or even things we saw along the way out of the comfort of our air-conditioned coach. All of that was bonus material, but it had a downside for me. Our time at each place was limited. I wanted to linger unsupervised in every place and soak in the whole scope of each site, savoring and capturing the essence of every detail. I felt like a selfish child, forced to leave a fun activity and tempted to resist the hectic nature of the schedule by talking back in a whine of discontent, "Pleeeeasee can't we stay loooonger?"

High hopes for what I would see at the next site renewed my expectation every time we rolled toward a new adventure, so the day we pulled into Tabgha, I was filled with anticipation. I was eager to see the Mount of Beatitudes because I had a feeling Jesus had a message for me there. Everyone piled out of the bus and headed out to explore the grounds before wandering to the meeting place where we would have our devotional speaker. I sat and listened with mediocre attentiveness as my mind wandered to the grassy hillside off in the distance that looked over the Sea of Galilee glistening in the valley below.

This was a highly trafficked stop for tourists on their pilgrimages through the Holy Land, so fences and barriers prevented me from living my daydream and sitting on the actual mount where Jesus had spoken from for a time of long reflection. Despite the confining structure of the visit, I received the personal and direct word from Jesus that I had needed to hear for a long time. With only ten minutes to reflect on what we had experienced in a quiet place of our choosing, I sat down to write so that both the message I received and the vision of this place were etched in my memory.

NOTES IN MY TRAVEL JOURNAL

Mount of Beatitudes, Day 4

"Lord, Jesus, you see and you know. Thank you for the way you clearly speak to me visually. As I walked into this garden, the first marker I saw was the one that said,

   "BLESSED ARE THOSE WHO MOURN,
   FOR THEY WILL BE COMFORTED."

I'm not even sure if that is the first one in the garden, but it's the one you drew my attention to. Thank you for powerfully speaking to me, for the peace you have given me in these days. You are answering my prayers for a deeper healing.

The verses that stood out to me today, as they were read by the group, were verse 8, "Your Father knows what you need before you ask Him." You are showing me so clearly that this is true, Lord. You knew I needed to SEE these things and walk where you walked. I receive this Truth from you today, Jesus. Keep me mindful of it even after this, that you do know what I need and when I need it. I trust you, Lord.

One version someone read of verse 6:21 said, "For where your treasure is, there the desires of your heart will be..." Lord, I confess that I have held onto the treasure of having a man to love me. Help me to let go of that treasure, trading it in for the GREATEST treasure, my eternal relationship with you.

QUMRAN

February 25, 2017

As the days unfolded, all that I saw overwhelmed me. It was as if each stop was more powerful than the last and added another layer of evidence to my mustard seed faith. Historical events that I had tucked away in my brain as "Bible stories" came to life as each detail described in God's Word was laid out before me, excavated by generations of archaeologists. Before this, I had never even dreamed of *standing* in front of the former gates of Jericho to *see* the walls of the city where they had stood tall and fortified unearthed in a pile of rubble. Even the layers of burn scar were easy to see in areas of the site. It felt like we had traveled there in a time machine as we turned from the site to the rooftop diner where we ate lunch with a view of the place where the *commander* of the Lord's army appeared to Joshua and said, "Take off your sandals, for the place where you are standing is holy."

Kabobs and hummus seemed an inadequate feast in a place of such significance, yet we sat on the patio and ate with a view of Jericho's ancient fallen walls baking in the desert sun. Filled with food and awe, we boarded our holy coach for what was promised to be the hike of a lifetime. After a brief walkabout at the remains of the two thousand year old Essene settlement, we rode on the bus to an unmarked part of a two-lane highway and disembarked, gathering in a huddle amid stones and dust on the side of the highway. Across the highway in the distance, the Dead Sea spread out like a mirage, but we would have to wait until later to touch it. Our next quest was to hike toward the rocky, jagged, camo-colored hills to go *inside* the first cave discovered in Qumran. It was the actual cave where a young shepherd tossed a rock in and heard a clunk, discovering the first pottery storage jars containing the Dead Sea Scrolls.

We gathered around Joel, the biblical archaeologist who was traveling with us for a brief introduction of what we were about to see. As he described it, I stood there flabbergasted that I was standing in a place "almost all archaeologists would agree is the most significant, impactful, important archaeological discovery of all time."

After being properly oriented about what we were going to see, I said, "See you soon" to Rachel who stayed on the bus with a few others who couldn't physically make the hike, and we set out like pilgrims across the barren, rocky landscape in front of us. Our destination loomed in front of us with eroded, vertical crags that rose up like tabernacles from the desert. My picture of the scene described in the Bible became sharp and clear in my mind as I studied the landscape. Suddenly, I understood why there are at *least* a hundred references to "dust" in the Word of God! The land we were trekking was nothing but dust! Well, there were plenty of rocks, too.

I had a sense the whole time we were tromping up the side of the remote, desolate hill toward the hidden cave that this wasn't a well-worn path. The way was clear enough, but it was obvious that we were about to see something epic. There were no signs of the bustling tourists and pilgrims who we rubbed shoulders with in other Holy Land locations. We were treading on ground that was less-traveled, but eternally significant.

As the narrow path turned sharply and got suddenly steeper, a small hole in the cliff came into view ahead. We were plodding slowly as we got closer and closer. Some in the group were short of breath by this time because of the incline we had just navigated, yet all of us had our eyes fixed on that dark opening. As I approached, a couple of people were already inside the cave and I could hear their voices echoing, increasing my determination to get inside and see it for myself. Hunching over to fit through the small opening, I stretched my legs one at a time into the coolness of the small cave. I stood and took in the simplicity of the hiding place that had been a shelter for the clay pots and scrolls that date back to one hundred years before Christ.

The scrolls found in the particular cave I stood in were the most intact of all of the scrolls that would eventually be found in the eleven caves that loomed over the ancient Essene settlement and contained the *whole* scroll of Isaiah. I struggled to keep up with the historical details our guide rattled off to us as my mind raced with the impact of what this meant for my faith.

"This is one of two archaeological finds that talk about the Messiah being nailed to the Cross. 125 years before Christ, they said he would be born in Bethlehem and pierced in his hands and feet!

The whole scroll of Isaiah was found in Cave 1 and it was a huge problem for scholars because it matched the records of those who lived through events from the same time period. This evidence made it harder to refute the Biblical account.

The ancient scrolls sat in these caves for thousands of years while the events unfolded a few miles away in Jericho! No man knows the future, so the hundreds of prophecies that came true show the reliability of Scripture and the fact that God speaks to us."

Then, this quote follows: "If you're gods, you should be able to tell the ancient past *and* the unseen future!" The Dead Sea scrolls do this with COMPLETE ACCURACY! I slipped and tripped down the trail, but my spirit was soaring. My thoughts raced with the impact of this realization, "If God spoke to the people who wrote on these scrolls when they sought Him, then He *is* the one talking to *me*! The Bible is true just like I've always believed!"

I climbed the steps onto the bus sweaty and covered in holy dust, excited to share the discoveries with Rachel. As I took my seat next to her, the bus driver's voice over the microphone reminded me that I was a tourist and snapped me back into the present. He was announcing the arrival of a jeweler who would be coming through to show us a pamphlet and give us an opportunity to order something custom made as a souvenir of our trip through the Holy Land. Once I pushed back my initial annoyance at the monetary focus of the moment, I was able to recognize it as the opportunity I had dreamed about from the very beginning of my preparation for the trip! *"Choose something special to buy and wear 'as a memorial to the LORD' for what He has done."*

As I thumbed through the brochure looking for something special to wear, it was clear what I needed to buy. I selected a silver ring with three sections. The center section of the ring was thicker to allow for engraving, and there were narrow silver bands on either side of that. I knew immediately what I wanted my keepsake ring to say. My memorial to the LORD for what He had done would be *this* silver ring with the word "beloved" engraved in Hebrew. I had no hesitation giving my credit card information for that purchase!

Days later, the finished ring arrived at our hotel in Jerusalem, and I got to hold it in my hands. Rolling it around and examining it made me even more thankful that I had splurged and treated myself to such a souvenir. As I considered the magnitude of the impact the trip had on me, my mind began to recall promises and truths God had spoken to me over the years. These messages came in pieces like broken pottery from ages past, but they were coming together into a new, more complete vision that I could grasp. The ring I held in my hand was bringing it into focus, but I had one thing to confirm. I lifted my eyes and scanned the lobby for a local person I could talk to.

The entryway to the bustling hotel was crowded with groups gathering for the day's adventures, so everyone was already fully engaged in conversations. The man who had delivered the jewelry still lingered in the corner near the window, so I approached him with my question. Holding out the ring he had handed over to me minutes before, I asked, "I know what I *want* this to say, but can you tell me what this word is?"

He took the silver piece and turned it in his weathered hand, "It says 'Beloved.' It means that you are loved."

"Thank you so much," was all I could squeak out past all of the random thoughts in my head. Years of buying things from street vendors in Mexico and Africa had trained me to be skeptical of the stories I heard about the mementos I purchased. Even as emotions welled up in me with the vision God was showing me, the relief I was feeling about the ring *actually* saying what I wanted it to say made me want to laugh hysterically. If I hadn't been by myself at that moment, I would have thrown out a list of other words that *could* have been mistakenly etched in my precious memorial. I could just picture meeting an Israeli friend sometime in the future who asked about my ring with a puzzled look on their face only to find out that it meant something nonsensical the whole time.

All of this played out in my head as I found a quiet place to place it on my finger. This wasn't just a frivolous decision after all. I still wore my wedding ring on my right hand, the modest band of channel set diamonds sandwiched between similar narrow, gold bands with my birthstone and other birthstones of the kids. Each ring was a gift from Chris until they were stacked on my sturdy finger as thick as a cigar band. Now I had to rearrange. Years of memories and longing filled me as I allowed those thoughts to mingle with new revelations. A vision came into focus. Removing all of my rings, I lined up the truth of my life story on the ring finger of my right hand.

As I held my diamond engagement band, I remembered that there was a sacred time when I was chosen by a man and asked to be his wife. When Chris asked me to marry him there was no ring, just a bent knee and a bouquet of my favorite flowers as a promise to get me diamonds when he could afford it. When we got married, and I put these wedding rings on my finger, we had vowed to love each other exclusively until one of us passed away. Now, with Chris gone, Jesus had been trying to get me to realize that I have *always* been His beloved, even as I was developing in my mother's womb.

Whether I met a man who would choose me as his wife again or not, Jesus would be with me forever. He would *never* leave me!

I slipped my engagement ring from Chris on the ring finger of my right hand and added the new ring beside it. With all I had learned on the trip, THIS was the eternal message God knew I needed to uncover, and now I had a visual reminder to help me push back the hopelessness and replace it with the overwhelming truth that I was, and always will be, BELOVED.

Pennsylvania

March 2017

One of the conditions for me being able to make the trip to Israel was that I would be able to honor my commitment to be the main speaker at a youth retreat in Pennsylvania, so my return to American soil had me landing on the East Coast rather than the West. The temperature wasn't the only shock to my system. Major delays in Tel Aviv because of broken luggage scanners left a group of us stranded there for an extra night and wiped out my only day of preparation and transition before jumping into the event. I landed in New York before the sun rose, bleary-eyed and dazed to a friend's welcome. These daylight hours would be my only time to recalibrate and go over my notes before speaking for the first session that very evening.

Thankfully, there wasn't anything that could erase the indelible lessons I had just learned on my pilgrImage through the Holy Land, and I was eager to share all that God had taught me. Although my body must have resembled the frozen, leafless trees that stood rigid in the cold, my mind and spirit were filled with new life. Over the course of the trip through Israel, the theme of this retreat, "BEYOND," had been in the back of my mind. As I carried the theme with me through each milestone archaeological site and held it up alongside the truths I experienced, it was clear that God was pulling together the five sessions I was about to speak, so I put my detailed outlines to the side and just listened.

By the time my friend picked me up from the airport, it was "go-time," and the first session was at hand. The title for the evening's opening session was "Beyond our Stories" and I only had a few hours to adjust to a new time zone, bundle up for below zero weather, and work up enough energy to captivate hundreds of teenagers with the first plot twists of our story and introduce them to the One who had carried me through.

It was a rigorous weekend schedule and the messages welled up in me from having JUST seen the evidence of the hope I had firsthand. The Spirit was already pulling all five of the sessions together inside of me, but my body was weary, and I was homesick for my kids. Two weeks had gone by, and I had a growing sense that it was time to get home to them. New lessons and clarity brought a distracted thoughtfulness that kept my mind racing from one context to the next: Israel, Pennsylvania, home, Israel, Pennsylvania, home... My mind was struggling to remain in the present when there was so much to process before transitioning back to my "normal" life. What I needed was prayer!

The retreat was at a retreat center designed for events like these. Cottages and dorm-style lodging sat on the outskirts of the campus on the southern end. A large cafeteria provided meals for attendees near the entrance, a huge gym-like meeting hall completed the circle of well-appointed buildings, and a fire pit rose up from the middle as the hub. Since a cold front had blown in a final dose of winter weather, all of the meetings took place indoors in the meeting hall. Multiple double doors opened to the vast room that was pre-set with rows of chairs and the emptiness of the huge space echoed with the loud chatter and laughter of the youth who bubbled over with adolescent energy. I had noticed after the first night's session that there was a hand-labeled sign on a room in the back of the hall that read, "Prayer Room." Peeking in, I could see that the volunteer prayer warriors were waiting there and available, filling their time with relaxed conversation.

"Hi there," I interrupted. "I'm about to get up to speak for the session, but I was wondering if you would have a few minutes to pray for me before I go up."

My request awoke an eagerness in them, and they immediately rose to gather around me. One of the women asked how they could pray for me, and I explained that I needed the Holy Spirit to focus my thoughts and speak through me. It was a general request, but I trusted that they would cover me with prayer in whatever way the

Spirit led them and it would calm me for the task ahead. What I didn't anticipate was that, out of this group of complete strangers, a woman would be given a vision directly from God that would prepare me for the whole road ahead, not just the next assembly. As their hands rested on my head, back, and shoulders, their calm voices rose to the God I knew was listening. One woman's voice interrupted with an apologetic question, "I'm seeing something in prayer that I'd like to share with you. May I tell you what I think Jesus wants to show you?"

Lifting my head to gain eye contact with her, I nodded my permission, and the woman I had never met began to share what she was seeing in prayer: *"I see you in the back of an old pick-up truck on a country road. It's a dirt road with a lot of ruts and rocks so the ride is bumpy. You are sitting facing backwards in the bed of the truck with your back against the cab. As you bump along, you decide to look at the road ahead. Getting onto your knees, you look through a window into the cab of the truck. It's a small, rectangular window that slides open.*

You look ahead and then to the driver's seat. The driver turns to look at you. It's Jesus at the wheel. He's looking back at you with a calm look on his face. You are filled with a sense of comfort and peace as he turns his face to you. Here's what he wants you to hear, 'Michelle, I'll drive. I know the way. You just sit back and let me take you where you need to go. Trust me.'"

Her voice trailed off there and she stroked my back as tears rolled down my face in awe. HOW did this woman who had never met me know that I had ridden in the back of an old pick-up truck down a bumpy dirt road for most of my childhood?! Through the Holy Spirit, God had *shown* her a vision that would prove to me that He saw me and had heard my cries! There was no human way possible she could have ever known how to describe the place where I grew up! Jesus had literally placed Himself in my dad's old pick-up to tell me He was in control, and I could trust Him to lead me where *He* wanted me to go!

Shock and awe replaced the nervousness I had felt before ducking into that prayer room of strangers. When the final "amen" was spoken, I thanked all of them and explained the reason for the tears. Words were insufficient in that moment, but I attempted to communicate the depth of my gratitude and then opened the door to face the waiting audience. Knowing the God of the Universe was with me was all I needed for the session *and* whatever I would face in my unknown future.

72 | Heart's Desire

"Delight yourself also in the Lord, And He shall give you the desires of your heart."
— Psalm 37:4

There are times when there aren't words in the English language that are strong enough to describe the emotions of grief. To say I "missed Chris" is a gross understatement. A word that is the opposite of hyperbole would be more appropriate here, but it doesn't exist. We had become "one" in a way that the rhythms of our days flowed together. When he was suddenly gone, I felt off-balance and his absence by my side created a dark hole that left me feeling weakened, as if my insides were hobbling along with a physical amputation of some kind.

I knew of no other outlet for my intense feelings other than to pray to God to relieve them. Occasionally, God allowed for my paths to cross with another widow, and I found respite in their understanding. In that safe place, I could pour out the ugliness of the pain and know that they'd "get it" without returning my cries with platitudes. I have a couple of least favorite things well-meaning people said that made me want to inflict bodily injury or something. I'll share a few here with the responses I would have *liked* to say. Instead, I chose to stare silently back at them with my frozen cry face peering back at them blankly as if I'd been punched in the gut.

"Time heals all wounds." "

"Oh, really? Well, at this moment, I'm hurting, and the pain is so intense that I can't even *sleep*. Sometimes I don't even know where to sit or what to eat. Time's not going to bring my husband back."

"God won't give you more than you can handle."

"Seriously?! Where is that in Scripture?! Grief PLUS raising six hurting kids, multiple moves across countries, work, AND life?! How is that comforting? I can't handle this!"

Here's the real kicker... This one was hardest because it's actually *in* the Bible and God had pointed it out to me way back in 2012 when Chris was still around.

"Jesus is your husband."

"How is this possible?! He doesn't have skin now! Even if He's everything to me, He's not *physically* with me and I need a hug *so badly!*"

"Someday, someone is going to hug you so tight that it will
squish all of your broken pieces back together."
– Anonymous quote jotted in my journal

My prayers often reflected this desperation and it's reflected in my journals over the years. I was learning who I was *individually* and finding my way toward contentment whether I had humans with me or not. Comfort was something I had to *seek* and the place I found it best was in the Word of God. These wrestling sessions often ended with me realizing that God had *made* me this way and He'd work out what was best for me. Honestly, though, the fact that my worst case scenario had happened made me wonder what that would look like. There was always the chance that it would bring God more glory if I remained weak and needy of Him.

The weakness happened as soon as Chris's symptoms worsened and my lack of control over our circumstances became painfully obvious. Then, once he was gone, losing him was so agonizing and holding life together so demanding that I felt delicate, ready to crumble at the slightest disturbance in our routine. I didn't *feel* strong, yet I needed strength because my life required it. I rested in believing that God would supply what I needed when I needed it, and He always came through. True to His nature, He was usually not early, but never late.

Looking back, I still felt married for the whole first year, but as the second year began, the longing for companionship became nearly unbearable. I knew I had Chris's blessing to marry again someday, so that providential freedom released me of any guilt in praying for it. No matter where I was, the aching craving to share life with someone worked its way into my spirit. Even my happy places evoked such joy that my instinct was to want to tell Chris about it, then I'd realize where he was, sink into despair, and then work my way out one Truth at a time. It was in the second year of solo life that my prayers became categorical.

"*I've got the lonely part down, Lord, bring me to the place of being content in You. Then, in Your timing, bring another man to that same place with You. Perhaps he is lonely and hurting even now. Comfort him and deepen his relationship with You, Lord. Then, allow our paths to cross in your perfect timing. Oh, that You would even lessen that desire in me so that I can be content in you.*"

73 | Mr. Wonderful

"Commit your way to the Lord;
trust in him and he will do this:
He will make your righteous reward shine like the dawn,
your vindication like the noonday sun."
— Psalm 37:5-7

It was a technological annoyance nearly a
year after my trip to the Promised Land that led to me being scolded
by my son, Jed, who was a man of eighteen at the time. I had been
exercising my due diligence in pouring over the transactions in my
bank account and a repeated charge of $8.99 kept showing up.
Wracking my brain over my bills and imagining what that could be
hadn't yielded a solution, but I had a feeling it was something to do
with my phone. As frustration built, I turned to my greatest, in-house
technology helpline, the closest young adult kid I could find. That
day, Jed was my tech savior, and I handed my phone over to him in
desperation.

Holding the device in one hand, he scrolled through my apps
and dug around like a detective looking for clues. Then, tasting
victory, his face lit up with a smirk. He had me on something. His face
revealed the fact that he had caught me in something that was going
to be good fodder for teasing —and perhaps blackmail. His eyes
widened and his smile grew into a broad grin as he launched into
his brief investigation, "Mom! Have you been doing on-line *dating*?!"

My face must have blushed every shade of pink and red, the
color of the sun rising on an embarrassing truth. I stammered, "Well,
I haven't gone on any *dates* with it, but I may have been doing a
little scrolling."

Once his laughter subsided, he composed himself to give me
an honest talking-to: "You meet so many people, Mom. You don't
need a dating app. What you need to do is stop treating every guy

you know as your best friend. You'll meet somebody, but you have to be open to it."

Who was this eighteen-year-old relationship miser?! How did he know my business? The answers were clear even as they flew through my flabbergasted mind. My son probably wasn't the only person watching my every move. I had a half-dozen onlookers to all of my friend choices, my comings and goings, my phone conversations, my cry sessions, and most of my private meltdowns. Although most of the time my struggles and the intensity of my emotions were overwhelming to them, they were witnesses to every choice that I made. This moment of reckoning revealed that some of them were old enough to have their own opinions about my personal life.

He was still a teenager, but in that split second, he was the one who had been chosen to intervene. He dug up the app, deleted it with a couple of confident swipes of his finger, and forbade me from ever considering on-line dating again. "Mom, from now on, if you're interested in a man, just LET HIM KNOW."

Relief and terror flooded me in simultaneous waves of anxious awareness. With this new awareness, accountability, and indirect permission from my son, I had to trust that God would put the *right* man in my path at the *right* time and, once he was in sight, it was up to me to let him know I was interested. What a dizzying thought!

On a Sunday shortly after that conversation, I entered church in the same manner I usually did when I felt obviously alone and without someone to sit with. I slinked in tardy, laying low and solo so that I didn't draw attention to myself. It was always easiest to slide into a seat in the back while one of the pastors was praying the opening prayer. Successfully planted in my seat in the back, I bowed my head until I heard the "amen." As I lifted my head, my attention was drawn to a man who was stretching his long arms to put them around the teenage boys seated on either side of him. I didn't remember seeing him before. Who was he? Then, I did what any single, searching woman would do. I found his left hand and checked for a wedding ring. While I knew the absence of a band on his left ring finger wasn't conclusive evidence that he wasn't married, I figured it gave me permission to at least do a little fact-finding.

I have to confess that I was distracted through the whole church service. My eyes kept sneaking a peek where the three of them sat listening. He was attentive and engaged in the sermon. It seemed like he was close to my age, handsome, clean-cut, and my first impression was that he was responsible. He had that air of being in charge for some reason. A woman never materialized, and it seemed as if he was there alone with his sons. I couldn't help but wonder who he was and what his circumstances were.

My preliminary inquiry into the identity of the handsome man from church continued when I returned home. Even before eating, I pulled the pictorial directory from the shelf and thumbed through its pages in hopeful anticipation. I had no idea what his name was, but I searched every face for that Image until at last I found him! There he was, pictured with the same young men and the names listed under the picture didn't list a woman. All I needed to do was ask a friend to pry a little bit with her husband to get information for me. It didn't take me long to turn to my church BFF, Lisa, for her next "friend mission." Her husband was serving on the board of elders at the time. He would surely know a little about this guy!

I continued with life a little distracted by the youthful preoccupation of a potential crush. The feelings were foreign and intriguing. While I went about my work and duties of the week, I waited for the report back from Lisa. When it came, my heart soared with hope. My assumption had been right. He wasn't married. He was divorced. The reason for his singleness brought a little slump in my initial Pollyanna fantasy. I had always figured that my ideal man would be someone who was also widowed. I figured that would make it easier to understand each other and give us freedom to honor our late spouses even as we moved forward with our new life together. Pushing the overthinking aside and remembering Jed's advice, I considered my next step.

The First Encounter

"... I knew I did from the first moment we met. It was... not love at first sight, exactly, but – familiarity. Like: oh, hello... it's you. It's going to be you. Game over."
– Mahairi McFarlane

With my outfit meticulously planned, I arrived at church the following Sunday and strategically selected my seat. This time I was on time. I needed to allow for ample time to get the open seat I needed. It seemed like the man in question was quite predictable. He sat in the same seat *every* Sunday. On this particular day, he sat alone. With butterflies tickling my stomach and nervous energy building, I took my place in the row behind him.

With twenty-eight years of church attendance in this same place, I could anticipate the order of service as well as my own daily schedule. We bowed to pray, next came the amen, and next was the moment... greeting time! AAAGH! What was I doing here?! Oh, no. It was about to happen... The pastor cheerfully greeted the congregation and uttered the familiar command I was anticipating. "Turn and greet the people around you and introduce yourself to someone you don't already know..."

My nervous system was out of control by then and I'm sure my hands were shaking as I watched him turn toward me. Our eyes met with something welcoming, almost like familiarity, although I didn't remember having ever talked to him. As his eyes peered into me, his deep and confident voice pronounced a sentence I wasn't expecting, "Good morning, Michelle. I'm Brent."

Thoughts came before words... "Oh, my gosh. He said my name! What should I do?! Why does he know my name?! What do I say? What do I say?"

With my hand still firmly in his warm, firm handshake, I stuttered, "Nice to meet you."

I'm sure I confessed my lack of attentiveness over the next hour to the Lord because I mentally missed *another* sermon. After church was over, I watched Brent leave and rallied to regain my composure as I searched for my kids. With my teens wrangled, we headed for the car. I feigned normalcy as we walked along chatting about our morning. Then, in the distance I spotted him again. He was parked in-between me and my car and was standing there chatting with some other guys I knew! I gave a falsely calm and confident wave toward the group and was met with waves and Brent's warm voice again: "Have a good evening!"

Evening?! It was morning! There it was. The first sign that he must have been feeling at least a *little* bit as shaken up as I was.

While my body went through the motions of normalcy, my insides were all a flutter, and my mind was distracted with excitement. It was as if that handshake had erased half of my years and I was a teenager again. Where was my reasoning and patience? Where was the dependence on God and the faithfulness to wait? I had this sense of urgency in me to at least connect with him and let him know I was interested. After all, that was what Jed had advised! The thought of leaning so heavily on my son's advice at that moment brought a giggle and I pondered who else I could turn to.

Once again, Lisa seemed like the best person for me to turn to. She balanced me. I could usually count on her to talk me down from the heights of my emotional intensity and back down to reason and reality. She answered 9-1-1 calls for a living, and this was an *emergency*! There was no time to waste.

She wasn't shocked by my Sunday afternoon call. I had already asked her to do the initial investigation into Brent's marital status and character, so she was ready for the next question. As soon as she answered, the fireworks of my feelings burst out and I begged her to help me make the next decision. "Tell me what to do. I can't think straight. Should I do nothing and leave this in God's hands to orchestrate, or should I send a benign, but friendly message to let him know I'd like to get to know him?"

I wasn't prepared for her answer. She was one of my accountability partners in life, a prayer warrior after God's heart and glory. I knew she'd remind me of what I had already vowed to do – TRUST GOD AND HIS TIMING.

"Send a message."

"What?! You think I should do it?!"

I felt like a child who was told they could get the puppy, "Ok! Thanks! Bye!"

I had prayed that God would nudge him to reach out, but still couldn't shake the strong leading to send him a message. Going about my daily duties, I mixed brainstorming with calls to God for His help and guidance. I went back over the scenes I had just lived as if they had played out with a musical score in a Romcom. He didn't strike me as a man who would be on social media. No...too refined looking. He seemed professional. There was NO WAY I was going to use the phone number listed in the church directory. That would be too forward. I wracked my brain. "What else? What else? LinkedIn! Perfect!"

I opened the app and searched for the name that was now on my mind constantly. In the next second, his face was in front of me in the form of a debonair profile photo and I had my chance! I tapped the message icon and summoned all of my communication skills so that this message would sound casual, friendly, and politely interested, but not desperate. Jed's words kept coming back to me: "Don't treat every guy like your best friend."

It was just a little message on a platform *meant* for people to connect with each other, but it felt like I was opening the door to a whole new chapter of my life. I typed the words, erased a few, added more, edited a bit, and then read the whole masterpiece. Once it seemed good enough, I took a deep breath, hit the paper airplane icon to send it on its fateful way, and went to get my nails done.

LinkedIn

Michelle Gennaro – 2:44 p.m. Monday

"Hey there! Just wanted to say it's always nice to see you at church and I was hoping to get to say hi after. It's usually a bit hectic. It would be great to get to talk to you sometime. Hope you have a good week!"

Brent Lapp – 4:14 p.m. Monday

"Hi, Michelle,

I was hoping to hear from you. This is a pleasant surprise. I would be happy to talk and/or meet for a coffee sometime. (PHONE NUMBER!) :-) Brent"

74 | The Fullness of Time

"There are times, seasons, and places where the plans
and promises of God meet up with the people of
God to create a fullness of time."
– Remnant Blog

Monday's messages led to a coffee date
on Thursday evening. When Brent gave me his phone number, I had resisted the temptation to call him and instead sent him my own number. I wanted him to be in control of the situation so that I had no doubt he was pursuing me in a romantic sense. I had no interest in entering into any kind of trivial dating game of Catch and Release.

My life hadn't been void of attention from men, but the year leading up to meeting Mr. Wonderful had brought a few social situations with men that had left me discouraged and hopeless. I had a platonic friend from college who was like an uncle to my kids. I had been a pen pal to a sensitive and godly man who was all the way on the east coast. I had hung out with a divorced man from church I had known for years, and I had even gone on a few dates with a man my friend had introduced me to. In every case, my feelings became confusing to me and I had to beg God to help me navigate the awkwardness.

Eventually, each friendship was defined as only that and I received the direction I needed from God. None of those were the one He was preparing for me. Indeed, they all seemed intimidated and terrified at the idea of having any kind of committed relationship. I was left feeling hopeless and undesirable. Who would *ever* have the guts to take on a woman like me?

With a background like that, I prepared for the coffee date with excitement and nervousness, but behind those butterflies were ominous, dark clouds of dread. As much as I wanted to be in love again, my heart was guarded. There had already been enough heartbreak and disappointment. This time, I was asking God to make it clear. I needed a man who would pursue me in a way that made it abundantly obvious that *he* was the one I had been waiting for. I wanted to be **wanted**.

The place he chose was only a couple of miles from my house and tucked back on a side street in an area of town that was a combination of industrial businesses and up and coming trendy Asian restaurants and international stores. The little teashop offered a comforting level of anonymity as people bustled in and out to meet friends for casual visiting over unique drinks.

As soon as I saw him waiting outside, the butterflies took flight in a flurry of flutters. I was alert to every move and expression he made. His tall frame stood in front of me as his broad smile greeted me. His eyes met mine in warm anticipation that seemed to match my own and he caught me up in a casual hug. All of the advice I had been given over the years seemed to scroll through my mind like a playbook of what to look for next. "If he offers to pay, that's a sign that this is romantic and not just friendship."

We ordered tea as if we'd never seen a menu before. Our minds were elsewhere, and the beverages were just a ruse for the time we intended to spend together. With our choices finally made, he took charge like a perfect gentleman: "Would you like anything else?"

"No, thank you."

There was no way I could put anything else in my stomach. His next move was one I had been trained to look for. He took his card and paid for our order. His chivalry pointed to the fact that this was indeed a first date. We made our way to a nearby tall table as I attempted to quell my overthinking,

The next three and a half hours played out like an interview more than flirtatious chatting. There was no delay in getting right down to real intentions. Brent led the way into topics that might have been covered in premarital counseling rather than on a first date. We shared our salvation testimonies and then the painful endings to our first marriages: mine through death and his through a painful divorce. Although we both came to the table with considerable baggage, we openly admitted our deep desires for being married again.

Opposite experiences in marriage had led us to the same longings. For me, marriage was a fulfilling and safe partnership, but for him, it had been a long, twenty-year journey of honoring a commitment to someone who he couldn't predict. Our marriage ended in the fulfillment of our vows to be together until death parted us, and his ended in divorce court. He dreamed of someday experiencing a marriage like the one I had enjoyed for twenty-three years, and I longed to have that again if God allowed.

Once we were on the same page about being married again, the grilling continued. He asked me about everything from what I was looking for in a husband, what my deal-breakers were, even daring to ask me about my comfort level with physical intimacy. There were few topics that Brent failed to mention. Over time, he helped me understand that he had no desire to waste time dating someone if she didn't have the character he was looking for. He had no desire to enter into a marriage that may end in divorce as his first one had. As the little restaurant neared closing time, I passed the initial test and Brent asked me if I'd like to get together again. Every part of me wanted to scream "YES! I'm yours!" Yet, my own guarded heart wanted more guidance. His situation wasn't as neat and tidy as I had assumed, and I wasn't sure I should boldly jump in with both feet.

My hesitation was met with the next sign that this man had the character and integrity I had been praying for. By Saturday morning, he was sitting in our pastor's office seeking wise counsel.

From that day forward, Pastor Kenny was our mutually trusted guide through every phase of our relationship. He had been Chris's accountability partner and my boss through most of our married life and had even counseled Brent and his former wife as they tried to save their marriage. He knew the intimate details of each of our lives and was the best person to give us honest and godly direction.

After months of being acquaintances, I entered my kitchen after returning home from a trip with my girlfriends to find the biggest flower arrangement I had ever received. The long-stemmed pink and red roses were nestled in delicate white baby's breath and together their beauty filled the whole counter with color and fragrance. I searched the floral display for a sign of who they were from. Then, in the very center, a small envelope held the answer to my question.

There, printed on a little card were the words I longed to hear: "*Will you be mine? Brent."*

Since he was on an extended trip with a friend checking another item off of his life list, the best I could do was to call him and give him my answer. Without hesitation, I gave him my boldest "YES!"

I felt like Hagar, the maidservant of Sarah, who fled to the desert and was comforted by God Himself. In the desert of her darkest hour, she had given God a name. I would have chosen the same name for my Heavenly Father as I stared at those words. God had shown up and answered my most intimate prayers, *"You are the God who SEES me. I have now seen the One who sees me." Genesis 16:13*

75 | "Wanted"

"Is ANYTHING too hard for the Lord?!" Genesis 18:14

There was no doubt I was in love again. The responsibilities of my life continued to demand every bit of my time and energy, but there was a new tingling in my heart, distracting thoughts of Brent in my mind, and new prayers for God's help in navigating all of it. On the inside, I felt like a teenager again. I hadn't dated "for real" since Chris and I met when I was barely twenty-one and that's exactly how I felt again. No matter what I was doing, thoughts of him filled my mind and I was constantly distracted by the desire to spend more and more time with him. Looking back, it was the vast differences between dating at twenty-years-old and being a widowed mother in her fifties with five young people in the house that kept me from throwing all of myself into our relationship with reckless abandon. My time was limited, and I lived my life out in front of an audience. Whether I wanted it or not, I had the accountability of parenthood.

Being a mom made it impossible for me to allow my feelings for Brent and my dreams of a future with him to grow without considering all of the implications. As soon as I found myself in the clouds of blissful romance, a practical question would enter my mind. Reality kept me grounded in the truth that neither road ahead of me would be easy. If I said yes to be head-over-heels committed to this man, it meant taking all of my kids with me on the ride. We had walked through trauma and grief together, had navigated every transition and move, and had figured out a routine. The answers to my prayers meant more change and another transition.

I had been persistent in my prayers to God for the man He was preparing for me, and I still needed Him to show me if Brent was the one. In my mind, I had to be either in or out. I couldn't drag my children along as I dated someone, allow them to get to know him, and then change my mind and start again. Besides, I had asked God for a sign that *this* man was the one I had been waiting for.

Since both of us had jobs that demanded a lot of our time and each of us still had kids at home, we communicated a lot through texts and phone conversations. On one particular day, as I was working in the kitchen, my attention was drawn to my phone as a notification popped up on the home screen and brought it to life. It was a message from Brent! The newness of our relationship and my developing feelings for him meant that a message from him had the power to reduce me instantly from a responsible adult to a wistful teenager with no self-control. I couldn't leave the message there; I had to read it. Drying my hands, I picked up my phone and opened the message. It was a link to a country song. A simple tap on the link swept me up into the next chapter of my life.

"Wanted"

You know I'd fall apart without you
I don't know how you do what you do
'Cause everything that don't make sense about me
Makes sense when I'm with you...
As good as you make me feel
I wanna make you feel better
Better than your fairy tales
Better than your best dreams
You're more than everything I need
You're all I ever wanted
All I ever wanted.
You'll always be wanted.[9]

Shock assailed me. *Where* did he find this song?! Did he realize the implications of it? More importantly, did he *mean* it?! *This isn't just a catchy song; these are the desires of my heart put to music!* I hadn't told him my intimate prayers to my Heavenly Father and yet they were reflected in the captivating ballad I was listening to. THIS WAS IT. There was no doubt God was showing me what I

---

[9] Hayes, Hunter. "Wanted," On *Wanted*, Atlantic, 2011, CD.

had been *begging* Him for. I had to know *why* Brent sent me this particular song! Without even thinking about it, I tapped the phone icon on the screen that would connect me to him. As the phone rang, my emotions surged until tears started flowing. By the time he answered, and his smooth, resonant voice answered, I was a mess of wracking sobs. It was difficult to force words out and I fought to gain my composure.

"Michelle. What's wrong? Are you there?"

I fumbled over my words as terror gripped me. "Why did you send me that song?"

"I'm sorry, Michelle. I can't understand you. Say it again."

My sobs were stealing my breath and making my throat tighten up. Each word that I tried to push out was accompanied by a raspy, gasping sound. Taking a deep breath, I repeated the words I was so afraid to speak: "Why did you send me that song?"

"I sent it because it describes how I feel. Is that bad? What's wrong?"

His answer only made the storm inside of me grow. As I continued to try to quell the crying fit, my thoughts flooded my mind as I desperately tried to form an intelligent response. My thoughts were in overdrive and I was having a conversation in my own head while silence hung between us. "He *wants* me?! He wants *me*! This is the sign I was asking for! *This* is the man I've been praying for. Am I going to do this again?! If I let myself love him, I might lose him and that hurts so bad. Do I want this? I don't want to grieve again, Lord! It hurts so badly."

Finally, with all of that going on in my head, I was able to squeeze out the truth of what I was going through and confess it to Brent. "It's not bad, it's really good. But if I love you, you might die. Don't die!"

How could a man respond to that?! The poor guy had sent me the perfect, romantic country song, and *this* was the response he got?! He wasn't in control of when Chris died! How could he promise me that he wouldn't die before I did?

"Michelle, I can't control when I die, but I know I love you."

There it was. This was the moment of decision. Did I want to receive my heart's desire that God had miraculously handed to me, or was I going to let fear steal my joy? I sat there for an extended moment as I faced my biggest fear again. Could I face my worst case scenario a second time? Is loving and being loved on this level worth it? The answer was obvious. God had shown me the way and I had learned of His faithfulness to keep His promises. He would be with me and would never leave me, even if I had to grieve again. That truth gave me the courage to respond and to jump into a new season with both feet despite my lack of control over the outcomes.

"I know that's true. I'm just scared. I love you too."

JOURNAL ENTRY

I have often been overwhelmed with the extravagant detail with which you have answered my prayers, Lord. How I praise you for SEEING each little detail of my journey. It's as if you let me "steep" in my pain while I learned and grew from it. Thank you for seeing fit to bring an end to that long season of loneliness.

As my feelings for Brent grew, huge waves of grief often assaulted my joy and pulled me back down into sorrow. My kids showed outward signs of that same process. I knew they were happy for me, but sometimes their behavior showed signs of dreariness and they spent large amounts of time in their rooms. One day, when I asked Silly how she was *really* doing, she gave me an honest answer that describes, with precision, the process all of us were going through. She confessed that it was hard for her to watch me get closer and closer to getting married again. She explained it this way: "I know Dad is gone and he's not coming back, but seeing you with someone else just makes it feel so *final*."

My own psyche was going through that same pattern of processing as we started talking about getting married. The truth was that the budding of a new season couldn't erase the last. Besides, I didn't want it to. In a strange sense, loving again and thinking about getting married again felt a lot like when I was pregnant with my second child. Julia was my first baby, the first child I had ever loved. How could I love another baby this much?! The answer to that question only came with the birth of another child. There was enough love for *every* one of them! Each time another baby was born, my heart grew to allow for more and more love. Not only that, but the same thing even happened when I became a mother through adoption!

I'm not sure how a human could handle all of that love without the supernatural help and power of their Creator. The magnitude of it was often too much for me to bear. Milestones don't have manners. They force themselves on you as surely as the sun rises in the east every morning. My growing relationship with Brent developed over the course of a year, so the kids and I continued to go through the highs and lows of memories that flooded in as the passing of time brought anniversaries, birthdays, and memories of our former life. Despite all of the new things that were happening in my life, grief still hung like a dark cloak over my shoulders.

Without warning, my mood would darken, and I'd notice that the whole household seemed "off." With nerves on edge, the kids and I were short with each other for no reason, the muscles in my back were too tight and painful to stretch out, and tension headaches furrowed my brow and caused me to squint my way through the day. Over the years, I eventually learned to recognize the symptoms. With a moment of awakening, I'd check the date to see if it was something my body was remembering causing trauma and grief to bubble up within us. January 24th, 2019 was the date that jumped off of my phone screen at me and it stopped me in my tracks. My body stood in my kitchen in San Diego, California, but every other part of me was bumping along a rocky, donkey path in a Land Rover in the mountains of Lesotho.

It has been six years since I drove Chris out of the village to the hospital. My logical mind could still do the math.

I saw myself downshifting over ruts as Chris suffered in the back. It was life and death. We had lived through a nightmare worse that I could have imagined on my most fear-filled days. I could almost make out the moans of the engine as it crawled over rocky ledges to carry us to help. Tears started falling, then the air left my lungs and my neck and throat tightened as I tried to choke back the sobs.

Chris was sick. He died. The truth of it hit me as I looked around and reminded myself of the present. My life was so different now, worlds away from the place we had left so suddenly. The changes were so drastic; it was hard to make sense of in times like those.

Even the day before my sudden flashback, I had been able to picture Chris alive and next to me like he'd never left. I could sense the energy of his presence and picture him in his tan pants. Every detail of his body and soul still seemed real, and I had to remind myself he was gone. Now, six years after we had lived through the thing I never wanted to happen, life was morphing into a new chapter. With tears streaming down my face, it was difficult to categorize my emotions. Tears of joy mingled with tears of profound sorrow. This was suffering in the midst of joy, and it took my mind back to a promise I had claimed all of those years ago. I was aware of the faithful way God had carried me one day at a time until 2,190 days later, I was still standing.

76 | Tell Your Heart to Beat Again

"They called on the Lord and he answered them."
–Psalm 99:6

One day at a time, the calendar ticked forward to spring. Life continued to bring forth trials and landmark events, signs that seasons were coming and going just like God promised. There were many days that my mind just could not compute that I was getting married, but each time my thoughts turned toward Brent, gratitude and praise washed over me. He was indeed the man God had prepared for me. Beneath his handsome, charming exterior, his loving heart drew me to him more than anything else did. Suffering had grown him into a man who continued to search for God and he was open to growth. Often, when he reflected on what God had brought him through, his eyes welled with tears as he expressed his gratitude. He sought God every morning at the start of the day and wasn't afraid to be stretched and to learn new ways of communicating and navigating relationships. Besides that, he was adventurous and fun to be with. It was easy for me to picture being with him for the next seasons of my life.

I loved having a special person in my life who thought of me, gave me butterflies, and who received my love with responsive thankfulness. With the weather warming into the delightful 70s and flowers blooming wherever I looked, I was eager to get out and enjoy the outdoors. Despite feeling a little sniffly and being road-weary from work travel, I eagerly drove the two miles to Brent's rented condo and skipped my way up the stairs to knock on his door. He opened it with a grand, sweeping motion and raised his voice to welcome me with a beaming smile, "Hey, Peach!"

Taking me into his arms and squeezing me tight enough to lift me off of the ground, he asked, "Whatcha want to do today?!"

I confessed my puniness and suggested, "Can we just take an easy walk somewhere nice?"

"That's a great idea! How about Balboa Park? I've been wanting to check on the cherry blossoms."

My retired navy, valiant aviator, thrill-seeking adventurer boyfriend loved the delicate, pink blossoms of cherry trees more than any other flower. It wasn't only for their captivating beauty; it was because they were a symbol of hope and honor to him. His favorite movie of all time, *The Last Samurai* (Edward Zwick, 2003), had swept him up in their significance within Japanese culture. As a symbol of times of revival and the fleeting nature of life, they held deep meaning to him and reminded him of the hope God had placed in his heart for the newness of life he was experiencing. Their feathery pink blooms only lasted for a couple of weeks, and he was curious to see them at least once if we could.

Arriving at the park that dated all the way back to the late 1800s, we strolled hand-in-hand past historical buildings and lush landscapes of mature trees and well-groomed gardens. As we approached the Japanese Tea Garden, he tugged my hand and pulled me toward the ticket booth. I was surprised because we usually just peered over the fence to check for the bright shock of pink that swathed the canyon below in color. "Let's go in this time," he suggested as he drew me closer toward the gate.

It was a simple gesture, but my spirits lifted with excitement. This was the perfect day to walk under the trellises of blooming, sweet-smelling, purple wisteria and wander the curving paths through the meticulously manicured gardens. We walked all the way through the gardens to the very end, stopping on the patio of a Japanese-style structure to gaze down into a pond filled with brilliantly colored koi fish. Orange, white, and peach-colored shapes turned and darted through the clear water. Stopping by the rail, we hugged and did what any couple would do who found themselves in such a romantic setting—we took a selfie.

With the moment documented, we headed back up the hill, winding through the shade of more than a hundred blooming cherry trees. When we were almost to the end of the grove of trees, Brent pulled me to the side of the path to look closer at the blossoms. Finding just the right one, he plucked it from the tree and turned to me. As he held it between his finger and thumb, he looked into my eyes and said something similar to what Katsumoto said in his favorite movie, this time replacing the word "blossom" with "woman." "The perfect woman is a rare thing. If you spent your whole life looking for her, it would not be a wasted life. Michelle, will you marry me?"

I had no words. It must have only been a second of silence, but it hung in the air like minutes ticking by slowly. Then, with my filter gone because of the shock of it, I answered with a question, "Are you being serious?"

"Do you think I'd joke about that?" he replied as a light-hearted giggle escaped from his smiling lips. "All I have is this bloom to give you today. The ring is being sized. But yes, I'm asking if you'll marry me, Michelle."

The tears started falling before my answer came, "Yes! Yes!"

Then, as if we needed any more evidence of God's favor, grace, and abounding love, a breeze swept through the canyon and the downy, light pink petals of the blossoms were caught up in the breeze and swirled around us magically. Not only was I wanted, but I was chosen and loved by the man I had been praying for even before I knew he existed. Ironically, for the second time in my life, I found myself engaged to the perfect man without a ring.

At our age and stage in life, we saw no reason to delay our wedding date. As we compared our calendars and prayerfully considered the best time for all eight of our combined kids, whether they were adults or still teenagers living at home, there were no gaps in our schedules. Life events that made their way onto stress inventories were coming up in both of our lives and we decided we'd rather navigate all of it together, rather than in two separate households. Silly's graduation was coming and then my mom was taking her to Rome. Duane was being promoted from junior high to high school. My dad was battling stage 4 rectal cancer. Each of our four teenage boys were starting their new sports seasons in four different sports, and Brent was coming to the end of his teaching job.

We had found each other and were confident in our relationship, knew we would be working hard to prepare for marriage with counseling, and figured we had what it took to navigate all of that *and* have a simple ceremony. We set the date for the middle of June and asked our trusted pastor to meet with us to lay the groundwork for our upcoming marriage.

Despite our intentional and conscientious prayers and planning, it was tricky to navigate plans for our wedding and come alongside our kids as they processed all that the upcoming, gargantuan change would mean for them. There was no way to know everything they were thinking and feeling and it seemed like there were times they withheld their feelings out of love for us. They wanted us to be happy, but they were well acquainted with transitions and were bracing themselves for the change.

With one week to go before our wedding, my prayers were equally balanced between praising God for answering my prayers and begging Him for help as we moved forward.

JOURNAL ENTRY

June 8, 2019

One week until our wedding!

Oh, my gosh, Lord, this time NEXT Saturday I will be getting up to get ready for my WEDDING! Wow, my heart may explode with excitement and anticipation! I thought I wouldn't survive waiting for Brent and now he is going to be my HUSBAND!

Be with our kids this week. Comfort them in any nervous or anxious thoughts they have and draw them to You, so that they can see your love clearly in our story. Loosen the last chords of woundedness from Brent's heart and free him to feel and to experience your peace and contentment as he steps into a new season.

Be with Silly in these days before graduation. Give her a sense of accomplishment and relief for what she has done. She spent her whole adolescence in grief and transition with a single mom and among a crowd of survivors. Help us CELEBRATE the way you have carried us!

The morning of our wedding dawned as incongruous as the experience of dating with teenagers in the household. Although most of my emotions and thoughts focused on the milestone ahead of me, the gargantuan miracle and answer to prayer that God had ordained, my rational and responsible self had to make sure all of the arrangements were made for the kids. We were leaving for a weekend away immediately following the wedding, so the house had to be stocked with food, there had to be someone present with them for the weekend, and some of them needed rides to the church and then home after the big event.

Sleep was difficult with so many details to think about, not to mention the nervousness of everything I was about to experience. Every aspect of my life was about to change and there was a myriad of emotions for each one. When I finally gave up on sleeping and my eyes opened on the morning of our wedding day, I knew the timing and the tasks I needed to accomplish, but my brain was lost in a dreamlike fog. I had made arrangements for everyone else, but I was alone in the house with nobody to ride to the church with me! How did I mess that up?! I couldn't do this by myself!

When I got married the first time at the age of twenty-three, I had all of my best friends piled in the bed with me on the night before my wedding. We giggled and talked late into the night and then rose together to primp and get ready. This time, I rose by myself and didn't even have a ride to the church! There were signs that I was a grown woman even though my insides felt as young and vulnerable as they did back then. I needed a friend! I picked up my phone and dialed Lisa as if on autopilot. As soon as she answered, I breathed a hopeful sigh of relief.

"I wondered how you were getting there!" Her immediate willingness was a comfort and freed me to continue getting ready. "I'll be right over."

Our goal was to have a simple and sacred ceremony with our closest local family and friends without all of the expense and stress of a big wedding. The beautiful simplicity of the morning was evident as our friends gifted us with their support and talents. One picked up Starbucks coffee, another picked up specially frosted Krispy Kreme donuts, my college friend documented everything brilliantly with his camera, Olivia took video, and my friend Kathy made me a bouquet more elegant that I would have ever designed for myself. The people surrounding us were the ones who had walked through our darkest times with us and were there supporting us in this new step.

427

My oldest son, Jed, took his place as the man of the house and walked me down the aisle of the church that had been a home to me through most of the seasons of our lives. The doors swung open, and as I caught sight of our friends and the familiar sanctuary, my whole life flashed before me. This was the same room where I had been baptized, where we had dedicated each of our babies to the Lord, and where Chris's standing-room-only memorial service had been held. The intensity of my emotions expanded within me as I scanned the crowd. I breathed through my nose to attempt to push back the tears, and as the piano music filled the room, my eyes met with Brent's at the end of the long aisle. I could see the moisture in his eyes as his smile lit up his face.

Our mutual friend, Nathan, was playing the piano and his smooth, clear voice sang out Danny Gokey's song that seemed like it had been written to tell our story.

"Tell Your Heart To Beat Again"

"Beginning,
Just let that word wash over you
It's alright now
Love's healing hands have pulled you through
So get back up, take step one
Leave the darkness, feel the sun
'Cause your story's far from over
And your journey's just begun
Tell your heart to beat again
Close your eyes and breathe it in...
Let every heartbreak
And every scar
Be a picture that reminds you
Who has carried you this far
'Cause love sees farther than you ever could
In this moment heaven's working
Everything for your good."[10]

---

[10] Gokey, Danny, "Tell Your Heart to Beat Again," by Bernie Herms, Randy Philipps, and Matthew West, on *Hope In Front of Me*, BMG-Chrysalis, 2014, CD.

Our trusted pastor, Kenny, officiated as we said our vows to each other and each of us made promises to our children. Brent's son, Josh, read the Bible passage, we exchanged rings, and then as the fullness of time played out, we were man and wife. Wife! I was a wife again! Chris's dad blessed us by doing the closing prayer and the amount of love we felt in those moments was like a foreshadow of Heaven. Each of us had lived through our own worst case scenarios; but God, in His mercy, hadn't forsaken us or left us there.

77 | More Like Chopping

"Family is like music,
Some high notes,
Some low notes,
But always a beautiful song."
— Unknown

If there's one thing I've learned from this crazy ride, it's that transitions are transitions. It doesn't matter if it's a plot twist that brings the deadliest blow you could have imagined or if it's something you've begged God for, change delivers ripple effects that can be overwhelming. Every step of our relationship was covered in prayer, guided with wise counsel, and walked out with deliberate and careful consideration. Yet, the stars in our eyes and our hope for the future made the consequences of our choices seem doable and altogether worth the effort. They *have* been worth it, but the stress of bringing two entirely different family cultures together under one roof has often felt just as foreign and intense as learning to live in a village where I didn't speak the language.

The brokenness of our journeys has left us stronger and wiser, but there are deep wounds that can still be easily triggered. When you add up the numbers of hurting people in our blended family, it's a recipe for what Brent calls "dynamic." One man coming from a broken marriage + one woman suddenly widowed + two wounded teen boys + six grieving young adults = a LOT of emotional baggage. One of our best friends who had walked a similar road before us gave us the BEST advice early on. He said, "It will often feel like the world is spinning in chaos around you, but as long as the two of you are united and on the same page, life will be good."

Truer words have never been spoken. Our kids will tell their own stories someday and it is our prayer that they will see God's loving hand writing theirs too. I'm sure we'd all testify to the same thing, though. As the adjustment to living under the same roof has played out, we've wondered why families like ours are referred to as "blended." That word evokes feelings of sweet concoctions, gently swirled, and combined into a tasty new creation. The truth is that some days the living out of bringing two families together who have completely different backgrounds feels a lot more like being chopped.

Each member brings a unique flavor to the mix. Some are sweet and open to new things. Others are spicy and prickly. A couple of them have been angry and resentful, bringing notes of bitterness to the mix. All of us have been guilty of being "salty" at times—our nerves worn thin from the work of trying to make things go smoothly. As I describe the recipe, I realize that the end result of the chopping and crushing under the pestle of remarriage is a lot like a savory and sweet salsa. Two of my favorites are mango and peach. As you partake of such unique blends, you can see and taste each ingredient because they're intact and visible in the mix. Yet, each essence has added something so that our family has a new flavor. It's bittersweet, spicy, savory, and delicious all at the same time.

Even good can be hard, but it's worth it.

"Taste and see that the Lord is good;
blessed is the one who takes refuge in him."
– Psalm 34:8

78 | Promises Kept
No longer a widow with orphans

"Sing to God, sing praise to his name, extol him who rides on the
clouds – his name is the LORD – and rejoice before him.
A father to the fatherless, a defender of widows,
is God in his holy dwelling."
– Psalm 68:4-5

A couple of years into our fully packed, flavorful life, with four boys left in high school, we set out to divide and conquer four required sports physicals. We showed up to the routine appointment with Joseph and Duane tagging along with the lackadaisical air of summer still lingering as they sauntered toward the medical building. I looked back at them and smiled, thankful to have an appointment to take them to, considering the circumstances.

We had received a last minute notification that Duane had to have documentation of a completed sports physical before he showed up to football practice that upcoming Friday. As soon as we saw the email in the inbox, Brent and I both automatically sprang into action, both of us flexing our Type A reflexes within our own unique, learned skill sets. I opened Google on my cell phone to look for local, low-cost, civilian clinics that offered quick sports physicals. Out of the corner of my eye, I could see him sitting at his desk with his phone in his hand. He was dialing the Navy Medical Clinic to see if he could get them an appointment. Times like these were like a race to see which of our backgrounds would work best for the "Crisis of the Day."

The Navy won. Brent was able to schedule appointments for *both* boys that Thursday, the day before the forms were due. In *our* world, that was plenty of time! My commander husband valiantly drove us to the navy clinic that was still unfamiliar to me, heady with his recent victory. We see ourselves as life coaches in this season of parenting. We're either on call for the twenty-somethings, ready to give advice, encouragement, or comfort when asked, or guiding the emergent young men toward doing life things independently. I hovered nearby as both boys checked themselves in for their appointments just in case there was a question they couldn't answer. Once that was done, everything felt routine.

When their names were called, both boys stood to be measured and weighed before being led to their exam room. In the spirit of independence and privacy, I asked if they wanted me to wait or come with them. My clearance came with a simple, "You can come" and I was handed two clipboards with more paperwork to fill out.

These were ordinary sports physicals, so there was an abundance of medical questions to answer: past injuries, current medications, height, weight, family history. It must have been that last one that took me back. As the gentle doctor listened to Joseph's chest with his stethoscope, I was suddenly transported back to when they were toddlers that fit in my arms. They were both small and vulnerable, full of parasites and delayed in almost every area of their lives. From the time we met them, it was as if they had the whole world to discover and catch up on. None of that deterred Chris or me. In our minds, God had given us all of the resources we needed to love them and raise them. We had health insurance and love. What more would we need?

Somehow, seventeen years had passed since that first glance into the little wooden crib Joseph was napping in when we first scooped him up in our arms. My life suddenly felt like I was caught up in a movie time warp sequence, scenes of my life rushing by me blurred with momentum and swirling together into a tornado-like storm of emotion. I sat awestruck at decorations in the pediatric exam room. My boys were young men, but there we were surrounded by Africanesque cartoon jungle decor. The trim around the ceiling of the well-appointed exam room was trimmed with little painted monkeys, vines, and bananas. The connections my brain was making packed enough power to categorize the vision that came together in those moments as more of an epiphany.

Suddenly, I could see the whole scope of Joseph and Duane's lives and the way God had literally plucked them out of their hopeless circumstances, rescued them, placed them in our family, and provided for them all the way to where we were now—sitting in the Navy medical clinic. The emotions that hit me in that moment were so sudden that I was left sitting there in wonder—*how in the world did we get here?*

It wasn't that God hadn't provided for my biological children. In fact, He had been present and generous with each of them in very individual and powerful ways. We had prayed for each of them and we considered each of them a miraculous gift. However, Joseph and Duane started their lives as orphans and now they were the size of grown men holding iPhones, playing sports, and working their own jobs. In those moments, it was as if God allowed me to see His timing in our lives, the fulfillment of His promises. They weren't just black and white on a page anymore, they were real, and the evidence sat in front of me living and breathing, whole and well. Not only had they caught up in their physical development and stature, but they were above average. The one with the club feet was here getting a *sports* physical because he *runs* track and cross country, and the itty bitty, sickly, premature, snot-nosed, silent one was the defensive lineman being told he should try to shed some of the pounds that had been helping him hold his ground on the defensive line.

I'm not sure what I looked like on the outside in those moments. I hope I looked like I had it all together because what was happening on the inside was supernatural. My Heavenly Father had flashed my life before me and was showing me the answers to my prayers and the evidence that He had kept His promises to us. God, who is the same yesterday, today, and forever, had shown up in the lives of these boys and done what He said He would do!

"God sets the lonely in families, He leads out the prisoners with singing..."
– Psalm 68:6

"For the LORD your God is God of gods and Lord of lords, the great God, mighty and awesome, who shows no partiality and accepts no bribes. He defends the cause of the fatherless and the widow, and loves the alien, giving him food and clothing."
– Deuteronomy 10:17-18

You see, when Chris and I committed to raise Joseph as our own and then he and Danyne decided it would be best for us to take Duane too, we were a "solid team." We had no idea what was ahead of us. I didn't know that Chris would go to Heaven just six years into their upbringing. Yet, God had defended our cause! As a couple, we did have the resources to take care of Joseph and Duane's medical and educational needs when they came home. Then, when Chris passed away, we had the providential life insurance policy and Social Security survivor benefits to help me with extra expenses. Finally, in the fullness of time, the man who was now my husband, the retired Navy commander with benefits for stepchildren that he didn't even know he had, materialized on the scene in front of me in church!

As I continued to let the vision play out, I allowed my mind to be transported back to the fence of our garden in the village. This time I was without Chris, and I was looking out over the whole of my life since the moment he had shared the inkling that we wouldn't be in the village as long as we thought. He had said that he had a sense that "God was doing something big." With the reality of our lives flashing past me in technicolor, I could see how far we had come.

Here were two young men who looked like ordinary, handsome, strong, middle class teenagers. Yet, I knew the *rest* of the story. They were created by God in wombs we didn't know, abandoned for reasons we couldn't figure out, and placed in our family through circumstances we couldn't have orchestrated on our own. They had an earthly father who held them and loved them long enough to pass on parts of him that are still with them today, a stepfather who had courageously entered into their lives and opened his heart to them, and a Heavenly Father who was *still* providing for them in ways that were beyond my own ability.

Not only that, but as I sat there in that exam room waiting for the doctor to knock and enter, I was aware that I no longer had six souls in tow. Each of the kids are now maturing and branching out on their own, making choices and taking steps into their own unseen futures. They have their own jobs and they're navigating love, relationships, marriage, and the highs and lows of life with increasing courage. The pain still lingers in all of us like an ache that remains under the surface and flares up unexpectedly in powerful swells of grief; but now they ebb and flow. We're moving forward and we're victorious.

There's no doubt in my mind that God told Chris ahead of time what He was about to do. We weren't there in the village as long as we thought, and He's sure done something big.

Epilogue

*"He who made the promise will find a way to keep it.
My part is simply to obey His commands, not to direct
His ways. I am His servant, not His advisor. I call upon Him and He
WILL deliver me."*
— *Charles Spurgeon*

My story isn't over, it's still being written.

I'm learning more and more to stay seated in the back of the truck, backside firmly planted in the present, and eyes glancing back only to reflect and remember, not to stir up shame or regret. Just like the vision given to me by the stranger who prayed over me at the youth camp in Pennsylvania, I'll listen to Jesus's admonition and leave the driving to Him. The road continues to be bumpy, and the route is often not what I expected it to be, but He's good and he sees the whole of my journey from womb to Heaven. I don't have that power. But He does.

Now I understand that people who said God wouldn't give me more than I could handle were just trying to make me feel better. In the discomfort of the moment, unable to sit in the awkwardness of the silence, they had caved in and sought comfort in meme-worthy platitudes. The truth of it is that God's ways are higher than ours, His power is made perfect in weakness, and the hard stuff still exists because we live in the time between the Fall and His return when He'll make everything new. At least He sits as a refiner, in control of the heat of the fire, and He turns down the heat in the nick of time when enough of the dross has been sizzled off of us.[11] I pray that by the time I see Him face to face He'll take my face into His hands and say, "Well done, Michelle. You've been faithful to use your journey

---

[11] Malachi 3:3 NIV

to bring others along with you. Come and rest. The rigors and toils of that life are all over."

That same God has even revealed some of the eternal fruit from our time in the village and Chris's life *and* death. After posting a letter to Chris on his Heaven Day this year, a comment from a dear friend in Lesotho answered many of the questions that had plagued me in my wrestling.

FACEBOOK COMMENT

February 16, 2022

Khotalo M - *Your faith and your family to God it's so amazing. I remember those days visiting your house in the village. As a young man looking for a good example, the faith you have in Christ, the life you sacrificed for the Kingdom of God, your love for the people, you did what Jesus would do. We always remember and pray for your family. Your faith has made us grow and be faithful to God. It's hard but you and your husband showed us how to trust and serve God no matter what. It's not easy sometimes but Jesus didn't say it would be either! Dying is a gain to live is Christ! Many shepherds are getting saved and being baptized in the name of the Lord. People in the village are getting saved too. You did a big job and I am sure it makes Chris/Ntate Thabang happy and Jesus never stops saying well done my faithful servants. May we get encouraged and persevere until we see Jesus face to face too.*

In the meantime, Brent and I have a new vision growing in our hearts for the time when our nest is empty. We long to see God use our brokenness for the healing of others who have had their own worst case scenarios leave them hurting and burnt out. We're taking steps of faith and trusting that God will continue to show up in unexpected, miraculous ways to provide a ranch that will be a safe place of rest, renewal, and the restoration of hope. Maybe by the time you turn the last page here we'll be walking down a dirt road toward you with our waving hands in the fresh air welcoming you in. Mountains will frame the horizon and forests of green trees will frame the scene. We'll make sure you can find us there. Beauty from ashes, that's our story. It'll be your story too. Don't take my word for it, trust His Word and His promises. If He said it, He'll do it.

Acknowledgements

To my children – We asked God for each of you and I can't imagine my life without you. Thank you for being brave and walking this journey with us despite the pain. I love you more than I ever thought was possible.

To my husband, Brent – I still have to look down at the sparkly ring on my finger to remind myself that it's all real. Beauty from ashes! The risk of loving you has already been worth it. Thank you for honoring Chris, being willing to grow with me, and for never giving up. I love you and can't wait to see what God has for our future!

To our parents, Latter's, "Dadzo" in Heaven, and Gennaro's – Thank you for all you have sacrificed on our behalf and for God's glory. You have been steadfast in your love, fervent in your prayers, and faithful and generous to provide a place to land with you, no matter where we've found ourselves.

To my brother, Geramy – You've been with me most of my life and I'm thankful for your loyal love and friendship. I know my choices made it hard for you at times, but you've never walked away. I'll always let you look out my window.

To the Gennaro family – Thank you for being our forever family. I consider it a great privilege to continue to bear your name. Always and forever.

To my church family at Clairemont Emmanuel – You've stood by us through decades, raised us up in the knowledge of the Lord, supported us in parenting, partnered with us in ministry, sent us where God called us, grieved our most devastating losses, and celebrated our greatest victories. What a comfort to know we'll be worshiping together for Eternity!

To my AIM family – There's no doubt in my mind that you're the ones God chose to be our team, our home away from home, our partners in the Gospel, my most trusted counsel, and my yoke-bearers in my toughest days. To God be the glory for all He's done in and through you!

To my beloved friends – You know who you are! There aren't enough pages to write about each one of you who has stood by me, encouraged me, shared life with me, and literally held my arms up. Whether you're named in these pages or not, I thank my God every time I remember you.

To my editors, Monica and Russell – This book is what it is because of your gifting, dedication, and love of the craft. Thank you for making sure God's story is the very best it can be! Mon, you get me! I love you with ALL CAPS!

To my Heavenly Father – May you receive ALL of the glory! Great things YOU have done!

Contact Page

You can send me a message, check my speaking schedule, or look for updates at my website: **michellegennarolapp.com**

Instagram @michelle_g_lapp

linkedin.com/in/michellegennarolapp

Look for my Facebook fan page and let's connect!

CPSIA information can be obtained
at www.ICGtesting.com
Printed in the USA
LVHW110806190223
739749LV00002BB/6

9 781662 869273